English Fiction, 1660-1800

AMERICAN LITERATURE, ENGLISH LITERATURE, AND WORL
LITERATURES IN ENGLISH: AN INFORMATION GUIDE SERIE

Series Editor: Theodore Grieder, Curator, Division of Special Collections,
Fales Library, New York University, New York, New York

Associate Editor: Duane DeVries, Associate Professor, Polytechnic Institute of
New York, Brooklyn, New York

Other books on English literature in this series:

ENGLISH DRAMA TO 1660 (EXCLUDING SHAKESPEARE)—*Edited by Frieda Elaine Penninger*

ENGLISH DRAMA, 1660-1800—*Edited by Frederick M. Link*

ENGLISH DRAMA AND THEATRE, 1800-1900—*Edited by L.W. Conolly and J.P. Wearing*

ENGLISH DRAMA, 1900-1950—*Edited by E.H. Mikhail*

CONTEMPORARY DRAMA IN AMERICA AND ENGLAND, 1950-1970—*Edited by Richard H. Harris**

ENGLISH FICTION, 1800-1850—*Edited by Duane DeVries**

ENGLISH FICTION, 1900-1950 (2 volumes)—*Edited by Thomas J. Rice**

ENGLISH NOVEL, 1851-1900—*Edited by Robert Schweik and Albert Dunn**

THE ENGLISH LITERARY JOURNAL TO 1900—*Edited by Robert B. White, Jr.*

ENGLISH PROSE, PROSE FICTION, AND CRITICISM TO 1660—*Edited by S.K. Heninger, Jr.*

OLD AND MIDDLE ENGLISH POETRY TO 1500—*Edited by Walter H. Beale*

ENGLISH POETRY, 1500-1660—*Edited by S.K. Heninger, Jr.**

ENGLISH POETRY, 1660-1800—*Edited by Donald C. Mell**

ENGLISH ROMANTIC POETRY, 1800-1835—*Edited by Donald H. Reiman**

VICTORIAN POETRY, 1835-1900—*Edited by Ronald E. Freeman**

ENGLISH POETRY, 1900-1950—*Edited by Emily Ann Anderson**

*in preparation

The above series is part of the
GALE INFORMATION GUIDE LIBRARY

The Library consists of a number of separate series of guides covering
major areas in the social sciences, humanities, and current affairs.

General Editor: Paul Wasserman, Professor and former Dean, School
of Library and Information Services, University of Maryland

Managing Editor: Denise Allard Adzigian, Gale Research Company

English Fiction, 1660-1800

A GUIDE TO INFORMATION SOURCES

Volume 14 in the American Literature, English Literature, and World Literatures in English Information Guide Series

Jerry C. Beasley

*Associate Professor of English
University of Delaware*

Gale Research Company
Book Tower, Detroit, Michigan 48226

137804

Library of Congress Cataloging in Publication Data

Beasley, Jerry C
    English fiction, 1660-1800.

    (Gale information guide library) (American literature,
English literature, and world literatures in English; v. 14)
    Bibliography; p. 313
    Includes index.
    1. English fiction—18th century—Bio-bibliography.
2. English fiction—Early modern, 1500-1700—Bio-bibli-
ography. 3. English fiction—18th century—History
and criticism—Bibliography. 4. English fiction—Early
modern, 1500-1700—History and criticism—Bibliography.
I. Title
Z2014.F5B42   [PR851]   o16.823   74-11526
ISBN 0-8103-1226-3

To the memory of my father
Guy E. Beasley

VITA

Jerry C. Beasley received his B.A. degree from George Peabody College, his M.A. from the University of Kansas, and his Ph.D. from Northwestern University. Since 1969 he has been teaching at the University of Delaware, where he is now associate professor of English. His special field of interest is the English novel of the eighteenth and nineteenth centuries; his articles have appeared in a number of learned journals. In 1972 the University Press of Virginia published his book, A CHECK LIST OF PROSE FICTION PUBLISHED IN ENGLAND, 1740-1749; he is at work on a new book, a critical study called NOVELS OF THE 1740'S. He presently serves as editorial supervisor of research for a new microfilm collection of BRITISH FICTION, 1700-1850, to be published by Research Publications, Inc. He is a member of the editorial board of the new standard edition of THE WORKS OF TOBIAS SMOLLETT, to be published by the University of Delaware Press.

CONTENTS

Acknowledgments   ix

Introduction   xi

Abbreviations   xv

Part I   General Bibliography
    Background Sources   3
        A.   General Reference Works   3
        B.   English Literature, 1660–1800:   General History and
            Criticism   5
    The English Novel: General Histories and Critical Surveys   11
    The Novel as Genre: Selected Studies in Form and Technique . . .   15
    English Fiction, 1660–1800:   History and Criticism   19
    Checklists and Other Bibliographical Resources   31
    Special Resources   39
        A.   Serials   39
        B.   Reprint Series and Selected Modern Collections   40
    Selected Background Readings   43

Part II   Individual Authors
    A Note on the Organization of Part II   51
    Robert Bage (1728–1801)   53
    William Beckford (1760–1844)   57
    Aphra Behn (1640–89)   63
    Henry Brooke (1703–83)   69
    John Bunyan (1628–88)   73
    Fanny Burney (1752–1840)   81
    John Cleland (1709–89)   87
    Thomas Day (1748–89)   91
    Daniel Defoe (1660–1731)   95
    Henry Fielding (1707–54)   111
    Sarah Fielding (1710–68)   135
    William Godwin (1756–1836)   139
    Oliver Goldsmith (1730–74)   147
    Richard Graves (1715–1804)   153

Contents

Eliza Haywood (1693-1756) 157
Thomas Holcroft (1745-1809). 161
Samuel Johnson (1709-84). 165
Charlotte Ramsay Lennox (1720-1804). 177
Matthew Gregory Lewis (1775-1818) 181
Henry Mackenzie (1745-1831). 185
Mary Delarivière Manley (1672-1724) 189
Ann Radcliffe (1764-1823) 193
Clara Reeve (1729-1807) 199
Samuel Richardson (1689-1761) 203
Charlotte Smith (1749-1806). 219
Tobias Smollett (1721-71). 223
Laurence Sterne (1713-68) 237
Jonathan Swift (1667-1745) 253
Horace Walpole (1717-97) 269

Index 277

ACKNOWLEDGMENTS

I should like to express my appreciation for all of the help I have received while preparing this volume. To my Delaware colleagues Donald Mell and Elaine Safer I am thankful for many suggestions and for a willingness to listen to me talk about my work. To the librarians at the Newberry Library and the libraries of the University of Pennsylvania, Harvard University, and the University of Delaware I am grateful for much kind assistance over the past several years. My special thanks go to Michael Shugrue for suggesting this project to me, and to Theodore Grieder for the encouragement he has so consistently given. The graduate students in my eighteenth-century novel seminar are due a considerable measure of gratitude, for they alerted me to a number of articles that might otherwise have escaped my notice. My greatest debt, however, is to my wife, Rita, whose patient support and honest criticism I value even more than she thinks I do.

J.C.B.
Newark, Delaware
September, 1976

INTRODUCTION

HOW TO USE THIS GUIDE

I hope this book will answer the needs of specialists and nonspecialists alike. The novice in the field will find listed throughout the following pages a variety of general resources and introductory studies, while the hundreds of specialized books and articles included among the entries will be of immediate interest to the advanced student and the practicing scholar. I have attempted to make this guide a convenient and reliable record of important scholarship, although I have of necessity been very selective. The fiction of the Restoration and the eighteenth century, or at least the major fiction, has generated enormous interest during the last few decades, and no book of this kind could possibly ever acknowledge all that critics, editors, and literary historians have achieved. I have chosen for inclusion, in part I (General Bibliography) and part II (Individual Authors), those items that I felt were most useful and significant and have meanwhile tried to provide a reasonably good representation of the range of scholarly endeavor. Limitations of space required me to omit many worthy pieces of work, among them a number of books and articles in languages other than English. I regret these omissions, which I hope may not seem merely arbitrary, and I regret almost as much the need to exclude from part II several novelists who, if this book could have been much, much longer, would have commanded my attention. I have ignored the likes of Sarah Scott, Frances Sheridan, Francis Coventry, John Shebbeare, Sophia Lee, and Elizabeth Inchbald only because I judged them to be less important than the twenty-nine authors whom I decided to include. I trust that the user who needs any sort of information beyond that which I have provided will find in this book such resources as will lead him to it. The various annual bibliographies listed in part I will be of particular value to anyone who wishes to know of scholarship too recent to be acknowledged here.

The organization of the guide is relatively simple, but a few hints about its contents may be helpful to the user. Part I lists a variety of general aids:

> (1) Background Sources. Included here are general reference works of special interest to students of English fiction, 1660-1800, and a selection of general histories and critical studies of the literature of the period.

(2) The English Novel: General Histories and Critical Surveys. The most basic and important studies of their kind are listed here; each is a work with which every student of British fiction should be familiar.

(3) The Novel as Genre: Selected Studies in Form and Technique. This section includes important theoretical studies, not necessarily limited to Restoration and eighteenth-century fiction.

(4) English Fiction, 1660-1800: History and Criticism. Listed here are books and articles specifically devoted to Restoration and eighteenth-century fiction, but not to any one author. A number of the items do contain extended discussions of individual novelists (the annotations indicate who they are), and many of these are important enough to be entered again at the appropriate places in part II of this guide.

(5) Checklists and Other Bibliographical Resources. This section includes a selective, but fairly comprehensive, list of bibliographical guides to important primary and secondary materials for the study of the period's fiction. Individual author bibliographies are not entered here, but they do appear in part II.

(6) Special Resources. Listed here are the periodicals and serials most pertinent to the study of the period and its fiction, and of the novel as a genre. This section also lists several important reprint series, and selected modern collections of rare Restoration and eighteenth-century novels.

(7) Selected Background Readings. Included here are significant books and articles on a variety of subjects, from social and political history to aesthetics and contemporary philosophy, from literary theory to the intricacies of publishing and the book trade.

Part II of this book is devoted to twenty-nine individual authors. For each of the lesser figures I have provided a brief headnote indicating the author's importance to the history of the period's fiction; it would have been presumptuous to have attempted the same for the major writers, and I have not done so. For all of the novelists I have regularly included several kinds of listings:

(1) Principal Works. The section on each author begins with a short-title list of the most important works in the canon, chronologically arranged. In the case of a very prolific writer the list is necessarily selective, and in all cases it is intended only to suggest the range of the writer's career and to provide a handy reference to titles and dates. It is not intended as an exact bibliographical record, and thus the only kind of publication information supplied is the first date of issue for each title; original punctuation is retained. Each work is described according to its type; I have used the label "novel" to indicate any extended narrative fiction in prose.

(2) Editions. These include collected works (when available), selections and specialized collections (when available), and important separate editions of individual works; in the last category, the emphasis is on available scholarly editions of the author's novels, although editions of works in other genres are included if they are particularly useful to the study of the fiction. I have not tried to provide a complete publishing and editing history of any author's work. Rather, I have identified the most important or useful editions and have tried to indicate which of these possess the greatest value for the student or scholar.

(3) Letters. The principal scholarly collections of letters, and sometimes the journals or diaries, are listed here. The letters of some authors, of course, have not survived, and those of others have never been collected or published in any form. In some instances the only immediate access to an author's letters is through articles describing the collections held by a library; such articles are listed.

(4) Bibliography. This section lists the available bibliographies and checklists of works by and about the author. I have omitted listings that are less complete than my own.

(5) Biography. Here I have included introductory biographical studies as well as the more sophisticated biographies and critical biographies intended for an audience of specialists.

(6) Critical Studies and Commentaries. This section includes important books, articles, and collections of essays on the author's work, with an emphasis on twentieth-century criticism. A majority of these studies are highly specialized discussions of the author's fiction, although book-length works on versatile writers like Samuel Johnson and Jonathan Swift generally range beyond the novels.

Almost all of the entries in the guide are annotated, the only exceptions being those items whose titles are so self-explanatory as to make any annotation superfluous. Many of the annotations are merely descriptive, but a majority are evaluative as well. Where I thought it might be helpful, I have quoted from the book or article being described. In the interest of saving space for annotations, I have as a rule not given chapter titles or page numbers in citations of books containing adequate tables of contents and indexes, and I have not usually troubled to identify the increasingly numerous reprints (as opposed to revisions) of the older scholarly works included. With this same purpose of economy in mind, I have sometimes omitted the general titles of series to which cited books and monographs belong, provided this could be done without inconveniencing the user. Series titles which might indicate something important about quality or format (Oxford English Novels, for example, or Twentieth Century Views) are supplied. Publishers' names are given in short form--for example, Scribner's instead of Charles Scribner's Sons, Macmillan instead of Macmillan Publishing Co., Inc. The guide follows the usual practice of omitting publishers' names when citing titles dated earlier than 1900.

Finally, a word about the specific arrangement of entries in the guide. All items in the various sections of part I are listed in alphabetical order, by author, editor, or in some cases by title. In part II, the primary materials relating to an individual author (that is to say, editions, including letters) appear in chronological order of publication, as is customary, while secondary materials (bibliographies, biographies, and critical studies) occur in alphabetical order. The index may be used to locate all references, throughout the book, to a given author or work.

ABBREVIATIONS

Titles marked by an asterisk (*) are annotated in the text; entry numbers for these are given in parentheses.

AUMLA   JOURNAL OF THE AUSTRALASIAN UNIVERSITIES MODERN LAN-
        GUAGE ASSOCIATION

BNYPL   BULLETIN OF THE NEW YORK PUBLIC LIBRARY

CBEL   *THE CAMBRIDGE BIBLIOGRAPHY OF ENGLISH LITERATURE
        (No. 162)

CE   COLLEGE ENGLISH

ECS   *EIGHTEENTH-CENTURY STUDIES (No. 198)

ELH   JOURNAL OF ENGLISH LITERARY HISTORY

ELN   ENGLISH LANGUAGE NOTES

FCE   *THE FEMINIST CONTROVERSY IN ENGLAND (No. 209)

FIN   *THE FLOWERING OF THE NOVEL (No. 210)

FoN   *FOUNDATIONS OF THE NOVEL (No. 211)

HLQ   HUNTINGTON LIBRARY QUARTERLY

JEGP   JOURNAL OF ENGLISH AND GERMANIC PHILOLOGY

JHI   JOURNAL OF THE HISTORY OF IDEAS

JNT   *JOURNAL OF NARRATIVE TECHNIQUE (No. 202)

MLN   MODERN LANGUAGE NOTES

MLQ   MODERN LANGUAGE QUARTERLY

Abbreviations

MLR	MODERN LANGUAGE REVIEW
MP	MODERN PHILOLOGY
N&Q	NOTES AND QUERIES
NCBEL	*THE NEW CAMBRIDGE BIBLIOGRAPHY OF ENGLISH LITERATURE (No. 187)
NOVEL	*NOVEL: A FORUM ON FICTION (No. 203)
PBSA	PAPERS OF THE BIBLIOGRAPHICAL SOCIETY OF AMERICA
PLL	PAPERS ON LANGUAGE AND LITERATURE
PMLA	PUBLICATIONS OF THE MODERN LANGUAGE ASSOCIATION OF AMERICA
PQ	PHILOLOGICAL QUARTERLY
REL	THE REVIEW OF ENGLISH LITERATURE
RES	REVIEW OF ENGLISH STUDIES
SB	STUDIES IN BIBLIOGRAPHY
SBHT	*STUDIES IN BURKE AND HIS TIME (No. 205)
SBrW	*THE LIFE AND TIMES OF SEVEN MAJOR BRITISH WRITERS (No. 214)
SEL	*STUDIES IN ENGLISH LITERATURE, 1500-1900 (No. 207)
SNNTS	*STUDIES IN THE NOVEL (No. 208)
SP	STUDIES IN PHILOLOGY
SSF	STUDIES IN SHORT FICTION
TLS	THE [LONDON] TIMES LITERARY SUPPLEMENT
TSL	TENNESSEE STUDIES IN LITERATURE
TSLL	TEXAS STUDIES IN LITERATURE AND LANGUAGE
UTQ	UNIVERSITY OF TORONTO QUARTERLY

Part I

GENERAL BIBLIOGRAPHY

BACKGROUND SOURCES

A. GENERAL REFERENCE WORKS

1 ABSTRACTS OF ENGLISH STUDIES. Urbana, Ill.: National Council of Teachers of English, 1958-- . 10/year.

Abstracts of current articles in scholarly journals; since 1972, abstracts of monographs as well.

2 Altick, Richard D., and Andrew Wright. SELECTIVE BIBLIOGRAPHY FOR THE STUDY OF ENGLISH AND AMERICAN LITERATURE. 5th ed. New York: Macmillan, 1975.

Listings of national bibliographies, literary histories and encyclopedias, library catalogues, and a large variety of other source materials. An indispensable aid.

3 BRITISH MUSEUM GENERAL CATALOGUE OF PRINTED BOOKS. London: 1959-- .

An invaluable resource; the 263 volumes published between 1959 and 1966 record the holdings through 1955, and periodic supplements bring the catalogue up to date.

4 DICTIONARY OF NATIONAL BIOGRAPHY. 21 vols., with supplements. London: Oxford University Press, 1917-71.

An invaluable source of information about major and minor literary figures of all periods; the 1951-60 supplement contains an index to the entire series.

5 DISSERTATION ABSTRACTS INTERNATIONAL. Ann Arbor, Mich.: University Microfilms, 1938-- . Monthly.

Abstracts of doctoral theses on all subjects; a retrospective index (1970) covers the years 1938-69.

6   Downs, Robert B. AMERICAN LIBRARY RESOURCES: A BIBLIOGRAPHI-
     CAL GUIDE. Chicago: American Library Association, 1951. Supple-
     ments: 2 vols., 1962, 1972.

     Contains leads useful to anyone interested in American library
     holdings in early English fiction.

7   _____. BRITISH LIBRARY RESOURCES: A BIBLIOGRAPHICAL GUIDE.
     Chicago: American Library Association, 1973.

     Similar to Downs's volume on American library holdings (see
     No. 6).

8   Harvey, Paul, ed. THE OXFORD COMPANION TO ENGLISH LITERA-
     TURE. 4th ed., rev. by Dorothy Eagle. Oxford: Clarendon Press, 1967.

     An indispensable aid that provides biographical and bibliographi-
     cal sketches of hundreds of writers, together with summaries of
     major works; includes brief discussions of literary movements
     and of pertinent extraliterary subjects.

9   Holman, C. Hugh, et al. A HANDBOOK TO LITERATURE. 3rd ed.
     New York: Odyssey Press, 1972.

     The most thorough and usable book of its kind; offers readable,
     authoritative definitions of literary terms and concepts.

10   Kunitz, Stanley J., and Howard Haycraft, eds. BRITISH AUTHORS BE-
     FORE 1800: A BIOGRAPHICAL DICTIONARY. New York: Wilson,
     1952.

11   MLA ABSTRACTS OF ARTICLES IN SCHOLARLY JOURNALS. New York:
     Modern Language Association, 1972-- . Annual.

     Coverage begins with the year 1970; published in conjunction
     with the annual MLA INTERNATIONAL BIBLIOGRAPHY OF
     BOOKS AND ARTICLES ON THE MODERN LANGUAGES
     AND LITERATURES (see No. 184).

12   THE NATIONAL UNION CATALOGUE. London: Mansell; Chicago:
     American Library Association, 1968.

     A most valuable resource for locating copies of old and rare
     books in American libraries. When completed, the NUC will
     contain some 610 volumes covering pre-1956 imprints. The
     various supplements covering post-1956 imprints provide addi-
     tional information.

B. ENGLISH LITERATURE, 1660-1800: GENERAL HISTORY AND CRITICISM

13 Anderson, Howard, and John S. Shea, eds. STUDIES IN CRITICISM AND AESTHETICS, 1660-1800: ESSAYS IN HONOR OF SAMUEL HOLT MONK. Minneapolis: University of Minnesota Press, 1967.

A collection of essays on eighteenth-century literature and art.

14 Battestin, Martin C. THE PROVIDENCE OF WIT: ASPECTS OF FORM IN AUGUSTAN LITERATURE AND THE ARTS. Oxford: Clarendon Press, 1974.

An extremely important (if controversial) book that emphasizes the theological basis for the characteristic formal ordering of Augustan writing. Battestin gives major attention to Pope, Gay, Fielding, and Goldsmith.

15 Brissenden, R.F., ed. STUDIES IN THE EIGHTEENTH CENTURY. Canberra: Australian National University Press, 1968.

A collection of papers presented at the David Nichol Smith Memorial Seminar, Canberra, 1966; the subjects range from the social to the philosophical to the literary, and the figures treated include Sterne.

16 _____. STUDIES IN THE EIGHTEENTH CENTURY II. Toronto: University of Toronto Press, 1973.

A collection of papers presented at the second David Nichol Smith Memorial Seminar, Canberra, 1970; includes studies of a variety of figures, among them Richardson, Sterne, Fielding, and Swift.

17 Butt, John. THE AUGUSTAN AGE. London: Hutchinson, 1950.

A brief but excellent survey of the literary history of the period.

18 Byrd, Max. VISITS TO BEDLAM: MADNESS AND LITERATURE IN THE EIGHTEENTH CENTURY. Columbia: University of South Carolina Press, 1974.

More ambitious in scope than DePorte's similar study (see No. 22) and sometimes capable of fresh insights on important writers of the period, whom Byrd sees working within a context that nearly always includes an awareness of lunacy as a threat or at least a palpable fact of life; but often disappointingly imprecise in its reading of texts.

19 Champion, Larry S., ed. QUICK SPRINGS OF SENSE: STUDIES IN THE EIGHTEENTH CENTURY. Athens: University of Georgia Press, 1974.

A collection of original essays, by important scholars, on eighteenth-century literature. The volume is weighted toward the fiction of the period, and among the essays are studies of Defoe, Swift, Fielding, Sterne, and Smollett.

20 Clifford, James L., ed. EIGHTEENTH-CENTURY ENGLISH LITERATURE: MODERN ESSAYS IN CRITICISM. New York: Oxford University Press, 1959.

A selection of reprinted essays on a variety of subjects and figures, including (among the novelists) Swift, Defoe, Fielding, Johnson, and Sterne.

21 Crane, Ronald S. "Suggestions toward a Genealogy of the 'Man of Feeling.'" THE IDEA OF THE HUMANITIES, I. Ed. Wayne C. Booth. Chicago: University of Chicago Press, 1967.

The very best discussion of how social, philosophical, and literary currents converged in the eighteenth century to produce the sentimental hero.

22 DePorte, Michael V. NIGHTMARES AND HOBBYHORSES: SWIFT, STERNE, AND AUGUSTAN IDEAS OF MADNESS. San Marino, Calif.: Huntington Library, 1974.

An illuminating discussion of the ways in which A TALE OF A TUB and TRISTRAM SHANDY reflect and respond to eighteenth-century notions of insanity; the notions themselves, and their general relation to literature of the period, receive considerable attention. (See also No. 18.)

23 Dobrée, Bonamy. ENGLISH LITERATURE IN THE EARLY EIGHTEENTH CENTURY, 1700-1740. The Oxford History of English Literature, vol. 7. Oxford: Clarendon Press, 1959.

24 Ehrenpreis, Irvin. LITERARY MEANING AND AUGUSTAN VALUES. Charlottesville: University Press of Virginia, 1974.

Selection of essays; includes a study of the "styles" of GULLIVER'S TRAVELS. Ehrenpreis attempts to counter what he sees as the recent tendency to impart modern values to Augustan writers. The essays in this book emphasize the explicitness, the straightforward didacticism, and the conventionality of a wide range of Augustan literature.

25 Foxon, David. LIBERTINE LITERATURE IN ENGLAND, 1660-1745. New Hyde Park, N.Y.: University Books, 1965.

A sweeping, quite valuable survey that includes treatment of some works regarded as pornographic; valuable background for the study of Cleland's FANNY HILL.

26 Frye, Northrop. "Towards Defining an Age of Sensibility." ELH, 23 (1956), 144-52.

An essential discussion that greatly illuminates the popular novels of sensibility published in the latter half of the eighteenth century.

27 Fussell, Paul. THE RHETORICAL WORLD OF AUGUSTAN HUMANISM: ETHICS AND IMAGERY FROM SWIFT TO BURKE. New York: Oxford University Press, 1965.

A valuable book, though its bearing on the period's fiction is limited.

28 Green, F.C. MINUET: A CRITICAL SURVEY OF FRENCH AND EN-GLISH LITERARY IDEAS IN THE EIGHTEENTH CENTURY. New York: Dutton, 1935.

Especially useful to anyone interested in the relationships between French and English fiction in the period.

29 Harth, Philip, ed. NEW APPROACHES TO EIGHTEENTH-CENTURY LIT-ERATURE. New York: Columbia University Press, 1974.

A half-dozen essays, selected from the English Institute papers of 1972 and 1973, on subjects ranging from characteristic forms and genres of the period to suggestions for new research. Samuel Richardson is among the novelists discussed.

30 Hilles, Frederick W., ed. THE AGE OF JOHNSON: ESSAYS PRE-SENTED TO CHAUNCEY BREWSTER TINKER. New Haven, Conn.: Yale University Press, 1949.

A very rich collection of modern essays on a variety of subjects and figures, including (among the novelists) Richardson, Fielding, Smollett, Sterne, Burney, and Radcliffe.

31 Loftis, John. COMEDY AND SOCIETY FROM CONGREVE TO FIELDING. Stanford, Calif.: Stanford University Press, 1959.

Specific emphasis on stage comedy. Of special interest to the student of the novel is the discussion of Fielding's plays.

32 McKillop, Alan Dugald. ENGLISH LITERATURE FROM DRYDEN TO BURNS. New York: Appleton-Century-Crofts, 1948.

Still one of the best brief literary histories of the period.

33 Miller, Henry Knight; Eric Rothstein; and George [S.] Rousseau, eds. THE AUGUSTAN MILIEU: ESSAYS PRESENTED TO LOUIS A. LANDA.

New York: Oxford University Press, 1970.

Essays on a variety of subjects and writers.

34   Price, Martin. TO THE PALACE OF WISDOM: STUDIES IN ORDER AND ENERGY FROM DRYDEN TO BLAKE. New York: Doubleday, 1964.

Includes important chapters on Defoe and Sterne.

35   Renwick, W.L. ENGLISH LITERATURE, 1789-1815. The Oxford History of English Literature, vol. 9. Oxford: Clarendon Press, 1963.

36   Rogers, Pat. THE AUGUSTAN VISION. London: Weidenfeld and Nicolson, 1974.

An excellent new survey of English political, social, philosophical, and literary concerns, 1688-1760.

37   Sherburn, George, and Donald F. Bond. THE RESTORATION AND EIGHTEENTH CENTURY (1660-1789). A Literary History of England, vol. 3. Ed. Albert C. Baugh. 2nd ed. New York: Appleton-Century-Crofts, 1967.

The most authoritative work of its kind; includes an extensive and invaluable bibliographical supplement.

38   Sutherland, James R. ENGLISH LITERATURE OF THE LATE SEVENTEENTH CENTURY. The Oxford History of English Literature, vol. 6. Oxford: Clarendon Press, 1969.

39   Tave, Stuart M. THE AMIABLE HUMORIST: A STUDY IN THE COMIC THEORY AND CRITICISM OF THE EIGHTEENTH AND EARLY NINETEENTH CENTURIES. Chicago: University of Chicago Press, 1960.

An attempt to show the development of characters who are comically "amiable"--who combine the heroic and the ridiculous in a mixture that makes them at once laughable and sympathetic. Includes important discussions of Fielding and Sterne.

40   Watt, Ian [P.], ed. THE AUGUSTAN AGE: APPROACHES TO ITS LITERATURE, LIFE, AND THOUGHT. Greenwich, Conn.: Fawcett Books, 1968.

A collection of reprinted essays, with a fine introduction by Watt. Includes brief excerpts from selected Augustan writers.

41   Webber, Joan. THE ELOQUENT "I": STYLE AND SELF IN SEVENTEENTH-CENTURY PROSE. Madison: University of Wisconsin Press, 1969.

A valuable study that includes a discussion of Bunyan.

42   Wellek, René. THE LATER EIGHTEENTH CENTURY. A HISTORY OF
      MODERN CRITICISM, 1750-1950, vol. 1. New Haven, Conn.: Yale
      University Press, 1955.

      Perhaps the most comprehensive and useful account of criticism
      in the age of Johnson.

43   Williams, Raymond. THE COUNTRY AND THE CITY. London: Chatto
      and Windus, 1973.

      A Marxist discussion partly focused on the eighteenth century,
      when country-city tensions were alive in literature and society;
      polemical and biased, yet provocative on economic and social
      issues, especially as reflected in Defoe, Richardson, and Field-
      ing, all of whom are discussed--but too briefly, tentatively,
      and superficially.

THE ENGLISH NOVEL:
GENERAL HISTORIES AND CRITICAL SURVEYS

44   Allen, Walter. THE ENGLISH NOVEL: A SHORT CRITICAL HISTORY.
      New York: Dutton, 1954.

      A succinct, readable, and insightful critical survey.

45   Alter, Robert. PARTIAL MAGIC: THE NOVEL AS A SELF-CONSCIOUS
      GENRE. Berkeley and Los Angeles: University of California Press, 1975.

      "A self-conscious novel . . . is a novel that systematically
      flaunts its own condition of artifice and that by so doing
      probes into the problematic relationship between real-seeming
      artifice and reality." Alter is interested in the "playful"
      novel in particular, and his essay on TRISTRAM SHANDY (the
      only eighteenth-century novel discussed at length) is especially
      illuminating.

46   Baker, Ernest A. THE HISTORY OF THE ENGLISH NOVEL. 10 vols.
      London: Witherby, 1924-39; Vol. 11 added by Lionel Stevenson. New
      York: Barnes and Noble, 1967.

      A superficial survey, valuable primarily for its sweep and its
      summaries of hundreds of novels, many of them quite obscure.

47   Brissenden, R.F. VIRTUE IN DISTRESS: STUDIES IN THE NOVEL OF
      SENTIMENT FROM RICHARDSON TO SADE. New York: Barnes and
      Noble, 1974.

      An interesting critical survey that touches on the major eighteenth-
      century novelists of sensibility; includes useful discussions of
      formal conventions and characteristic themes.

48   Donovan, Robert Alan. THE SHAPING VISION: IMAGINATION IN
      THE ENGLISH NOVEL FROM DEFOE TO DICKENS. Ithaca, N.Y.:
      Cornell University Press, 1966.

      An impressive and very valuable book that brings modern techniques of formal analysis to bear on early novels in an attempt to give them the respectful attention they deserve but have not always received from twentieth-century critics. Donovan takes the novels on their own terms and his approach provides for extremely insightful discussions of works by Defoe, Richardson, Fielding, Sterne, Smollett, Austen, Scott, Thackeray, and Dickens.

49   Kettle, Arnold. AN INTRODUCTION TO THE ENGLISH NOVEL. 2 vols. London: Hutchinson, 1951; rev. ed., 1967.

Largely devoted to fiction after 1800, and slightly Marxist in its bias; but provocative on Defoe, Richardson, Fielding, and Sterne.

50   Kiely, Robert. THE ROMANTIC NOVEL IN ENGLAND. Cambridge, Mass.: Harvard University Press, 1972.

Includes essays on several nineteenth-century novels, and on THE CASTLE OF OTRANTO, VATHEK, THE MYSTERIES OF UDOLPHO, CALEB WILLIAMS, and THE MONK; an excellent study, perhaps the best of its kind, that emphasizes the shared conventions, themes, and innovations of these disparate novels.

51   Leavis, F.R. THE GREAT TRADITION. London: Chatto and Windus, 1948.

Provocative and interesting, but doctrinaire; eccentric in its summary dismissal of eighteenth-century novelists.

52   Mack, Maynard, and Ian Gregor, eds. IMAGINED WORLDS: ESSAYS ON SOME ENGLISH NOVELS AND NOVELISTS IN HONOUR OF JOHN BUTT. London: Methuen, 1968.

Includes essays on Defoe, Fielding, Swift, and Johnson.

53   Stevenson, Lionel. THE ENGLISH NOVEL: A PANORAMA. Boston: Houghton Mifflin, 1960.

The most comprehensive of the modern one-volume studies of the development of the English novel; includes a rudimentary bibliography of secondary sources and a chronological summary listing 218 novelists and their important roles.

54   Van Ghent, Dorothy. THE ENGLISH NOVEL: FORM AND FUNCTION. New York: Rinehart, 1953.

Includes provocative discussions of DON QUIXOTE, THE PIL-GRIM'S PROGRESS, MOLL FLANDERS, CLARISSA, TOM JONES, and TRISTRAM SHANDY. These and later novels are discussed in chronological sequence, to suggest the "special juxtaposition" of each "with its neighbors."

55   Wagenknecht, Edward. CAVALCADE OF THE ENGLISH NOVEL. New York: Holt, 1943; rev. ed., 1954.

A lively, readable study now largely superseded by Allen (No. 44) and Stevenson (No. 53); includes useful bibliographies of authors, their principal works, and scholarship devoted to them.

THE NOVEL AS GENRE:
SELECTED STUDIES IN FORM AND TECHNIQUE

56   Allott, Miriam, ed. NOVELISTS ON THE NOVEL. New York: Columbia University Press, 1959.

> An extensive collection of critical statements on the novel, taken (often in excerpt) from novelists themselves.

57   Alter, Robert. ROGUE'S PROGRESS: STUDIES IN THE PICARESQUE NOVEL. Cambridge, Mass.: Harvard University Press, 1964.

> An excellent study of the picaresque tradition; includes valuable essays on Defoe, Fielding, and Smollett.

58   Booth, Wayne C. THE RHETORIC OF FICTION. Chicago: University of Chicago Press, 1961.

> A crucial study of point of view in fiction; includes especially illuminating, extended discussions of Fielding and Sterne. The bibliography lists scores of critical studies whose subjects are related to Booth's own.

59   Chandler, Frank Wadleigh. THE LITERATURE OF ROGUERY. 2 vols. Boston: Houghton Mifflin, 1907.

> Still the most comprehensive survey of a large field; offers an abundance of information on criminal "lives" and picaresque fictions, from the Renaissance onward.

60   Forster, E.M. ASPECTS OF THE NOVEL. New York: Harcourt, Brace, 1927.

> A witty, somewhat eccentric, but crucial little book.

61   Frye, Northrop. ANATOMY OF CRITICISM: FOUR ESSAYS. Princeton, N.J.: Princeton University Press, 1957.

> Essential to all students of every literary form; the first essay,

on four modes of fiction, is of greatest interest to students of
the novel.

62   Gove, Philip Babcock. THE IMAGINARY VOYAGE IN PROSE FICTION:
A HISTORY OF ITS CRITICISM AND A GUIDE FOR ITS STUDY, WITH
AN ANNOTATED CHECK LIST OF 215 IMAGINARY VOYAGES FROM
1700 TO 1800. New York: Columbia University Press, 1941.

An authoritative discussion; the checklist identifies many narratives, both native and foreign, that were published in England during the period covered.

63   Grossvogel, David I. LIMITS OF THE NOVEL: EVOLUTIONS OF A
FORM FROM CHAUCER TO ROBBE-GRILLET. Ithaca, N.Y.: Cornell
University Press, 1968.

An ambitious and sometimes puzzling study that treats the novel
as metaphor moving the reader from mere belief to a response
that may be called "esthetic commentary"; includes discussions
of Cervantes, Lafayette, Sterne, and Defoe.

64   Halperin, John, ed. THE THEORY OF THE NOVEL: NEW ESSAYS.
New York: Oxford University Press, 1974.

A valuable collection of new essays by various modern critics.

65   Hardy, Barbara. THE APPROPRIATE FORM: AN ESSAY ON THE NOVEL.
London: Athlone Press, 1964.

A fresh, insightful study of the "variety of narrative form";
the "dogmatic form" of Defoe receives brief but helpful treatment.

66   Harvey, W.J. CHARACTER AND THE NOVEL. Ithaca, N.Y.: Cornell
University Press, 1965.

A fine, widely ranging discussion of characterization as it affects the connections between fiction and reality.

67   James, Henry. THE ART OF THE NOVEL: CRITICAL PREFACES. Ed.
R.P. Blackmur. New York: Scribner's, 1934.

A gathering of James's prefaces; Blackmur's preliminary discussion
is almost as valuable as the essays it introduces.

68   Kermode, Frank. THE SENSE OF AN ENDING: STUDIES IN THE THE-
ORY OF FICTION. New York: Oxford University Press, 1967.

As much a study of culture and aesthetics as of the novel; begins with the Apocalypse as model and attempts to tie the

"theory of literary fictions to the theory of fictions in general."

69   Lodge, David. LANGUAGE OF FICTION: ESSAYS IN CRITICISM AND VERBAL ANALYSIS OF THE ENGLISH NOVEL. London: Routledge and Kegan Paul, 1966.

    An extremely insightful study of language and style in fiction.

70   Lubbock, Percy. THE CRAFT OF FICTION. London: J. Cape, 1921.

    An essential, very influential study of the techniques of the novelist; written from a Jamesian bias.

71   Miller, Stuart. THE PICARESQUE NOVEL. Cleveland: Case Western Reserve University Press, 1967.

    An attempt to "construct an 'ideal genre type'" for the picaresque novel through discussions of formal devices found in works by several continental writers and in Defoe's MOLL FLANDERS and Smollett's RODERICK RANDOM; marred by Miller's refusal to see the picaresque as social commentary or literary satire.

72   Muir, Edwin. THE STRUCTURE OF THE NOVEL. London: Hogarth Press, 1928.

    A very important formal analysis of the variety of conventional fictional structures.

73   Richter, David H. FABLE'S END: COMPLETENESS AND CLOSURE IN RHETORICAL FICTION. Chicago: University of Chicago Press, 1974.

    Exploration of the "architectonic principles of coherence, completeness, and closure in a group of novels whose structure is generated not by plot but by doctrines, themes, attitudes, or theses"; eighteenth-century rhetorical fiction receives brief attention.

74   Scholes, Robert, and Robert Kellogg. THE NATURE OF NARRATIVE. New York: Oxford University Press, 1966.

    A fine treatment of the major narrative forms in literature, of which the novel is but one.

75   Shepperson, Archibald Bolling. THE NOVEL IN MOTLEY: A HISTORY OF THE BURLESQUE NOVEL IN ENGLISH. Cambridge, Mass.: Harvard University Press, 1936.

    A thorough study of its subject; gives major attention to eighteenth-century writers of parodic fiction, including Fielding.

76 Stevick, Philip. THE CHAPTER IN FICTION: THEORIES OF NARRATIVE DIVISION. Syracuse, N.Y.: Syracuse University Press, 1970.

> Wide-ranging, generalized discussion of the practices of novelists from Defoe through Barth.

77 _____, ed. THE THEORY OF THE NOVEL. New York: Free Press, 1967.

> A collection of fifty-three critical statements on the novel, taken from both novelists and critics; includes an extensive annotated bibliography of theoretical criticism of the novel.

78 Tillyard, E.M.W. THE EPIC STRAIN IN THE ENGLISH NOVEL. London: Chatto and Windus, 1958.

> An attempt to trace the legacy of the epic, as adapted by various novelists, from the earliest stages in the history of English prose fiction; includes an extended discussion of Fielding.

79 Trilling, Lionel. "Manners, Morals, and The Novel." THE LIBERAL IMAGINATION: ESSAYS ON LITERATURE AND SOCIETY. New York: Viking Press, 1950.

> An important essay on the novel as the vehicle of "moral realism," the agent of the "moral imagination."

80 Wellek, René, and Austin Warren. "The Nature and Modes of Narrative Fiction." THEORY OF LITERATURE. 3rd ed. New York: Harcourt, Brace, 1962.

> This entire book is essential for any student of literature; includes a valuable bibliography of works on literary theory.

ENGLISH FICTION, 1660-1800: HISTORY AND CRITICISM

81   Adams, Percy G. TRAVELERS AND TRAVEL-LIARS, 1660-1800. Berkeley and Los Angeles: University of California Press, 1962.

   An analytical survey of the period's large body of travel narratives, many of which were fictional or semifictional.

82   Alter, Robert. ROGUE'S PROGRESS: STUDIES IN THE PICARESQUE NOVEL. Cambridge, Mass.: Harvard University Press, 1964.

   See No. 57 for annotation.

83   Auty, Susan G. THE COMIC SPIRIT OF EIGHTEENTH-CENTURY NOVELS. Port Washington, N.Y.: Kennikat Press, 1975.

   This book takes the promising view that the major novels of Fielding, Smollett, and Sterne are "antisplenetic" comedies; but the discussion is somewhat derivative, and it suffers also from a muddled definition of comedy. The pursuit of the "antisplenetic" through major and minor novels does have the virtue of synthesizing various eighteenth-century notions of comic fiction.

84   Baker, Sheridan. "Ideas of Romance in Eighteenth-Century Fiction." PUBLICATIONS OF THE MICHIGAN ACADEMY OF ARTS, SCIENCES, AND LETTERS, 49 (1964), 507-22.

   A useful general study, especially for students of Richardson, Fielding, and Smollett.

85   Barnett, George, ed. EIGHTEENTH-CENTURY BRITISH NOVELISTS ON THE NOVEL. New York: Appleton-Century-Crofts, 1968.

   An anthology drawn from primary sources.

86   Beasley, Jerry C. "English Fiction in the 1740's: Some Glances at the Major and Minor Novels." SNNTS, 5 (1973), 155-75.

An attempt to assess the contemporaneity of Richardson, Fielding, and Smollett; emphasizes their common uses of conventional themes, methods, and types of fiction.

87   Black, Frank Gees. THE EPISTOLARY NOVEL IN THE LATE EIGHTEENTH CENTURY: A DESCRIPTIVE AND BIBLIOGRAPHICAL STUDY. Eugene: University of Oregon Press, 1940.

A detailed survey covering the years 1740 to about 1840; includes an extensive bibliographical listing of primary sources.

88   Black, Sidney J. "Eighteenth-Century 'Histories' as a Fictional Mode." BOSTON UNIVERSITY STUDIES IN ENGLISH, 1 (1955), 38-44.

A general discussion of the reasons why so many eighteenth-century novelists called their fictions "histories."

89   Boyce, Benjamin, ed. PREFACES TO FICTION. Augustan Reprint Society Publications, no. 32. Los Angeles: William Andrews Clark Memorial Library, 1952.

Reprints of important early prefaces by Georges de Scudéry, Manley, d'Argens, William Warburton, and Samuel Derrick.

90   Braudy, Leo. "The Form of the Sentimental Novel." NOVEL, 7 (1973), 5-13.

A persuasive attempt to show that the sentimental novels of the 1760's and 1770's were "neither the resurgence of a cultural stream that had somehow gone underground for half a century, nor part of an essentially discontinuous novelistic tradition."

91   _____. NARRATIVE FORM IN HISTORY AND FICTION: HUME, FIELDING, AND GIBBON. Princeton, N.J.: Princeton University Press, 1970.

An excellent study, in the course of which Braudy develops an unusually fresh approach to Fielding's method.

92   Brooks, Douglas. NUMBER AND PATTERN IN THE EIGHTEENTH-CENTURY NOVEL: DEFOE, FIELDING, SMOLLETT, AND STERNE. London: Routledge and Kegan Paul, 1973.

A numerologist's approach to the novels, coupled with that of the literary critic; the numerological analyses fail because they force patterns that seem not to exist, but when Brooks discusses orderly design in the works, he is on sure ground.

93   Conant, Martha Pike. THE ORIENTAL TALE IN ENGLAND IN THE EIGHTEENTH CENTURY. New York: Columbia University Press, 1908.

Still the most comprehensive survey of its field; includes a
bibliographical listing of foreign and native oriental tales.

94   Day, Robert Adams. TOLD IN LETTERS: EPISTOLARY FICTION BEFORE
RICHARDSON. Ann Arbor: University of Michigan Press, 1966.

An intelligent, thorough critical survey covering the years
1660-1740; includes an exhaustive chronological listing of English epistolary fiction published during those years.

95   Duncan, Jeffrey L. "The Rural Ideal in Eighteenth-Century Fiction."
SEL, 8 (1968), 517-35.

A general discussion; gives its chief attention to Fielding,
Smollett, Sterne, and Goldsmith.

96   Dussinger, John A. THE DISCOURSE OF THE MIND IN EIGHTEENTH-
CENTURY FICTION. The Hague: Mouton, 1974.

A study of the "dialectical relationship between eighteenth-
century empiricism and the 'new species of writing' that is
centered in the problem of knowledge"; the purpose is to account for "the anxiety and ambivalence in the dynamics of
representing the self in fiction." Included are essays on
Richardson, Johnson, Goldsmith, and Sterne.

97   Foster, James R. "The Abbé Prévost and the English Novel." PMLA, 42
(1927), 443-64.

Important to the study of the relationships between eighteenth-
century French and English fiction.

98   _____. HISTORY OF THE PRE-ROMANTIC NOVEL IN ENGLAND.
New York: Modern Language Association, 1949.

An exhaustive, detailed discussion of those major and minor
eighteenth-century novels and novelists who seem to anticipate
most directly the romanticism of the early nineteenth century.

99   Gove, Philip Babcock. THE IMAGINARY VOYAGE IN PROSE FICTION:
A HISTORY OF ITS CRITICISM AND A GUIDE FOR ITS STUDY, WITH
AN ANNOTATED CHECK LIST OF 215 IMAGINARY VOYAGES FROM
1700 TO 1800. New York: Columbia University Press, 1941.

See No. 62 for annotation.

100   Gregory, Allene. THE FRENCH REVOLUTION AND THE ENGLISH
NOVEL. New York: Putnam's, 1915.

Still a very useful discussion; novels by Holcroft, Godwin, and others seem to have been written partly in response to the Revolution.

101 Greiner, Walter F., ed. ENGLISH THEORIES OF THE NOVEL. VOL. 2: EIGHTEENTH CENTURY. Tübingen, W. Germany: Niemeyer, 1970.

A selection drawn from contemporary sources.

102 Grieder, Josephine. TRANSLATIONS OF FRENCH SENTIMENTAL PROSE FICTION IN LATE EIGHTEENTH-CENTURY ENGLAND: THE HISTORY OF A LITERARY VOGUE. Durham, N.C.: Duke University Press, 1975.

A thorough study of the popularity and importance of French sentimental fiction as it was read in translation in late eighteenth-century England. Grieder's principal object is to "describe the literary milieu in which this foreign fiction was produced, to indicate the conditions which made such translations feasible and attractive, and to present the reactions of the British critics and public towards it."

103 Haas, Gaylord R. "The English Novel from 1731 to 1740: A Decade Study." Ph.D. dissertation, Northwestern University, 1966.

A survey that offers extended summaries of and commentaries on the forgotten fiction of the 1730's.

104 Hart, Francis R. "The Experience of Character in the English Gothic Novel." EXPERIENCE IN THE NOVEL: SELECTED PAPERS FROM THE ENGLISH INSTITUTE. Ed. Roy Harvey Pearce. New York: Columbia University Press, 1968.

On methods of characterization and on the conventional means of defining the experience of terror or pathos in what are often stock characters.

105 Haviland, Thomas Philip. "The 'Roman de Longue Haleine' on English Soil." Ph.D. dissertation, University of Pennsylvania, 1931.

A study of the reception and the literary influence of French heroic romances.

106 Heidler, Joseph Bunn. THE HISTORY, FROM 1700 TO 1800, OF ENGLISH CRITICISM OF PROSE FICTION. Urbana: University of Illinois Press, 1928.

A chronological survey.

107 Horner, Joyce M. THE ENGLISH WOMEN NOVELISTS AND THEIR CONNECTION WITH THE FEMINIST MOVEMENT (1688-1797). Smith College

Studies in Modern Languages, vol. 11, no. 1-3 (1929-30). Northampton, Mass.: 1930.

> An often astute critical survey that includes fine discussions of Behn, Manley, Sarah Fielding, Lennox, Burney, and some lesser figures.

108 Hughes, Helen Sard. "The Middle-Class Reader and the English Novel." JEGP, 25 (1926), 362-78.

> A discussion of how the new prominence and literacy of the middle classes greatly influenced the early development of the novel.

109 _____. "Translations of the Vie de Marianne and their Relation to Contemporary English Fiction." MP, 15 (1917), 491-512.

> An assessment of the influence of Marivaux's novel upon English fiction-writers, especially Richardson and Fielding.

110 Hume, Robert D. "Gothic Versus Romantic: A Revaluation of the Gothic Novel." PMLA, 84 (1969), 282-90.

> An interesting, somewhat speculative essay. The Gothic is defined not merely by "the presence of some stock devices," but by the creation of an atmosphere of moral and emotional ambiguity; the chief interest is psychological.

111 Karl, Frederick R. A READER'S GUIDE TO THE EIGHTEENTH-CENTURY ENGLISH NOVEL. New York: Noonday Press, 1974.

> A readable survey of the works of major novelists and some minor ones.

112 Kay, Donald. SHORT FICTION IN THE SPECTATOR. University: University of Alabama Press, 1975.

> A systematic study of a previously neglected subject.

113 MacCarthy, Bridget G. THE LATER WOMEN NOVELISTS, 1744-1818. New York: William Salloch, 1948.

> A continuation of No. 114.

114 _____. WOMEN WRITERS: THEIR CONTRIBUTION TO THE ENGLISH NOVEL 1621-1744. Cork, Engl.: Cork University Press, 1944.

> A good study; very helpful on Behn, Manley, Haywood, and Sarah Fielding. (See also No. 113.)

115 McKillop, Alan Dugald. THE EARLY MASTERS OF ENGLISH FICTION.

Lawrence: University of Kansas Press, 1956.

Includes essays that are among the best general assessments of the novels of Defoe, Richardson, Fielding, Smollett, and Sterne.

116 _____. "English Circulating Libraries, 1725-1750." THE LIBRARY, Fourth Series, 14 (1934), 477-85.

Still an excellent account of the beginnings of what became a major means of distributing novels.

117 Major, John Campbell. THE ROLE OF PERSONAL MEMOIRS IN EN-GLISH BIOGRAPHY AND NOVEL. Philadelphia: University of Pennsylvania Press, 1934.

Useful to anyone interested in eighteenth-century fiction's increasing emphasis on the individual life.

118 Maresca, Thomas E. EPIC TO NOVEL. Columbus: Ohio State University Press, 1974.

An attempt to explain how the novel supplemented the epic in the eighteenth century; learned and interesting, but marred by its profusion of plot summaries and its blurred definition of epic.

119 Mayo, Robert D. THE ENGLISH NOVEL IN THE MAGAZINES, 1740-1815. WITH A CATALOGUE OF 1375 MAGAZINE NOVELS AND NOVELISTS. Evanston, Ill.: Northwestern University Press, 1962.

A critical and historical study of the beginnings of serial fiction; the catalogue is amply annotated and is invaluable. For some additions to the catalogue, see Edward W. Pitcher, "Robert Mayo's THE ENGLISH NOVEL IN THE MAGAZINES, 1740-1815: New Facts." THE LIBRARY, Fifth Series, 31 (1976), 20-30.

120 Mish, Charles C. "English Short Fiction in the Seventeenth Century." SSF, 6 (1969), 233-330.

A monograph-length article offering detailed analysis of the conventions of early short fiction.

121 Morgan, Charlotte E. THE RISE OF THE NOVEL OF MANNERS: A STUDY OF ENGLISH PROSE FICTION BETWEEN 1600 AND 1740. New York: Columbia University Press, 1911.

A historical survey, somewhat outdated because Morgan did not have the benefit of more recent bibliographical scholarship; includes a bibliography of some 650 works.

122 Niehus, Edward L. "The Nature and Development of the Quixote Figure in the Eighteenth-Century English Novel." Ph.D. dissertation, University of Minnesota, 1971.

> Traces the varying reflections of the extremely influential Quixote figure as seen in the major novels of the century.

123 Park, William. "Change in the Criticism of the Novel after 1760." PQ, 46 (1967), 34-41.

> The early emphasis on "nature as it is" gave way (among reviewers) to an appreciation for "imagination and wonderful incidents."

124 _____. "Fielding and Richardson." PMLA, 81 (1966), 381-88.

> Convincing argument that the novelists of the mid-eighteenth century, including a number of minor writers, shared a common body of assumptions and conventions.

125 _____. "What Was New About the 'New Species of Writing'?" SNNTS, 2 (1970), 112-30.

> An attempt to justify the claims of "newness" made by Fielding and Richardson, and to place those claims in their general contemporary contexts.

126 Paulson, Ronald. THE FICTIONS OF SATIRE. Baltimore: Johns Hopkins University Press, 1967.

> An important study that traces the mimetic drift of Augustan satire "away from formal satires" toward a kind that is a "specifically fictional construct, both in the sense that it pretends to be something that it is not, and in the sense that it produces stories, plots, and character relationships"; this leads to "the satiric novels of Fielding, Smollett, and Sterne."

127 _____. SATIRE AND THE NOVEL IN EIGHTEENTH-CENTURY ENGLAND. New Haven, Conn.: Yale University Press, 1967.

> An attempt to define Augustan satire, to chart its decline, and to explore its manifestations in the major English novels of the eighteenth century; includes excellent chapters on Fielding, Swift, Smollett, and Sterne.

128 Preston, John. THE CREATED SELF: THE READER'S ROLE IN EIGHTEENTH-CENTURY FICTION. New York: Barnes and Noble, 1970.

> A study emphasizing the relationships between the fictional world and "the 'created self,' the 'reader' invented by the

author in order to make his fictional world work"; includes
valuable essays on MOLL FLANDERS, CLARISSA, TOM JONES,
and TRISTRAM SHANDY.

129 Richetti, John J. POPULAR FICTION BEFORE RICHARDSON: NARRA-
TIVE PATTERNS 1700-1739. Oxford: Clarendon Press, 1969.

A serious analysis of the characteristic plots, stereotypes, and
moral concerns exhibited in very early eighteenth-century fiction; emphasizes the contribution of "unreadable" writers (among
them Manley and Haywood) to the beginnings of the English
novel.

130 Rothstein, Eric. SYSTEMS OF ORDER AND INQUIRY IN LATER
EIGHTEENTH-CENTURY FICTION. Berkeley and Los Angeles: University
of California Press, 1975.

Essays on RASSELAS, TRISTRAM SHANDY, HUMPHRY CLINKER,
AMELIA, and CALEB WILLIAMS. Rothstein's thesis is that,
despite their marked differences, "radical similarities of method"
inform these five major works.

131 Sacks, Sheldon. FICTION AND THE SHAPE OF BELIEF: A STUDY OF
HENRY FIELDING WITH GLANCES AT SWIFT, JOHNSON AND RICHARD-
SON. Berkeley and Los Angeles: University of California Press, 1964.

A study of how the novelists named in the title (especially
Fielding) shaped their moral convictions into satisfying aesthetic
forms.

132 Schulz, Dieter. "'Novel,' 'Romance,' and Popular Fiction in the First
Half of the Eighteenth Century." SP, 70 (1973), 77-91.

An examination of some minor early fiction, and a reevaluation
of the tirades of Richardson and Fielding against "novel" and
"romance" as attacks on subliterary "hybrids" instead of on
chivalric and heroic romance.

133 Shepperson, Archibald Bolling. THE NOVEL IN MOTLEY: A HISTORY
OF THE BURLESQUE NOVEL IN ENGLISH. Cambridge, Mass.: Harvard
University Press, 1936.

See No. 75 for annotation.

134 Sherbo, Arthur. STUDIES IN THE EIGHTEENTH CENTURY NOVEL. East
Lansing: Michigan State University Press, 1969.

An argumentative book attacking the views of many academic
commentators on the works of the major novelists, particularly
Fielding and Defoe.

135   Singer, Godfrey Frank. THE EPISTOLARY NOVEL: ITS ORIGIN, DE-
VELOPMENT, DECLINE, AND RESIDUARY INFLUENCE. Philadelphia:
University of Pennsylvania Press, 1933.

> A sweeping survey of the mode, from its beginnings to the
> twentieth century, with major attention inevitably given to the
> years 1660-1800; the discussions of material from the years
> 1660-1740 are superseded by Black, THE EPISTOLARY NOVEL
> IN THE LATE EIGHTEENTH CENTURY (No. 87), and Day,
> TOLD IN LETTERS (No. 94).

136   Slagle, Kenneth Chester. THE ENGLISH COUNTRY SQUIRE AS DE-
PICTED IN ENGLISH PROSE FICTION FROM 1740 TO 1800. Philadelphia: University of Pennsylvania Press, 1938.

> A useful study of a minor but important aspect of eighteenth-
> century fiction.

137   Spector, Robert Donald, ed. ESSAYS ON THE EIGHTEENTH-CENTURY
NOVEL. Bloomington: Indiana University Press, 1965.

> A collection of important essays, by various hands, on Defoe,
> Richardson, Fielding, Smollett, and Sterne.

138   Starkie, Walter F. "Miguel de Cervantes and the English Novel." ES-
SAYS BY DIVERS HANDS, 34 (1966), 159-79.

> A very important assessment of the influence of Cervantes,
> which was greatest during the eighteenth century.

139   STUDIES IN THE NOVEL, 2 (Summer 1970). Special Number: British
Neo-Classical Novel.

> Essays by various modern scholars.

140   Summers, Montague. THE GOTHIC QUEST: A HISTORY OF THE GOTHIC
NOVEL. London: Fortune Press, 1938.

> A readable, sweeping treatment, often more appreciative than
> critical.

141   Swedenberg, Hugh T. THE THEORY OF THE EPIC IN ENGLAND 1650-
1800. Berkeley and Los Angeles: University of California Press, 1944.

> Especially valuable to the student of Fielding.

142   _____, ed. THE USES OF IRONY: PAPERS ON DEFOE AND SWIFT
READ AT A CLARK LIBRARY SEMINAR. Berkeley and Los Angeles: University of California Press, 1966.

> Papers delivered by various distinguished scholars.

143   Taylor, John Tinnon. EARLY OPPOSITION TO THE ENGLISH NOVEL:
      THE POPULAR REACTION FROM 1760 TO 1830. New York: King's
      Crown Press, 1943.

      A study of the reputation of early fiction, which is an important
      part of its history.

144   Tieje, Arthur Jerrold. "A Peculiar Phase of the Theory of Realism in
      Pre-Richardsonian Fiction." PMLA, 28 (1913), 213-52.

      A discussion of the literary implications of the early preoccupa-
      tion with the "wickedness of lying" and the "utility of veri-
      fied narrative."

145   Tompkins, J.M.S. THE POPULAR NOVEL IN ENGLAND 1770-1800.
      London: Constable, 1932.

      An extensive critical survey that gives major emphasis to the
      great mass of "tenth-rate fiction" published during the period
      covered.

146   Utter, Robert P., and Gwendolyn B. Needham. PAMELA'S DAUGHTERS.
      New York: Macmillan, 1937.

      An entertaining, scholarly history of the sentimental heroine
      in English fiction from 1740 to about 1900.

147   Varma, Devendra P. THE GOTHIC FLAME: BEING A HISTORY OF THE
      GOTHIC NOVEL IN ENGLAND. London: Arthur Barker, 1957.

      Comprehensive but superficial.

148   Watt, Ian [P.]. THE RISE OF THE NOVEL: STUDIES IN DEFOE, RICH-
      ARDSON, AND FIELDING. London: Chatto and Windus, 1957.

      An invaluable study emphasizing the "enduring connections be-
      tween the distinctive literary qualities of the novel" and the
      "society in which it began and flourished."

149   Williams, Ioan. NOVEL AND ROMANCE, 1700-1800: A DOCUMEN-
      TARY RECORD. New York: Barnes and Noble, 1970.

      A valuable collection of early comments on fiction, gathered
      from prefaces, letters, magazines, and other primary sources; the
      table of contents serves almost as a bibliographical guide to
      early criticism of novels.

150   Wright, Walter Francis. SENSIBILITY IN ENGLISH PROSE FICTION,
      1760-1814: A REINTERPRETATION. Urbana: University of Illinois Press,
      1937.

A "new" interpretation, no longer very new but still interesting, of the "full significance of sensibility as a creative impulse in the novelists of the period." This study should be read along with the discussions by Crane (No. 21) and Frye (No. 26).

CHECKLISTS AND OTHER BIBLIOGRAPHICAL RESOURCES

151 ABSTRACTS OF ENGLISH STUDIES. Urbana, Ill.: National Council of Teachers of English, 1958-- . 10/year.

   See No. 1 for annotation.

152 Altick, Richard D., and Andrew Wright. SELECTIVE BIBLIOGRAPHY FOR THE STUDY OF ENGLISH AND AMERICAN LITERATURE. 5th ed. New York: Macmillan, 1975.

   See No. 2 for annotation.

153 Beasley, Jerry C. A CHECK LIST OF PROSE FICTION PUBLISHED IN ENGLAND, 1740-1749. Charlottesville: University Press of Virginia, 1972.

   Some 338 entries, with (for most titles) original publication data, library locations of extant copies, and descriptive annotations.

154 Bell, Inglis F., and Donald Baird. THE ENGLISH NOVEL 1578-1956: A CHECKLIST OF TWENTIETH-CENTURY CRITICISMS. Denver, Colo.: Alan Swallow, 1958.

   An unannotated listing of modern critical articles and books on novelists from Lyly to Graham Greene. Supplemented by Helen H. Palmer and Anne Jane Dyson, ENGLISH NOVEL EXPLICA-TION: CRITICISMS TO 1972 (Hamden, Conn.: Shoe String Press, 1973); further supplemented by Peter L. Abernethy et al., ENGLISH NOVEL EXPLICATION: SUPPLEMENT I (Hamden, Conn.: Shoe String Press, 1976). The 1976 supplement covers the years 1972-74.

155 Black, Frank Gees. THE EPISTOLARY NOVEL IN THE LATE EIGHTEENTH CENTURY: A DESCRIPTIVE AND BIBLIOGRAPHICAL STUDY. Eugene: University of Oregon Press, 1940.

   See No. 87 for annotation.

156 Blakey, Dorothy. THE MINERVA PRESS, 1790-1820. London: Bibliographical Society, 1939.

> A history of the Minerva Press, chief provider of novels (es-
> pecially Gothic novels) for the circulating libraries; includes
> also extensive bibliographical listings of the Minerva's publi-
> cations.

157 Block, Andrew. THE ENGLISH NOVEL, 1740-1850: A CATALOGUE.
2nd ed. London: William Dawson, 1961.

> Ambitious, but incomplete, inaccurate, and difficult to use
> because of its strictly alphabetical arrangement.

158 Bond, Donald F. THE EIGHTEENTH CENTURY. Arlington Heights, Ill.:
AHM, 1975.

> One volume in the "Goldentree" series of bibliographies; pro-
> vides listings for general topics and for some one hundred writ-
> ers of the period; excludes the novelists, who will soon have
> a volume all their own: THE BRITISH NOVEL THROUGH
> JANE AUSTEN, ed. Wayne C. Booth and Gwin J. Kolb.

159 Bonheim, Helmut W. THE ENGLISH NOVEL BEFORE RICHARDSON: A
CHECKLIST OF TEXTS AND CRITICISMS TO 1970. Metuchen, N.J.:
Scarecrow Press, 1971.

> Brief, highly selective, unannotated listings for twenty-six
> writers; includes also a general list covering anthologies, check-
> lists, and subject areas.

160 Booth, Wayne C. THE RHETORIC OF FICTION. Chicago: University
of Chicago Press, 1961.

> See No. 58 for annotation.

161 BRITISH MUSEUM GENERAL CATALOGUE OF PRINTED BOOKS. London:
1959-- .

> See No. 3 for annotation.

162 THE CAMBRIDGE BIBLIOGRAPHY OF ENGLISH LITERATURE. VOL. II:
1660-1800. Ed. F.W. Bateson. Cambridge: At the University Press,
1941.

> A basic bibliographical resource, especially valuable for its
> author bibliographies of primary and secondary sources. See
> also NCBEL, the recent revision (No. 187).

163 Conant, Martha Pike. THE ORIENTAL TALE IN ENGLAND IN THE EIGH-

TEENTH CENTURY. New York: Columbia University Press, 1908.

See No. 93 for annotation.

164 Cordasco, Francesco. EIGHTEENTH CENTURY BIBLIOGRAPHIES. Metuchen, N.J.: Scarecrow Press, 1970.

Includes bibliographies of the major eighteenth-century novelists.

165 Cox, Edward Godfrey. A REFERENCE GUIDE TO THE LITERATURE OF TRAVEL. 3 vols. Seattle: University of Washington Press, 1935-49.

A comprehensive bibliography relevant to the study of the imaginary voyage.

166 Day, Robert Adams. TOLD IN LETTERS: EPISTOLARY FICTION BEFORE RICHARDSON. Ann Arbor: University of Michigan Press, 1966.

See No. 94 for annotation.

167 DISSERTATION ABSTRACTS INTERNATIONAL. Ann Arbor, Mich.: University Microfilms, 1938-- . Monthly.

See No. 5 for annotation.

168 Downs, Robert B. AMERICAN LIBRARY RESOURCES: A BIBLIOGRAPHICAL GUIDE. Chicago: American Library Association, 1951. Supplements: 2 vols., 1962, 1972.

See No. 6 for annotation.

169 _____. BRITISH LIBRARY RESOURCES: A BIBLIOGRAPHICAL GUIDE. Chicago: American Library Association, 1973.

See No. 7 for annotation.

170 Dyson, A.E., ed. THE ENGLISH NOVEL: SELECT BIBLIOGRAPHICAL GUIDES. London: Oxford University Press, 1974.

Extensive and authoritative bibliographical essays on twenty English novelists, including Bunyan, Defoe, Swift, Richardson, Fielding, Sterne, and Smollett.

171 THE EIGHTEENTH CENTURY: A CURRENT BIBLIOGRAPHY. PQ, 1926-- . Annual.

A comprehensive listing, with extensive descriptive and evaluative annotations, of books, articles, and book reviews in the field. As of 1976, this bibliography is published directly by the American Society for Eighteenth-Century Studies. The bibliographies for 1925-60 have been collected in six volumes by

Louis A. Landa et al. as ENGLISH LITERATURE, 1660-1800:
A BIBLIOGRAPHY OF MODERN STUDIES (Princeton, N.J.:
Princeton University Press, 1950-72).

172 Esdaile, Arundell. A LIST OF ENGLISH TALES AND PROSE ROMANCES
PRINTED BEFORE 1740. London: Bibliographical Society, 1912.

Out of date and incomplete, but still very useful.

173 Gecker, Sidney. ENGLISH FICTION TO 1820 IN THE UNIVERSITY OF
PENNSYLVANIA LIBRARY. Philadelphia: University of Pennsylvania
Press, 1954.

A useful record of the Pennsylvania holdings, though woefully
out of date; still more valuable as a listing of primary texts.

174 THE GENTLEMAN'S MAGAZINE, 1731-51: THE LISTS OF BOOKS,
COLLECTED WITH ANNUAL INDEXES AND THE INDEX TO THE FIRST
TWENTY YEARS COMPILED BY EDWARD KIMBER (1752). London: Gregg-
Archive, 1966.

An extremely handy tool for the user who wishes to explore
the GENTLEMAN'S valuable monthly registers of new books.

175 Gove, Philip Babcock. THE IMAGINARY VOYAGE IN PROSE FICTION:
A HISTORY OF ITS CRITICISM AND A GUIDE FOR ITS STUDY, WITH AN
ANNOTATED CHECK LIST OF 215 IMAGINARY VOYAGES FROM 1700
TO 1800. New York: Columbia University Press, 1941.

See No. 62 for annotation.

176 Greenough, C.N. "Catalogue of English Prose Fiction, 1470-1832" (card-
index at the Widener Library of Harvard University).

Useful because it ranges so widely, but erratic and incomplete.

177 Jones, S. Paul. A LIST OF FRENCH PROSE FICTION FROM 1700 TO
1750. New York: Wilson, 1939.

An aid to the exploration of relationships between French and
English fiction of the early eighteenth century.

178 McBurney, William Harlin. A CHECK LIST OF ENGLISH PROSE FICTION,
1700-1739. Cambridge, Mass.: Harvard University Press, 1960.

Almost 400 entries, with full titles, publication information,
and library locations of extant copies. For some additions and
corrections to McBurney's listings, see the review by Donald
F. Bond, MP, 59 (1962), 231-34.

179 _____ . ENGLISH PROSE FICTION, 1700-1800, IN THE UNIVERSITY OF ILLINOIS LIBRARY. Urbana: University of Illinois Press, 1965.

Valuable as a record of the Illinois holdings, but even more valuable as a listing of primary texts.

180 McNutt, Dan J. THE EIGHTEENTH-CENTURY GOTHIC NOVEL: AN ANNOTATED BIBLIOGRAPHY OF CRITICISM AND SELECTED TEXTS. New York: Garland, 1975.

A helpful, amply annotated listing; includes a general bibliography as well as separate listings for Walpole, Lewis, Beckford, Reeve, Charlotte Smith, and Radcliffe.

181 Mayo, Robert D. THE ENGLISH NOVEL IN THE MAGAZINES, 1740-1815. WITH A CATALOGUE OF 1375 MAGAZINE NOVELS AND NOVELISTS. Evanston, Ill.: Northwestern University Press, 1962.

See No. 119 for annotation.

182 MHRA ANNUAL BIBLIOGRAPHY OF ENGLISH LANGUAGE AND LITERATURE. Cambridge, Engl.: Modern Humanities Research Association, 1921-- .

An unannotated listing of scholarly publications; coverage begins with the year 1920.

183 Mish, Charles C. ENGLISH PROSE FICTION, 1600-1700: A CHRONOLOGICAL CHECKLIST. Charlottesville: University Press of Virginia, 1967.

An invaluable listing; no annotations.

184 MLA INTERNATIONAL BIBLIOGRAPHY OF BOOKS AND ARTICLES ON THE MODERN LANGUAGES AND LITERATURES. New York: Modern Language Association, 1922-- . Annual.

No annotations. Prior to 1956, listed the work of American scholars only, and until 1970 always appeared in PMLA; issued separately since 1970, and since 1972 accompanied by the annual publication of MLA ABSTRACTS (see No. 11).

185 Morgan, Charlotte E. THE RISE OF THE NOVEL OF MANNERS: A STUDY OF ENGLISH PROSE FICTION BETWEEN 1600 AND 1740. New York: Columbia University Press, 1911.

See No. 121 for annotation.

186 THE NATIONAL UNION CATALOGUE. London: Mansell; Chicago: American Library Association, 1968.

See No. 12 for annotation.

187 THE NEW CAMBRIDGE BIBLIOGRAPHY OF ENGLISH LITERATURE.
VOL. II: 1660-1800. Ed. George Watson. Cambridge: At the University Press, 1971.

> Revision of CBEL (No. 162); a basic bibliographical resource, but should be supplemented with more specialized bibliographies.

188 "Recent Studies in the Restoration and Eighteenth Century." SEL, 1961-- .

> A bibliographical essay published annually in the summer number of SEL; devoted primarily to the discussion of book-length studies.

189 Sherburn, George, and Donald F. Bond. THE RESTORATION AND EIGHTEENTH CENTURY (1660-1789). A Literary History of England, vol. 3. Ed. Albert C. Baugh. 2nd ed. New York: Appleton-Century-Crofts, 1967.

> See No. 37 for annotation.

190 Stauffer, Donald A. THE ART OF BIOGRAPHY IN EIGHTEENTH CENTURY ENGLAND. WITH A BIBLIOGRAPHICAL SUPPLEMENT. Princeton, N.J.: Princeton University Press, 1941.

> See No. 246 for annotation.

191 Stevenson, Lionel. THE ENGLISH NOVEL: A PANORAMA. Boston: Houghton Mifflin, 1960.

> See No. 53 for annotation.

192 Stevick, Philip, ed. THE THEORY OF THE NOVEL. New York: Free Press, 1967.

> See No. 77 for annotation.

193 Streeter, Harold Wade. THE EIGHTEENTH CENTURY ENGLISH NOVEL IN FRENCH TRANSLATION: A BIBLIOGRAPHICAL STUDY. New York: Publications of the Institute of French Studies, 1936.

> One half of this study deals with the reception of English novelists in eighteenth-century France; the rest is a bibliographical record.

194 Summers, Montague. A GOTHIC BIBLIOGRAPHY. London: Fortune Press, 1941.

> A selective listing of Gothic fiction, 1728-1916.

195 Wagenknecht, Edward. CAVALCADE OF THE ENGLISH NOVEL. New

York: Holt, 1943; rev. ed., 1954.

See No. 55 for annotation.

196 Williams, Ioan. NOVEL AND ROMANCE, 1700-1800: A DOCUMEN-
TARY RECORD. New York: Barnes and Noble, 1970.

See No. 149 for annotation.

197 THE YEAR'S WORK IN ENGLISH STUDIES. London: English Association,
1921-- . Annual.

A record, with brief descriptive and evaluative annotations, of
scholarly publications; coverage begins with the year 1919.

SPECIAL RESOURCES

A. SERIALS

198 EIGHTEENTH-CENTURY STUDIES. 1967-- . Quarterly.

An interdisciplinary journal; since 1970, the official journal of the American Society for Eighteenth-Century Studies. Regularly publishes review articles and book reviews.

199 ENLIGHTENMENT ESSAYS. 1970-- . Quarterly.

200 GENRE. 1968-- . Quarterly.

Critical essays on all genres.

201 JOHNSONIAN NEWS LETTER. 1940-- . Quarterly.

Includes news of professional meetings, of recent eighteenth-century scholarship, and of ongoing research in the field.

202 JOURNAL OF NARRATIVE TECHNIQUE. 1971-- . 3/year.

203 NOVEL: A FORUM ON FICTION. 1967-- . 3/year.

Mainly devoted to articles on the theory of fiction; regularly features review articles and book reviews.

204 THE SCRIBLERIAN: A NEWSLETTER DEVOTED TO POPE, SWIFT, AND THEIR CIRCLE. 1968-- . 2/year.

205 STUDIES IN BURKE AND HIS TIME. 1959-- . 3/year.

Interdisciplinary journal; devoted to all aspects of late eighteenth-century culture. Volumes 1-8 were published under the title BURKE NEWSLETTER.

206 STUDIES IN EIGHTEENTH-CENTURY CULTURE. 1971-- . Annual.

> Gathers together the best papers (on various aspects of eighteenth-century culture) from the national and regional meetings of the American Society for Eighteenth-Century Studies.

207 STUDIES IN ENGLISH LITERATURE, 1500-1900. 1961-- . Quarterly.

> The summer number of each volume is devoted to eighteenth-century literature and includes a review essay covering recent scholarship in the field (see No. 188).

208 STUDIES IN THE NOVEL. 1969-- . Quarterly.

> Regularly publishes book reviews.

B. REPRINT SERIES AND SELECTED MODERN COLLECTIONS

209 THE FEMINIST CONTROVERSY IN ENGLAND 1788-1810. Ed. Gina Luria. 89 vols. New York: Garland, 1974-75.

> A collection of forty-four titles, with introductions by Gina Luria; reprints are in photofacsimile from first editions. The series includes works of fiction by Beckford, Godwin, and Charlotte Smith.

> For a catalogue of titles, write to Garland Publishing Inc., 545 Madison Ave., New York, N.Y. 10022.

210 THE FLOWERING OF THE NOVEL: REPRESENTATIVE MID-EIGHTEENTH-CENTURY FICTION 1740-1775. Selected and arranged by Michael F. Shugrue, Jerry C. Beasley, and Malcolm J. Bosse. 121 vols. New York: Garland, 1974-75.

> Photofacsimile reprints of 121 titles, many of them extremely rare. This series is now available with No. 211 under the general title THE NOVEL IN ENGLAND 1700-1775. (See also No. 214.)

> For a catalogue of titles, write to Garland Publishing Inc., 545 Madison Ave., New York, N.Y. 10022.

211 FOUNDATIONS OF THE NOVEL: REPRESENTATIVE EARLY EIGHTEENTH-CENTURY FICTION. Comp. and Ed. Michael F. Shugrue. Intro. Michael F. Shugrue, Malcolm J. Bosse, William Graves, and Josephine Grieder. 71 vols. New York: Garland, 1972-73.

> Photofacsimile reprints of 101 titles, 1700-1739. Now available with No. 210 under the general title THE NOVEL IN ENGLAND 1700-1775. (See also No. 214.)

For a catalogue of titles, write to Garland Publishing Inc.,
545 Madison Ave., New York, N.Y. 10022.

212 FOUR BEFORE RICHARDSON: SELECTED ENGLISH NOVELS, 1720-1727.
Ed. William H[arlin] McBurney. Lincoln: University of Nebraska Press,
1963.

Includes an excellent general introduction by McBurney, and
four novels by precursors of Richardson, Fielding, and Smollett:
Arthur Blackamore, LUCK AT LAST: OR, THE HAPPY UNFOR-
TUNATE (1723); W.P., THE JAMAICA LADY; OR, THE LIFE
OF BAVIA (1720); Eliza Haywood, PHILIDORE AND PLACEN-
TIA; OR, L'AMOUR TROP DELICAT (1727); Mary Davys, THE
ACCOMPLISHED RAKE; OR, MODERN FINE GENTLEMAN
(1727).

213 GOTHIC NOVELS. Ed. Devendra P. Varma. 49 vols. New York:
Arno Press, 1972-74.

Includes twenty titles, published under the general editorship
of Varma, who, along with other scholars, provides excellent
introductions to the selections.

For a catalogue of titles, write to Arno Press, 330 Madison Ave.,
New York, N.Y. 10017.

214 THE LIFE AND TIMES OF SEVEN MAJOR BRITISH WRITERS: DRYDEN,
POPE, SWIFT, RICHARDSON, STERNE, JOHNSON, GIBBON. 147 vols.
New York: Garland, 1974-76.

A collection of reprints, in photofacsimile, of 370 contemporary
books, pamphlets, and broadsides, most of them written in response to the works of the seven writers represented in the collection. (See also Nos. 210 and 211.)

For a catalogue of titles, write to Garland Publishing Inc.,
545 Madison Ave., New York, N.Y. 10022.

215 THE NOVEL IN LETTERS: EPISTOLARY FICTION IN THE EARLY EN-
GLISH NOVEL, 1678-1740. Ed. Natascha Wurzbach. Coral Gables,
Fla.: University of Miami Press, 1969.

Nine anonymous novels, with an informative general introduction.

216 RESTORATION PROSE FICTION, 1666-1700: AN ANTHOLOGY OF REP-
RESENTATIVE PIECES. Ed. Charles C. Mish. Lincoln: University of
Nebraska Press, 1970.

Includes a dozen short works of fiction, among them Behn's
THE HISTORY OF THE NUN.

SELECTED BACKGROUND READINGS

217 Altick, Richard D. THE ENGLISH COMMON READER: A SOCIAL HIS-
TORY OF THE MASS READING PUBLIC 1800-1900. Chicago: University
of Chicago Press, 1957.

An important study whose opening chapter deals succinctly and
usefully with "The Background: 1477-1800."

218 Anderson, Howard, et al., eds. THE FAMILIAR LETTER IN THE EIGH-
TEENTH CENTURY. Lawrence: University of Kansas Press, 1966.

Essays on the conventions of letter writing, and on the great
letter writers; especially useful to students of the novels of
Richardson and Burney.

219 Auerbach, Erich. MIMESIS: THE REPRESENTATION OF REALITY IN
WESTERN LITERATURE. Trans. Willard R. Trask. Princeton, N.J.:
Princeton University Press, 1953.

Auerbach does not focus on fiction, but the brilliant treatment
of his subject makes this book essential to the study of novels
of any period.

220 Bate, Walter Jackson. FROM CLASSIC TO ROMANTIC: PREMISES OF
TASTE IN EIGHTEENTH-CENTURY ENGLAND. Cambridge, Mass.: Harvard University Press, 1946.

An essential study of the period's changing aesthetics.

221 Blakey, Dorothy. THE MINERVA PRESS, 1790-1820. London: Bibliographical Society, 1939.

See No. 156 for annotation.

222 Byrd, Max. VISITS TO BEDLAM: MADNESS AND LITERATURE IN THE
EIGHTEENTH CENTURY. Columbia: University of South Carolina Press,
1974.

See No. 18 for annotation.

223 Clifford, James L., ed. MAN VERSUS SOCIETY IN EIGHTEENTH-CENTURY BRITAIN. Cambridge: At the University Press, 1968.

> Essays by various hands on political, economic, clerical, and artistic issues.

224 Collins, Arthur S. AUTHORSHIP IN THE DAYS OF JOHNSON: BEING A STUDY OF THE RELATION BETWEEN AUTHOR, PATRON, PUBLISHER AND PUBLIC, 1726-1780. New York: Dutton, 1929.

> Still a valuable study of matters that greatly affected the professional habits of novelists in the period.

225 Crane, Ronald S. "Suggestions toward a Genealogy of the 'Man of Feeling.'" THE IDEA OF THE HUMANITIES, I. Ed. Wayne C. Booth. Chicago: University of Chicago Press, 1967.

> See No. 21 for annotation.

226 DePorte, Michael V. NIGHTMARES AND HOBBYHORSES: SWIFT, STERNE, AND AUGUSTAN IDEAS OF MADNESS. San Marino, Calif.: Huntington Library, 1974.

> See No. 22 for annotation.

227 Frantz, R.W. THE ENGLISH TRAVELLER AND THE MOVEMENT OF IDEAS, 1660-1732. Lincoln: University of Nebraska Press, 1934.

> Helpful to our understanding of the reasons for the period's growing interest in the travel narrative and the imaginary voyage.

228 George, M. Dorothy. ENGLAND IN TRANSITION: LIFE AND WORK IN THE EIGHTEENTH CENTURY. London: Routledge, 1931.

> An important study of the period's social history.

229 _____. LONDON LIFE IN THE EIGHTEENTH CENTURY. London, 1925; rpt. New York: Harper Torchbooks, 1964.

> An essential study. The Harper reprint includes a supplement to the original bibliography.

230 Greene, Donald. THE AGE OF EXUBERANCE: BACKGROUNDS TO EIGHTEENTH-CENTURY ENGLISH LITERATURE. New York: Random House, 1970.

> An excellent little book that surveys the history of English aesthetics, philosophy, politics, and society from the Restoration to the 1780's.

231 Hipple, Walter J. THE BEAUTIFUL, THE SUBLIME, AND THE PICTUR-
ESQUE. Carbondale: Southern Illinois University Press, 1957.

   A philosophical investigation of late eighteenth-century tastes
   and aesthetics; should be read along with Monk's THE SUB-
   LIME (No. 241).

232 Hughes, Peter, and David Williams, eds. THE VARIED PATTERN: STUD-
IES IN THE EIGHTEENTH CENTURY. Toronto: Hakkert, 1971.

   An anthology of modern essays on several aspects of eighteenth-
   century culture.

233 Kliger, Samuel. "Whig Aesthetics: A Phase of Eighteenth-Century Taste."
ELH, 16 (1949), 135-50.

   A discussion of the very significant influence of Whig political
   philosophy (and its Lockean content) on eighteenth-century
   aesthetics.

234 Korshin, Paul J., ed. STUDIES IN CHANGE AND REVOLUTION: AS-
PECTS OF ENGLISH INTELLECTUAL HISTORY 1640-1800. London: Scolar
Press, 1972.

   Essays by various scholars on several subjects in the general
   area of intellectual history.

235 Leavis, Q.D. FICTION AND THE READING PUBLIC. London: Chatto
and Windus, 1939.

   A provocative study of the quality of fiction and its audience
   from the eighteenth century through the twentieth; the judgments on the general sophistication of eighteenth-century novelists and their readers are challenged by more recent scholarship.

236 Lovejoy, Arthur O. THE GREAT CHAIN OF BEING. Cambridge, Mass.:
Harvard University Press, 1936.

   An essential study of important early philosophical assumptions.

237 MacLean, Kenneth. JOHN LOCKE AND ENGLISH LITERATURE OF THE
EIGHTEENTH CENTURY. New Haven, Conn.: Yale University Press,
1936.

   A valuable study, if somewhat uneven; the writers whose work
   is treated include Sterne.

238 Manwaring, Elizabeth. ITALIAN LANDSCAPE IN EIGHTEENTH CENTURY
ENGLAND: A STUDY CHIEFLY OF THE INFLUENCE OF CLAUDE LOR-
RAIN AND SALVATOR ROSA ON ENGLISH TASTE 1700-1800. London:
Frank Cass, 1925.

Indispensable to the study of Gothic fiction.

239 Mazzeo, J.A., ed. REASON AND THE IMAGINATION: STUDIES IN THE HISTORY OF IDEAS, 1600-1800. New York: Columbia University Press, 1962.

Various essays by modern scholars; includes important studies of Swift and Sterne.

240 Mingay, G.E. ENGLISH LANDED SOCIETY IN THE EIGHTEENTH CENTURY. London: Routledge and Kegan Paul, 1963.

A very helpful study of an aspect of social history important to the student of eighteenth-century fiction.

241 Monk, Samuel Holt. THE SUBLIME: A STUDY OF CRITICAL THEORIES IN XVIII-CENTURY ENGLAND. New York: Modern Language Association, 1935.

An essential study of an important aspect of eighteenth-century taste and aesthetics; extremely relevant to the study of the Gothic novel, and should be read along with Hipple's THE BEAUTIFUL, THE SUBLIME, AND THE PICTURESQUE (No. 231).

242 Ogg, David. ENGLAND IN THE REIGN OF CHARLES II. 2nd ed. 2 vols. Oxford: Clarendon Press, 1956.

The standard history of this period.

243 Plant, Marjorie. THE ENGLISH BOOK TRADE: AN ECONOMIC HISTORY OF THE MAKING AND SALE OF BOOKS. London: Allen and Unwin, 1939.

Useful because it sheds light on the practice of booksellers, who powerfully influenced the early history of the novel.

244 Plumb, J.H. SIR ROBERT WALPOLE. 2 vols. London: Cresset Press, 1960.

The standard biography of the man who dominated English politics from 1720 to 1742 and who figured so prominently in the fiction of the period.

245 Schlatter, Richard B. THE SOCIAL IDEAS OF RELIGIOUS LEADERS, 1660-1688. London: Oxford University Press, 1940.

Emphasis on Puritan social philosophy.

246 Stauffer, Donald A. THE ART OF BIOGRAPHY IN EIGHTEENTH CEN-

TURY ENGLAND. WITH A BIBLIOGRAPHICAL SUPPLEMENT. Princeton, N.J.: Princeton University Press, 1941.

As Stauffer shows, biography and fiction often merged in this period. The bibliographical supplement lists hundreds of biographical and quasi-biographical works. (See also No. 247.)

247 _____. ENGLISH BIOGRAPHY BEFORE 1700. Cambridge, Mass.: Harvard University Press, 1930.

A history and survey. (See also No. 246.)

248. Stephen, Leslie. HISTORY OF ENGLISH THOUGHT IN THE EIGHTEENTH CENTURY. 3rd ed., rev. 2 vols. London: Smith, Elder, 1902.

First published in 1876; comprehensive, readable, and still indispensable to students of Restoration and eighteenth-century literature.

249 Stromberg, Roland N. RELIGIOUS LIBERALISM IN EIGHTEENTH-CENTURY ENGLAND. London: Oxford University Press, 1954.

Useful study of the optimistic philosophy that began with the Latitudinarians and ultimately helped to encourage the so-called cult of sensibility.

250 STUDIES IN BURKE AND HIS TIME. 1959-- . 3/year.

See No. 205 for annotation.

251 STUDIES IN EIGHTEENTH-CENTURY CULTURE. 1971-- . Annual.

See No. 206 for annotation.

252 Trevelyan, George Macaulay. HISTORY OF ENGLAND. 3 vols. Garden City, N.Y.: Doubleday, 1953.

First published in 1926; this history remains the most useful for the nonspecialist.

253 _____. ILLUSTRATED ENGLISH SOCIAL HISTORY. VOL. III: THE EIGHTEENTH CENTURY. London: Longmans, Green, 1951.

The most comprehensive and useful study of this subject.

254 Varma, Devendra P. THE EVERGREEN TREE OF DIABOLICAL KNOWLEDGE. Washington, D.C.: Consortium Press, 1972.

A discussion of the circulating libraries of the late eighteenth and nineteenth centuries, with major attention to popular Gothic fiction and to the reading tastes of the period.

255   Willey, Basil. THE EIGHTEENTH CENTURY BACKGROUND: STUDIES ON THE IDEA OF NATURE IN THE THOUGHT OF THE PERIOD. London: Chatto and Windus, 1940.

> An essential study of important philosophical currents in the period; continues No. 256.

256   _____. THE SEVENTEENTH CENTURY BACKGROUND: STUDIES IN THE THOUGHT OF THE AGE IN RELATION TO POETRY AND RELIGION. London: Chatto and Windus, 1934.

> See also No. 255.

257   Williams, Basil. THE WHIG SUPREMACY: 1714-1760. Oxford: Clarendon Press, 1939.

> A fine study; the political history it records is extremely important to any student of the period's fiction.

Part II

INDIVIDUAL AUTHORS

A NOTE ON THE ORGANIZATION OF PART II

The listings for each author are arranged according to the following scheme:

    (1) Principal Works. This is a short-title list of works and their dates of original publication. It is usually quite selective and is intended only as a convenient reference and an indication of the range of the author's work.

    (2) Editions. These include the collected works (when available), selections and specialized collections (when available), and important separate editions of the novels and of closely related works in other genres. The listings are selective and are restricted to the most important or useful editions.

    (3) Letters. The available scholarly editions of the author's letters, and sometimes the journals or diaries, are listed in this section.

    (4) Bibliography. Included here are the available bibliographies and checklists of works by and about the author.

    (5) Biography. This section typically lists introductory biographical studies as well as the more sophisticated biographies and critical biographies intended for an audience of specialists.

    (6) Critical Studies and Commentaries. In this section are important books, articles, and collections of essays on the author's work, with an emphasis on twentieth-century criticism.

All editions, including collections of letters, appear in chronological order of publication, while bibliographies, biographies, and critical studies are arranged alphabetically within their separate categories. For a fuller discussion of the format of part II, see the introduction with which this book begins.

ROBERT BAGE (1728-1801)

As a political and social radical, Bage wrote several early, anonymously published doctrinaire novels that anticipated the work of his more famous contemporary, William Godwin. His last work, HERMSPRONG (1796), is a satirical survey of late eighteenth-century political and social controversies. Bage, an important minor writer, has been almost totally neglected by editors and critics.

PRINCIPAL WORKS

MOUNT HENNETH. A NOVEL, IN A SERIES OF LETTERS, 1781
BARHAM DOWNS. A NOVEL, 1784
THE FAIR SYRIAN, A NOVEL, 1787
JAMES WALLACE, A NOVEL, 1788
MAN AS HE IS. A NOVEL, 1792
HERMSPRONG, OR MAN AS HE IS NOT. A NOVEL, 1796

EDITIONS

A. Selections

258 MOUNT HENNETH, BARHAM DOWNS, JAMES WALLACE. Ballantyne's Novelists' Library, vol. 9. With a Prefatory MEMOIR by Sir Walter Scott. London, 1821.

B. Individual Works

HERMSPRONG

259 HERMSPRONG: OR, MAN AS HE IS NOT. Ed. Vaughan Wilkins. London: Turnstile Press, 1951.

260 HERMSPRONG, OR, MAN AS HE IS NOT. Drawings by Cecil Keeling. London: Folio Society, 1960.

A handsome edition.

BIOGRAPHY

261 See No. 258.

CRITICAL STUDIES AND COMMENTARIES

Commentary on Bage and his fiction must be sought primarily in the standard histories of the novel, which should be consulted along with the studies entered here.

262 Crouch, William G. "The Novels of Robert Bage." Ph.D. dissertation, Princeton University, 1937.

A sensible, readable critical survey.

263 Fletcher, Theodore T. "Robert Bage: A Representative Revolutionary Novelist." Ph.D. dissertation, New York University, 1945.

An overview that emphasizes Bage's politics, with little attention to his art.

264 Foster, James R. HISTORY OF THE PRE-ROMANTIC NOVEL IN ENGLAND. New York: Modern Language Association, 1949.

Brief but insightful treatment of Bage's novels, which, according to Foster, have been unjustly neglected.

265 Grabo, C.H. "Robert Bage, a Forgotten Novelist." MIDWEST QUARTERLY, 5 (1917), 201-26.

A survey that attempts to recover the work of Bage from oblivion.

266 McCracken, David. "Godwin's Literary Theory: The Alliance between Fiction and Political Philosophy." PQ, 49 (1970), 113-33.

A discussion distinguishing between Godwin and other contemporary doctrinaire novelists, including Bage.

267 Sutherland, John H. "Robert Bage, Novelist of Ideas." PQ, 36 (1957), 211-20.

A thorough study of the doctrinaire aspects of Bage's fiction.

268   Tompkins, J.M.S.   THE POPULAR NOVEL IN ENGLAND 1770-1800.
      London: Constable, 1932.

> Various sections of this fine study offer sensitive discussions of
> the six novels of Bage, who, Tompkins claims, brought to fic-
> tion a "great increase of intellectual content."

WILLIAM BECKFORD (1760-1844)

Beckford was the eccentric, extremely wealthy son of a lord mayor of London. A painter and musician (he studied under Mozart), he also dabbled in architecture and constructed a fantastic palace called Fonthill, which inspired the setting for VATHEK (1786). Beckford's remarkable book, originally written in French, at once continues and burlesques the oriental and Gothic fashions in the fiction of his day.

PRINCIPAL WORKS

BIOGRAPHICAL MEMOIRS OF EXTRAORDINARY PAINTERS, 1780
VATHEK, 1786 (Novel)
POPULAR TALES OF THE GERMANS, by Musaeus, 1791 (Translation)
MODERN NOVEL WRITING, 1796 (Novel/burlesque)
AZEMIA: A DESCRIPTIVE AND SENTIMENTAL NOVEL, 1797 (Burlesque)
ITALY: WITH SKETCHES OF SPAIN AND PORTUGAL, 1834 (Travel diaries)
RECOLLECTIONS OF AN EXCURSION TO THE MONASTERIES OF ALCOBACA
          AND BATALHA, 1835 (Travel diaries)

EDITIONS

VATHEK

269 VATHEK. Ed. Richard Garnett. London, 1893.

>   An English text based on the Samuel Henley translation (from Beckford's original French) of 1786; it includes Henley's elaborate, learned notes.

270 VATHEK. Ed. Guy Chapman. 2 vols. London: Constable, 1929.

>   The French text of the 1787 Paris edition; it includes the EPISODES omitted from early English editions (see Nos. 274 and 275).

271 VATHEK: AN ARABIAN TALE. Trans. Herbert Grimsditch. New York: Limited Editions Club, 1945.

> A new translation in an elegant collector's edition; this translation was first published in 1929 by the Nonesuch Press.

272 VATHEK. Ed. Roger Londsdale. Oxford English Novels. London: Oxford University Press, 1970.

> Includes an excellent critical and biographical introduction, a select bibliography, a chronological record of Beckford's life, and explanatory notes. The text is that of the 1816 London edition, for which Beckford himself "corrected" Henley's translation.

273 VATHEK: THE ENGLISH TRANSLATION OF HENLEY AND THE FRENCH EDITIONS OF LAUSANNE AND PARIS. Delmar, N.Y.: Scholars' Facsimiles and Reprints, 1972.

274 THE EPISODES OF VATHEK. Ed. Lewis Melville [L.S. Benjamin]. Trans. Sir Frank T. Marzials. Philadelphia: Lippincott, 1912.

> The first translation of three episodes not published in earlier English editions, although Beckford intended them to be included in the original English version.

275 THE EPISODES OF VATHEK. Ed. Robert J. Gemmett. Rutherford, N.J.: Fairleigh Dickinson University Press, 1975.

> A new scholarly edition.

MODERN NOVEL WRITING

276 MODERN NOVEL WRITING AND AZEMIA. Intro. Herman Mittle Levy, Jr. Gainesville, Fla.: Scholars' Facsimiles and Reprints, 1970.

277 MODERN NOVEL WRITING: OR THE ELEGANT ENTHUSIAST. 2 vols. FCE.

> A photofacsimile reprint of the first edition, 1796.

AZEMIA

278 AZEMIA: A DESCRIPTIVE AND SENTIMENTAL NOVEL. 2 vols. FCE.

> A photofacsimile reprint of the first edition, 1797.

279 See No. 276.

LETTERS AND JOURNALS

280 ITALY, WITH SKETCHES OF SPAIN AND PORTUGAL. 2 vols. London, 1834.

Travel diaries.

281 THE TRAVEL-DIARIES OF WILLIAM BECKFORD. Ed. Guy Chapman. 2 vols. Cambridge: At the University Press, 1928.

Includes a memoir discussing Beckford's life, his career, and the importance of his travel writings.

282 THE JOURNAL OF WILLIAM BECKFORD IN PORTUGAL AND SPAIN, 1787-1788. Ed. Boyd Alexander. London: Hart-Davis, 1954.

283 EXCURSION A ALCOBACA ET BATALHA. Ed. André Parreaux. Pref. Guy Chapman. Paris: Societé d'Editions "Les Belles Lettres," 1956.

Travel diaries, in French, with a parallel-text translation.

284 LIFE AT FONTHILL, 1807-1822, WITH INTERLUDES IN PARIS AND LON-DON: FROM THE CORRESPONDENCE OF WILLIAM BECKFORD. Ed. Boyd Alexander. London: Hart-Davis, 1957.

285 RECOLLECTIONS OF THE LATE WILLIAM BECKFORD: LETTERS TO HIS DAUGHTER. Ed. Charlotte Landsdown. West Orange, N.J.: Albert Saifer, 1970.

286 DREAMS, WAKING THOUGHTS AND INCIDENTS. Ed. Robert J. Gemmett. Rutherford, N.J.: Fairleigh Dickinson University Press, 1971.

Letters from Europe (1783).

287 RECOLLECTIONS OF AN EXCURSION TO THE MONASTERIES OF ALCO-BACA AND BATALHA. Ed. Boyd Alexander. London: Centaur Press, 1972.

A new English edition of a manuscript journal kept in 1794.

288 See No. 291.

BIBLIOGRAPHY

289 Chapman, Guy, and John Hodgkin, eds. A BIBLIOGRAPHY OF WILLIAM BECKFORD OF FONTHILL. London: Constable, 1930; rpt. 1974.

Scholarly and useful, but now out of date.

290   Gemmett, Robert J. "An Annotated Checklist of the Works of William Beckford." PBSA, 61 (1967), 243-58.

Includes information on the various editions of VATHEK.

291   Gotlieb, Howard B. WILLIAM BECKFORD OF FONTHILL: WRITER, TRAVELLER, COLLECTOR, CALIPH, 1760-1844. A BRIEF NARRATIVE AND CATALOGUE OF AN EXHIBITION TO MARK THE TWO HUNDREDTH ANNIVERSARY OF BECKFORD'S BIRTH. New Haven, Conn.: Yale University Press, 1960.

Includes also a previously unpublished JOURNAL (1794), edited by Boyd Alexander.

292   McNutt, Dan J. THE EIGHTEENTH-CENTURY GOTHIC NOVEL: AN ANNOTATED BIBLIOGRAPHY OF CRITICISM AND SELECTED TEXTS. New York: Garland, 1975.

Includes a bibliography of Beckford.

293   See Nos. 296, 297, and 299.

BIOGRAPHY

294   Alexander, Boyd. ENGLAND'S WEALTHIEST SON: A STUDY OF WILLIAM BECKFORD. London: Centaur Press, 1962.

The best scholarly biography to date.

295   Brockman, Harold A.N. THE CALIPH OF FONTHILL. London: W. Laurie, 1956.

A sophisticated study of the life; not a critical biography.

296   Chapman, Guy. BECKFORD. New York: Scribner's, 1937; rev. ed., 1952.

Until recently, the best biography available; includes a bibliography of Beckford. (See also No. 281.)

297   Melville, Lewis [L.S. Benjamin]. LIFE AND LETTERS OF BECKFORD. New York: Duffield, 1910.

An early attempt at a scholarly biography, but unreliable because it fails in thoroughness and accuracy; includes a bibliography.

298   Oliver, John W. LIFE OF BECKFORD. Oxford: Oxford University Press, 1932.

Readable, but somewhat routine and superficial.

299 Parreaux, André. WILLIAM BECKFORD, AUTEUR DE VATHEK (1760-
     1844): ÉTUDE DE LA CRÉATION LITTERAIRE. Paris: Nizet, 1960.

> A fine critical biography, despite Parreaux's tendency to over-
> state the importance and the quality of VATHEK; a "Bibliogra-
> phie Sommaire" lists Beckford's works, as well as editions of
> VATHEK and works devoted to or mentioning Beckford.

300 Redding, Cyrus. MEMOIRS OF WILLIAM BECKFORD OF FONTHILL.
     2 vols. London, 1859.

> The first full-length biography; uncritical, but valuable be-
> cause of Redding's personal acquaintance with Beckford.

301 Sitwell, Sacheverell. BECKFORD AND BECKFORDISM: AN ESSAY.
     London: Duckworth, 1930.

> A routine assessment of Beckford's life, accompanied by inter-
> esting speculations on the literary and social effects of his
> various eccentricities.

302 Thompson, Karl F. "Beckford, Byron and Henley." ÉTUDES ANGLAISES,
     14 (1961), 225-28.

> On the relationship among these three in Europe; Byron dubbed
> Beckford "England's wealthiest son."

CRITICAL STUDIES AND COMMENTARIES

In the last few years, some scholars have begun to study VATHEK independently
of its author's spectacular life; but most early criticism of the novel is embedded
in the biographies listed above, and these should be consulted along with the
various critical studies entered below.

303 Conant, Martha Pike. THE ORIENTAL TALE IN ENGLAND IN THE
     EIGHTEENTH CENTURY. New York: Columbia University Press, 1908.

> The discussion of VATHEK is superficial, but Conant does place
> the novel in its contexts.

304 Folsom, James K. "Beckford's VATHEK and the Tradition of Oriental
     Satire." CRITICISM, 6 (1964), 53-69.

> Places VATHEK in the tradition that, in England and France,
> was firmly established by the second quarter of the eighteenth
> century.

305 Graham, Kenneth W. "Beckford's VATHEK: A Study in Ironic Dissonance."
     CRITICISM, 14 (1972), 243-52.

One of several recent articles to study the ingenuities and un-
certainties of Beckford's style.

306   Kiely, Robert. THE ROMANTIC NOVEL IN ENGLAND. Cambridge,
Mass.: Harvard University Press, 1972.

VATHEK is among the eighteenth-century novels treated in this
excellent study of the themes, conventions, and innovations of
a number of disparate romantic novels.

307   Mahmoud, Fatma Moussa, ed. WILLIAM BECKFORD OF FONTHILL: BI-
CENTENARY ESSAYS. Cairo, 1960.

Supplement to CAIRO STUDIES IN ENGLISH; includes essays
by various hands.

308   Mallarmé, Stephen. Preface to VATHEK. Paris, 1876.

Important early critical discussion of Beckford's novel; introduces the 1876 French edition.

309   Rieger, James Henry. "Au pied de la lettre: Stylistic Uncertainty in
VATHEK." CRITICISM, 4 (1962), 302-12.

On the unevenness of tone and general manner in Beckford's
novel, which seems torn between burlesque and serious fantasy.

310   Solomon, Stanley J. "Subverting Propriety as a Pattern of Irony in Three
Eighteenth-Century Novels: THE CASTLE OF OTRANTO, VATHEK, and
FANNY HILL." ERASMUS REVIEW, 1 (1971), 107-16.

An interesting and generally sound treatment of one method of
irony in the three novels. Solomon perhaps assumes too much
about the intentions of Walpole and Cleland.

311   Thompson, Karl F. "Henley's Share in Beckford's VATHEK." PQ, 31
(1952), 75-80.

An assessment of the degree to which Beckford's appointed trans-
lator put his own stamp on VATHEK.

312   Varma, Devendra P. THE GOTHIC FLAME: BEING A HISTORY OF THE
GOTHIC NOVEL IN ENGLAND. London: Arthur Barker, 1957.

Includes a useful discussion of VATHEK as it relates to and re-
flects Gothic themes and conventions.

APHRA BEHN (1640-89)

Aphra Behn was the first professional woman writer born in England; the "incomparable Astrea," as she was called, turned to fiction from writing for the stage. A gifted storyteller with a penchant for exotic settings and romantic plots, Behn always described her narratives as "true," and in this she anticipated a favorite practice of English novelists for the next half-century. Her tale of OROONOKO, OR, THE ROYAL SLAVE (1688), which introduced the idea of the "noble savage" into English fiction, has endured, and today enjoys the status of a minor classic.

PRINCIPAL WORKS

THE FORCED MARRIAGE, 1671 (Tragicomedy)
THE ROVER, 1677 (Comedy)
THE TOWN FOP, 1677 (Comedy)
THE FEIGNED COURTESANS, 1679 (Comedy)
THE ROUNDHEADS, 1682 (Political Comedy)
LOVE LETTERS BETWEEN A NOBLEMAN AND HIS SISTER, 1684 (Novel)
POEMS UPON SEVERAL OCCASIONS, 1684
AGNES DE CASTRO, 1688 (Novel)
THE FAIR JILT, 1688 (Novel)
OROONOKO, OR, THE ROYAL SLAVE, 1688 (Novel)
THE HISTORY OF THE NUN, 1689 (Novel)
THE LUCKY MISTAKE, 1689 (Novel)
A PINDARIC POEM TO THE REVEREND DR. BURNET, 1689
THE YOUNGER BROTHER, 1696 (Comedy)
THE UNFORTUNATE BRIDE, 1698 (Novel)
THE UNFORTUNATE HAPPY LADY, 1698 (Novel)
THE WANDERING BEAUTY, 1698 (Novel)
THE DUMB VIRGIN, 1700 (Novel)
THE UNHAPPY MISTAKE, 1700 (Novel)

EDITIONS

A. Collected Works

313 THE HISTORIES AND NOVELS OF THE LATE INGENIOUS MRS. BEHN. London, 1696.

> A posthumous collection compiled by Charles Gildon; includes "The History of the Life and Memoirs of Mrs. Behn, Written by One of the Fair Sex."

314 THE PLAYS, HISTORIES, AND NOVELS OF THE INGENIOUS MRS. APHRA BEHN. 6 vols. London, 1871.

315 THE NOVELS OF MRS. APHRA BEHN. Intro. Ernest A. Baker. London: Routledge, 1905.

> Incomplete.

316 THE WORKS OF APHRA BEHN. Ed. Montague Summers. 6 vols. London: W. Heinemann, 1915.

> The only modern collected edition, though it is incomplete and the editing is faulty; it includes a biographical and critical introduction. This edition is available in reprint from the Arno Press; volume 5 only has been reprinted as OROONOKO AND OTHER PROSE NARRATIVES. New York: B. Blom, 1967.

B. Selections

317 SELECTED WRITINGS OF THE INGENIOUS MRS. APHRA BEHN. Intro. Robert Phelps. New York: Grove Press, 1950.

> Includes four stories, a play, and poems.

C. Individual Works

THE FAIR JILT

318 TWO TALES. THE ROYAL SLAVE AND THE FAIR JILT. London: Folio Society, 1953.

OROONOKO

319 OROONOKO. SHORTER NOVELS, vol. 2. Everyman's Library. London: J.M. Dent, 1929-30.

320 OROONOKO: OR, THE ROYAL SLAVE. Ed. Lore Metzger. New York: W.W. Norton, 1973.

> An inexpensive paperback edition; good text, with brief intro-
> ductory comments, but no scholarly apparatus.

321. See No. 318.

THE HISTORY OF THE NUN

322 THE HISTORY OF THE NUN. RESTORATION PROSE FICTION, 1666-1700: AN ANTHOLOGY OF REPRESENTATIVE PIECES. Ed. Charles C. Mish. Lincoln: University of Nebraska Press, 1970.

BIBLIOGRAPHY

323 See No. 329

BIOGRAPHY

324 Bernbaum, Ernest. "Mrs. Behn's Biography a Fiction." PMLA, 28 (1913), 432-53.

> The first persuasive challenge to the anonymous "History" pub-
> lished in THE HISTORIES AND NOVELS, 1696 (see No. 313).
> Bernbaum's claim that Behn was never in Surinam, advanced
> here and in No. 325, is no longer justifiable. (See Nos. 326
> and 330.)

325 _____. "Mrs. Behn's OROONOKO." ANNIVERSARY PAPERS BY COL-LEAGUES AND PUPILS OF GEORGE LYMAN KITTREDGE. Boston: Ginn, 1913.

> See also No. 324.

326 Cameron, William J. NEW LIGHT ON APHRA BEHN. Auckland, New Zealand: University of Auckland Press, 1961.

> A good account of Behn in her role as spy, and of her travels
> to Surinam.

327 Hargreaves, Henry A. "The Life and Plays of Mrs. Behn." Ph.D. disser-tation, Duke University, 1961.

> The first chapter offers an account of all the biographical in-
> formation and sources available, through 1960.

328 "The History of the Life and Memoirs of Mrs. Behn, Written by One of the Fair Sex." THE HISTORIES AND NOVELS OF THE LATE INGE-NIOUS MRS. BEHN. London, 1696.

> (See No. 313.) An interesting, unreliable, early biographical essay, based on the supposed "autobiographical" hints contained in Behn's fiction; until this century, generally accepted as a truthful account.

329 Link, Frederick M. APHRA BEHN. New York: Twayne, 1968.

> A critical biography, written for the nonspecialist; includes a bibliography of primary and secondary sources.

330 Platt, Harrison Gray, Jr. "Astrea and Celadon: An Untouched Portrait of Aphra Behn." PMLA, 49 (1934), 544-59.

> A forceful argument, based partly on circumstantial evidence, that Behn did live for a time in Surinam, as she claimed, and that the characters in OROONOKO may therefore have been drawn from firsthand observation.

331 Woodcock, George. THE INCOMPARABLE APHRA. London: Boardman, 1948.

> A critical biography.

CRITICAL STUDIES AND COMMENTARIES

Studies of Behn's fiction tend to focus on OROONOKO; and, to a degree unusual even for criticism of the novel, they concentrate on a biographical question: whether the author ever lived in Surinam, the setting for the novel. Thus, much of the criticism of Behn's work is to be found in the biographical studies listed above, and these should be consulted along with the critical studies enumerated here.

332 Guffey, George Robert, and Andrew Wright. TWO ENGLISH NOVELISTS: APHRA BEHN AND ANTHONY TROLLOPE: PAPERS READ AT A CLARK LIBRARY SEMINAR. Berkeley and Los Angeles: University of California Press, 1974.

> Guffey's paper is a good general assessment of Behn's fiction.

333 Hargreaves, Henry A. "New Evidence of the Realism of Mrs. Behn's OROONOKO." BNYPL, 74 (1970), 437-44.

> More biographical criticism.

334 Hill, Rowland M. "Aphra Behn's Use of Setting." MLQ, 7 (1946), 189-203.

A discussion of Behn's techniques in the "use of realistic lo-
cale."

335 Horner, Joyce M. THE ENGLISH WOMEN NOVELISTS AND THEIR CON-
NECTION WITH THE FEMINIST MOVEMENT (1688-1797). Smith College
Studies in Modern Languages, vol. 11; no. 1-3 (1929-30). Northampton,
Mass.: 1930.

Astute comments on Behn's importance as an early woman novelist whose "way to success," paradoxically enough, was "to
write like a man."

336 MacCarthy, Bridget G. WOMEN WRITERS: THEIR CONTRIBUTION TO THE
ENGLISH NOVEL 1621-1744. Cork, Engl.: Cork University Press, 1944.

An extended, helpful discussion that treats Behn as one of the
earliest writers to introduce realism, however tentative, into
English fiction.

337 Seeber, Edward D. "Oroonoko and Crusoe's Man Friday." MLQ, 12
(1951), 286-91.

Behn's novel may have been the source for Defoe's character.

338 _____. "OROONOKO in France in the XVIIIth Century." PMLA, 51
(1936), 953-59.

A consideration of the influence of Behn's "noble savage" on
French thought and literature.

339 Sheffey, Ruthe T. "The Literary Reputation of Aphra Behn." Ph.D. dissertation, University of Pennsylvania, 1959.

A good study; coverage begins with Behn's own day and ends
with the 1950's.

340 Sypher, Wylie. "A Note on the Realism of Mrs. Behn's OROONOKO."
MLQ, 3 (1942), 401-5.

Assessment of the degree of verisimilitude in Behn's story of
the royal slave of Surinam.

HENRY BROOKE (1703-83)

Henry Brooke was an Irish lawyer who, during and after his university years in London, was the friend of Pope, Lyttelton, and other members of the Opposition to Prime Minister Walpole and George II. His tragedy, GUSTAVUS VASA (1739), could not be performed because it was treasonous. The latter half of his life he spent in Ireland, where he became an advocate for Irish rights and privileges. THE FOOL OF QUALITY (1764-70) was a celebrated sentimental novel that revealed Brooke's reverence for the substance of Rousseau's ÉMILE (1762) and the form of Sterne's TRISTRAM SHANDY (1759-67); it was reissued in 1781, as abridged by John Wesley, who greatly admired its benevolist teachings. A second, less successful (though similar) novel, JULIET GRENVILLE, appeared in 1774.

PRINCIPAL WORKS

UNIVERSAL BEAUTY, 1735 (Poem)
GUSTAVUS VASA, 1739 (Tragedy)
THE FARMER'S SIX LETTERS TO THE PROTESTANTS OF IRELAND, 1745 (Political tracts)
THE CASE OF THE ROMAN CATHOLICS OF IRELAND, 1760 (Political/religious treatise)
THE FOOL OF QUALITY: OR THE HISTORY OF HENRY EARL OF MORELAND, 1764-70 (Novel)
JULIET GRENVILLE: OR, THE HISTORY OF THE HUMAN HEART, 1774 (Novel)
A COLLECTION OF PLAYS AND POEMS, 1778

EDITIONS

THE FOOL OF QUALITY

341 THE FOOL OF QUALITY: OR, THE HISTORY OF HENRY, EARL OF MORELAND. Ed. Charles Kingsley. 2 vols. London, 1859.

Includes a somewhat effusive introduction, or "biographical preface."

342 THE FOOL OF QUALITY. Ed. Ernest A. Baker. London: Routledge, 1906.

> Includes Kingsley's biographical preface (see No. 341), together with a new life of Brooke by Baker, and a bibliography.

JULIET GRENVILLE

343 JULIET GRENVILLE: OR, THE HISTORY OF THE HUMAN HEART. Louisville, Ky.: Lost Cause Press, 1960.

> A microcard republication of the 1774 edition.

BIBLIOGRAPHY

344 See Nos. 342 and 345.

BIOGRAPHY

345 Scurr, Helen Margaret. HENRY BROOKE. Minneapolis: University of Minnesota Press, 1927.

> A brief, uncritical biography, written as a thesis; includes a bibliography.

346 See Nos. 341 and 342.

CRITICAL STUDIES AND COMMENTARIES

Brooke has been slighted by critics; except for the few studies listed below, discussion of his work is limited to the standard histories of the English novel.

347 Darbee, Richard H. "Henry Brooke: A Study of His Ideas and of His Position in the Pre-Romantic Movement." Ph.D. dissertation, University of New Mexico, 1953.

> A good study that emphasizes Brooke's historical importance as a polemical novelist of sensibility.

348 Foster, James R. HISTORY OF THE PRE-ROMANTIC NOVEL IN ENGLAND. New York: Modern Language Association, 1949.

> Foster accounts for the origins and importance of THE FOOL OF QUALITY, which was "the first, or almost the first, full-length portrait of a boy," but which evinces throughout an excess of "deliberate pathos and unrestrained emotion."

349 Tompkins, J.M.S. THE POPULAR NOVEL IN ENGLAND 1770-1800. London: Constable, 1932.

> Includes a brief but excellent critical discussion of Brooke's two novels.

JOHN BUNYAN (1628-88)

PRINCIPAL WORKS

A FEW SIGHS FROM HELL, 1658 (Theological treatise)
THE DOCTRINE OF THE LAW AND GRACE UNFOLDED, 1659 (Theological
     treatise)
PRISON MEDITATIONS, 1665 (Verses)
GRACE ABOUNDING TO THE CHIEF OF SINNERS, 1666 (Spiritual autobiog-
     raphy)
THE PILGRIM'S PROGRESS, 1678; Part Two, 1684 (Novel)
THE LIFE AND DEATH OF MR. BADMAN, 1680 (Novel)
THE HOLY WAR, 1682 (Novel)
A BOOK FOR BOYS AND GIRLS: OR, COUNTRY RHIMES FOR CHILDREN,
     1686 (Emblem book)
THE WATER OF LIFE, 1688 (Theological treatise)
THE HEAVENLY FOOTMAN, 1698 (Theological treatise)

EDITIONS

A. Collected Works

350　THE COMPLETE WORKS OF JOHN BUNYAN. Ed. George Offor. 3 vols.
    London, 1852.

> Inaccurate texts, but still a valuable edition because Offor was
> a collector of early editions of Bunyan's works and a student
> of Puritan theology; his commentaries provide much historical
> information. This and Offor's second edition (1860–62) are rare.

351　THE COMPLETE WORKS OF JOHN BUNYAN. Ed. Henry Stebbing.
    4 vols. London, 1859.

> Includes an introduction, memoir, and notes; this edition has
> been reprinted, in facsimile, by the Johnson Reprint Corp.
> (London, 1970).

352 THE MISCELLANEOUS WORKS OF JOHN BUNYAN. Ed. Roger Sharrock et al. Oxford: Clarendon Press, 1976-- .

> This collection, now in progress, will be definitive; it will provide the very first critical editions of a large number of Bunyan's theological and controversial works.

B. Individual Works

Of Bunyan's three works of fiction, only THE PILGRIM'S PROGRESS has been adequately edited. Critical editions of THE LIFE AND DEATH OF MR. BADMAN and THE HOLY WAR will be included in the new MISCELLANEOUS WORKS, now in progress (see No. 352).

GRACE ABOUNDING

353 GRACE ABOUNDING TO THE CHIEF OF SINNERS AND THE PILGRIM'S PROGRESS FROM THIS WORLD TO THAT WHICH IS TO COME. Ed. Roger Sharrock. London: Oxford University Press, 1966.

354 See No. 356.

PILGRIM'S PROGRESS

355 THE PILGRIM'S PROGRESS. Ed. J.B. Wharey. Oxford: Clarendon Press, 1928; rev. by Roger Sharrock. Oxford: Clarendon Press, 1960; 2nd ed., 1968.

> Sharrock's 1968 revision is the standard text.

356 THE PILGRIM'S PROGRESS FROM THIS WORLD TO THAT WHICH IS TO COME. Ed. James Thorpe. Boston: Houghton Mifflin, 1969.

> Reliable text, nicely introduced; also includes GRACE ABOUND-ING.

357 See Nos. 353 and 358.

THE LIFE AND DEATH OF MR. BADMAN

358 THE LIFE AND DEATH OF MR. BADMAN. Ed. John Brown. Cambridge: At the University Press, 1905.

> The 1680 text, but with some later variants; this volume includes a reprint of Brown's 1887 edition of THE PILGRIM'S PROGRESS.

359 THE LIFE AND DEATH OF MR. BADMAN. Ed. G.B. Harrison. Intro. Bonamy Dobrée. London: Nonesuch Press, 1928.

>A modern old-spelling edition; no notes.

THE HOLY WAR

360 THE HOLY WAR. Ed. Mabel Peacock. Oxford, 1892.

361 THE HOLY WAR. Ed. James F. Forrest. New York: New York University Press, 1967.

>Supersedes all previous editions; provides a reliable text, with modernized spelling and punctuation.

BIBLIOGRAPHY

362 Harrison, Frank M. A BIBLIOGRAPHY OF THE WORKS OF JOHN BUNYAN. Oxford: Bibliographical Society, 1932.

>The standard bibliography of primary materials.

363 Sharrock, Roger. "Bunyan." THE ENGLISH NOVEL: SELECT BIBLIOGRAPHICAL GUIDES. Ed. A.E. Dyson. London: Oxford University Press, 1974.

>A fine bibliographical essay that identifies primary sources and discusses selected secondary materials; Sharrock lists nothing published after 1968.

BIOGRAPHY

364 Brown, John. JOHN BUNYAN: HIS LIFE, TIMES, AND WORK. London, 1885; rev. by Frank M. Harrison. London: Hulbert, 1928.

>Frequently called the standard life, though cluttered, superficial, and impressionistic.

365 Godber, Joyce. "The Imprisonments of John Bunyan." TRANSACTIONS OF THE CONGREGATIONAL HISTORICAL SOCIETY, 16 (1949), 23-32.

>Questions whether the first part of THE PILGRIM'S PROGRESS could actually have been written during Bunyan's second imprisonment, as was long assumed.

366 Harrison, G.B. JOHN BUNYAN: A STUDY IN PERSONALITY. London: J.M. Dent, 1928.

A psychological approach, partly dependent upon the works;
Bunyan's conversion is seen as the central fact of his life and
his writings.

367   Talon, Henri A. BUNYAN. Writers and Their Work, No. 73. London:
Longmans, Green, 1964.

An excellent, brief "biocritical" introduction to Bunyan's life
and works.

368   _____. JOHN BUNYAN: THE MAN AND HIS WORKS. Trans. Barbara
Wall. Cambridge, Mass.: Harvard University Press, 1951.

An excellent "biocritical" study that focuses on the religious
visionary in Bunyan and his works.

369   Winslow, Ola E. JOHN BUNYAN. New York: Macmillan, 1961.

A solid scholarly biography.

CRITICAL STUDIES AND COMMENTARIES

Much Bunyan criticism has been biographical, probably because his works are
all products of an intensely religious orientation to human experience. The
critical biographies listed above should be consulted along with the studies enumerated in this section, some of which are themselves partly biographical.

370   Fish, Stanley E. "Progress in THE PILGRIM'S PROGRESS." SELF-
CONSUMING ARTIFACTS: THE EXPERIENCE OF SEVENTEENTH-CENTURY
LITERATURE. Berkeley and Los Angeles: University of California Press,
1972.

The pilgrim's sense of his progress is illusory, and this is "a
large part of Bunyan's point"; a tedious but persuasive argument.

371   Frye, Roland M. GOD, MAN AND SATAN: PATTERNS OF CHRISTIAN
THOUGHT AND LIFE IN PARADISE LOST, PILGRIM'S PROGRESS, AND
THE GREAT THEOLOGIANS. Princeton, N.J.: Princeton University
Press, 1960.

A small but invaluable book; Frye, a critic and theologian,
studies the theology of Milton and Bunyan.

372   Gibson, Daniel, Jr. "On the Genesis of PILGRIM'S PROGRESS." MP,
32 (1935), 365-82.

A source study of the background (in Puritan thought and writings) for episodes of Bunyan's work.

373 Golder, Harold. "Bunyan and Spenser." PMLA, 45 (1930), 216-37.

A comparative study in search of sources for Bunyan's work.

374 _____. "Bunyan's Giant Despair." JEGP, 30 (1931), 361-68.

A source study.

375 Greaves, Richard L. JOHN BUNYAN. Grand Rapids, Mich.: William B. Erdmans, 1969.

A discussion of Bunyan's theology, with particular reference to his polemical tracts; indirectly illuminates the fiction.

376 Hardin, Richard F. "Bunyan, Mr. Ignorance, and the Quakers." SP, 69 (1972), 496-508.

Mr. Ignorance is meant to suggest the Quakers.

377 Kaufmann, U. Milo. THE PILGRIM'S PROGRESS AND TRADITIONS IN PURITAN MEDITATION. New Haven, Conn.: Yale University Press, 1966.

An elaborate study, useful for its comparative method of treating the literary conventions and techniques of Bunyan's book alongside their counterparts and (in the case of certain image patterns) their originals in devotional literature.

378 Kelman, John. THE ROAD: A STUDY OF JOHN BUNYAN'S PILGRIM'S PROGRESS. 2 vols. London: Oliphant, 1911-12.

A Nonconformist scholar's sensitive study, featuring analysis of the individual episodes of Bunyan's book.

379 Lamont, Daniel. "Bunyan's HOLY WAR: A Study in Christian Experience." THEOLOGY TODAY, 3 (1946-47), 459-72.

A discussion of THE HOLY WAR as an analogue to the archetypal Christian experience in the personal war against evil.

380 Leavis, F.R. "The Pilgrim's Progress." ANNA KARENINA AND OTHER ESSAYS. London: Chatto and Windus, 1967.

On the universal appeal and psychological relevance of THE PILGRIM'S PROGRESS, which gives enduring form to the power "outside ourselves" that makes for "righteousness."

381 Mandel, Barrett S. "Bunyan and the Autobiographer's Artistic Purpose." CRITICISM, 10 (1968), 225-43.

Primarily concerned with GRACE ABOUNDING, but the formal

considerations shed light on Bunyan's three fictional works as
well.

382   Pascal, Roy. "The Present Tense in THE PILGRIM'S PROGRESS." MLR,
      60 (1965), 13-16.

      An interesting essay on Bunyan's language (especially certain
      grammatical forms) in relation to his images and their effective-
      ness.

383   Sharrock, Roger. "Bunyan and the English Emblem Writers." RES, 21
      (1945), 105-16.

      The traditional emblem book as an important source of the
      method and some of the episodes of THE PILGRIM'S PROGRESS.

384   _____. JOHN BUNYAN. Rev. ed. London: Edward Arnold, 1968.

      A brief introductory study of the life and work, with emphasis
      on THE PILGRIM'S PROGRESS.

385   _____. "Spiritual Autobiography in THE PILGRIM'S PROGRESS." RES,
      24 (1948), 102-20.

      An analysis of the echoes, in the fictional work, of the charac-
      teristic themes, images, and structural properties of the devo-
      tional form.

386   Tindall, William York. JOHN BUNYAN, MECHANICK PREACHER. New
      York: Columbia University Press, 1934.

      Tindall brings to this study great knowledge of Bunyan's charac-
      teristic genres: the spiritual autobiography and the emblematic
      or symbolic fiction. The comparisons of Bunyan's writings with
      other contemporary works in these genres are extremely able
      and useful, though Tindall is annoyingly hostile to the Puritan
      Bunyan and his "tinker's" genius.

387   Van Ghent, Dorothy. "On THE PILGRIM'S PROGRESS." THE ENGLISH
      NOVEL: FORM AND FUNCTION. New York: Rinehart, 1953.

      A stimulating essay on the powerful allegory of THE PILGRIM'S
      PROGRESS as "a landscape of dream or of nightmare inhabited
      by our very solid neighbors."

388   Webber, Joan. THE ELOQUENT "I": STYLE AND SELF IN SEVENTEENTH-
      CENTURY PROSE. Madison: University of Wisconsin Press, 1969.

      The chapter on Bunyan gives superb critical treatment to the spiri-
      tual autobiography and is helpful for the study of THE PILGRIM'S
      PROGRESS and (especially) GRACE ABOUNDING.

389 Wharey, J.B. A STUDY OF THE SOURCES OF BUNYAN'S ALLEGORIES.
     Baltimore: J.H. Furst, 1904.

     A thorough, extremely useful investigation of the backgrounds
     in Puritan theology and popular literature; includes extended
     analyses of individual episodes in THE PILGRIM'S PROGRESS.

390 Whyte, Alexander. BUNYAN CHARACTERS. 4 vols. Edinburgh, 1893.

     This study emphasizes the devotional purpose of Bunyan's work,
     but is still among the best critical treatments of Bunyan's tech-
     niques of shaping moral abstractions into characters.

FANNY BURNEY (1752-1840)

Daughter of a distinguished music master (Dr. Charles Burney), friend of Dr. Johnson, Joshua Reynolds, Edmund Burke, and Hester Thrale, Frances (Fanny) Burney was the most highly respected--and the most accomplished--novelist of the last quarter of the eighteenth century. Her epistolary novel EVELINA (1778) took London by storm, and it is indeed a fine performance. Burney was an imitator of Richardson who nonetheless copied Smollett in her caricatures of vulgar, pretentious people. CECILIA (1782), a sprawling work, abandons the epistolary form; though it contains some delightful comic strokes, it is inferior to EVELINA, as are CAMILLA (1796) and THE WANDERER (1814). From 1786 to 1791 Burney was second keeper of the robes to Queen Charlotte, and in 1793 she became the wife of a French refugee, General Alexandre d'Arblay. Her last years were spent in quiet gentility. She was among Austen's favorite novelists, and it is generally conceded that EVELINA and CECILIA greatly influenced the author of PRIDE AND PREJUDICE and EMMA.

PRINCIPAL WORKS

EVELINA; OR, THE HISTORY OF A YOUNG LADY'S ENTRANCE INTO THE
      WORLD, 1778 (Novel)
CECILIA, OR, MEMOIRS OF AN HEIRESS, 1782 (Novel)
CAMILLA: OR, A PICTURE OF YOUTH, 1796 (Novel)
THE WANDERER; OR, FEMALE DIFFICULTIES, 1814 (Novel)
MEMOIRS OF DOCTOR BURNEY, 1832

EDITIONS

EVELINA

391   EVELINA, OR, THE HISTORY OF A YOUNG LADY'S ENTRANCE INTO
      THE WORLD. Ed. Austin Dobson. Illus. Hugh Thomson. London: Mac-
      millan, 1920.

392   EVELINA; OR, THE HISTORY OF A YOUNG LADY'S ENTRANCE INTO

THE WORLD. Ed. Sir Frank D. Mackinnon. Oxford: Clarendon Press, 1930.

A reliable critical edition.

393 EVELINA. Everyman's Library. London: J.M. Dent, 1931.

Includes a helpful introduction by Ernest Rhys.

394 EVELINA, OR THE HISTORY OF A YOUNG LADY'S ENTRANCE INTO THE WORLD. Ed. Edward A. Bloom. Oxford English Novels. London: Oxford University Press, 1968.

An excellent scholarly edition, with a solid critical introduction, a brief select bibliography, and a chronological record of Burney's career.

CECILIA

395 CECILIA, OR MEMOIRS OF AN HEIRESS. Ed. Annie Raine Ellis. 2 vols. London, 1890.

396 CECILIA; OR, MEMOIRS OF AN HEIRESS. Ed. R. Brimley Johnson. 3 vols. London, 1893.

CAMILLA

397 CAMILLA: OR, A PICTURE OF YOUTH. Ed. Edward A. Bloom and Lillian D. Bloom. Oxford English Novels. London: Oxford University Press, 1972.

Includes apparatus similar to that found in No. 394.

LETTERS AND JOURNALS

398 THE DIARY AND LETTERS OF MADAME D'ARBLAY. Ed. Charlotte Barrett. Pref. and notes by Austin Dobson. 6 vols. London: Macmillan, 1904-5.

Incomplete and out of date; superseded by No. 400. These six volumes reprint, with Dobson's notes, the collection edited by Charlotte Barrett (Burney's niece) and published in 1842-46.

399 THE EARLY DIARY OF FRANCES BURNEY, 1768-1778. Ed. Annie Raine Ellis. 2 vols. London: G. Bell, 1913.

Superseded by No. 400.

400 THE JOURNALS AND LETTERS OF FANNY BURNEY (MADAME D'ARBLAY).

Ed. Joyce Hemlow et al. Oxford: Clarendon Press, 1972-- .

The definitive edition; in progress.

401 A CATALOGUE OF THE BURNEY FAMILY CORRESPONDENCE, 1749-1878. Ed. Joyce Hemlow et al. New York: New York Public Library, 1971.

BIBLIOGRAPHY

402 See Nos. 403, 407, and 408.

BIOGRAPHY

403 Adelstein, Michael [E.]. FANNY BURNEY. New York: Twayne, 1968.

An adequate, though brief, critical biography; includes a bibliography.

404 Dobson, Austin. FANNY BURNEY. London: Macmillan, 1903.

A readable biography, more appreciative than critical.

405 Gerin, Winifred. THE YOUNG FANNY BURNEY: A BIOGRAPHY. London: Nelson, 1961.

A good account of the early years: the home life, the reading, the family friendships, and the background for the novels.

406 Hahn, Emily. A DEGREE OF PRUDERY: A BIOGRAPHY OF FANNY BURNEY. Garden City, N.Y.: Doubleday, 1950.

An unsympathetic biography.

407 Hemlow, Joyce. THE HISTORY OF FANNY BURNEY. Oxford: Clarendon Press, 1958.

The standard life, and a model scholarly biography; an appendix provides a bibliography of Burney manuscripts.

408 Tourtellot, A.B. BE LOVED NO MORE: THE LIFE AND ENVIRONMENT OF FANNY BURNEY. Boston: Houghton Mifflin, 1938.

A "life-and-times" study, with special emphasis on the Burney family relationships; uncritical and (as the title hints) a bit impressionistic. Includes a bibliography.

CRITICAL STUDIES AND COMMENTARIES

409 Beasley, Jerry C. "Fanny Burney and Jane Austen's PRIDE AND PREJU-DICE." ENGLISH MISCELLANY, 24 (1973-74), 153-66.

> On Austen's "borrowings" from EVELINA and CECILIA.

410 Bradbrook, Frank W. JANE AUSTEN AND HER PREDECESSORS. Cambridge: At the University Press, 1966.

> See especially chapter VI, which places Burney in the "feminist tradition" that Austen inherited.

411 Cecil, David. POETS AND STORY-TELLERS. New York: Macmillan, 1949.

> The discussion of Burney is an excellent critical overview of her novels.

412 Erickson, James P. "EVELINA and BETSY THOUGHTLESS." TSLL, 6 (1964), 96-103.

> The plot and theme of Haywood's novel anticipate EVELINA.

413 Hale, Will T. MADAME D'ARBLAY'S PLACE IN THE DEVELOPMENT OF THE ENGLISH NOVEL. Bloomington: Indiana University Press, 1916.

> A rather superficial study; however, it does indicate Burney's debts, influences, and importance.

414 Hemlow, Joyce. "Fanny Burney and the Courtesy Books." PMLA, 65 (1950), 732-61.

> A discussion of Burney's knowledge of, and indebtedness to, this popular form.

415 Horner, Joyce M. THE ENGLISH WOMEN NOVELISTS AND THEIR CON-NECTION WITH THE FEMINIST MOVEMENT (1688-1797). Smith College Studies in Modern Languages, vol. 11, no. 1-3 (1929-30). Northampton, Mass.: 1930.

> Includes an excellent critical discussion of Burney as the first major female novelist.

416 MacCarthy, Bridget G. THE LATER WOMEN NOVELISTS, 1744-1818. New York: William Salloch, 1948.

> Especially interesting on the personal and literary influence of the important people who constantly visited Burney's home; good discussion of the novels.

417 Malone, Kemp. "EVELINA Revisited." PLL, 1 (1965), 3-19.

A pleasant, readable discussion that offers astute observations on Burney's techniques.

418 Montague, Edwine, and Louis L. Martz. "Fanny Burney's EVELINA." THE AGE OF JOHNSON: ESSAYS PRESENTED TO CHAUNCEY BREWSTER TINKER. Ed. Frederick W. Hilles. New Haven, Conn.: Yale University Press, 1949.

A "conversation" between Montague and Martz, who are trying to decide upon the particular literary merits of EVELINA.

419 Tinker, Chauncey Brewster. DR. JOHNSON AND FANNY BURNEY, BEING THE JOHNSONIAN PASSAGES FROM THE WORKS OF MME. D'ARBLAY. New York: Moffat, 1912.

The introduction is still valuable because of its author's vast knowledge of Johnson and his circle.

420 Tompkins, J.M.S. THE POPULAR NOVEL IN ENGLAND 1770-1800. London: Constable, 1932.

Tompkins does not concentrate on Burney, but her discussions of other novelists of the time are essential to the study of EVELINA and CECILIA.

421 White, Eugene. FANNY BURNEY, NOVELIST: A STUDY IN TECHNIQUE. Hamden, Conn.: Shoe String Press, 1960.

A study of Burney's technical achievement, which was at its height in EVELINA, her first novel; interesting on the origins (in the likes of Richardson and Smollett) and uses, both original and derivative, of her characteristic narrative conventions.

JOHN CLELAND (1709-89)

John Cleland was a notorious figure in his own time, primarily because of his FANNY HILL (1748-49), an obscene "imitation" of Richardson's PAMELA (1740) and CLARISSA (1747-48). But he was nonetheless the acquaintance of Garrick and Boswell, and he was a philologist and gifted stylist as well as a pornographer. Although he remains somewhat notorious today, his work--FANNY HILL, at least--is taken rather more seriously than it used to be.

PRINCIPAL WORKS

FANNY HILL; OR, MEMOIRS OF A WOMAN OF PLEASURE, 1748-49 (Novel)
MEMOIRS OF A COXCOMB, 1751 (Novel)
TITUS VESPASIAN, 1755 (Tragedy)
SURPRISES OF LOVE, 1764 (Novel)
THE WAY TO THINGS BY WORDS, AND TO WORDS BY THINGS, 1766
      (Philological treatise)
SPECIMEN OF AN ETYMOLOGICAL VOCABULARY, 1768 (Philological Treatise)
THE WOMAN OF HONOUR, 1768 (Novel)

EDITIONS

FANNY HILL

422   MEMOIRS OF A WOMAN OF PLEASURE. Ed. Peter Quennell. New York: Putnam's, 1963.

     Modern popular edition; provides a sensible introduction and a modest bibliography, but relies on a copy text that, unknown to the editor and publisher, had been expurgated.

423   FANNY HILL. London: Mayflower Books, 1970.

     Not a scholarly edition, but a more accurate text than Mayflower's previously published editions of FANNY HILL (1963 and 1966), both printed from an expurgated text.

MEMOIRS OF A COXCOMB

424 MEMOIRS OF A COXCOMB. New York: Lancer Books, 1963.

425 MEMOIRS OF A COXCOMB. Ed. P.R.A. Lingham. London: Roberts and Vinter, 1964.

> Includes a brief but helpful introduction by Lingham.

426 MEMOIRS OF A COXCOMB. FIN.

> A photofacsimile reprint of the first edition, 1751.

LETTERS

427 See No. 429.

BIBLIOGRAPHY

428 See No. 429.

BIOGRAPHY

429 Epstein, William H. JOHN CLELAND: IMAGES OF A LIFE. New York: Columbia University Press, 1974.

> An admirable scholarly biography; includes a bibliography. Epstein quotes from, lists, and locates a good many of Cleland's letters.

CRITICAL STUDIES AND COMMENTARIES

Until recently, the author of FANNY HILL seems to have been regarded as a distressing aberration in the history of English fiction, while his controversial novel enjoyed only the status of a widely read underground work. In the last few years, however, Cleland has received modest but serious attention from scholars, most of whom have been interested either in the relationships between FANNY HILL and the works of major writers or in the place of Cleland's novel in the history of English pornography and censorship.

430 Bradbury, Malcolm. "FANNY HILL and the Comic Novel." CRITICAL QUARTERLY, 13 (1971), 263-75.

> An interesting discussion of Cleland's apparently deliberate uses of formal comic structure and conventions; emphasizes some

eighteenth-century difficulties with the novel as a distinct genre.

431   Braudy, Leo. "FANNY HILL and Materialism." ECS, 4 (1970), 21-40.

A judicious discussion of Cleland's novel as an ironic commentary upon contemporary middle-class values.

432   Copeland, Edward W. "Clarissa and Fanny Hill: Sisters in Distress." SNNTS, 4 (1972), 343-52.

According to Copeland, Cleland's novel repeats, in parody, the themes and conventions of the early volumes of CLARISSA (although in many respects it more closely parallels the story of PAMELA), and addresses some of the same social issues that concerned Richardson. The comparison illuminates the "sexual energy that animates the rhetorical fantasies" of Richardson's characters.

433   Foxon, David. "John Cleland and the Publication of MEMOIRS OF A WOMAN OF PLEASURE." BOOK COLLECTOR, 12 (1963), 476-87.

Thorough examination of the details of the complications and the controversies surrounding the publication of FANNY HILL; also provides information about the earliest editions. Included in No. 434.

434   _____. LIBERTINE LITERATURE IN ENGLAND, 1660-1745. New Hyde Park, N.Y.: University Books, 1965.

A sweeping, quite valuable survey that includes treatment of some works regarded as pornographic; valuable background for the study of FANNY HILL. Includes No. 433.

435   Hollander, John. "The Old Last Act: Some Observations on FANNY HILL." ENCOUNTER, 21 (1963), 69-77.

A review essay discussing 1963 editions of Cleland's novel (see Nos. 422 and 423), but also a general discussion of the work itself. Hollander regards Cleland's "heroine" as an important female character in English literature, and he admires Cleland's clever use of language.

436   Morrissey, L.J., and B. Slepian. "What Is FANNY HILL?" ESSAYS IN CRITICISM, 14 (1964), 65-75.

A review article discussing 1963 editions of Cleland's FANNY HILL (see Nos. 422 and 423), but an interesting critical discussion as well, especially for its observations on Cleland's euphemistic language.

437   Rembar, Charles. THE END OF OBSCENITY: THE TRIALS OF LADY
      CHATTERLEY, TROPIC OF CANCER, AND FANNY HILL. New York:
      Random House, 1968.

      Graphic accounts, including many of the testimonies given.

438   Shinagel, Michael. "MEMOIRS OF A WOMAN OF PLEASURE: Pornog-
      raphy and the Mid-Eighteenth-Century English Novel." STUDIES IN
      CHANGE AND REVOLUTION: ASPECTS OF ENGLISH INTELLECTUAL
      HISTORY, 1640-1800. Ed. Paul J. Korshin. London: Scolar Press, 1972.

      A slight essay discussing Shinagel's enjoyment of FANNY HILL;
      some emphasis on the degree to which the novel intends to be
      seriously "instructive."

439   Solomon, Stanley J. "Subverting Propriety as a Pattern of Irony in Three
      Eighteenth-Century Novels: THE CASTLE OF OTRANTO, VATHEK, and
      FANNY HILL." ERASMUS REVIEW, 1 (1971), 107-16.

      An interesting and generally sound treatment of one method of
      irony in the three novels. Solomon perhaps assumes too much
      about the intentions of Walpole and Cleland.

440   Taube, Myron. "MOLL FLANDERS and FANNY HILL: A Comparison."
      BALL STATE UNIVERSITY FORUM, 9 (1968), 76-80.

      Identifies the obvious relationships between Defoe's roguish
      heroine and Cleland's.

441   Thompson, Ralph. "Deathless Lady." THE COLOPHON, 1 (1935), 207-
      20.

      A thorough treatment of the publishing history of FANNY HILL,
      but Thompson refuses to grant the novel any literary value.

THOMAS DAY (1748-89)

Day was a philanthropist, political radical, and avid disciple of Rousseau; he turned to didactic fiction as a means of proclaiming his views of society, and particularly of education. THE HISTORY OF SANDFORD AND MERTON (1783-89) borrowed much from the educational theories advanced in Rousseau's ÉMILE (1762) and was for a century the most widely read of all children's books.

PRINCIPAL WORKS

THE DYING NEGRO, 1773 (Poem)
THE HISTORY OF SANDFORD AND MERTON, 1783-89 (Novel)
THE LETTERS OF MARIUS, 1784 (Political treatise)
THE HISTORY OF LITTLE JACK, 1788 (Novel)

EDITIONS

SANDFORD AND MERTON

442   THE HISTORY OF SANDFORD AND MERTON. Ed. Cecil Hartley. London, 1874.

> Hartley tampered with the text, but this is the nearest thing to a scholarly edition available.

443   THE HISTORY OF SANDFORD AND MERTON. London: Blackie, 1910.

LITTLE JACK

444   THE HISTORY OF LITTLE JACK, AND OTHER STORIES. New York: McLoughlin, 1906.

LETTERS

445   See No. 447.

BIBLIOGRAPHY

446   See No. 447.

BIOGRAPHY

447   Gignilliat, George Warren.   THE AUTHOR OF SANDFORD AND MERTON:
      A LIFE OF THOMAS DAY, ESQ.   New York: Columbia University Press,
      1932.

         A critical biography; includes a bibliography. Gignilliat quotes,
         lists, and locates a number of Day's letters.

448   Keir, James.   AN ACCOUNT OF THE LIFE AND WRITINGS OF THOMAS
      DAY, ESQ.   London, 1791; rpt. New York: Garland, 1970.

         The earliest biography, written by Day's friend; the Garland
         reprint is a photofacsimile of the first edition.

449   Scott, Sir H.W.   THE EXEMPLARY MR. DAY, 1748-1789.   London: Faber
      and Faber, 1935.

         A critical biography.

CRITICAL STUDIES AND COMMENTARIES

Day has been all but ignored by critics; most discussions of his work are found
in the critical biographies listed above and in the standard histories of the English novel.

450   Foster, James R.   HISTORY OF THE PRE-ROMANTIC NOVEL IN EN-
      GLAND.   New York: Modern Language Association, 1949.

         Foster gives little attention to Day, but the background he de-
         scribes is indispensable to the reading of SANDFORD AND
         MERTON.

451   Pritchett, V.S.   THE LIVING NOVEL.   New York: Reynal and Hitch-
      cock, 1947.

         Includes a brief, general, but helpful discussion of SANDFORD
         AND MERTON.

452 Sadler, Michael. THOMAS DAY: AN ENGLISH DISCIPLE OF ROUS-
SEAU. Cambridge: At the University Press, 1928.

A sound critical overview that emphasizes the relationships between SANDFORD AND MERTON and ÉMILE.

DANIEL DEFOE (1660-1731)

PRINCIPAL WORKS

Defoe is known to have written some 550 books and pamphlets, not to mention his many periodical essays. The listing here therefore represents only the smallest fraction of the whole canon.

AN ESSAY UPON PROJECTS, 1697
THE TRUE-BORN ENGLISHMAN, 1701 (Poem)
THE SHORTEST WAY WITH THE DISSENTERS, 1702 (Prose satire)
A REVIEW OF THE AFFAIRS OF FRANCE; later A REVIEW OF THE STATE OF
      THE BRITISH NATION, 1704-13 (Periodical)
THE CONSOLIDATOR, OR MEMOIRS OF SUNDRY TRANSACTIONS FROM THE
      WORLD IN THE MOON, 1705 (Imaginary voyage)
JURE DIVINO, 1706 (Poem)
THE TRUE RELATION OF THE APPARITION OF ONE MRS. VEAL, 1706 (Re-
      portage)
THE FAMILY INSTRUCTOR, 1715 (Conduct book)
ROBINSON CRUSOE, 1719 (Novel)
THE FARTHER ADVENTURES OF ROBINSON CRUSOE, 1719
SERIOUS REFLECTIONS OF ROBINSON CRUSOE, 1720
THE LIFE, ADVENTURES, AND PYRACIES OF THE FAMOUS CAPTAIN SINGLE-
      TON, 1720 (Novel)
MEMOIRS OF A CAVALIER, 1720 (Novel)
THE FORTUNES AND MISFORTUNES OF THE FAMOUS MOLL FLANDERS, 1722
      (Novel)
THE HISTORY AND REMARKABLE LIFE OF . . . COLONEL JACQUE, 1722
      (Novel)
A JOURNAL OF THE PLAGUE YEAR, 1722 (Novel)
RELIGIOUS COURTSHIP, 1722 (Conduct book)
A NEW VOYAGE ROUND THE WORLD, 1724 (Imaginary voyage)
ROXANA, OR THE FORTUNATE MISTRESS, 1724 (Novel)
A TOUR THROUGH THE WHOLE ISLAND OF GREAT BRITAIN, 1724-27 (Travel
      narrative)
THE FOUR YEARS VOYAGES OF CAPTAIN GEORGE ROBERTS, 1726 (Imaginary
      voyage)
A GENERAL HISTORY OF THE PYRATES, 1726-28 (Voyages)
MADAGASCAR: OR ROBERT DRURY'S JOURNAL, 1729 (Imaginary voyage)

EDITIONS

A. Collected Works

453   ROMANCES AND NARRATIVES BY DANIEL DEFOE. Ed. George A.
Aitken. 16 vols. London, 1895.

> Contains all of the novels, plus many of the pamphlets, in
> modernized texts.

454   THE WORKS OF DANIEL DEFOE. Ed. Gustavus H. Maynadier. 16 vols.
New York: Brainard, 1905.

> Very similar in contents to the Aitken edition (No. 453); THE
> TRUE-BORN ENGLISHMAN and THE SHORTEST WAY, both
> omitted by Aitken, are included in this edition.

455   THE SHAKESPEARE HEAD EDITION OF THE NOVELS AND SELECTED
WRITINGS OF DANIEL DEFOE. 14 vols. Oxford: Basil Blackwell,
1927-28.

> Less complete than the Aitken edition (No. 453), and occa-
> sionally poor in the choice of copy texts (especially for COL-
> ONEL JACK); but Defoe's language is unmodernized, and the
> scholarly historical and explanatory notes, although placed in-
> conveniently at the end of the collection, are helpful.

456   A new edition of the collected works of Daniel Defoe. Ed. Manuel
Schonhorn and Maximillian E. Novak. Carbondale: Southern Illinois
University Press, forthcoming.

> This scholarly edition, now in the early stages of preparation,
> will be more complete and reliable than any previous collec-
> tion.

B. Selections and Specialized Collections

457   A REVIEW OF THE AFFAIRS OF FRANCE. Ed. A.W. Secord. 22 vols.
New York: Facsimile Text Society, 1938.

> The only complete set of the REVIEW available; a facsimile edi-
> tion, with useful notes and introduction by Secord. See also
> William L. Payne, INDEX TO DEFOE'S REVIEW (New York:
> Columbia University Press, 1948).

458   DANIEL DEFOE. Ed. James T. Boulton. New York: Schocken Books,
1965.

> A collection of representative excerpts from Defoe's writings,

accompanied by Boulton's biographical and interpretive commentaries.

459 SELECTED POETRY AND PROSE OF DANIEL DEFOE. Ed. Michael F. Shugrue. New York: Holt, Rinehart and Winston, 1968.

An intelligent selection of representative works, including some pieces of journalism and poetry difficult to find in other collections.

C. Individual Works

THE CONSOLIDATOR

460 THE CONSOLIDATOR: OR, MEMOIRS OF SUNDRY TRANSACTIONS FROM THE WORLD IN THE MOON. FoN.

A photofacsimile reprint of the first edition, 1705.

ROBINSON CRUSOE

Modern separate editions of the novel do not include THE FARTHER ADVENTURES (1719) or SERIOUS REFLECTIONS (1720), Defoe's continuations; these may be read in the collected editions of the WORKS.

461 THE LIFE AND ADVENTURES OF ROBINSON CRUSOE. Ed. Angus Ross. Harmondsworth, Engl.: Penguin Books, 1965.

Includes an excellent critical introduction, with an appendix on Alexander Selkirk, explanatory notes, and a brief but useful glossary.

462 THE LIFE AND STRANGE SURPRIZING ADVENTURES OF ROBINSON CRUSOE OF YORK, MARINER. Ed. J. Donald Crowley. Oxford English Novels. London: Oxford University Press, 1972.

Includes a brief critical introduction, a select bibliography, a chronology of Defoe's life and career, and explanatory notes.

463 ROBINSON CRUSOE. Ed. Michael Shinagel. Norton Critical Edition. New York: W.W. Norton, 1975.

Includes a reliable text, a short gathering of excerpts from important background sources, and a selection of critical commentaries from the eighteenth century through the twentieth.

CAPTAIN SINGLETON

464 THE LIFE, ADVENTURES AND PIRACIES OF THE FAMOUS CAPTAIN
SINGLETON. Ed. James R. Sutherland. Everyman's Library. London:
J.M. Dent, 1963.

Includes a valuable introduction by Sutherland.

465 THE LIFE, ADVENTURES, AND PYRACIES OF THE FAMOUS CAPTAIN
SINGLETON. Ed. Shiv K. Kumar. Oxford English Novels. London:
Oxford University Press, 1969.

Includes a brief, very general introduction to the novel, and
other apparatus similar to that found in No. 462.

466 THE LIFE, ADVENTURES, AND PYRACIES, OF THE FAMOUS CAPTAIN
SINGLETON. FoN.

A photofacsimile reprint of the first edition, 720.

MEMOIRS OF A CAVALIER

467 MEMOIRS OF A CAVALIER. Ed. James T. Boulton. Oxford English
Novels. London: Oxford University Press, 1973.

Includes apparatus similar to that found in No. 462.

468 MEMOIRS OF A CAVALIER. FoN.

A photofacsimile reprint of the first edition, 1720.

MOLL FLANDERS

469 MOLL FLANDERS. Ed. James R. Sutherland. Boston: Houghton Mifflin,
1959.

Excellent edition; includes a brief but solid critical introduction and useful explanatory notes.

470 MOLL FLANDERS. Ed. J. Paul Hunter. Crowell Critical Library. New
York: Crowell, 1970.

A most convenient edition for textual comparison. Hunter includes parallel passages from the first and third editions; the
latter, "corrected" (but, it is now thought, probably not by
Defoe), has been the most widely reprinted text, though the
first edition is more authoritative. Also included is a selection
of critical commentaries on MOLL FLANDERS.

471 THE FORTUNES AND MISFORTUNES OF THE FAMOUS MOLL FLANDERS.

Ed. George A. Starr. Oxford English Novels. London: Oxford University Press, 1971.

>Includes apparatus similar to that found in No. 462. The introduction and explanatory notes are particularly noteworthy.

472 MOLL FLANDERS. Ed. Edward Kelly. Norton Critical Edition. New York: W.W. Norton, 1973.

>Includes apparatus similar to that found in No. 463.

COLONEL JACK

473 THE HISTORY AND REMARKABLE LIFE OF THE TRULY HONOURABLE COLONEL JACQUE. Ed. Samuel Holt Monk. Oxford English Novels. London: Oxford University Press, 1965.

>Includes apparatus similar to that found in No. 462.

JOURNAL OF THE PLAGUE YEAR

474 A JOURNAL OF THE PLAGUE YEAR. Ed. Anthony Burgess and Christopher Bristow. Harmondsworth, Engl.: Penguin Books, 1966.

>Includes a sensible introduction by Burgess, a "Clinical Summary" of the plague, and explanatory notes.

475 A JOURNAL OF THE PLAGUE YEAR. Ed. Louis A. Landa. Oxford English Novels. London: Oxford University Press, 1969.

>Includes apparatus similar to that found in No. 462.

ROXANA

476 ROXANA, THE FORTUNATE MISTRESS. Ed. Jane Jack. Oxford English Novels. London: Oxford University Press, 1964.

>Includes apparatus similar to that found in No. 462.

A TOUR THRO' THE WHOLE ISLAND OF GREAT BRITAIN

477 A TOUR THRO' THE WHOLE ISLAND OF GREAT BRITAIN. Ed. G.D.H. Cole and D.C. Browning. Rev. ed. 2 vols. Everyman's Library. London: J.M. Dent, 1963.

>A fine scholarly edition.

478 A TOUR THRO' THE WHOLE ISLAND OF GREAT BRITAIN. Ed. Pat Rogers. Harmondsworth, Engl.: Penguin Books, 1965.

CAPTAIN GEORGE ROBERTS

479 THE FOUR YEARS VOYAGES OF CAPTAIN GEORGE ROBERTS. FoN.

A photofacsimile of the first edition, 1726.

A GENERAL HISTORY OF THE PYRATES

480 A GENERAL HISTORY OF THE PYRATES. Ed. Manuel Schonhorn. London: J.M. Dent, 1972.

A gathering in one volume of the two-volume compendium of "histories" and anecdotes of famous pirates; includes comprehensive notes and a valuable introduction recounting the history of piracy in the early 1700's and assessing Defoe's interest in it.

LETTERS

481 THE LETTERS OF DANIEL DEFOE. Ed. George Harris Healey. Oxford: Clarendon Press, 1955.

Includes 251 letters, 235 of them by Defoe and 16 of them addressed to him; ample and helpful annotations and index.

BIBLIOGRAPHY

Defoe signed only a very few of his hundreds of works, while he lent his name to a good many things he did not write. Defoe bibliography has therefore always been something of a muddle; the canon probably never will be finally established, and bibliographers doubtless will continue to disagree about it. The books below listing Defoe's works are sometimes at odds with one another, and only by surveying them all may one get a complete picture of the attributions.

482 Alden, John, ed. A CATALOG OF THE DEFOE COLLECTION IN THE BOSTON PUBLIC LIBRARY. Boston: Hall, 1966.

483 Hutchins, Henry C. ROBINSON CRUSOE AND ITS PRINTING, 1719-1731. New York: Columbia University Press, 1925.

A thorough bibliographical account of all of the editions published during Defoe's lifetime.

484 Moore, John Robert. A CHECKLIST OF THE WRITINGS OF DANIEL DEFOE. 2nd ed. Hamden, Conn.: Archon Books, 1971.

The first edition was published in 1960 by Indiana University

Press, with a new printing in 1962 (adding several more titles);
the most recent edition includes supplements containing more
than 200 corrections, and 22 new titles. See also M[aximillian]
E. Novak, "Daniel Defoe," in NCBEL, vol. II, for additional
suggestions on the Defoe canon.

485 Novak, M[aximillian] E. "Defoe." THE ENGLISH NOVEL: SELECT BIBLIO-
GRAPHICAL GUIDES. Ed. A.E. Dyson. London: Oxford University
Press, 1974.

A very helpful bibliographical essay that identifies and briefly
discusses important primary and secondary materials.

486 See also Nos. 488, 490, 526, and 539.

BIOGRAPHY

487 Defoe, Daniel. "An Appeal to Honor and Justice." London, 1715.

Defoe's most extensive autobiographical piece; reprinted in
No. 458.

488 Dottin, Paul. DANIEL DEFOE ET SES ROMANS. 3 vols. Paris: Les
Presses Universitaires de France, 1924.

Fine critical biography; includes bibliographical appendixes.

489 Fitzgerald, Brian. DANIEL DEFOE: A STUDY IN CONFLICT. London:
Secker and Warburg, 1954.

A Marxist study that adds nothing to our knowledge of Defoe.
As biographer and critic, Fitzgerald is inept; unfortunately his
book is the most extensive Marxist study available.

490 Lee, William. DANIEL DEFOE: HIS LIFE AND RECENTLY DISCOVERED
WRITINGS 1716-1729. 3 vols. London, 1869.

Still a valuable biography; volume I concludes with a chronological listing of Defoe's works. Volumes II and III reprint
numerous short pieces not previously attributed to Defoe.

491 Moore, John Robert. DANIEL DEFOE: CITIZEN OF THE MODERN
WORLD. Chicago: University of Chicago Press, 1958.

Extremely important book; treats Defoe as a "prophet" of the
modern world that, in the author's view, he anticipated and
helped to create. Moore adds new facts about Defoe's life,
but organizes his study around a number of topics, each representing an area of major achievement. An appendix provides
an exhaustive chronological outline of Defoe's life and career.

492 Payne, William Lytton. MR. REVIEW: DANIEL DEFOE AS AUTHOR OF THE REVIEW. New York: King's Crown Press, 1947.

> An intriguing account of an important aspect of Defoe's career.

493 Shinagel, Michael. DANIEL DEFOE AND MIDDLE-CLASS GENTILITY. Cambridge, Mass.: Harvard University Press, 1968.

> An interesting, energetic, but finally unsatisfying argument that Defoe was (rather like Moll Flanders) perpetually engaged in the pursuit of genteel respectability.

494 Sutherland, James R. DEFOE. London: Methuen, 1937; rev. ed., 1950.

> The best biography of Defoe.

495 _____. DEFOE. Writers and Their Work, No. 51. London: Longmans, Green, 1965.

> An excellent, brief "biocritical" introduction to Defoe's life and works.

CRITICAL STUDIES AND COMMENTARIES

496 Alter, Robert. "A Bourgeois Picaroon." ROGUE'S PROGRESS: STUDIES IN THE PICARESQUE NOVEL. Cambridge, Mass.: Harvard University Press, 1964.

> Alter concludes that MOLL FLANDERS actually derives "from the English criminal biography," and that it is therefore "more misleading than instructive" to call it a picaresque novel.

497 Ayers, Robert W. "ROBINSON CRUSOE: 'Allusive Allegorick History.'" PMLA, 82 (1967), 399–407.

> Defoe, "an artist in the Puritan tradition," must be taken seriously when he speaks of CRUSOE as an "allusive allegorick history."

498 Baine, Rodney M. DANIEL DEFOE AND THE SUPERNATURAL. Athens: University of Georgia Press, 1968.

> An examination of Defoe's angelology and occult writings, such as AN ESSAY ON THE HISTORY AND REALITY OF APPARITIONS (1727); interesting and ambitious, but not terribly helpful to the student of the novels.

499 Bastian, Frank. "Defoe's JOURNAL OF THE PLAGUE YEAR Reconsidered." RES, NS 16 (1965), 151–73.

On the vague boundaries between fiction and history in the work of Defoe, with glances at some of his contemporaries.

500 Benjamin, Edwin B. "Symbolic Elements in ROBINSON CRUSOE." PQ, 30 (1951), 206-11.

The novel is a "symbolic account of a spiritual experience."

501 Boyce, Benjamin. "The Question of Emotion in Defoe." SP, 1 (1953), 45-58.

On a subject rarely discussed in Defoe studies; emphasis on the feelings of Crusoe, Moll, and (especially) Roxana.

502 Brown, Homer O. "The Displaced Self in the Novels of Daniel Defoe." ELH, 38 (1971), 562-90.

An extremely provocative (if almost impenetrable) essay that addresses Defoe's habitual practice of dividing his narrators' impulses between revelation and disguise of the self; they and the novels they inhabit are apt representatives for "a society of mutually suspicious individuals."

503 Byrd, Max, ed. DANIEL DEFOE: A COLLECTION OF CRITICAL ESSAYS. Twentieth Century Views. Englewood Cliffs, N.J.: Prentice-Hall, 1976.

A selection of reprinted essays by Defoe scholars.

504 Donovan, Robert Alan. THE SHAPING VISION: IMAGINATION IN THE ENGLISH NOVEL FROM DEFOE TO DICKENS. Ithaca, N.Y.: Cornell University Press, 1966.

Excellent chapter on MOLL FLANDERS; attempts "not to perform an act of historical reconstruction" but to analyze the novel's form by closely examining "the verbal texture in which the novelist's imaginative vision is embedded, for it is here that one encounters the selection and arrangement of details, the modulations of tone, and the very rhythms of thought which make the narrated incidents significant." From this perspective, Donovan considers the ironic tensions between the novel's "two heroines," the Moll who narrates and the Moll who acts.

505 Elliott, Robert C., ed. TWENTIETH CENTURY INTERPRETATIONS OF MOLL FLANDERS. Englewood Cliffs, N.J.: Prentice-Hall, 1970.

A selection of reprinted essays by modern Defoe scholars.

506 Ellis, Frank, ed. TWENTIETH CENTURY INTERPRETATIONS OF ROBINSON CRUSOE. Englewood Cliffs, N.J.: Prentice-Hall, 1969.

A selection of reprinted essays by modern Defoe scholars.

507 Forster, E.M. ASPECTS OF THE NOVEL. New York: Harcourt, Brace, 1927.

Forster takes MOLL FLANDERS as his major example of the "novel of character."

508 Halewood, William. "Religion and Invention in ROBINSON CRUSOE." ESSAYS IN CRITICISM, 14 (1964), 339-51.

An argument anticipating that advanced by Hunter (No. 510) and Starr (No. 542).

509 Hume, Robert D. "The Conclusion of Defoe's ROXANA: Fiasco or Tour de Force?" ECS, 3 (1970), 475-90.

The ending is just as "Defoe wanted and conceived it." (See also No. 512.)

510 Hunter, J. Paul. THE RELUCTANT PILGRIM: DEFOE'S EMBLEMATIC METHOD AND QUEST FOR FORM IN ROBINSON CRUSOE. Baltimore: Johns Hopkins University Press, 1966.

Sees the artistic power of ROBINSON CRUSOE as the result of Defoe's reliance upon Puritan subliterary traditions: the "Guide-Book," the "Providence" tradition, spiritual biography and autobiography, allegories, and emblem books. (See also Nos. 508 and 542.)

511 James, E. Anthony. DANIEL DEFOE'S MANY VOICES: A RHETORICAL STUDY OF PROSE STYLE AND LITERARY METHOD. Amsterdam: Editions Rodopi, 1972.

Analysis of Defoe's language; throws light on his remarkable versatility and inventiveness in the creation of personae.

512 Jenkins, Ralph E. "The Structure of ROXANA." SNNTS, 2 (1970), 145-58.

An attempt to show that the ending of ROXANA, usually judged to be inept or at least inappropriate and incomplete, is actually right for this novel, which is really a complicated "allegorical structure." (See also No. 509.)

513 Johnson, Clifford. "Defoe's Reaction to Enlightened Secularism: A JOURNAL OF THE PLAGUE YEAR." ENLIGHTENMENT ESSAYS, 3 (1972), 169-77.

Despite his interest in science and technology, Defoe remained

always convinced of the actions of providence in the affairs
of mankind.

514 Koonce, Howard L. "Moll's Muddle: Defoe's Use of Irony in MOLL
FLANDERS." ELH, 30 (1963), 377-94.

On the conscious and complex ironies in Defoe's novel. (See
also Nos. 520 and 547.)

515 McBurney, William H[arlin]. "Colonel Jacque: Defoe's Definition of the
Complete Gentleman." SEL, 2 (1962), 321-36.

A fine essay that explains in detail Defoe's conception of gentility, and its manifestation in Colonel Jacque.

516 McKillop, Alan Dugald. THE EARLY MASTERS OF ENGLISH FICTION.
Lawrence: University of Kansas Press, 1956.

Includes a chapter on Defoe that is the best single critical
survey of his novels, short though it is. McKillop sees Defoe
as a serious artist and conscious moralist.

517 McMaster, Juliet. "The Equation of Love and Money in MOLL FLAN-
DERS." SNNTS, 2 (1970), 131-44.

Defoe's novel ironically exposes Moll as a woman representing
a "world view where financial considerations have taken the
place of sexual, moral and spiritual ones."

518 Moore, John Robert. DEFOE IN THE PILLORY AND OTHER STUDIES.
Bloomington: Indiana University Press, 1939.

Varied essays on several of Defoe's more obscure works, for
each of which a synopsis is provided.

519 Nicholson, Watson. THE HISTORICAL SOURCES OF DEFOE'S JOURNAL
OF THE PLAGUE YEAR. Boston: Stratford, 1919.

Still a very useful study.

520 Novak, Maximillian E. "Conscious Irony in MOLL FLANDERS: Facts
and Problems." CE, 26 (1964), 198-204.

An excellent contribution to the debate over the question of
whether Defoe was a conscious ironist; Novak believes he was.
(See also Nos. 514 and 547.)

521 _____. "Crime and Punishment in Defoe's ROXANA." JEGP, 65 (1966),
445-65.

ROXANA is a novel of "moral decay"; its moral and technical sophistication make it, in certain respects, Defoe's "furthest advance" in fictional form, though its ending is "truncated."

522 _____. DEFOE AND THE NATURE OF MAN. Oxford: Oxford University Press, 1963.

Emphasizes Defoe's embodiment of natural law in the worlds of his fictions: those worlds are thus rationally organized, touched by occasional Providential interventions, and peopled by characters possessing a powerful, "natural" instinct for self-preservation.

523 _____. "Defoe's 'Indifferent Monitor': The Complexity of MOLL FLANDERS." ECS, 3 (1970), 351-65.

On the intricacies of Defoe's narrative techniques.

524 _____. "Defoe's Theory of Fiction." SP, 61 (1964), 650-68.

Assembles and comments on Defoe's various published statements on fiction.

525 _____. "Defoe's Use of Irony." THE USES OF IRONY: PAPERS ON DEFOE AND SWIFT READ AT A CLARK LIBRARY SEMINAR. Ed. Hugh T. Swedenberg. Berkeley and Los Angeles: University of California Press, 1966.

An account of the ironies in a number of Defoe's works and of the contemporary reactions to them.

526 _____. ECONOMICS AND THE FICTION OF DANIEL DEFOE. Berkeley and Los Angeles: University of California Press, 1962.

A study of Defoe as the able exponent of a number of contemporary economic theories, synthesized and made coherent in the novels; includes a bibliography of Defoe's economic writings.

527 _____. "Imaginary Islands and Real Beasts: The Imaginative Genesis of ROBINSON CRUSOE." TSL, 19 (1974), 57-78.

An important contribution to the discussion of the origins and composition of ROBINSON CRUSOE.

528 Peterson, Spiro. "The Matrimonial Theme of Defoe's ROXANA." PMLA, 70 (1955), 166-91.

ROXANA, says Peterson, provides a deliberate contrast to MOLL FLANDERS--the two novels feature alternative views of marriage espoused by carefully differentiated types of heroines.

529 Piper, William B. "MOLL FLANDERS as a Structure of Topics." SEL, 9 (1969), 489-502.

> A discussion arguing the simplicity of the novel's structure; runs counter to much recent criticism.

530 Preston, John. THE CREATED SELF: THE READER'S ROLE IN EIGHTEENTH-CENTURY FICTION. New York: Barnes and Noble, 1970.

> Chapter on MOLL FLANDERS; investigates the ways in which Defoe's ironies work to "re-route" his readers' "social thinking and motives."

531 Price, Martin. TO THE PALACE OF WISDOM: STUDIES IN ORDER AND ENERGY FROM DRYDEN TO BLAKE. New York: Doubleday, 1964.

> Includes a discussion of MOLL FLANDERS that emphasizes the formlessness of the novel, and--on the basis of the book's end-ing--asserts that "ultimately, one might call Defoe a comic artist."

532 Raleigh, John Henry. "Style and Structure and Their Import in Defoe's ROXANA." UNIVERSITY OF KANSAS CITY REVIEW, 20 (1953), 128-35.

> Praise for Defoe's careful artistry in the construction of this novel.

533 Richetti, John J. DEFOE'S NARRATIVES: SITUATIONS AND STRUC-TURES. Oxford: Clarendon Press, 1975.

> A study of the major novels; emphasis on the narratives as fic-tions instead of historical or biographical documents. Richetti's purpose is to see the works as "instinctively coherent and cul-turally functional acts of the mimetic-historical imagination."

534 _____. POPULAR FICTION BEFORE RICHARDSON: NARRATIVE PAT-TERNS 1700-1739. Oxford: Clarendon Press, 1969.

> Chapter III places Defoe's travel narratives and pirate adven-tures in the context of other contemporary works in these popu-lar modes and examines ROBINSON CRUSOE in connection with other desert-island tales.

535 Rogal, Samuel J. "The Profit and Loss of Moll Flanders." SNNTS, 5 (1973), 98-103.

> An account (complete with ledger charts) of the "at least sixty-five separate occasions in the novel on which Moll receives and pays out cash money."

536 Rogers, Pat, ed. DEFOE: THE CRITICAL HERITAGE. London: Routledge and Kegan Paul, 1972.

> A useful collection of critical commentaries on Defoe, from his own time and later.

537 Schonhorn, Manuel. "Defoe's CAPTAIN SINGLETON: A Reassessment with Observations." PLL, 7 (1971), 38-51.

> An interesting and valuable discussion of Defoe's treatment of his pirates, whom he modeled on real persons and the characters of popular pirate tales, but significantly softened and gentled; his realism, Schonhorn suggests, is thus a modified realism that does not always simply mirror or "photograph" the actual world.

538 Secord, Arthur W. ROBERT DRURY'S JOURNAL AND OTHER STUDIES. Urbana: University of Illinois Press, 1961.

> Like Secord's earlier book (No. 539), a study in Defoe's sources; the third essay gives extensive treatment to the sources (in three contemporary histories) of MEMOIRS OF A CAVALIER.

539 _____. STUDIES IN THE NARRATIVE METHOD OF DEFOE. Urbana: University of Illinois Press, 1924.

> Emphasis on Defoe's use of sources, suggesting (perhaps unwittingly) that he was resourceful but not very original; includes a lengthy bibliography of sources for Defoe's travel narratives.

540 Sen, Sri C. DANIEL DEFOE: HIS MIND AND HIS ART. Calcutta: University of Calcutta Press, 1948.

> An enthusiastic, if somewhat impressionistic, discussion endorsing the view of Defoe as conscious artist.

541 Starr, George A. DEFOE AND CASUISTRY. Princeton, N.J.: Princeton University Press, 1971.

> An analysis of the moral dilemmas and the sometimes contradictory ethical currents running throughout Defoe's work; especially informative on the philosophical backgrounds.

542 _____. DEFOE AND SPIRITUAL AUTOBIOGRAPHY. Princeton, N.J.: Princeton University Press, 1965.

> A valuable study linking the form and meaning of ROBINSON CRUSOE and MOLL FLANDERS to a popular Puritan subliterary form. (See also Nos. 508 and 510.)

543 _____. "Defoe's Prose Style: 1. The Language of Interpretation." MP, 71 (1974), 277-94.

A sensitive and important contribution to the discussion of Defoe's "plain style" and its richness of texture and meaning.

544 Sutherland, James R. DANIEL DEFOE: A CRITICAL STUDY. Cambridge, Mass.: Harvard University Press, 1971.

A readable, perceptive discussion of the artistry in Defoe's fiction; especially illuminating on the poems, essays, and tracts as they relate to the fiction.

545 _____. "The Relation of Defoe's Fiction to His Non-Fictional Writings." IMAGINED WORLDS: ESSAYS ON SOME ENGLISH NOVELS AND NOVELISTS IN HONOUR OF JOHN BUTT. Ed. Maynard Mack and Ian Gregor. London: Methuen, 1968.

A very perceptive discussion; especially sound on the sometimes blurred distinctions between the real and the imagined in Defoe's work.

546 Taube, Myron. "MOLL FLANDERS and FANNY HILL: A Comparison." BALL STATE UNIVERSITY FORUM, 9 (1968), 76-80.

Identifies the obvious relationships between Defoe's roguish heroine and Cleland's.

547 Van Ghent, Dorothy. "On MOLL FLANDERS." THE ENGLISH NOVEL: FORM AND FUNCTION. New York: Rinehart, 1953.

One of the major essays in the recent debate over the question of whether Defoe was a conscious or "accidental" ironist. Van Ghent argues that MOLL FLANDERS is an intricate, coherent structure of particular and overriding ironies. (See also Nos. 514 and 520.)

548 Watt, Ian P. "The Naming of Characters in Defoe, Richardson, and Fielding." RES, 25 (1949), 322-38.

A discussion of the significance of names.

549 _____. "The Recent Critical Fortunes of MOLL FLANDERS." ECS, 1 (1967), 109-26.

A survey of the critical controversies surrounding the novel in the late 1950's and 1960's.

550 _____. THE RISE OF THE NOVEL: STUDIES IN DEFOE, RICHARDSON, AND FIELDING. London: Chatto and Windus, 1957.

Includes discussions of ROBINSON CRUSOE and MOLL FLAN-
DERS that have been very influential. Watt sees Defoe as an
economic individualist whose narratives lack fully coherent
form, as a writer who is not the first novelist, but rather the
"master of the brilliant episode."

551 _____. "ROBINSON CRUSOE as a Myth." ESSAYS IN CRITICISM, 1
(1951), 95-119.

An essay that admits, but is somewhat hostile to, the apotheo-
sis of homo economicus achieved by Defoe's fiction and accepted by two hundred years of readers. Crusoe, as culture-
hero, crowds out of the pantheon of myth those "other figures,
whether comic or tragic," who represent more generous aspira-
tions than he.

552 Zimmerman, Everett. DEFOE AND THE NOVEL. Berkeley and Los Angeles: University of California Press, 1975.

A useful general discussion that emphasizes Defoe's artistry in
the novel, and particularly his relationship, as author, with
the psychology and the language of his characters.

553 _____. "H.F.'s Meditations: A JOURNAL OF THE PLAGUE YEAR."
PMLA, 87 (1972), 417-23.

The journal is rich not only because Defoe made brilliant use
of historical sources, but because the book really focuses on
H.F. himself, who becomes a complex and psychologically interesting character.

HENRY FIELDING (1707-54)

PRINCIPAL WORKS

LOVE IN SEVERAL MASQUES, 1728 (Comedy)
THE AUTHOR'S FARCE, 1730 (Farce)
THE TRAGEDY OF TRAGEDIES [TOM THUMB], 1731 (Farce/burlesque)
THE MODERN HUSBAND, 1732 (Comedy)
DON QUIXOTE IN ENGLAND, 1734 (Comedy)
PASQUIN, 1736 (Farce)
THE HISTORICAL REGISTER FOR 1736, 1737 (Political farce)
THE CHAMPION, 1739-41 (Periodical)
AN APOLOGY FOR THE LIFE OF MRS. SHAMELA ANDREWS, 1741 (Burlesque
          of Richardson's PAMELA)
JOSEPH ANDREWS, 1742 (Novel)
MISCELLANIES, 1743 (Includes: poems and essays; JONATHAN WILD; JOUR-
          NEY FROM THIS WORLD TO THE NEXT)
THE TRUE PATRIOT, 1745-46 (Periodical)
THE JACOBITE'S JOURNAL, 1747-48 (Periodical)
TOM JONES, 1749 (Novel)
AMELIA, 1751 (Novel)
THE COVENT-GARDEN JOURNAL, 1752 (Periodical)
JOURNAL OF A VOYAGE TO LISBON, 1755

EDITIONS

A. Collected Works

Presently available editions of Fielding's collected works are all incomplete and
unscholarly. None includes SHAMELA, and all are scanty on the periodical
essays and the social pamphlets; the texts, and the explanatory notes (when they
exist at all), are unreliable. The new Wesleyan edition (see No. 558), now in
progress, will supersede all of the others and will answer the need for a complete, scholarly collection of Fielding's writings.

554 THE WORKS OF HENRY FIELDING, ESQ.; WITH THE LIFE OF THE AUTHOR. Ed. Arthur Murphy. 4 and 8 vols. London, 1762.

> The earliest collection of Fielding's works, published simultaneously in two separate editions, one in four volumes quarto and the other in eight volumes octavo. Incomplete; and the "Essay on the Life and Genius of Henry Fielding, Esq.," which is at its worst slanderous, is even at its best marred by Murphy's garrulousness and inaccuracies.

555 THE WORKS OF HENRY FIELDING, ESQ. Ed. Thomas Roscoe. London, 1840.

> A bulky edition, "Complete in One Volume," that is based on Murphy (No. 554) and is incomplete.

556 THE WORKS OF HENRY FIELDING, ESQ. EDITED WITH A BIOGRAPHICAL ESSAY. Ed. Leslie Stephen. 10 vols. London, 1882.

> More nearly complete than earlier editions; the "Life" is readable, sympathetic, and interesting, but it repeats many of Murphy's old inaccuracies of fact (see No. 554).

557 THE COMPLETE WORKS OF HENRY FIELDING, ESQ. WITH AN ESSAY ON THE LIFE, GENIUS AND ACHIEVEMENT OF THE AUTHOR. Ed. William E. Henley. 16 vols. New York, 1902; rpt. New York: Barnes and Noble, 1967.

> At present, the most nearly complete of all the collected editions; based on the Leslie Stephen edition (No. 556), although it adds a few poems and pamphlets and an edited version of the JOURNAL OF A VOYAGE TO LISBON.

558 THE WESLEYAN EDITION OF THE WORKS OF HENRY FIELDING. Ed. W.B. Coley et al. 16 vols. projected. Middletown, Conn.: Wesleyan University Press, 1967-- .

> This edition, now in progress, will be definitive; the titles thus far published include JOSEPH ANDREWS (1967) and TOM JONES (1975), both edited by Martin C. Battestin.

B. Selections and Specialized Collections

559 THE COVENT-GARDEN JOURNAL. Ed. Gerard E. Jensen. 2 vols. New Haven, Conn.: Yale University Press, 1915.

> Still the standard edition, but it will be superseded by the Wesleyan edition (No. 558).

560 THE VOYAGES OF MR. JOB VINEGAR. Ed. S.J. Sackett. Augustan

Reprint Society Publications, No. 67. Los Angeles: William Andrews Clark Memorial Library, 1958.

The "Job Vinegar" papers from THE CHAMPION.

561 THE FEMALE HUSBAND AND OTHER WRITINGS. Ed. Claude E. Jones. Liverpool: Liverpool University Press, 1960.

A carelessly edited collection of representative minor pieces by Fielding.

562 THE TRUE PATRIOT: AND THE HISTORY OF OUR OWN TIMES. Ed. Miriam A. Locke. University: University of Alabama Press, 1964.

An annotated edition.

563 LITERARY AND SOCIAL CRITICISM OF HENRY FIELDING. Ed. Ioan Williams. London: Routledge and Kegan Paul, 1970.

An extremely useful collection of Fielding's literary and social criticism, gathered from his prefaces, introductory chapters, pamphlets, and periodical essays; includes an extensive bibliography.

C. Individual Works

SHAMELA

564 AN APOLOGY FOR THE LIFE OF MRS. SHAMELA ANDREWS. Ed. Ian [P.] Watt. Augustan Reprint Society Publications, No. 57. Los Angeles: William Andrews Clark Memorial Library, 1956.

A facsimile of the second edition, 1741.

565 AN APOLOGY FOR THE LIFE OF MRS. SHAMELA ANDREWS. FIN; also SBrW.

Garland series reprints, in photofacsimile, of the first edition, 1741.

566 See Nos. 568 and 569.

JOSEPH ANDREWS

567 THE HISTORY OF THE ADVENTURES OF JOSEPH ANDREWS AND OF HIS FRIEND MR. ABRAHAM ADAMS. Ed. Maynard Mack. New York: Holt, Rinehart and Winston, 1948.

Includes a fine critical introduction.

568 JOSEPH ANDREWS AND SHAMELA. Ed. Martin C. Battestin. Boston: Houghton Mifflin, 1961.

> Includes a critical introduction that is among the finest of all commentaries on Fielding's first two works of fiction.

569 JOSEPH ANDREWS AND SHAMELA. Ed. Douglas Brooks. Oxford English Novels. London: Oxford University Press, 1970.

> Includes a critical introduction, a select bibliography, a chronology of Fielding's life and career, and explanatory notes; the text is reliable.

JONATHAN WILD

First published in THE MISCELLANIES, vol. III (1743), this work was revised by Fielding and reissued separately in 1754. Modern editions have used the later version as a copy text.

570 THE LIFE OF MR. JONATHAN WILD THE GREAT. Ed. J.H. Plumb. New York: New American Library, 1962.

> Includes an excellent foreword by Plumb.

571 JONATHAN WILD THE GREAT AND THE JOURNAL OF A VOYAGE TO LISBON. Ed. Douglas Brooks. Intro. A.R. Humphreys. Everyman's Library. London: J.M. Dent, 1973.

> Includes an excellent, though brief, critical introduction; the notes are helpful.

572 THE LIFE OF MR. JONATHAN WILD THE GREAT. FIN.

> A reprint, in photofacsimile, of the revised edition of 1754.

TOM JONES

573 THE HISTORY OF TOM JONES, A FOUNDLING. Ed. George Sherburn. New York: Random House, 1950.

> Includes a brief but excellent critical introduction by Sherburn.

574 THE HISTORY OF TOM JONES. Ed. A.R. Humphreys. 2 vols. Everyman's Library. London: J.M. Dent, 1962.

575 THE HISTORY OF TOM JONES. Ed. R.P.C. Mutter. Harmondsworth, Engl.: Penguin Books, 1966.

> Includes a good general introduction to the novel, and useful (though relatively scarce) explanatory notes.

576 TOM JONES. Ed. Sheridan Baker. Norton Critical Edition. New York: W.W. Norton, 1973.

> Includes a reliable text, a short gathering of excerpts from important background sources, and a selection of critical commentaries from the eighteenth through the twentieth centuries.

AMELIA

577 AMELIA. Ed. George Saintsbury. 2 vols. Everyman's Library. London: J.M. Dent, 1930; rpt., with new introduction by A.R. Humphreys, 1962.

JOURNAL OF A VOYAGE TO LISBON

578 THE JOURNAL OF A VOYAGE TO LISBON. Ed. Harold Pagliaro. New York: Nardon Press, 1963.

> The best modern edition of Fielding's often moving personal record of his travels to the city where he died.

579 See No. 571.

LETTERS

Only some twenty letters by Fielding have survived. These have never been collected; a number of them may be found in the British Library, while the rest are scattered among private collections and various other library holdings. The Cross biography (No. 588) reprints several of the letters.

580 McAdam, E[dward] L., [Jr.]. "A New Letter from Fielding." YALE REVIEW, 38 (1949), 300-310.

> A documentation of the discovery of a now famous letter to Richardson, praising CLARISSA; the letter is reprinted.

BIBLIOGRAPHY

581 Battestin, Martin C. "Fielding." THE ENGLISH NOVEL: SELECT BIBLIOGRAPHICAL GUIDES. Ed. A.E. Dyson. London: Oxford University Press, 1974.

> A fine bibliographical essay covering both primary and secondary sources.

582 Cordasco, Francesco. HENRY FIELDING: A LIST OF CRITICAL STUDIES

PUBLISHED FROM 1895 TO 1946. Brooklyn, N.Y.: Long Island University Press, 1948.

A seventeen-page pamphlet, quite selective in its listings; no annotations.

583 Jobe, Alice. "Fielding's Novels: Selected Criticism (1940-1969)." SNNTS, 2 (1970), 246-59.

A helpful listing; no annotations.

584 See Nos. 563, 588, 590, 608, 670, and 684.

BIOGRAPHY

585 Banerji, H.K. HENRY FIELDING: PLAYWRIGHT, JOURNALIST, AND MASTER OF THE ART OF FICTION, HIS LIFE AND WORKS. Oxford: Basil Blackwell, 1929.

Erratic and incomplete on the life, superficial and whimsical in discussion of the works; valuable only for its many summaries of Fielding's minor writings.

586 Battestin, Martin C. "Fielding's Changing Politics and JOSEPH ANDREWS." PQ, 39 (1960), 39-55.

One of the first attempts to challenge the traditional notion that Fielding was the perpetual enemy of Prime Minister Walpole.

587 Butt, John. FIELDING. Writers and Their Work, No. 57. London: Longmans, Green, 1954.

The best brief introduction to Fielding's life and works. Butt uses JOSEPH ANDREWS as a touchstone for discussion of Fielding's theories of fiction and of his responses as an artist to contemporary political, social, intellectual, and literary currents.

588 Cross, Wilbur L. THE HISTORY OF HENRY FIELDING. 3 vols. New Haven, Conn.: Yale University Press, 1918.

Still the best and most authoritative biography, though it is sometimes wrong on the facts and effusive in its defense of Fielding's personal character. Cross reprints several of Fielding's surviving letters; his bibliography of primary works and principal editions (volume III) is extensive and usually reliable.

589 Dobson, Austin. HENRY FIELDING. London, 1883.

An impressionistic biography, but nonetheless important as a

pioneering attempt to rescue Fielding's reputation as a man
from the smug, censorious Victorian view of him as a wanton,
vulgar libertine.

590 Dudden, F. Homes. HENRY FIELDING: HIS LIFE, WORKS, AND
TIMES. 2 vols. Oxford: Clarendon Press, 1952.

A massive but disappointing biography that fails to correct the
inaccuracies of Cross (No. 588) or to add significantly to our
knowledge of Fielding; includes a lengthy bibliography of primary and secondary materials.

591 Grundy, Isobel. "New Verse by Henry Fielding." PMLA, 87 (1972),
213-45.

A very important article; prints some 800 lines of verse from a
recently discovered holograph manuscript. Composed in 1729
and 1733, the verses show Fielding's early attempts at mock
epic and burlesque, and because the verses support the Whig
government and satirize the anti-Walpole Scriblerus group, they
challenge the notion that Fielding was always on the side of
the Opposition.

592 Jones, B. Maelor. HENRY FIELDING: NOVELIST AND MAGISTRATE.
London: Allen and Unwin, 1933.

A sound, but by no means definitive, study; the emphasis is
on Fielding the magistrate, but Jones illuminates the legal
themes, motifs, and issues that arise in the novels.

593 See Nos. 554 and 556.

CRITICAL STUDIES AND COMMENTARIES

594 Alter, Robert. FIELDING AND THE NATURE OF THE NOVEL. Cambridge, Mass.: Harvard University Press, 1968.

An attempt to rescue Fielding from the neglect or sneers of
some modern critics, and to define both his particular conception and practice of novelistic form and his proper place within
the genre as a whole. The discussion focuses on style, characterization, and structure in JOSEPH ANDREWS and TOM JONES
and relates these works to a tradition of the "art-novel."

595 _____. "The Picaroon Domesticated." ROGUE'S PROGRESS: STUD-
IES IN THE PICARESQUE NOVEL. Cambridge, Mass.: Harvard University Press, 1964.

An excellent discussion of TOM JONES in relation to picaresque tradition.

596   Anderson, Howard. "Answers to the Author of CLARISSA: Theme and Narrative Technique in TOM JONES and TRISTRAM SHANDY." PQ, 51 (1972), 859-73.

> The masterpieces of Fielding and Sterne are seen as deliberate responses, or alternatives in substance and form, to Richardson's masterpiece.

597   Baker, Sheridan. "Henry Fielding's Comic Romances." PAPERS OF THE MICHIGAN ACADEMY OF SCIENCES, ARTS, AND LETTERS, 45 (1960), 411-19.

> The proper term for Fielding's works is "comic romance," not "comic prose epic."

598   Battestin, Martin C. "Fielding's Definition of Wisdom: Some Functions of Ambiguity and Emblem in TOM JONES." ELH, 35 (1968), 188-217.

> A discussion of Fielding's use of verbal ambiguity and an emblematic method to convey the theme of the need for prudence and "Virtue," or "moral Wisdom," which are in Fielding's view our "true Interest."

599   _____. "Fielding's Revisions of JOSEPH ANDREWS." SB, 16 (1963), 81-117.

> An account of the many changes made by Fielding in the second edition of the novel; includes a complete list of variant readings.

600   _____. THE MORAL BASIS OF FIELDING'S ART: A STUDY OF JOSEPH ANDREWS. Middletown, Conn.: Wesleyan University Press, 1959.

> Demonstration of the profound influence of Latitudinarian divines--especially Barrow, Tillotson, Clarke, and Hoadly--on Fielding's morality and ethics as they inform, shape, and direct his fiction; the emphasis in on JOSEPH ANDREWS, but the implications for Fielding's other novels are important. For a challenge to Battestin's view, see No. 611.

601   _____. "Tom Jones and 'His Egyptian Majesty': Fielding's Parable of Government." PMLA, 82 (1967), 68-77.

> The episode during which Tom and Partridge fall in with a band of gypsies (Book XII) is really a commentary on Jacobite political philosophy.

602   _____. "TOM JONES: The Argument of Design." THE AUGUSTAN MILIEU: ESSAYS PRESENTED TO LOUIS A. LANDA. Ed. Henry Knight Miller et al. New York: Oxford University Press, 1970.

An important essay that examines, among other things, the philosophical and religious influences that helped to shape Fielding's novel.

603 _____, ed. TWENTIETH CENTURY INTERPRETATIONS OF TOM JONES. Englewood Cliffs, N.J.: Prentice-Hall, 1968.

A collection of reprinted essays by modern Fielding scholars.

604 Beasley, Jerry C. "English Fiction in the 1740's: Some Glances at the Major and Minor Novels." SNNTS, 5 (1973), 155-75.

An attempt to show that, despite their differences, Fielding, Richardson, and Smollett all exploited contemporary themes, methods, and types of fiction.

605 _____. "Romance and the 'New' Novels of Richardson, Fielding, and Smollett." SEL, 16 (1976), 437-50.

The three major novelists of the 1740's all borrowed to some extent from the themes and conventions of romance.

606 Bell, Michael. "A Note on Drama and the Novel: Fielding's Contribution." NOVEL, 3 (1970), 119-28.

An unexceptional but informative essay on Fielding as "scenic artist" whose episodes frequently draw heavily but subtly on dramatic techniques; Fielding's "contribution" is the "complete fusion" of two aesthetic modes.

607 Bissell, Frederick Olds. FIELDING'S THEORY OF THE NOVEL. Ithaca, N.Y.: Cornell University Press, 1933.

Emphasizes Fielding's theory of the "comic-prose-epic," especially as applied in JOSEPH ANDREWS.

608 Blanchard, Frederic T. FIELDING THE NOVELIST: A STUDY IN HISTORICAL CRITICISM. New Haven, Conn.: Yale University Press, 1926.

An exhaustive and indispensable study of the reception and influence of Fielding's novels, through the early years of the twentieth century; Richardson's reputation, as it relates to Fielding's, also receives considerable attention. The bibliography of sources is extremely valuable.

609 Bloch, Tuvia. "AMELIA and Booth's Doctrine of the Passions." SEL, 13 (1973), 461-73.

Argues that Booth and Fielding agree on the doctrine of the prevailing passion governing men's behavior.

610 Booth, Wayne C. THE RHETORIC OF FICTION. Chicago: University of Chicago Press, 1961.

Includes an excellent discussion of the narrator in TOM JONES.

611 Braudy, Leo. NARRATIVE FORM IN HISTORY AND FICTION: HUME, FIELDING, AND GIBBON. Princeton, N.J.: Princeton University Press, 1970.

Includes an excellent discussion of Fielding's notions of the relationships between fiction and history; the latter becomes the "skeleton of method and ideal" for the former, and because the facts of experience are confusing, Fielding is led to the portrayal of the "atmosphere of epistemological uncertainty in which we live." For a different view of Fielding's purpose and methods, see No. 600.

612 Brooks, Douglas. "The Interpolated Tales in JOSEPH ANDREWS Again." MP, 65 (1968), 208-13.

A discussion of the appropriateness of the first and last digressions to the novel as a whole. (See also Nos. 613, 628, and 689.)

613 Cauthen, I.B., Jr. "Fielding's Digressions in JOSEPH ANDREWS." CE, 17 (1956), 379-82.

A brief defense of the interpolated tales. (See also Nos. 612, 628, and 689.)

614 Coley, William B. "The Background of Fielding's Laughter." ELH, 26 (1959), 229-52.

A discussion of Fielding's comic vision and techniques and of their connections to the philosophical theories of Shaftesbury and the satires of Swift.

615 Cooke, Arthur L. "Henry Fielding and the Writers of Romance." PMLA, 62 (1947), 984-94.

Fielding's knowledge of the heroic romance was considerable and influenced the development of his theory of the comic prose epic.

616 Coolidge, John S. "Fielding and 'Conservation of Character.'" MP, 57 (1960), 245-59.

AMELIA differs from Fielding's earlier novels not only because of its more subdued tone but also because it "conserves" character by revealing personality in a developmental fashion.

617 Crane, Ronald S. "The Plot of TOM JONES." JOURNAL OF GENERAL EDUCATION, 4 (1950), 112-30; rev. and rpt. as "The Concept of Plot and the Plot of TOM JONES." CRITICS AND CRITICISM: ANCIENT AND MODERN. Ed. Ronald S. Crane. Chicago: University of Chicago Press, 1952.

> An excellent and influential essay, widely reprinted; emphasizes an Aristotelian view of the organic function of plot as the "particular temporal synthesis effected by the writer among the elements of action, character, and thought that constitute the matter of his invention."

618 Digeon, Aurélien. LES ROMANS DE FIELDING. Paris, 1923; trans. as THE NOVELS OF FIELDING. London: Routledge and Kegan Paul, 1925.

> One of the very best general studies of Fielding's fiction.

619 Donovan, Robert Alan. THE SHAPING VISION: IMAGINATION IN THE ENGLISH NOVEL FROM DEFOE TO DICKENS. Ithaca, N.Y.: Cornell University Press, 1966.

> The fine chapter on JOSEPH ANDREWS takes the unusual view that Fielding's novel continues throughout its parody of Richardson's PAMELA and that this aim helps to account for the "coherence, or lack of it, in the imaginative vision which shapes the novel."

620 Dyson, A.E. "Satiric and Comic Theory in Relation to Fielding." MLQ, 18 (1957), 225-37.

> An examination of Fielding's work reveals that he was a comic writer rather than a satirist, for he judges against a norm of behavior instead of an ideal.

621 Ehrenpreis, Irvin. FIELDING: TOM JONES. London: Edward Arnold, 1964.

> A fine general introduction to the novel's form and substance; written for the nonspecialist.

622 Empson, William. "TOM JONES." KENYON REVIEW, 20 (1958), 217-49.

> An essential study of TOM JONES as a thesis novel, rich in the complexity of ironies and double ironies, promoting a doctrine of "imaginative sympathy."

623 Farrell, William J. "The Mock-Heroic Form of JONATHAN WILD." MP, 63 (1966), 216-26.

> An excellent discussion of Fielding's ironic use of the established

methods of panegyric biography to create a mock-heroic narrative.

624 Folkenflik, Robert. "Purpose and Narration in Fielding's AMELIA."
NOVEL, 7 (1974), 168–74.

In part, an answer to the article by Hassall (see No. 631);
Folkenflik also attempts to explain why Fielding chose to avoid
authorial narration in AMELIA.

625 Goggin, L.P. "Development of Techniques in Fielding's Comedies."
PMLA, 67 (1952), 769–81.

The comedies of manners are Fielding's best plays, and they
directly anticipate the novels.

626 Goldberg, Homer. THE ART OF JOSEPH ANDREWS. Chicago: University of Chicago Press, 1969.

An excellent study; analyzes the literary background of the
novel and the use Fielding made of that background; particular
emphasis on the importance of Cervantes, Scarron, and Marivaux
and on the validity of Fielding's theory of the comic prose epic
as defined in the preface to JOSEPH ANDREWS.

627 _____. "Comic Prose Epic or Comic Romance: The Argument of the
Preface to JOSEPH ANDREWS." PQ, 43 (1964), 193–215.

A detailed analysis of the preface. Goldberg, more ably than
anyone else, shows what Fielding meant. The article answers
the faulty reading of Ian Watt in THE RISE OF THE NOVEL
(see No. 691). See also Goldberg's book on JOSEPH AN-
DREWS (No. 626), which is in part an elaboration upon the
analysis presented in this article.

628 _____. "The Interpolated Stories in JOSEPH ANDREWS or 'The History
of the World in General' Satirically Revised." MP, 63 (1966), 295–310.

Discussion of the relevance of the digressions, emphasizing
their indebtedness to similar interludes in DON QUIXOTE.
(See also Nos. 612, 613, and 689.)

629 Golden, Morris. FIELDING'S MORAL PSYCHOLOGY. Amherst: University of Massachusetts Press, 1966.

The central crisis of Fielding's novels is the psychological problem of the "enclosed self": naturally egocentric man must es-
tablish outgoing sympathy. In intellectual terms, the paradox
involves a conflict between the ideas of Hobbes, Locke, and
Mandeville on one side, and Shaftesbury and the Latitudinarian
theologians on the other.

630   Guthrie, William B. "The Comic Celebrant of Life in TOM JONES."
      TSL, 19 (1974), 91-105.

> In his masterpiece, Fielding suspends moral judgment in a comic
> celebration of life, the principal celebrants being the narrator
> and the hero. Guthrie gives considerable attention to the
> feasting and drinking motifs and to sexuality in the novel.

631   Hassall, Anthony. "Fielding's AMELIA: Dramatic and Authorial Narra-
      tion." NOVEL, 5 (1972), 225-33.

> "AMELIA is tentative and uncertain on the basic structural
> level of narrative method: it alternates between authorial and
> dramatic narration, and in such a way that the two methods
> inhibit one another." For an answer to this argument, see
> No. 624.

632   Hatfield, Glenn W. HENRY FIELDING AND THE LANGUAGE OF
      IRONY. Chicago: University of Chicago Press, 1968.

> A fine study of Fielding's theories of language, his ironic at-
> tacks on the abuses of language, and his own attempts at an
> "honest" use of words.

633   Hilles, Frederick W. "Art and Artifice in TOM JONES." IMAGINED
      WORLDS: ESSAYS ON SOME ENGLISH NOVELS AND NOVELISTS IN
      HONOUR OF JOHN BUTT. Ed. Maynard Mack and Ian Gregor. Lon-
      don: Methuen, 1968.

> A fine explanation and defense of the artful symmetries of
> Fielding's novel.

634   Humphreys, A.R. "Fielding's Irony: Its Method and Effects." RES, 18
      (1942), 183-96.

> An important study that emphasizes Fielding's verbal ironies,
> particularly in JONATHAN WILD.

635   Hunter, J. Paul. "The Lesson of AMELIA." QUICK SPRINGS OF SENSE:
      STUDIES IN THE EIGHTEENTH CENTURY. Ed. Larry S. Champion. Athens:
      University of Georgia Press, 1974.

> An essay that is in large part an attempt to suggest, in the
> midst of a whirlwind of Fielding scholarship, that a new bal-
> ance, a new perspective on Fielding's importance and achieve-
> ment, may be necessary. "Perhaps the ultimate guarantee that
> Fielding will not be overrated is AMELIA," a novel in which
> his "limitations stand forth boldly."

636   _____. OCCASIONAL FORM: HENRY FIELDING AND THE CHAINS

OF CIRCUMSTANCE. Baltimore: Johns Hopkins University Press, 1975.

A fine discussion of Fielding's novels, which places them in relation to the drama and to "historical forces operating on his mind and art, chronicling his anxiety" and his adjustment to changing literary and historical circumstance.

637 Hutchens, Eleanor Newman. IRONY IN TOM JONES. University: University of Alabama Press, 1965.

Detailed examinations of situational, verbal, and dramatic ironies in the novel; for Fielding, irony was a habit of mind as well as a technique. The brief survey of Fieldingesque ironies in later writers, including Austen, Dickens, and Thackeray, is useful.

638 Irwin, Michael. HENRY FIELDING: THE TENTATIVE REALIST. New York: Oxford University Press, 1967.

A strained and debatable argument that Fielding's art developed in complexity as his didactic impulses became more intense. Irwin's adaptation of Gombrich's method (in ART AND ILLUSION) is ingenious but unsatisfactory because it leads to capricious judgments about the textures of Fielding's novels.

639 Irwin, William R. THE MAKING OF JONATHAN WILD: A STUDY IN THE LITERARY METHOD OF HENRY FIELDING. New York: Columbia University Press, 1941.

An excellent treatment of the literary, social, and political contexts within which Fielding composed his novel; especially illuminating on his use of epic analogy, on the adaptations from the tradition of criminal biography, and on the transformations of political history and the facts of the real-life Jonathan Wild's biography into the stuff of art.

640 _____. "Satire and Comedy in the Works of Henry Fielding." ELH, 13 (1946), 168-88.

Enumerates Fielding's favorite objects of mockery--corrupt lawyers, trading justices, pedants, and so on--and shows how his treatment of them harmonizes with his theory of the comic prose epic.

641 Johnson, Maurice. FIELDING'S ART OF FICTION: ELEVEN ESSAYS ON SHAMELA, JOSEPH ANDREWS, TOM JONES, AND AMELIA. Philadelphia: University of Pennsylvania Press, 1961.

An uneven set of essays by a formalist critic; the discussion of symbolic images (such as Sophia's muff) in TOM JONES is especially noteworthy.

642   Kaplan, Fred. "Fielding's Novel About Novels: The 'Prefaces' and the 'Plot' of TOM JONES." SEL, 13 (1973), 535-49.

> A useful summary account of the prefaces and their connections with the various books of Fielding's novel.

643   Kermode, Frank. "Richardson and Fielding." CAMBRIDGE JOURNAL, 4 (1950), 106-14.

> A stimulating but prejudicial argument stressing the differences between Richardson and Fielding and exalting Richardson's searching introspection and authorial distance at the expense of Fielding's comic vision and methods. For different views of, and approaches to, the relationships between the two novelists, see Nos. 604, 605, 657, and 658.

644   Knowles, A.S., Jr. "Defoe, Swift, and Fielding: Notes on the Retirement Theme." QUICK SPRINGS OF SENSE: STUDIES IN THE EIGHTEENTH CENTURY. Ed. Larry S. Champion. Athens: University of Georgia Press, 1974.

> A discussion of the "Horatian-Augustan ideal" of retirement to country life as reflected in the work of these novelists; Fielding receives greatest emphasis.

645   Kreissman, Bernard. PAMELA-SHAMELA: A STUDY OF THE CRITICISMS, BURLESQUES, PARODIES, AND ADAPTATIONS OF RICHARDSON'S PAMELA. Lincoln: University of Nebraska Press, 1960.

> SHAMELA, clearly the best of the anti-Pamelas, receives considerable attention from Kreissman; the comparisons of SHAMELA to other works like it are especially noteworthy.

646   Kropf, C.R. "Educational Theory and Human Nature in Fielding's Works." PMLA, 89 (1974), 113-20.

> An examination of Fielding's changing views on, and uses of, contemporary theories concerning the relationship between human nature and the value of education.

647   Levine, George R. HENRY FIELDING AND THE DRY MOCK: A STUDY OF THE TECHNIQUES OF IRONY IN HIS EARLY WORK. The Hague: Mouton, 1967.

> A useful discussion of the devices of irony in the plays and in JOSEPH ANDREWS and JONATHAN WILD.

648   Loftis, John. COMEDY AND SOCIETY FROM CONGREVE TO FIELDING. Stanford, Calif.: Stanford University Press, 1959.

> Includes a good discussion of Fielding's plays in relation to their social and historical backgrounds.

649 McKillop, Alan Dugald. THE EARLY MASTERS OF ENGLISH FICTION. Lawrence: University of Kansas Press, 1956.

 Chapter III offers the best general critical assessment of Fielding's novels.

650 _____. "The Personal Relations between Fielding and Richardson." MP, 28 (1931), 423–33.

 The best brief discussion of this subject.

651 _____. "Some Recent Views of TOM JONES." CE, 21 (1959), 17–22.

 A survey of commentaries published during the few years prior to 1959.

652 _____, ed. AN ESSAY ON THE NEW SPECIES OF WRITING FOUNDED BY MR. FIELDING, 1751. Augustan Reprint Society Publications, No. 95. Los Angeles: William Andrews Clark Memorial Library, 1962.

 This essay, often attributed to Francis Coventry (author of the Fieldingesque HISTORY OF POMPEY THE LITTLE, 1751), is the best contemporary critical assessment of Fielding's work.

653 Miller, Henry Knight. "Some Functions of Rhetoric in TOM JONES." PQ, 45 (1966), 209–35.

 A fine discussion of Fielding's uses of the devices of classical rhetoric in the development of his comic fiction and its themes.

654 _____. "The Voices of Henry Fielding: Style in TOM JONES." THE AUGUSTAN MILIEU: ESSAYS PRESENTED TO LOUIS A. LANDA. Ed. Henry Knight Miller et al. New York: Oxford University Press, 1970.

 An important essay on Fielding's narrative techniques.

655 Moore, Robert Etheridge. "Dr. Johnson on Fielding and Richardson." PMLA, 66 (1951), 162–81.

 Moore takes the view that, despite Dr. Johnson's public comments on the two writers, Fielding's novels are much closer to Johnson's most "deeply-felt" literary principles than are Richardson's.

656 Palmer, Eustace. "AMELIA--The Decline of Fielding's Art." ESSAYS IN CRITICISM, 21 (1971), 135–51.

 Palmer takes the conventional position, not always now accepted, that as the high comedy, the irony, and the mock-epic machinery vanished from AMELIA, Fielding's performance as a novelist declined.

657　Park, William. "Fielding and Richardson." PMLA, 81 (1966), 381-88.

　　　A convincing argument that the novelists of the mid-eighteenth
　　　century shared a common body of assumptions and conventions.
　　　For a very different view of the relationships between Fielding
　　　and Richardson, see No. 643; for views similar to those ex-
　　　pressed in this article, see Nos. 604, 605, and 658.

658　_____. "What Was New About the 'New Species of Writing'?" SNNTS,
　　　2 (1970), 112-30.

　　　An attempt to justify the claims of artistic "newness" made by
　　　Fielding and Richardson, who were in many respects not so
　　　different as has sometimes been thought. (See also No. 657.)

659　Paulson, Ronald. SATIRE AND THE NOVEL IN EIGHTEENTH-CENTURY
　　　ENGLAND. New Haven, Conn.: Yale University Press, 1967.

　　　The three excellent chapters on Fielding show how his major nov-
　　　els (especially TOM JONES) progressively transcend the sati-
　　　rist's art to develop not just the exposure of individual actions
　　　but the assessment of whole beings and abstract codes of thought
　　　and behavior.

660　_____, ed. FIELDING: A COLLECTION OF CRITICAL ESSAYS. Twen-
　　　tieth Century Views. Englewood Cliffs, N.J.: Prentice-Hall, 1962.

　　　Reprinted essays by various modern Fielding scholars.

661　Paulson, Ronald, and Thomas Lockwood, eds. FIELDING: THE CRITICAL
　　　HERITAGE. London: Routledge and Kegan Paul, 1968.

　　　A collection of critical commentaries on Fielding, from his
　　　own time and later.

662　Powers, Lyall H. "The Influence of the AENEID on Fielding's AMELIA."
　　　MLN, 71 (1956), 330-36.

　　　A study of parallels.

663　Preston, John. THE CREATED SELF: THE READER'S ROLE IN EIGHTEENTH-
　　　CENTURY FICTION. New York: Barnes and Noble, 1970.

　　　The two chapters on Fielding examine the means by which TOM
　　　JONES uses ironic plot to engage the reader's attention and
　　　sympathies, and by which the novel pursues its moral purpose
　　　of defining "true judgment."

664　Rawson, Claude J. HENRY FIELDING. London: Routledge and Kegan
　　　Paul, 1968.

A general introduction to Fielding's works, together with illustrative excerpts; for the nonspecialist.

665 _____. HENRY FIELDING AND THE AUGUSTAN IDEAL UNDER STRESS. London: Routledge and Kegan Paul, 1972.

A provocative study of the "moral, social, and aesthetic ideals" of Augustan literature and literary style, as their "harmonies" came under threat from "disruptive pressures" and "radical insecurities" that manifested themselves in some of the "most confident, and some of the most conservative, writing of the period." The emphasis is on Fielding, and the discussion of JONATHAN WILD in the second half of the book is especially fresh and stimulating.

666 _____, ed. HENRY FIELDING: A CRITICAL ANTHOLOGY. Harmondsworth, Engl.: Penguin Books, 1973.

A collection of critical commentaries, many of them extracts, from Fielding's own time forward.

667 Rogers, Winfield H. "Fielding's Early Aesthetic and Technique." SP, 40 (1943), 529-51.

A study of the apprenticeship years, 1729 to 1740, with emphasis on the important comedies and farces; these, says Rogers, helped Fielding to develop "the aesthetic and techniques upon which his great works were written."

668 Rothstein, Eric. "The Framework of SHAMELA." ELH, 35 (1968), 381-402.

An extended analysis of the Oliver-Tickletext framework of letters that "surrounds" the main plot of Fielding's parody.

669 _____. SYSTEMS OF ORDER AND INQUIRY IN LATER EIGHTEENTH-CENTURY FICTION. Berkeley and Los Angeles: University of California Press, 1975.

The essay on AMELIA treats the epistemological and aesthetic principles that govern Fielding's careful ordering of the novel.

670 Rundus, Raymond J. "TOM JONES in Adaptation: A Chronology and Criticism." BNYPL, 77 (1974), 329-41.

A listing and critical evaluation of seventeen authenticated adaptations, with citation of a dozen additional nonauthenticated adaptations. This list adds importantly to Cross's bibliography (see No. 588).

671 Ruthven, K.K. "Fielding, Square, and the Fitness of Things." ECS, 5 (1971), 243-55.

A discussion of the characterization of Square in relation to the antideism of the polemics of Samuel Clarke (1675-1729).

672 Sacks, Sheldon. FICTION AND THE SHAPE OF BELIEF: A STUDY OF HENRY FIELDING WITH GLANCES AT SWIFT, JOHNSON, AND RICHARDSON. Berkeley and Los Angeles: University of California Press, 1964.

Neo-Aristotelian rhetorical criticism. Sacks emphasizes the devices by which Fielding's characters are designed (as "fallible paragons," "species characters," "walking concepts," and so on) to give formal expression to the author's beliefs.

673 Schonhorn, Manuel. "Heroic Allusion in TOM JONES: Hamlet and the Temptations of Jesus." SNNTS, 6 (1974), 218-27.

On the interesting parallels between Tom Jones and the most familiar eighteenth-century interpretation of Hamlet as the embodiment of filial piety. Schonhorn draws similar parallels between the temptations of Christ and Tom Jones's temptation during his own forty days in the wilderness.

674 Shepperson, Archibald Bolling. THE NOVEL IN MOTLEY: A HISTORY OF THE BURLESQUE NOVEL IN ENGLISH. Cambridge, Mass.: Harvard University Press, 1936.

Includes an excellent discussion of SHAMELA.

675 Sherburn, George. "Fielding's AMELIA: An Interpretation." ELH, 3 (1936), 1-14.

In AMELIA, Fielding turns from the "comic" to a more sober mode of prose epic that depicts (with echoes of the AENEID) moral nobility undergoing the test of serious adversity.

676 _____. "Fielding's Social Outlook." PQ, 35 (1956), 1-23.

Fielding was "fundamentally a moralist," and this essential essay attempts to show how his ethical and social ideas "shape his work, both as a whole and as seen in individual episodes."

677 Shesgreen, Sean. LITERARY PORTRAITS IN THE NOVELS OF HENRY FIELDING. DeKalb: Northern Illinois University Press, 1972.

A "sister arts" approach to Fielding's pictorial habits of characterization; includes detailed and thoughtful analyses.

678 _____. "The Moral Function of Thwackum, Square, and Allworthy." SNNTS, 2 (1970), 159-67.

Fielding defined three possible motivations for benevolence:

sympathy, philosophic love of virtue, and religious terrors and allurements. In TOM JONES, Allworthy represents the first motivation, Square and Thwackum the other two.

679 Spilka, Mark. "Comic Resolution in Fielding's JOSEPH ANDREWS." CE, 15 (1953), 11-19.

The late scenes in Booby Hall are essential to the completion of Fielding's comic design.

680 Stevick, Philip. "Fielding and the Meaning of History." PMLA, 79 (1964), 561-68.

An account of Fielding's views of history, and of his novels as "histories."

681 Tave, Stuart M. THE AMIABLE HUMORIST: A STUDY IN THE COMIC THEORY AND CRITICISM OF THE EIGHTEENTH AND EARLY NINETEENTH CENTURIES. Chicago: University of Chicago Press, 1960.

Includes a discussion of Fielding that emphasizes his contribution to the development of the comic characterization combining the heroic and the ridiculous in a mixture producing the simultaneous effects of laughter and sympathy.

682 Taylor, Dick, Jr. "Joseph as Hero in JOSEPH ANDREWS." TULANE STUDIES IN ENGLISH, 7 (1957), 91-109.

Argument that, on the basis of Joseph's growth and development, he (and not Parson Adams) is the hero of the novel.

683 Thackeray, William Makepeace. THE ENGLISH HUMOURISTS OF THE EIGHTEENTH CENTURY. Everyman's Library. London: J.M. Dent, 1929.

Lecture V (1853) includes a discussion of Fielding; it is at once an expression of admiration for the "astonishing" ingenuity of TOM JONES and a denunciation of Fielding's morality. Thackeray's views were extremely influential in the nineteenth century.

684 Thornbury, Ethel M. HENRY FIELDING'S THEORY OF THE COMIC PROSE EPIC. Madison: University of Wisconsin Press, 1931.

A study of the literary backgrounds (primarily in French criticism) for Fielding's theory and of Fielding's application of the theory in JOSEPH ANDREWS and TOM JONES. An appendix contains the sale catalogue of Fielding's library.

685 Towers, A.R. "AMELIA and the State of Matrimony." RES, NS 5 (1954), 144-57.

An important discussion of the marriage theme in AMELIA.

686 Van Ghent, Dorothy. "On TOM JONES." THE ENGLISH NOVEL: FORM AND FUNCTION. New York: Rinehart, 1953.

A study of the functions of "form" and "feeling" as they represent clashes between appearance and reality in TOM JONES.

687 Vopat, James B. "Narrative Technique in TOM JONES: The Balance of Art and Nature." JNT, 4 (1974), 144-54.

The lesson of Tom's experience in the novel is that good nature must be balanced by self-control; but it is the narrator who most fully embodies the art of control, and it is the consciousness of the narrator's formal design that makes the novel so artistically effective.

688 Wallace, Robert M. "Fielding's Knowledge of History and Biography." SP, 44 (1947), 89-107.

A useful discussion for the student of Fielding's novelistic adaptations of the techniques of "history"-writing.

689 Warner, John M. "The Interpolated Narratives in the Fiction of Fielding and Smollett: An Epistemological View." SNNTS, 5 (1973), 271-83.

Fielding's digressions, Warner believes, provide for a dialectical relationship with the main narrative, successfully supporting structures based on a principle of "epistemological uncertainty"; Smollett attempts the same, and fails in all but his last novel (HUMPHRY CLINKER), where he finally achieves the kind of balance Fielding had reached in JOSEPH ANDREWS and TOM JONES. (See also Nos. 612, 613, and 628.)

690 Watt, Ian P. "The Naming of Characters in Defoe, Richardson, and Fielding." RES, 25 (1949), 322-38.

A discussion of the significance of names.

691 _____. THE RISE OF THE NOVEL: STUDIES IN DEFOE, RICHARDSON, AND FIELDING. London: Chatto and Windus, 1957.

Includes the controversial two chapters on Fielding that offer a provocative but prejudicial argument: Watt examines the preface to JOSEPH ANDREWS, finds it unconvincing as a definition of "comic prose epic," and questions the integrity of Fielding's theory; finally, he finds Richardson's "realism of presentation" preferable to Fielding's "realism of assessment." (See also No. 627.)

692 Wendt, Allan. "The Moral Allegory of JONATHAN WILD." ELH, 24 (1957), 306-20.

Fine essay; identifies and analyzes the ethical extremes represented by Wild and Heartfree and suggests that a synthesis of energetic greatness and active goodness, as described in the preface to the MISCELLANIES, is what Fielding was promoting.

693 _____. "The Naked Virtue of Amelia." ELH, 27 (1960), 131-48.

A study of Fielding's heroine as a symbolic figure of suffering womanhood.

694 Wess, Robert V. "The Probable and the Marvelous in TOM JONES." MP, 68 (1970), 32-45.

A consideration of Fielding's various statements on probability and the marvelous and of his mixture of those two effects.

695 Williams, Aubrey. "Interpositions of Providence and the Design of Fielding's Novels." SOUTH ATLANTIC QUARTERLY, 70 (1971), 265-86.

An impressive but controversial argument that Fielding's personal Christian vision dictated the active intervention of providence in the novels, presumably to the extent of inspiring the coincidences of plot and the system of rewards and punishments.

696 Williams, Murial Brittain. MARRIAGE: FIELDING'S MIRROR OF MORALITY. University: University of Alabama Press, 1973.

A sketchy study of the marriage themes in Fielding's plays and novels, with some attention to relevant periodical essays.

697 Woods, Charles B. "Fielding and the Authorship of SHAMELA." PQ, 25 (1946), 248-72.

An expertly documented article that established beyond question that Fielding wrote SHAMELA.

698 Work, James A. "Henry Fielding: Christian Censor." THE AGE OF JOHNSON: ESSAYS PRESENTED TO CHAUNCEY BREWSTER TINKER. Ed. Frederick W. Hilles. New Haven, Conn.: Yale University Press, 1949.

A landmark essay; inspired a reevaluation of the moral and ethical content of Fielding's novels. From THE CHAMPION on, Fielding's works reveal the influence of the Latitudinarians and advocate a distinctly Christian morality.

699 Wright, Andrew. HENRY FIELDING: MASK AND FEAST. Berkeley and

Los Angeles: University of California Press, 1965.

A fine example of rhetorical criticism. Wright emphasizes the comic devices by which Fielding develops his celebratory view of life: the real world, when seen through the mask of comedy, is transformed into the feast.

SARAH FIELDING (1710-68)

Sarah Fielding was an important minor novelist who has always been obscured by the brilliance of her brother Henry. In her own time she earned with her novels a considerable measure of popularity and respect, and the quality of DAVID SIMPLE (1744), her first and best work of fiction, suggests that she has been unjustly neglected. She was a humorist, like Henry Fielding, but oddly enough her tone and manner make her fictions resemble Richardson's PAMELA and CLARISSA more nearly than her brother's JOSEPH ANDREWS and TOM JONES. She was the friend of Richardson, who admired her work, as did his rival, Henry Fielding, who suggested revisions and provided a laudatory preface for the second edition of DAVID SIMPLE.

PRINCIPAL WORKS

THE ADVENTURES OF DAVID SIMPLE, 1744 (Novel)
FAMILIAR LETTERS BETWEEN THE PRINCIPAL CHARACTERS IN DAVID SIMPLE, 1747 (Miscellaneous tales and essays)
THE GOVERNESS, OR, THE LITTLE FEMALE ACADEMY, 1749 (Educational novel)
THE ADVENTURES OF DAVID SIMPLE. VOLUME THE LAST, 1753
THE CRY: A NEW DRAMATIC FABLE, with Jane Collier, 1754
THE LIVES OF CLEOPATRA AND OCTAVIA, 1757 (Novel)
THE HISTORY OF THE COUNTESS OF DELLWYN, 1759 (Novel)
THE HISTORY OF OPHELIA, 1760 (Novel)
MEMOIRS OF SOCRATES, by Xenophon, 1762 (Translation)

EDITIONS

DAVID SIMPLE

700 THE ADVENTURES OF DAVID SIMPLE. Ed. Ernest A. Baker. London: Routledge, 1904.

> Printed from the second edition, 1744; includes Henry Fielding's preface.

701 THE ADVENTURES OF DAVID SIMPLE. Ed. Malcolm Kelsall. Oxford English Novels. London: Oxford University Press, 1969.

> Includes an excellent critical introduction, a brief bibliographical note, and a chronology of the life and career of Sarah Fielding; the text is that of the second edition, 1744, as revised by Henry Fielding and adorned by his preface. The rare "Volume the Last," 1753, is also included.

702 THE ADVENTURES OF DAVID SIMPLE. FIN.

> A photofacsimile reprint of the second (revised) edition, 1744, with Henry Fielding's preface.

THE GOVERNESS

703 THE GOVERNESS: OR, LITTLE FEMALE ACADEMY. Ed. Jill E. Grey. London: Oxford University Press, 1968.

> A reprint, in facsimile, of the first edition, 1749. Includes an introduction touching on the importance of this book as one of the first "educational" novels; also includes a bibliography.

CLEOPATRA AND OCTAVIA

704 THE LIVES OF CLEOPATRA AND OCTAVIA. Ed. R. Brimley Johnson. London: Scholartis Press, 1929.

705 THE LIVES OF CLEOPATRA AND OCTAVIA. FIN.

> A photofacsimile reprint of the first edition, 1757.

COUNTESS OF DELLWYN

706 THE HISTORY OF THE COUNTESS OF DELLWYN. FIN.

> A photofacsimile reprint of the first edition, 1759.

HISTORY OF OPHELIA

707 THE HISTORY OF OPHELIA. FIN.

> A photofacsimile reprint of the first edition, 1760.

BIBLIOGRAPHY

708 See Nos. 701 and 703.

BIOGRAPHY

709   Barbauld, Anna L., ed. THE CORRESPONDENCE OF SAMUEL RICHARD-
SON. 6 vols. London, 1804; rpt. New York: AMS Press, 1968.

> Volume II supplies scattered but interesting information about
> Sarah Fielding's life as it touched Richardson's.

710   Cross, Wilbur L. THE HISTORY OF HENRY FIELDING. 3 vols. New
Haven, Conn.: Yale University Press, 1918.

> A study of Henry Fielding that remains the best source of in-
> formation about his sister's life.

711   Werner, Herman Oscar, Jr. "The Life and Works of Sarah Fielding."
Ph.D. dissertation, Harvard University, 1939.

> Werner's treatment of the life is superficial and derivative,
> but it does gather together the information scattered about in
> Barbauld and Cross (Nos. 709 and 710). The detailed descrip-
> tions of the novels are useful (if generally uncritical) because
> of the unfamiliarity of so much of the material.

CRITICAL STUDIES AND COMMENTARIES

Sarah Fielding has received only the scantiest critical attention, and most commentary on her works is to be found in the standard histories of the English
novel.

712   Horner, Joyce M. THE ENGLISH WOMEN NOVELISTS AND THEIR CON-
NECTION WITH THE FEMINIST MOVEMENT (1688-1797). Smith College
Studies in Modern Languages, vol. 11, no. 1-3 (1929-30). Northampton,
Mass.: 1930.

> Includes a valuable discussion of Sarah Fielding's contribution
> to the eighteenth-century novel.

713   Kelsall, Malcolm. "Introduction" to THE ADVENTURES OF DAVID SIMPLE.
Oxford English Novels. London: Oxford University Press, 1969.

> See No. 701.

714   MacCarthy, Bridget D. WOMEN WRITERS: THEIR CONTRIBUTION TO THE
ENGLISH NOVEL 1621-1744. Cork, Engl.: Cork University Press, 1944.

> Includes brief, general discussion of Sarah Fielding's work, es-
> pecially DAVID SIMPLE.

715   Raynal, Margaret Isabel. "A Study of Sarah Fielding's Novels." Ph.D.

dissertation, University of North Carolina at Chapel Hill, 1970.

The only full-length study to concentrate on the novels themselves.

716   See No. 711.

WILLIAM GODWIN (1756-1836)

Godwin, the son of a Calvinist minister, trained to be a preacher but abandoned this career in favor of political philosophy and novel-writing. His radical politics made him notorious upon the publication of POLITICAL JUSTICE (1793), just four years after the outbreak of the French Revolution, but also helped to earn him friendships with Thomas Holcroft, Mary Wollstonecraft (whom he married), Hazlitt, Coleridge, and Shelley (his son-in-law). He wrote some nine novels; of these CALEB WILLIAMS (1794), which effectively combines fine tragic plotting with Gothic mystery and radical politics, is deservedly the best remembered.

PRINCIPAL WORKS

THE HISTORY OF THE LIFE OF WILLIAM PITT, EARL OF CHATHAM, 1783
IMOGEN, A PASTORAL ROMANCE. FROM THE ANCIENT BRITISH, 1783
    (Novel)
ITALIAN LETTERS: OR, THE HISTORY OF THE COUNT DE ST. JULIAN, 1784
    (Novel)
DAMON AND DELIA: A TALE, 1784 (Novel)
ENQUIRY CONCERNING THE PRINCIPLES OF POLITICAL JUSTICE, 1793
    (Political treatise)
THINGS AS THEY ARE; OR, THE ADVENTURES OF CALEB WILLIAMS, 1794
    (Novel)
THE ENQUIRER: REFLECTIONS OF EDUCATION, MANNERS AND LITERATURE,
    1797 (Essays)
MEMOIRS OF THE AUTHOR OF A VINDICATION OF THE RIGHTS OF WOMEN
    [Mary Wollstonecraft], 1798
ST. LEON, 1799 (Novel)
LIFE OF GEOFFREY CHAUCER, 1803-1804
FLEETWOOD; OR, THE NEW MAN OF FEELING, 1805 (Novel)
MANDEVILLE. A TALE OF THE SEVENTEENTH CENTURY, 1817 (Novel)
OF POPULATION, 1820 (Treatise)
CLOUDESLEY: A NOVEL, 1830
DELORAINE, A TALE, 1833 (Novel)

EDITIONS

A. Selections

717 ENQUIRY CONCERNING POLITICAL JUSTICE. WITH SELECTIONS FROM
GODWIN'S OTHER WRITINGS. Ed. K. Odell Carter. Oxford: Clarendon Press, 1971.

> Includes an intelligent abridgment of POLITICAL JUSTICE.

B. Individual Works

IMOGEN

718 IMOGEN: A PASTORAL ROMANCE FROM THE ANCIENT BRITISH. Ed.
Jack W. Marken et al. New York: New York Public Library, 1963.

> Reprinted from the 1784 edition, with an introduction by Marken
> and critical commentaries by Martha Winburn England, Burton
> R. Pollin, and Irwin Primer.

ITALIAN LETTERS

719 ITALIAN LETTERS; OR, THE HISTORY OF THE COUNT DE ST. JULIAN.
Ed. Burton R. Pollin. Lincoln: University of Nebraska Press, 1965.

> A scholarly edition.

POLITICAL JUSTICE

720 ENQUIRY CONCERNING POLITICAL JUSTICE AND ITS INFLUENCE ON
MORALS AND HAPPINESS. Ed. F.E.L. Priestly. 3 vols. Toronto: University of Toronto Press, 1946.

> An excellent scholarly edition.

721 See No. 717.

CALEB WILLIAMS

722 CALEB WILLIAMS, OR THINGS AS THEY ARE. Ed. Ernest A. Baker.
London: Routledge, 1903.

723 THE ADVENTURES OF CALEB WILLIAMS, OR THINGS AS THEY ARE.
Ed. George Sherburn. New York: Holt, Rinehart and Winston, 1960.

A fine edition featuring an excellent introduction, biographical and bibliographical information, a reliable text, and Godwin's own account of the novel's composition.

724 THE ADVENTURES OF CALEB WILLIAMS, OR, THINGS AS THEY ARE. Ed. Herbert Van Thal. Intro. Walter Allen. London: Cassell, 1966.

Includes a critical introduction that is astute and informative.

725 CALEB WILLIAMS. Ed. David McCracken. Oxford English Novels. London: Oxford University Press, 1970.

Includes a brief introduction, a select bibliography, and a chronology of Godwin's life.

ST. LEON

726 ST. LEON: A TALE OF THE SIXTEENTH CENTURY. Foreword by Devendra P. Varma. Intro. Juliet Beckett. Arno Gothic Novels. New York: Arno Press, 1972.

A reprint of the London edition of 1831, with an excellent critical introduction.

727 ST. LEON: A TALE OF THE SIXTEENTH CENTURY. 4 vols. FCE.

A photofacsimile reprint of the first edition, 1799.

FLEETWOOD

728 FLEETWOOD: OR, THE NEW MAN OF FEELING. Bentley's Standard Novels, No. 22. London, 1832.

A relatively rare, early edition but still the most widely available.

LETTERS

729 GODWIN AND MARY: THE CORRESPONDENCE OF WILLIAM GODWIN AND MARY WOLLSTONECRAFT. Ed. Ralph M. Wardle. Lawrence: University of Kansas Press, 1966.

BIBLIOGRAPHY

730 Marken, Jack W. "The Canon and Chronology of William Godwin's Early Works." MLN, 69 (1954), 176-80.

An attempt to provide an accurate account of Godwin's obscure early novels, sermons, and journalistic writings.

731 Pollin, Burton R. GODWIN CRITICISM: A SYNOPTIC BIBLIOGRAPHY. Toronto: University of Toronto Press, 1967.

The most comprehensive listing (prepared with computer assistance) of Godwin criticism; includes contemporary as well as nineteenth- and twentieth-century materials, all of which are summarized.

732 See Nos. 734 and 758.

BIOGRAPHY

733 Brailsford, H.N. SHELLEY, GODWIN, AND THEIR CIRCLE. New York: Holt, 1913.

Mainly concerned with Godwin's political life and his part in the reaction to the French Revolution; little attention to the novels.

734 Brown, Ford K. THE LIFE OF WILLIAM GODWIN. London: J.M. Dent, 1926.

Routine, reasonably thorough biography; distinguished primarily for its long, yet incomplete, list of Godwin's works.

735 Fleisher, David. WILLIAM GODWIN: A STUDY IN LIBERALISM. London: Allen and Unwin, 1951.

Heavy emphasis on POLITICAL JUSTICE; essentially an estimate of Godwin's personality, politics, and political friendships, this book illuminates both the life and the novels.

736 Grylls, Rosalie Glynn. WILLIAM GODWIN AND HIS WORLD. London: Oldhams Press, 1952.

A "life-and-times" approach to Godwin's biography; readable but unscholarly.

737 Hazlitt, William. "William Godwin." THE SPIRIT OF THE AGE. London, 1825.

One of the most valuable biographical treatments of Godwin, by his close friend.

738 Paul, C. Kegan. WILLIAM GODWIN, HIS FRIENDS AND CONTEMPORARIES. 2 vols. London, 1876.

Still the most important biographical study.

739 Woodcock, George. WILLIAM GODWIN: A BIOGRAPHICAL STUDY. London: Porcupine Press, 1946.

A reliable study of the life.

CRITICAL STUDIES AND COMMENTARIES

740 Allen, B. Sprague. "William Godwin and the Stage." PMLA, 35 (1920), 358-74.

On dramatizations of Godwin's novels and some of the actors influenced by their roles in such adaptations.

741 _____. "William Godwin as a Sentimentalist." PMLA, 33 (1918), 1-29.

Godwin's fiery radicalism bore a natural relationship to eighteenth-century sentimentalism, which encouraged individualism and introspection, prized delicate feelings, and promoted a kind of emotional egalitarianism based on the Christian ethic of brotherly love.

742 Barker, Gerard A. "Justice to CALEB WILLIAMS." SNNTS, 6 (1974), 377-88.

An argument that the published (or "revised") ending of the novel is superior to the recently discovered original; see No. 756 for a similar argument and No. 746 for a different one.

743 Boulton, James T. "William Godwin, Philosopher and Novelist." THE LANGUAGE OF POLITICS IN THE AGE OF WILKES AND BURKE. London: Routledge and Kegan Paul, 1963.

A provocative essay; concerned mainly with relationships between the rhetoric of Godwin's novels (especially CALEB WILLIAMS) and his pamphlets on political philosophy.

744 Cobb, Joann P. "Godwin's Novels and POLITICAL JUSTICE." ENLIGHTENMENT ESSAYS, 4 (1973), 15-28.

Cobb's subject is tired, but her essay revives it and develops a useful investigation of the connections between the treatise and the novel, especially their differing treatments of the problem of evil.

745 Cruttwell, Patrick. "On CALEB WILLIAMS." HUDSON REVIEW, 11 (1958), 87-95.

Cruttwell's main purpose is to argue the need for a new, scholarly edition of the novel.

746 Dumas, D. Gilbert. "Things As They Were: The Original Ending of CALEB WILLIAMS." SEL, 6 (1966), 575-97.

The original manuscript ending, which leaves Caleb as victim and Falkland as triumphant, was not even mentioned in Godwin's account of the novel; Dumas argues that the revised ending weakens the novel--an interesting but debatable claim. (See also Nos. 742 and 756.)

747 Evans, Frank B. III. "Shelley, Godwin, Hume, and the Doctrine of Necessity." SP, 37 (1940), 632-40.

Shelley, in Queen Mab, draws not only upon Godwin, but also upon Godwin's own source (for the "Necessitarianism" of POLITICAL JUSTICE), David Hume.

748 Furbank, P.N. "Godwin's Novels." ESSAYS IN CRITICISM, 5 (1955), 214-28.

A very substantial treatment of all but the most obscure of Godwin's novels; the works are "confessional" in form, obsessed with guilt and outlaws, and they anticipate Dickens and Dostoyevsky.

749 Gregory, Allene. THE FRENCH REVOLUTION AND THE ENGLISH NOVEL. New York: Putnam's, 1915.

Includes an extended discussion of Godwin that places him second only to Thomas Holcroft in importance as a revolutionary novelist. CALEB WILLIAMS, as Gregory describes it, is a "tendency" novel.

750 Gross, Harvey. "The Pursuer and the Pursued: A Study of CALEB WILLIAMS." TSLL, 1 (1959), 401-11.

Godwin's anarchism derived logically from Rousseau's doctrine of natural goodness, and the plot of his novel served as an analogue to his belief that the government was determined to hunt out and destroy the individual.

751 Kiely, Robert. THE ROMANTIC NOVEL IN ENGLAND. Cambridge, Mass.: Harvard University Press, 1972.

CALEB WILLIAMS is among the late eighteenth-century works treated in this excellent study of the themes, conventions, and innovations of a number of disparate "romantic" novels.

752 McCracken, David. "Godwin's CALEB WILLIAMS: A Fictional Rebuttal

of Burke." SBHT, 11 (1969-70), 1442-52.

> On Godwin's novel as a reaction to Burke's REFLECTIONS
> ON THE REVOLUTION IN FRANCE. (See also No. 754.)

753 _____. "Godwin's Literary Theory: The Alliance between Fiction and
Political Philosophy." PQ, 49 (1970), 113-33.

> A discussion distinguishing between Godwin and other contem-
> porary doctrinaire novelists such as Bage and Holcroft.

754 _____. "Godwin's Reading in Burke." ELN, 7 (1970), 264-70.

> A valuable survey. (See also No. 752.)

755 Monro, D.H. GODWIN'S MORAL PHILOSOPHY: AN INTERPRETATION
OF WILLIAM GODWIN. London: Oxford University Press, 1953.

> Monro's purpose is not quite that of the literary critic, but
> the novels (especially CALEB WILLIAMS and ST. LEON) pro-
> vide major evidence for his analysis of Godwin as a moralist
> whose political and social thought derived from Hutcheson and
> Hume.

756 Myers, Mitzi. "Godwin's Changing Conception of CALEB WILLIAMS."
SEL, 12 (1972), 591-628.

> An argument in favor of the published (or "revised") ending
> of the novel. (See also Nos. 742 and 746.)

757 Ousby, Ian. "'My Servant Caleb': Godwin's CALEB WILLIAMS and the
Political Trials of the 1790's." UTQ, 44 (1974), 47-55.

> The discussion of the political atmosphere of the 1790's, as
> reflected in celebrated political trials, sheds new light on
> Godwin's novel, especially its ending.

758 Pollin, Burton R. EDUCATION AND ENLIGHTENMENT IN THE WORKS
OF WILLIAM GODWIN. New York: Las Americas, 1962.

> A superb study of Godwin's views of the elite; includes a
> checklist of several hundred critiques of Godwin's works, as
> well as a record of all of Godwin's works and their editions,
> variants, and translations.

759 Preu, James A. THE DEAN AND THE ANARCHIST. Tallahassee: Florida
State University Press, 1959.

> A study of Swift's influence on Godwin's doctrine of anarchism;
> a strained (though interesting) argument, based on Godwin's
> own comments and a great deal of conjecture.

760   Rothstein, Eric. "Allusion and Analogy in the Romance of CALEB WIL-
        LIAMS." UTQ, 37 (1967), 18-30.

        Allusion and analogy as systematic method; Rothstein also iden-
        tifies some hitherto unexplained allusions. An expanded ver-
        sion of this article appears in Rothstein's book, SYSTEMS OF
        ORDER AND INQUIRY IN LATER EIGHTEENTH-CENTURY
        FICTION (Berkeley and Los Angeles: University of California
        Press, 1975).

761   Sherburn, George. "Godwin's Later Novels." STUDIES IN ROMANTI-
        CISM, 1 (1962), 65-82.

        A study of Godwin's last five novels makes Sherburn suspect
        that their author's first love may have been fiction; includes
        treatment of the themes and conventions common to all five
        books.

762   Stamper, Rexford. "CALEB WILLIAMS: The Bondage of Truth." SOUTH-
        ERN QUARTERLY, 12 (1973), 39-50.

        As Caleb's character is revealed, he develops an "awakening
        moral sense," and this helps to define and support the artistic
        coherence of the novel.

763   Stephen, Leslie. "William Godwin's Novels." STUDIES OF A BIOG-
        RAPHER, III. New York: Putnam's, 1907.

        A readable, interesting discussion, more in the manner of a
        "gentleman's essay" than real scholarship.

OLIVER GOLDSMITH (1730-74)

PRINCIPAL WORKS

THE BEE, 1759 (Periodical)
ENQUIRY INTO THE PRESENT STATE OF POLITE LEARNING IN EUROPE, 1759
THE CITIZEN OF THE WORLD, 1762 ("Spy"-letter fiction)
HISTORY OF ENGLAND, 1764-71
THE TRAVELLER, 1764 (Poem)
ESSAYS, 1765 (Miscellaneous collection)
THE VICAR OF WAKEFIELD, 1766 (Novel)
THE GOOD NATUR'D MAN, 1768 (Comedy)
THE DESERTED VILLAGE, 1770 (Poem)
A COMPARISON BETWEEN LAUGHING AND SENTIMENTAL COMEDY, 1773
    (Essay)
SHE STOOPS TO CONQUER, 1773 (Comedy)
A HISTORY OF THE EARTH AND ANIMATED NATURE, 1774 (Scientific history)
RETALIATION, 1774 (Verse caricatures)

EDITIONS

A. Collected Works

764 THE MISCELLANEOUS WORKS OF OLIVER GOLDSMITH. 5 vols. London, 1801.

> The first volume of this early collection includes Thomas Percy's famous "Life" of Goldsmith.

765 THE MISCELLANEOUS WORKS OF OLIVER GOLDSMITH. Ed. Sir James Prior. 4 vols. London, 1837.

> A scholarly but incomplete edition by the author of the most authoritative early biography of Goldsmith (see No. 787).

766 THE WORKS OF OLIVER GOLDSMITH. Ed. J.M.W. Gibbs. 5 vols. London, 1885-86.

Until recently, the most authoritative collection.

767 COLLECTED WORKS OF OLIVER GOLDSMITH. Ed. Arthur Friedman. 5 vols. Oxford: Clarendon Press, 1966.

> The standard edition; not complete, but everything essential is included: the "reviews, essays, biographies, novel, poems, plays, prefaces, introductions, and a few miscellaneous pieces."

B. Selections

768 GOLDSMITH: SELECTED WORKS. Ed. Richard Garnett. Cambridge, Mass.: Harvard University Press, 1951.

> Includes important representative pieces, nicely introduced.

769 THE VICAR OF WAKEFIELD AND OTHER WRITINGS. Ed. Frederick W. Hilles. New York: Random House, 1955.

> Includes (besides the VICAR) more than a dozen poems, as well as SHE STOOPS TO CONQUER and excerpts from THE CITIZEN OF THE WORLD. The introduction is an important critical statement.

C. Individual Works

THE CITIZEN OF THE WORLD

770 THE CITIZEN OF THE WORLD. Ed. Austin Dobson. London, 1891.

771 See No. 769.

THE VICAR OF WAKEFIELD

772 THE VICAR OF WAKEFIELD. Ed. Austin Dobson. London, 1883.

> Includes an excellent critical introduction.

773 THE VICAR OF WAKEFIELD. Ed. Oswald Doughty. London: Scholartis Press, 1928.

> Includes a sound critical introduction.

774 THE VICAR OF WAKEFIELD. Ed. Frederick W. Hilles. Everyman's Library. New York: Dutton, 1951.

> The introduction to this "New American Edition" in the Every-

man's Library series is an important critical discussion of the novel's structural unity.

775 THE VICAR OF WAKEFIELD: A TALE SUPPOSED TO BE WRITTEN BY HIMSELF. Ed. Arthur Friedman. Oxford English Novels. London: Oxford University Press, 1974.

Includes a reliable text, with a fine critical introduction, a select bibliography, and a chronology of Goldsmith's life and career.

776 See No. 769.

LETTERS

777 THE COLLECTED LETTERS OF OLIVER GOLDSMITH. Ed. Katharine C. Balderston. Cambridge: At the University Press, 1928.

Still the standard collection.

BIBLIOGRAPHY

778 Friedman, Arthur. "Oliver Goldsmith." NCBEL, II.

The most complete listing (up to 1968) of works by and about Goldsmith. See also Ronald S. Crane's entry on Goldsmith in CBEL, II.

779 Scott, Temple. OLIVER GOLDSMITH BIBLIOGRAPHICALLY AND BIO-GRAPHICALLY CONSIDERED. London: Maggs, 1928.

Based on the collection in the library of W.M. Wilkins; incomplete, and now superseded bibliographically by No. 778 and biographically by No. 788.

780 Williams, Iolo A. "Oliver Goldsmith." SEVEN XVIIITH CENTURY BIBLIOGRAPHIES. New York, 1924; rpt. New York: Burt Franklin, 1968.

Superseded by No. 778.

BIOGRAPHY

781 Dobson, Austin. THE LIFE OF OLIVER GOLDSMITH. London, 1888.

Brief, readable, accurate.

782   Forster, John. THE LIFE AND TIMES OF OLIVER GOLDSMITH. 2 vols. London, 1854.

>An important, if opinionated, study by the biographer of Dickens; extremely popular during the last century.

783   Irving, Washington. THE LIFE OF OLIVER GOLDSMITH. New York, 1849.

>Goldsmith interestingly viewed through the eyes of a distinguished American writer.

784   Jeffares, A. Norman. GOLDSMITH. Writers and Their Work, No. 107. London: Longmans, Green, 1959.

>Brief "biocritical" study; excellent as an introduction for the nonspecialist.

785   Kirk, Clara M. OLIVER GOLDSMITH. New York: Twayne, 1967.

>A routine critical biography; useful for the nonspecialist.

786   Percy, Thomas. "The Life of Dr. Oliver Goldsmith." THE MISCELLANEOUS WORKS OF OLIVER GOLDSMITH, vol. 1. London, 1801.

>(See No. 764.) Percy's "Life" is still an invaluable source of information.

787   Prior, Sir James. THE LIFE OF OLIVER GOLDSMITH. 2 vols. London, 1837.

>For many years, regarded as the most reliable biography.

788   Wardle, Ralph M. OLIVER GOLDSMITH. Lawrence: University of Kansas Press, 1957.

>The most detailed and impressive critical biography to date.

CRITICAL STUDIES AND COMMENTARIES

789   Adelstein, Michael E. "Duality of Theme in THE VICAR OF WAKEFIELD." CE, 22 (1961), 315-21.

>An interesting discussion of the themes of prudence and fortitude.

790   Backman, Sven. THIS SINGULAR TALE: A STUDY OF THE VICAR OF WAKEFIELD AND ITS LITERARY BACKGROUND. Lund, Sweden: Gleerup, 1971.

>A specialized study of the literary sources and antecedents of

Goldsmith's novel; emphasis on the novel, the periodical essay, and the drama.

791 Bell, Howard J., Jr. "THE DESERTED VILLAGE and Goldsmith's Social Doctrines." PMLA, 59 (1944), 747-72.

Goldsmith's major poem is Bell's chief subject, but the discussion of its humane responses to the pain, the poverty, and the glory of the threatened rural life bears upon THE VICAR OF WAKEFIELD.

792 Dahl, Curtis. "Patterns in Disguise in THE VICAR OF WAKEFIELD." ELH, 25 (1958), 90-104.

An argument for the "hidden" coherence of Goldsmith's novel.

793 Emslie, Macdonald. GOLDSMITH: THE VICAR OF WAKEFIELD. London: Edward Arnold, 1963.

A general study for the nonspecialist.

794 Foster, James R. HISTORY OF THE PRE-ROMANTIC NOVEL IN ENGLAND. New York: Modern Language Association, 1949.

Includes a short but excellently balanced discussion of THE VICAR OF WAKEFIELD and its author; Goldsmith rejected the cult of melancholy, while he purged his sentimentality of "affectation and excesses" and based it on a "normal and healthy development of the sympathetic imagination."

795 Gallaway, W.F. "The Sentimentalism of Goldsmith." PMLA, 48 (1933), 1167-81.

THE VICAR OF WAKEFIELD is chief among several works discussed; Goldsmith wished to provoke tears and benevolent impulses but also feelings of strength derived from the fortitude of admirable characters in distress.

796 Hilles, Frederick W. "Introduction" to THE VICAR OF WAKEFIELD. Everyman's Library. New York: Dutton, 1951.

(See No. 774.) This essay was seminal to subsequent discussion of the novel's structural unity.

797 Hopkins, Robert H. THE TRUE GENIUS OF OLIVER GOLDSMITH. Baltimore, Md.: Johns Hopkins University Press, 1969.

A systematic study of Goldsmith's nondramatic works, ending with an analysis of the VICAR. Hopkins defends Goldsmith against those who do not take him seriously, arguing that his "true genius" is revealed through his craftsmanship, his amiable irony and satire, and the "good sense" that they serve.

798 Hunting, Robert. "The Poems in THE VICAR OF WAKEFIELD." CRITI-
CISM, 15 (1973), 234-41.

An interesting analysis of the poetic interludes as satiric devices.

799 Jefferson, D.W. "Observations on THE VICAR OF WAKEFIELD." CAM-
BRIDGE JOURNAL, 4 (1950), 621-28.

An essential study, especially useful for the understanding of
satire in Goldsmith's novel.

800 McAdam, Edward L., Jr. "Goldsmith, the Good-Natured Man." THE
AGE OF JOHNSON: ESSAYS PRESENTED TO CHAUNCEY BREWSTER
TINKER. Ed. Frederick W. Hilles. New Haven, Conn.: Yale Uni-
versity Press, 1949.

A general essay emphasizing the interesting relationship between Goldsmith's insecurity and genuine sweetness and his
most enduring and excellent works, which almost inevitably
promote a doctrine of benevolence and good nature.

801 Quintana, Ricardo. OLIVER GOLDSMITH: A GEORGIAN STUDY.
New York: Macmillan, 1967.

An essential book; the discussion of the VICAR is especially
valuable for its observations on Goldsmith's gentle but firm
satiric comedy and its objects, including the clergy.

802 Rousseau, George S., ed. GOLDSMITH: THE CRITICAL HERITAGE.
London: Routledge and Kegan Paul, 1974.

A collection of commentaries from the eighteenth and nineteenth centuries.

803 Sells, Arthur Lytton. OLIVER GOLDSMITH: HIS LIFE AND WORKS.
New York: Barnes and Noble, 1974.

An excellent general introduction; more critical than biographical.

RICHARD GRAVES (1715-1804)

Graves was a jolly, pleasure-loving vicar, a learned man who consorted with poets; his novel COLUMELLA (1779) is based on the life of William Shenstone. THE SPIRITUAL QUIXOTE (1773), his best and most memorable work, is an able imitation of Cervantes that uses a central character named Geoffrey Wildgoose to satirize Whitefield and the Methodist enthusiasts. This novel enjoys the status of an important minor work and is the only one of Graves's fictions to be given serious notice by modern editors and critics.

PRINCIPAL WORKS

THE FESTOON, 1765 (Epigrams)
THE SPIRITUAL QUIXOTE, 1773 (Novel)
THE PROGRESS OF GALLANTRY, 1774 (Poem)
EUPHROSYNE, 1776-80 (Poems)
COLUMELLA, 1779 (Novel)
EUGENIUS, 1785 (Novel)
RECOLLECTION OF WILLIAM SHENSTONE, 1788 (Biography)
PLEXIPPUS, 1790 (Novel)
THE REVERIES OF SOLITUDE, 1793 (Essays and poems)
THE COALITION, 1794 (Comedy)
SERMONS, 1799

EDITIONS

THE SPIRITUAL QUIXOTE

804 THE SPIRITUAL QUIXOTE: OR, THE SUMMER'S RAMBLE OF MR. GEOFFREY WILDGOOSE. A COMIC ROMANCE. Ed. Charles Whibley. London: Davies, 1926.

   A handsome edition, with a fine introduction.

805 THE SPIRITUAL QUIXOTE. Ed. Clarence Tracy. Oxford English Novels.

London: Oxford University Press, 1967.

Includes a fine critical introduction, a chronology of Graves's life and career, and a bibliographical note on primary and secondary materials.

806 THE SPIRITUAL QUIXOTE. 3 vols. FIN.

A photofacsimile reprint of the first edition, 1773.

LETTERS

807 Hill, Charles Jarvis. "Applause for Dodsley's CLEONE." PQ, 14 (1935), 181-84.

Includes letters written by Graves in praise of Dodsley's work.

BIBLIOGRAPHY

808 See Nos. 805 and 809.

BIOGRAPHY

809 Hill, Charles Jarvis. THE LITERARY CAREER OF RICHARD GRAVES. Smith College Studies in Modern Languages, vol. xvi, no. 1-3, (1934-35). Northampton, Mass.: 1935.

An astute, thorough critical biography in monograph form; includes a bibliography of Graves's works.

CRITICAL STUDIES AND COMMENTARIES

Graves has been largely ignored by modern critics, although he figures in the standard histories of the English novel, where most discussion of his work must be sought.

810 Ellis, Havelock. "Richard Graves and THE SPIRITUAL QUIXOTE." NINE-TEENTH CENTURY, 77 (1915), 848-60.

With an eye on Graves's genial but effective ridicule of Methodist excesses, Ellis calls THE SPIRITUAL QUIXOTE a "comic masterpiece."

811 Hill, Charles Jarvis. "Shenstone and Richard Graves's COLUMELLA." PMLA, 49 (1934), 566-76.

An account of the biographical details in COLUMELLA, which
is based on the life of William Shenstone.

812 Lyons, N.J. "THE SPIRITUAL QUIXOTE: A New Key to the Characters
in Graves's Novel." N&Q, 216 (1971), 63-67.

The list of identifications is taken from a handwritten version
in a copy of the 1810 edition of the novel.

813 Rymer, Michael. "Satiric Technique in THE SPIRITUAL QUIXOTE."
DURHAM UNIVERSITY JOURNAL, 34 (1972), 54-64.

A systematic study of Graves's satiric devices.

814 Tompkins, J.M.S. THE POPULAR NOVEL IN ENGLAND 1770-1800.
London: Constable, 1932.

Mentions Graves repeatedly, always briefly; the comments are
not detailed, but they do place Graves's novels in their proper
context.

815 Tracy, Clarence. "Introduction" to THE SPIRITUAL QUIXOTE. Oxford
English Novels. London: Oxford University Press, 1967.

See No. 805.

ELIZA HAYWOOD (1693-1756)

Like many other early women novelists, the extremely prolific Eliza Haywood began as a playwright, failed, and turned to fiction for a livelihood. Her first novel, LOVE IN EXCESS (1719), was an astonishing success; it was followed shortly by numerous other brief, extravagantly passionate amatory tales, and by several outrageous "scandal chronicles" (or "secret histories") that earned Haywood a brutally scornful allusion in Pope's DUNCIAD (1728). After Pope's blast, Haywood's career faltered for a time, but it was renewed in the 1740's and early 1750's in mature novels that, following the example of Richardson and Fielding, were both artful and more subdued.

PRINCIPAL WORKS

LOVE IN EXCESS, 1719 (Novel)
THE BRITISH RECLUSE, 1722 (Novel)
IDALIA, 1723 (Novel)
LASSELIA, 1723 (Novel)
THE RASH RESOLVE, 1724 (Novel)
MEMOIRS OF A CERTAIN ISLAND ADJACENT TO THE KINGDOM OF UTOPIA,
         1725 (Novel/scandal chronicle)
SECRET HISTORIES, NOVELS AND POEMS, 1725 (Collected early works)
THE DISTRESS'D ORPHAN, 1726 (Novel)
THE MERCENARY LOVER, 1726 (Novel)
PHILIDORE AND PLACENTIA, 1727 (Novel)
SECRET HISTORY OF THE PRESENT INTRIGUES OF THE COURT OF CARA-
         MANIA, 1727 (Novel/scandal chronicle)
ADVENTURES OF EOVAII, 1736 (Novel/political satire)
ANTI-PAMELA, 1741 (Parody of Richardson's PAMELA; questionable attribution)
THE FEMALE SPECTATOR, 1744-46 (Periodical)
THE FORTUNATE FOUNDLINGS, 1744 (Novel)
LIFE'S PROGRESS THROUGH THE PASSIONS, 1748 (Novel)
EPISTLES FOR THE LADIES, 1749 (Epistolary sketches)
THE HISTORY OF MISS BETSY THOUGHTLESS, 1751 (Novel)
THE HISTORY OF JEMMY AND JENNY JESSAMY, 1753 (Novel)

EDITIONS

RASH RESOLVE

816   THE RASH RESOLVE: OR, THE UNTIMELY DISCOVERY. FoN.
A photofacsimile reprint of the first edition, 1724.

MEMOIRS OF . . . UTOPIA

817   MEMOIRS OF A CERTAIN ISLAND ADJACENT TO THE KINGDOM OF UTOPIA. FoN.
A photofacsimile reprint of the first edition, 1725.

MERCENARY LOVER

818   THE MERCENARY LOVER: OR, THE UNFORTUNATE HEIRESSES. FoN.
A photofacsimile reprint of the first edition, 1726.

PHILIDORE AND PLACENTIA

819   PHILIDORE AND PLACENTIA; OR, L'AMOUR TROP DELICAT. FOUR BEFORE RICHARDSON: SELECTED ENGLISH NOVELS, 1720-1727. Ed. William H[arlin] McBurney. Lincoln: University of Nebraska Press, 1963.

SECRET HISTORY OF . . . CARAMANIA

820   THE SECRET HISTORY OF THE PRESENT INTRIGUES OF THE COURT OF CARAMANIA. FoN.
A photofacsimile reprint of the first edition, 1727.

ADVENTURES OF EOVAII

821   ADVENTURES OF EOVAII, PRINCESS OF IJAVEO. FoN.
A photofacsimile reprint of the first edition, 1736.

ANTI-PAMELA

822   ANTI-PAMELA: OR, FEIGNED INNOCENCE DETECTED; IN A SERIES OF SYRENA'S ADVENTURES. SBrW.

Probably by Haywood. A photofacsimile reprint of the first edition, 1741.

THE FEMALE SPECTATOR

823 THE FEMALE SPECTATOR; BEING SELECTIONS FROM MRS. HEYWOOD'S PERIODICAL (1744-1746). Ed. Mary Priestley. London: John Lane, 1929.

Includes among the selections a number of brief stories that will be of interest to students of Haywood's novels.

FORTUNATE FOUNDLINGS

824 THE FORTUNATE FOUNDLINGS. FIN.

A photofacsimile reprint of the first edition, 1744.

LIFE'S PROGRESS THROUGH THE PASSIONS

825 LIFE'S PROGRESS THROUGH THE PASSIONS, OR, THE ADVENTURES OF NATURA. FIN.

A photofacsimile reprint of the first edition, 1748.

JEMMY AND JENNY JESSAMY

826 THE HISTORY OF JEMMY AND JENNY JESSAMY. 3 vols. FIN.

A photofacsimile reprint of the first edition, 1753.

BIBLIOGRAPHY

827 See No. 828.

BIOGRAPHY

828 Whicher, George Frisbie. THE LIFE AND ROMANCES OF MRS. ELIZA HAYWOOD. New York: Columbia University Press, 1915.

A critical biography. Still the most ample source of information on Haywood; includes an extensive bibliography of her works.

CRITICAL STUDIES AND COMMENTARIES

The deplorable quality of most of Haywood's fiction explains why it has been largely ignored by critics. Yet Haywood was a very productive and popular novelist whose early works helped to shape public attitudes toward fiction and whose later efforts importantly registered the powerful impact of Richardson and Fielding on their fellow novelists. Viewed in this light, her work seems to have been unduly neglected.

829 Erickson, James P. "EVELINA and BETSY THOUGHTLESS." TSLL, 6 (1964), 96-103.

A discussion of the similarities between the two works by Burney and Haywood.

830 _____. "The Novels of Eliza Haywood." Ph.D. dissertation, University of Minnesota, 1961.

A critical survey that gives major attention to numerous representative samples from Haywood's canon.

831 Horner, Joyce M. THE ENGLISH WOMEN NOVELISTS AND THEIR CONNECTION WITH THE FEMINIST MOVEMENT (1688-1797). Smith College Studies in Modern Languages, vol. 11, no. 1-3 (1929-30). Northampton, Mass.: 1930.

Haywood's novels briefly viewed in light of their feminist urgings. May be profitably studied along with No. 832.

832 MacCarthy, Bridget G. WOMEN WRITERS: THEIR CONTRIBUTION TO THE ENGLISH NOVEL (1621-1744). Cork, Engl.: Cork University Press, 1944.

May be profitably studied along with No. 831.

833 Richetti, John J. POPULAR FICTION BEFORE RICHARDSON: NARRATIVE PATTERNS 1700-1739. Oxford: Clarendon Press, 1969.

Haywood figures frequently in Richetti's fine discussions of the themes, conventions, and stereotypes of the period's fiction; but see especially chapters IV and V, which treat the scandal chronicles and the amatory tales, respectively.

834 See No. 828.

THOMAS HOLCROFT (1745-1809)

Thomas Holcroft was a friend of William Godwin, and one of the most vocal of the group of political radicals; his activities caused his arrest for high treason in 1794. His plays and novels typically champion the cause of democratic social reform, and his novel ANNA ST. IVES (1792) features a character usually thought to be the first proletarian hero in English fiction. Holcroft himself is regarded by many critics as England's first revolutionary novelist.

PRINCIPAL WORKS

ALWYN: OR THE GENTLEMAN COMEDIAN, 1780 (Novel)
DUPLICITY, 1781 (Comedy)
POSTHUMOUS WORKS OF FREDERICK THE GREAT, 1789 (Translation)
THE SCHOOL FOR ARROGANCE, 1791 (Comedy)
ANNA ST. IVES, 1792 (Novel)
THE ROAD TO RUIN, 1792 (Melodrama)
THE ADVENTURES OF HUGH TREVOR, 1794-97 (Novel)
KNAVE OR NOT?, 1798 (Comedy)
A TALE OF MYSTERY, 1802 (Melodrama)
TRAVELS THROUGH FRANCE, 1804
THE MEMOIRS OF BRYAN PERDUE, 1805 (Novel)

EDITIONS

ANNA ST. IVES

835   ANNA ST. IVES. Ed. Peter Faulkner. Oxford English Novels. London: Oxford University Press, 1970.

> Includes a brief critical introduction, a select bibliography, and a chronological record of Holcroft's life and career.

HUGH TREVOR

836 THE ADVENTURES OF HUGH TREVOR. Ed. Seamus Deane. Oxford
English Novels. London: Oxford University Press, 1973.

Includes apparatus similar to that found in No. 835.

LETTERS AND JOURNALS

837 See No. 840.

BIBLIOGRAPHY

838 Colby, Elbridge. A BIBLIOGRAPHY OF THOMAS HOLCROFT. New
York: New York Public Library, 1922.

The standard bibliography.

BIOGRAPHY

839 Colby, Elbridge. "Thomas Holcroft, Man of Letters." SOUTH ATLANTIC
QUARTERLY, 22 (1923), 53-70.

A biographical essay; emphasizes Holcroft's literary career but
does consider the political motives behind the plays and novels.

840 _____, ed. THE LIFE OF THOMAS HOLCROFT. 2 vols. London:
Constable, 1925.

An expanded edition of William Hazlitt's MEMOIRS OF THE
LATE THOMAS HOLCROFT (London, 1816), which included
Holcroft's autobiography and Hazlitt's continuation, "To the
Time of His Death." In the continuation Hazlitt relied heavily
on Holcroft's diaries and journals, and Colby introduces into
the modern edition a number of Holcroft's letters. Colby's
annotations are extensive and valuable.

841 Paul, C. Kegan. WILLIAM GODWIN, HIS FRIENDS AND CONTEMPO-
RARIES. 2 vols. London, 1876.

A chief source of information about Holcroft.

CRITICAL STUDIES AND COMMENTARIES

842 Baine, Rodney M. "The Novels of Thomas Holcroft." Ph.D. dissertation,
Harvard University, 1951.

A sound critical study. (See also No. 843.)

843 _____. THOMAS HOLCROFT AND THE REVOLUTIONARY NOVEL.
Athens: University of Georgia Press, 1965.

A sensible study of Holcroft's fiction and its importance to the
beginnings of what has become a minor tradition in English
fiction, the protest novel. Includes interesting discussions of
the relationships between Holcroft the craftsman and Holcroft
the thinker who used the novel as a vehicle for argument.

844 Gregory, Allene. THE FRENCH REVOLUTION AND THE ENGLISH
NOVEL. New York: Putnam's, 1915.

According to Gregory, Holcroft was the most important of the
several revolutionary novelists (among them William Godwin)
spurred into action by the French Revolution.

845 McCracken, David. "Godwin's Literary Theory: The Alliance between
Fiction and Political Philosophy." PQ, 49 (1970), 113-33.

A discussion that distinguishes between Godwin and other contemporary doctrinaire novelists, including Holcroft.

846 Stallbaumer, Virgil R. "Holcroft's Influence on POLITICAL JUSTICE."
MLQ, 14 (1953), 21-30.

Some have assumed that ANNA ST. IVES prepared the way
for Godwin's treatise; Stallbaumer finds the two similar in
thought, but dissimilar in style--Godwin is lucid and cogent
while Holcroft annoys the reader with his "rambling and dis-
cursive" manner.

847 _____. "Thomas Holcroft: A Satirist in the Stream of Sentimentalism."
ELH, 3 (1936), 31-62.

Holcroft as satirist, his political radicalism given shape by the
familiar forms and themes of sentimental fiction and drama.

848 _____. "Thomas Holcroft as a Novelist." ELH, 15 (1948), 194-218.

A critical survey of Holcroft's novels, with heaviest emphasis
on ALWYN, ANNA ST. IVES, and HUGH TREVOR.

849 Teissedou, Janie. "Thomas Holcroft: A Radical Novelist." POLITICS
IN LITERATURE IN THE NINETEENTH CENTURY. Lille, France: Uni-
versité de Lille, 1974.

A general discussion of the political content of Holcroft's fiction.

850 Tompkins, J.M.S. THE POPULAR NOVEL IN ENGLAND 1770-1800. London: Constable, 1932.

Comments quickly but astutely on all of Holcroft's fiction.

SAMUEL JOHNSON (1709-84)

According to some literary historians, it is doubtful whether THE HISTORY OF RASSELAS, PRINCE OF ABYSSINIA (1759) even belongs to the history of the novel in England. Whether it does or not, RASSELAS is still the most important and excellent example of a popular eighteenth-century fictional form, the philosophical romance. RASSELAS is Johnson's only work of prose fiction; he did not regard the genre of the novel highly, although he gave it serious attention in RAMBLER NO. 4 (31 March 1750), one of the landmark mid-century statements on prose fiction.

PRINCIPAL WORKS

VOYAGE TO ABYSSINIA, by Lobo, 1735 (Translation)
LONDON, A POEM, 1738
AN ACCOUNT OF THE LIFE OF MR. RICHARD SAVAGE, 1744
THE PLAN OF A DICTIONARY OF THE ENGLISH LANGUAGE, 1747
IRENE: A TRAGEDY, 1749
THE VANITY OF HUMAN WISHES, 1749 (Poem)
THE RAMBLER, 1750-52 (Periodical)
A DICTIONARY OF THE ENGLISH LANGUAGE, 1755
THE IDLER, 1758-60 (Periodical essays)
THE HISTORY OF RASSELAS, PRINCE OF ABYSSINIA, 1759 (Novel)
THE PLAYS OF WILLIAM SHAKESPEARE, 1765 (Edition)
A JOURNEY TO THE WESTERN ISLANDS OF SCOTLAND, 1775
PREFACES, BIOGRAPHICAL AND CRITICAL TO THE WORKS OF THE ENGLISH
        POETS [THE LIVES OF THE POETS], 1779-81

EDITIONS

A. Collected Works

851 THE WORKS OF SAMUEL JOHNSON, L.L.D. 11 vols. Oxford, 1825.

> For more than a century, the standard edition; will be superseded by No. 852.

852 THE WORKS OF SAMUEL JOHNSON. Ed. Walter Jackson Bate et al. New Haven, Conn.: Yale University Press, 1958-- .

> This is the "Yale Edition," now in progress; it is to be definitive.

B. Selections and Specialized Collections

853 SELECTIONS FROM SAMUEL JOHNSON, 1709-1784. Ed. R.W. Chapman. London: Oxford University Press, 1955.

854 RASSELAS, POEMS, AND SELECTED PROSE. Ed. Bertrand H. Bronson. 2nd ed. New York: Holt, Rinehart and Winston, 1958.

> A fine representative sampling, with a brief but excellent critical introduction.

855 A JOHNSON READER. Ed. E[dward] L. McAdam, Jr. and George Milne. New York: Pantheon Books, 1964.

856 RASSELAS AND ESSAYS. Ed. Charles Peake. London: Routledge and Kegan Paul, 1967.

> Reliable texts, with an excellent introduction and notes; the essays are intelligently selected.

857 JOHNSON AS CRITIC. Ed. John Wain. London: Routledge and Kegan Paul, 1973.

> A collection of Johnson's critical statements, drawn from the periodical essays, the Shakespeare preface and notes, and the LIVES OF THE POETS.

C. Individual Works

RASSELAS

858 HISTORY OF RASSELAS, PRINCE OF ABYSSINIA. Ed. O.F. Emerson. New York, 1895.

859 THE HISTORY OF RASSELAS, PRINCE OF ABYSSINIA. Ed. R.W. Chapman. Oxford: Clarendon Press, 1927.

> A fine scholarly edition; includes abundant textual notes but no literary or historical commentary.

860 THE HISTORY OF RASSELAS, PRINCE OF ABYSSINIA. Ed. Gwin J. Kolb. New York: Appleton-Century-Crofts, 1962.

> A nicely edited popular edition.

861 THE HISTORY OF RASSELAS, PRINCE OF ABYSSINIA. Ed. John P. Hardy. London: Oxford University Press, 1968.

A good critical edition, with an excellent introduction.

862 THE HISTORY OF RASSELAS, PRINCE OF ABISSINIA. Ed. Geoffrey Tillotson and Brian Jenkins. Oxford English Novels. London: Oxford University Press, 1971.

A reliable text, with an excellent critical introduction; includes a select bibliography and a chronological record of Johnson's life and career.

863 THE PRINCE OF ABISSINIA. A TALE. FIN.

A photofacsimile reprint of the first edition, 1759; bound with Voltaire, CANDIDE.

864 See Nos. 854 and 856.

LETTERS AND JOURNALS

865 THE LETTERS OF SAMUEL JOHNSON. Ed. R.W. Chapman. 3 vols. Oxford: Clarendon Press, 1952.

The standard edition.

866 THE WORKS OF SAMUEL JOHNSON. Vol. 1. DIARIES, PRAYERS, AND ANNALS. Ed. Edward L. McAdam, Jr. et. al. New Haven, Conn.: Yale University Press, 1958.

(See No. 852.) This volume in the Yale Edition contains the definitive text.

867 DR. JOHNSON: HIS LIFE IN LETTERS. Ed. David Littlejohn. Englewood Cliffs, N.J.: Prentice-Hall, 1965.

Selected letters, with biographical notes.

BIBLIOGRAPHY

868 Chapman, R.W., and Allen T. Hazen. "Johnsonian Bibliography: A Supplement to Courtney." PROCEEDINGS OF THE OXFORD BIBLIOGRAPHICAL SOCIETY, 5 (1939), 119-66.

See also No. 872.

869 Clifford, James L. JOHNSONIAN STUDIES, 1887-1950: A SURVEY

AND BIBLIOGRAPHY. Minneapolis: University of Minnesota Press, 1951.

This bibliography and its successors (Nos. 870 and 871) are indispensable.

870 Clifford, James L., and Donald J. Greene. "A Bibliography of Johnsonian Studies, 1950-1960." JOHNSONIAN STUDIES. Ed. Magdi Wahba. Cairo: Societe orientale de publicite, 1962.

871 _____. SAMUEL JOHNSON: A SURVEY AND BIBLIOGRAPHY OF CRITICAL STUDIES. Minneapolis: University of Minnesota Press, 1970.

This new "Survey and Bibliography" includes the contents of Nos. 869 and 870 (with corrections) and extends coverage through about 1968; it includes material published prior to 1887.

872 Courtney, W.P., and D. Nichol Smith. A BIBLIOGRAPHY OF SAMUEL JOHNSON. Oxford, 1915; rpt. Oxford: Clarendon Press, 1968.

Johnson's writings. (See also No. 868.)

873 Lascelles, Mary. "RASSELAS: A Rejoinder." RES, NS 21 (1970), 49-56.

A bibliographical essay surveying studies of RASSELAS since 1951.

BIOGRAPHY

874 Boswell, James. THE LIFE OF SAMUEL JOHNSON, L.L.D. Ed. G.B. Hill and L.F. Powell. 6 vols. Oxford: Clarendon Press, 1934-50.

The standard edition of Boswell's LIFE (1791), with which Johnson studies must begin.

875 Brack, O.M., Jr., and Robert E. Kelley. THE EARLY BIOGRAPHIES OF SAMUEL JOHNSON. Iowa City: University of Iowa Press, 1974.

An annotated collection of fourteen brief biographies of Johnson, all of them published between 1762 and 1786.

876 _____. SAMUEL JOHNSON'S EARLY BIOGRAPHIES. Iowa City: University of Iowa Press, 1971.

An evaluative discussion of the first biographers and their biographies, a number of which were published before Johnson's death.

877 Clifford, James L. YOUNG SAM JOHNSON. New York: McGraw-Hill, 1955.

An invaluable study of the early years of Johnson's life and career, through age forty.

878 Greene, Donald J. SAMUEL JOHNSON. New York: Twayne, 1970.

An excellent general introduction to Johnson's life and works.

879 Hawkins, Sir John. THE LIFE OF SAMUEL JOHNSON, L.L.D. Ed. Bertram H. Davis. New York: Macmillan, 1961.

The early Life (1787) by Hawkins, although overshadowed by Boswell's great work, is still valuable; Hawkins was Johnson's friend and executor. This edition is abridged.

880 Irwin, George. SAMUEL JOHNSON: A PERSONALITY IN CONFLICT. Auckland, New Zealand: University of Auckland Press, 1971.

A stimulating study of Johnson as a deeply disturbed and troubled man whose works, with their fine wisdom and clear good sense, represent a remarkable achievement.

881 Krutch, Joseph Wood. SAMUEL JOHNSON. New York: Holt, 1944.

A good critical biography.

882 Reade, Aleyn Lyell. JOHNSONIAN GLEANINGS. 10 pts. London, 1909–46; rpt. New York: Octagon Books, 1968.

Invaluable source of miscellaneous information on Johnson's family connections and relationships, and on the early years of his life. Part XI of the GLEANINGS (CONSOLIDATED INDEX OF PERSONS TO PARTS I-X) appeared in 1952.

883 Roberts, Sydney Castle. SAMUEL JOHNSON. Rev. ed. Writers and Their Work, No. 47. London: Longmans, Green, 1965.

A brief "biocritical" study; excellent as an introduction for the nonspecialist.

884 Wain, John. SAMUEL JOHNSON. New York: Viking Press, 1974.

Not a scholarly biography, but a remarkably perceptive and readable one.

CRITICAL STUDIES AND COMMENTARIES

885 Baker, Sheridan. "RASSELAS: Psychological Irony and Romance." PQ, 45 (1966), 249–61.

An interesting discussion of RASSELAS as a philosophical romance promoting a deeply ironic psychological interpretation of man's quest for happiness.

886 Balderston, Katharine C. "Johnson's Vile Melancholy." THE AGE OF JOHNSON: ESSAYS PRESENTED TO CHAUNCEY BREWSTER TINKER. Ed. Frederick W. Hilles. New Haven, Conn.: Yale University Press, 1949.

A reinterpretation of Johnson's recurring periods of deep depression; essentially biographical, this article sheds light indirectly on Johnson's writings, including RASSELAS.

887 Bate, Walter Jackson. THE ACHIEVEMENT OF SAMUEL JOHNSON. New York: Oxford University Press, 1955.

An excellent general study of Johnson's work.

888 Boulton, James T., ed. JOHNSON: THE CRITICAL HERITAGE. London: Routledge and Kegan Paul, 1971.

A collection of early critical statements on Johnson, many of them quite unfamiliar.

889 Chapin, Chester F. THE RELIGIOUS THOUGHT OF SAMUEL JOHNSON. Ann Arbor: University of Michigan Press, 1968.

Valuable for the study of RASSELAS, although the purpose and organization are somewhat muddled.

890 Conant, Martha Pike. THE ORIENTAL TALE IN ENGLAND IN THE EIGHTEENTH CENTURY. New York: Columbia University Press, 1908.

Includes an extended discussion of RASSELAS as an oriental romance.

891 Fussell, Paul. SAMUEL JOHNSON AND THE LIFE OF WRITING. New York: Harcourt, Brace, 1971.

A serious attempt to show Johnson as a serious writer; includes examination of his conceptions of writing, his methods, and his obsession with genres. The interpretive remarks (that RASSELAS is actually a boy's book, for example) are sometimes curious.

892 Greene, Donald J. THE POLITICS OF SAMUEL JOHNSON. New Haven, Conn.: Yale University Press, 1960.

Despite its specialized subject matter, one of the best books on Johnson.

893 _____, ed. SAMUEL JOHNSON: A COLLECTION OF CRITICAL ESSAYS. Twentieth Century Views. Englewood Cliffs, N.J.: Prentice-Hall, 1965.

Reprinted essays by various Johnson scholars.

894 Hagstrum, Jean H. SAMUEL JOHNSON'S LITERARY CRITICISM. Minneapolis: University of Minnesota Press, 1952.

A detailed survey and analysis of Johnson's critical stances and his critical writings; touches on Imlac's famous speech (in RASSELAS, chapter X) on "the business of a poet."

895 Hilles, Frederick W. "RASSELAS, an 'Uninstructive Tale.'" JOHNSON, BOSWELL, AND THEIR CIRCLE: ESSAYS PRESENTED TO LAWRENCE FITZROY POWELL IN HONOUR OF HIS EIGHTY-FOURTH BIRTHDAY. Oxford: Clarendon Press, 1965.

A penetrating discussion of the didactic function of Johnson's tale. (See No. 905.)

896 _____, ed. NEW LIGHT ON DR. JOHNSON: ESSAYS ON THE OCCASION OF HIS 250TH BIRTHDAY. New Haven, Conn.: Yale University Press, 1959.

Twenty essays (some of them reprinted) by various hands.

897 Jenkins, H.D. "Some Aspects of the Background of RASSELAS." STUDIES IN ENGLISH IN HONOR OF RAPHAEL DORMAN O'LEARY AND SELDEN LINCOLN WHITCOMB. Lawrence: University of Kansas Press, 1940.

On the literary and philosophical backgrounds.

898 JOHNSONIANA. 25 vols. SBrW.

Photofacsimile reprints of a variety of early criticisms, commentaries, and biographies of Johnson; many of these items were first published during Johnson's lifetime.

899 JOHNSONIAN NEWS LETTER. 1940-- . Quarterly.

News of eighteenth-century scholarship in progress, notes on discoveries about Johnson, and notices of recent articles on Johnson and other eighteenth-century writers.

900 Jones, Emrys. "The Artistic Form of RASSELAS." RES, NS 18 (1967), 387-401.

Comparison of RASSELAS with TRISTRAM SHANDY, another seemingly "formless" work, and description of Johnson's tale in terms of its subtle design of three sections with sixteen chapters each.

901   Kenney, William. "RASSELAS and the Theme of Diversification." PQ, 38 (1959), 84-89.

RASSELAS teaches that, since happiness is at best impermanent, man's best hope is contentment, attained by "diversifying his activities in such a way that both satiety and the consequent withdrawal into an unhealthy solitude can be avoided."

902   Kolb, Gwin J. "The 'Paradise' in Abyssinia and the 'Happy Valley' in RASSELAS." MP, 56 (1958), 10-16.

On the source of Johnson's setting and its use in RASSELAS. (See also No. 907.)

903   _____. "RASSELAS: Purchase Price, Proprietors, and Printings." SB, 15 (1962), 256-59.

904   _____. "The Structure of RASSELAS." PMLA, 66 (1951), 608-717.

A detailed analysis; very useful.

905   Lascelles, Mary, et al., eds. JOHNSON, BOSWELL AND THEIR CIRCLE: ESSAYS PRESENTED TO LAWRENCE FITZROY POWELL IN HONOUR OF HIS EIGHTY-FOURTH BIRTHDAY. Oxford: Clarendon Press, 1965.

An excellent collection of essays by modern Johnson scholars.

906   Leyburn, Ellen Douglas. "'No Romantick Absurdities or Incredible Fictions': The Relation of Johnson's RASSELAS to Lobo's VOYAGE TO ABYSSINIA." PMLA, 70 (1955), 1059-67.

A penetrating discussion of the relationships between RASSELAS and one of its main sources, a work that Johnson had translated earlier in his career.

907   Lockhart, Donald M. "'The Fourth Son of the Mighty Emperor': The Ethiopian Background of Johnson's RASSELAS." PMLA, 78 (1963), 516-28.

See also No. 902.

908   McIntosh, Carey. THE CHOICE OF LIFE: SAMUEL JOHNSON AND THE WORLD OF FICTION. New Haven, Conn.: Yale University Press, 1973.

A widely ranging study of Johnson's ideas on fiction, of his stories in the periodical essays, and of RASSELAS. This is the only full-length treatment of Johnson and fiction, and as such is of particular interest to students of RASSELAS.

909 Misenheimer, James B., Jr. "Dr. Johnson on Prose Fiction." NEW
     RAMBLER, 4, Ser. C (1968), 12–18.

     A record and analysis of Johnson's statements on the novel.

910 Moore, Robert Etheridge. "Dr. Johnson on Fielding and Richardson."
     PMLA, 66 (1951), 162–81.

     Takes the view that, despite Dr. Johnson's comments on the
     two novelists, Fielding's novels are much closer to Johnson's
     most "deeply-felt" literary principles than are Richardson's.

911 O'Flaherty, Patrick. "Dr. Johnson as Equivocator: The Meaning of RAS-
     SELAS." MLQ, 31 (1970), 195–208.

     RASSELAS, as a reaction to religious disquiet occasioned by
     the death of Johnson's mother, is "a kind of catharsis," a
     purgative for sorrow in the form of "absurd comedy."

912 Pagliaro, Harold. "Structural Patterns of Control in RASSELAS." EN-
     GLISH WRITERS OF THE EIGHTEENTH CENTURY. Ed. John H. Midden-
     dorf. New York: Columbia University Press, 1971.

     RASSELAS as a tale of contrasts and opposing principles, lead-
     ing inevitably to an "unconcluded" conclusion.

913 Preston, Thomas R. "The Biblical Context of Johnson's RASSELAS."
     PMLA, 84 (1969), 274–81.

     Preston, taking his cue from Boswell's LIFE OF JOHNSON,
     argues that RASSELAS echoes the vanitas vanitatum theme of
     Ecclesiastes as interpreted by early British theologians, includ-
     ing William Lowth and Bishop Simon Patrick.

914 Rothstein, Eric. SYSTEMS OF ORDER AND INQUIRY IN LATER EIGHTEENTH-
     CENTURY FICTION. Berkeley and Los Angeles: University of California
     Press, 1975.

     Includes an essay on RASSELAS that treats, among other things,
     Johnson's use of the devices of "modification" (contradiction
     and change) and "analogy" to construct a book that serves
     "to promote and to confute human wisdom," and to mount a
     "successful argument for . . . the vanity of human wishes."

915 Sachs, Arieh. "Generality and Particularity in Johnson's Thought." SEL,
     5 (1965), 491–511.

     Imlac's speech (in RASSELAS, chapter X) on "the business of
     a poet" centers on generality and particularity; Sachs provides
     a broad context within which this speech--and RASSELAS it-
     self, as the work of a poet--may be seen.

916   Sacks, Sheldon. FICTION AND THE SHAPE OF BELIEF: A STUDY OF
      HENRY FIELDING WITH GLANCES AT SWIFT, JOHNSON, AND RICH-
      ARDSON. Berkeley and Los Angeles: University of California Press,
      1964.

      The discussion of RASSELAS as an "apologue" provides a fresh
      approach to the tale's moral structure and function.

917   Schwartz, Richard B. SAMUEL JOHNSON AND THE PROBLEM OF
      EVIL. Madison: University of Wisconsin Press, 1975.

      A sometimes puzzling but generally interesting study; useful to
      the student of RASSELAS.

918   Sherburn, George. "Rasselas Returns--to What?" PQ, 38 (1959), 383-
      84.

      A brief note on the (to some) problematical ending of John-
      son's tale.

919   Tillotson, Geoffrey. "Imlac and the Business of a Poet." STUDIES IN
      CRITICISM AND AESTHETICS, 1660-1800: ESSAYS IN HONOR OF
      SAMUEL HOLT MONK. Ed. Howard Anderson and John S. Shea. Min-
      neapolis: University of Minnesota Press, 1967.

      A discussion of the aesthetic implications, for RASSELAS and
      for eighteenth-century literature, of Imlac's famous speech in
      chapter X.

920   _____. "RASSELAS." AUGUSTAN STUDIES. London: Athlone Press,
      1961.

      A general introduction to Johnson's tale, which Tillotson takes
      to be the most obvious evidence of Johnson's lasting and genu-
      ine interest in narrative.

921   _____. "RASSELAS and the Persian Tales." ESSAYS IN CRITICISM
      AND RESEARCH. Cambridge: At the University Press, 1942.

      RASSELAS, like most orientalized stories of its day, uses an
      exotic setting to obscure specific locality and impart univer-
      sality to a moral tale; one of Johnson's sources was Pétis de
      la Croix's popular collection of PERSIAN TALES, which was
      translated in 1714.

922   _____. "Time in RASSELAS." AUGUSTAN STUDIES. London: Athlone
      Press, 1961.

      The "notifications of time" in RASSELAS are "part of the

meaning of the story," which sees time as a "prime condition governing human life."

923 Voitle, Robert. SAMUEL JOHNSON THE MORALIST. Cambridge, Mass.: Harvard University Press, 1961.

A detailed study of Johnson's moral philosophy: the backgrounds and sources, the substance, and the formal manifestations in the writings.

924 Wahba, Magdi, ed. BICENTENARY ESSAYS ON RASSELAS. Cairo, 1959.

A supplement to CAIRO STUDIES IN ENGLISH; contains a rich variety of essays by experts on Johnson.

925 Weinbrot, Howard D. "The Reader, the General, and the Particular: Johnson and Imlac in Chapter Ten of RASSELAS." ECS, 5 (1971), 80-96.

A discussion questioning whether Johnson would agree with Imlac's every statement on "the business of a poet."

926 Whitley, Alvin. "The Comedy of RASSELAS." ELH, 23 (1956), 48-70.

An unorthodox but generally persuasive argument that, despite its sober message, RASSELAS is formally a comic work.

927 Wimsatt, W.K. "In Praise of RASSELAS." IMAGINED WORLDS: ESSAYS ON SOME ENGLISH NOVELS AND NOVELISTS IN HONOUR OF JOHN BUTT. Ed. Maynard Mack and Ian Gregor. London: Methuen, 1968.

An excellent "defense" of RASSELAS as a finely crafted fantasy.

928 _____. THE PROSE STYLE CF SAMUEL JOHNSON. New Haven, Conn.: Yale University Press, 1941.

A tediously detailed but judicious treatment of the intricacies of Johnson's language.

CHARLOTTE RAMSAY LENNOX (1720-1804)

Charlotte Lennox began writing fiction after failing as an actress. Her first novel, HARRIOT STUART (1750), in part dramatized her early childhood in America as the daughter of an English officer. THE FEMALE QUIXOTE (1752), an assault on the foolishness of romance-reading, is her best work, and it earned her the praise of Fielding, Richardson, and Dr. Johnson; Richardson and John son actually advised and assisted in the composition of the work. Later, this novel was one of Austen's favorites. Lennox must be counted among the more accomplished minor novelists of the latter half of the eighteenth century, al though in the forty years of fiction-writing that followed the publication of THE FEMALE QUIXOTE she never equaled that early triumph.

PRINCIPAL WORKS

POEMS ON SEVERAL OCCASIONS, 1747
THE LIFE OF HARRIOT STUART, 1750 (Novel)
MEMOIRS OF THE DUKE OF SULLY, by M. de Bethune, 1751 (Translation)
THE AGE OF LEWIS XIV, by Voltaire, 1752 (Translation)
THE FEMALE QUIXOTE, OR THE ADVENTURES OF ARABELLA, 1752 (Novel)
SHAKESPEAR ILLUSTRATED, 1753-54
MEMOIRS OF THE COUNTESS OF BERRI, by d'Audiguier, 1756 (Translation)
PHILANDER, 1757 (Pastoral drama)
HENRIETTA, 1758 (Novel)
THE GREEK THEATRE OF FATHER BRUMOY, by P. Brumoy, 1760 (Translation)
THE HISTORY OF HARRIOT AND SOPHIA, 1760-61; reissued, 1762, as SOPHIA
      (Novel)
THE SISTER, 1769 (Comedy based on HENRIETTA)
OLD CITY MANNERS, 1775 (Comedy based on EASTWARD HOE, by Chapman,
      Jonson, and Marston)
EUPHEMIA, 1790 (Novel)

EDITIONS

FEMALE QUIXOTE

929   THE FEMALE QUIXOTE, OR THE ADVENTURES OF ARABELLA.   Ed.
Margaret Dalziel.   Oxford English Novels.   London: Oxford University
Press, 1970.

> Includes an excellently edited text, a sound critical introduc-
> tion, a brief select bibliography, and a chronological record
> of Lennox's life and career; an appendix by Duncan Isles,
> "Johnson, Richardson, and THE FEMALE QUIXOTE," discusses
> the various contributions made by these two major figures to
> the composition of Lennox's novel.

930   THE FEMALE QUIXOTE; OR, THE ADVENTURES OF ARABELLA.   FIN.

> A photofacsimile reprint of the first edition, 1752.

HENRIETTA

931   HENRIETTA.   FIN.

> A photofacsimile reprint of the first edition, 1758.

SOPHIA

932   SOPHIA.   FIN.

> A photofacsimile reprint of the 1762 edition.

LETTERS

933   Isles, Duncan E.   "The Lennox Collection."   HARVARD LIBRARY BULLE-
TIN, 18 (1970), 317-44.

> A description and discussion of a collection of forty-two let-
> ters written to Lennox, most of them by literary friends and
> associates.   The collection is now at Harvard's Houghton Li-
> brary.

934   _____.   "Other Letters in the Lennox Collection."   TLS, August 5,
1965, p. 685.

> This and No. 935 both discuss the Houghton Library collection
> at Harvard; several letters that passed between Johnson and
> Lennox are included, and these concern the composition of
> THE FEMALE QUIXOTE.   See also Isles, "Appendix" to THE

FEMALE QUIXOTE (No. 929) for a brief account of correspondence between Lennox and Richardson.

935 _____. "Unpublished Johnson Letters." TLS, July 29, 1965, p. 666. See No. 934.

BIBLIOGRAPHY

936 See No. 939.

BIOGRAPHY

937 Isles, Duncan. "Johnson and Charlotte Lennox." NEW RAMBLER, 3, Ser. C (1967), 34-48.

On Johnson's friendship with Lennox and the large part he played in advancing her career.

938 Maynadier, Gustavus Howard. THE FIRST AMERICAN NOVELIST? Cambridge, Mass.: Harvard University Press, 1940.

A biographical study emphasizing the question of whether Lennox, who was born in the colonies, can be claimed as the first American novelist; excellent on the early years of her life.

939 Small, Miriam R. CHARLOTTE RAMSAY LENNOX: AN EIGHTEENTH-CENTURY LADY OF LETTERS. New Haven, Conn.: Yale University Press, 1935.

A critical biography; not always trustworthy, but still the only full-length study of Lennox. Includes a bibliography.

CRITICAL STUDIES AND COMMENTARIES

940 Bradbrook, Frank W. JANE AUSTEN AND HER PREDECESSORS. Cambridge: At the University Press, 1966.

The treatment of Lennox is limited, but useful for its illumination of her importance as an influence upon Jane Austen, who greatly admired her.

941 Dalziel, Margaret. "Introduction" to THE FEMALE QUIXOTE, OR THE ADVENTURES OF ARABELLA. Oxford English Novels. London: Oxford University Press, 1970.

See No. 929.

942 Fielding, Henry. Review of THE FEMALE QUIXOTE. THE COVENT-
GARDEN JOURNAL. Ed. Gerard E. Jensen. 2 vols. New Haven,
Conn.: Yale University Press, 1915.

> Review from the number for 24 March 1752. Fielding's obser-
> vations on the relationships between Lennox's novel and DON
> QUIXOTE are among the most astute of all commentaries on
> THE FEMALE QUIXOTE, a work that the review recommends
> as "a most extraordinary and most excellent Performance," and
> a "Work of true Humour."

943 Horner, Joyce M. THE ENGLISH WOMEN NOVELISTS AND THEIR
CONNECTION WITH THE FEMINIST MOVEMENT (1688-1797). Smith
College Studies in Modern Languages, vol. 11, no. 1-3 (1929-30).
Northampton, Mass.: 1930.

> Includes excellent discussions of Lennox's novels, especially
> THE FEMALE QUIXOTE.

944 Isles, Duncan. "Appendix" to THE FEMALE QUIXOTE, OR THE ADVEN-
TURES OF ARABELLA. Ed. Margaret Dalziel. Oxford English Novels.
London: Oxford University Press, 1970.

> See No. 929.

945 Kauvar, Elaine M. "Jane Austen and THE FEMALE QUIXOTE." SNNTS,
2 (1970), 211-21.

> Lennox exerted an influence not only on NORTHANGER AB-
> BEY, as is generally allowed, but variously on Austen's other
> novels--especially PRIDE AND PREJUDICE and EMMA, with
> their quixotic heroines.

946 MacCarthy, Bridget G. THE LATER WOMEN NOVELISTS, 1744-1818.
New York: William Salloch, 1948.

> Includes a useful discussion of Lennox and her novels, with
> emphasis on THE FEMALE QUIXOTE.

947 Small, Miriam R. CHARLOTTE RAMSAY LENNOX: AN EIGHTEENTH-
CENTURY LADY OF LETTERS. New Haven, Conn.: Yale University
Press, 1935.

> (See No. 939.) This biography contains the most extensive
> of all critical discussions of Lennox's novels.

MATTHEW GREGORY LEWIS (1775-1818)

"Monk" Lewis combined lasciviousness and horror in his Gothic romance of THE MONK (1796), a work copied after Radcliffe's MYSTERIES OF UDOLPHO (1794) but so scandalously immoral its author was threatened with legal action; he withdrew the novel, revised it, and reissued it in 1797. Lewis wallowed in the macabre and greatly admired Tieck, Schiller, and other German purveyors of the horrible and the grotesque. Lewis was himself admired in turn by Southey and Scott, who contributed verses to his anthology of TALES OF WONDER (1801); he called Byron and Shelley his friends. Lewis was a successful playwright and the wealthy owner of a Jamaica plantation, where he instituted reforms in the treatment of slaves.

PRINCIPAL WORKS

THE MONK: A ROMANCE, 1796; revised and reissued, 1797
THE MINISTER, 1797 (Tragedy)
THE CASTLE SPECTRE, 1798 (Gothic drama)
THE EAST INDIAN, 1800 (Comedy)
TALES OF WONDER, 1801 (Verse anthology; with Scott and Southey)
THE BRAVO OF VENICE: A ROMANCE, 1805
ADELGITHA; OR, THE FRUIT OF A SINGLE ERROR, 1806 (Tragedy)
FEUDAL TYRANTS, 1806 (Novel)
TIMOUR THE TARTAR: A GRAND ROMANTIC MELO-DRAMA, 1811
POEMS, 1812
RICH AND POOR: A COMIC OPERA, 1812
JOURNAL OF A WEST-INDIA PROPRIETOR, 1834

EDITIONS

THE MONK

948 THE MONK: A ROMANCE. Ed. Ernest A. Baker. London: Routledge, 1907.

949 THE MONK. Ed. Louis F. Peck. New York: Grove Press, 1952.

> Reprints the original text from the earliest edition of the novel (1796) and includes variant readings, a "Note on the Text," and an interesting introduction by John Berryman.

950 THE MONK: A ROMANCE. Ed. Howard Anderson. Oxford English Novels. London: Oxford University Press, 1973.

> This edition is the first since 1796 to be set from Lewis' own manuscript. Anderson provides an excellent critical introduction, a select bibliography, and a chronological record of Lewis' life and career.

THE BRAVO OF VENICE

951 THE BRAVO OF VENICE, A ROMANCE. Intro. Devendra P. Varma. Arno Gothic Novels. New York: Arno Press, 1972.

> A reprint of the London edition, 1805. Varma's introduction approaches the fulsome, but it remains one of the few statements anywhere on this novel.

LETTERS AND JOURNALS

952 THE LIFE AND CORRESPONDENCE OF M.G. LEWIS. Ed. Margaret Baron-Wilson. 2 vols. London, 1839.

> The biography is too laudatory; not all of the correspondence is collected here.

953 JOURNAL OF A WEST-INDIA PROPRIETOR, 1815-17. Ed. Mona Wilson. Boston: Houghton Mifflin, 1929.

> A scholarly edition.

954 Guthke, Karl S. "Some Unpublished Letters of M.G. Lewis." N&Q, 202 (1957), 217-19.

> For corrections see the note by "A Friend of Accuracy," page 389 of this same volume of N&Q.

955 See No. 959.

BIBLIOGRAPHY

956 McNutt, Dan J. THE EIGHTEENTH-CENTURY GOTHIC NOVEL: AN

ANNOTATED BIBLIOGRAPHY OF CRITICISM AND SELECTED TEXTS. New York: Garland, 1975.

Includes a bibliography of Lewis.

957 Todd, William B. "The Early Editions and Issues of THE MONK, with a Bibliography." SB, 2 (1949-50), 4-24.

958 See Nos. 959 and 967.

BIOGRAPHY

959 Peck, Louis F. A LIFE OF MATTHEW GREGORY LEWIS. Cambridge, Mass.: Harvard University Press, 1961.

The standard biography; includes a number of letters, many of them never before published. The bibliography offers a lengthy list of works by and about Lewis.

960 See No. 952.

CRITICAL STUDIES AND COMMENTARIES

961 Anderson, Howard. "Introduction" to THE MONK: A ROMANCE. Oxford English Novels. London: Oxford University Press, 1973.

See No. 950.

962 _____. "The Manuscript of M.G. Lewis's THE MONK: Some Preliminary Notes." PBSA, 62 (1968), 427-34.

A description of the manuscript; until 1973, no edition except the first had been set from this manuscript (see No. 950).

963 Brooks, Peter. "Virtue and Terror: THE MONK." ELH, 40 (1973), 249-63.

THE MONK symbolically challenges the "confident rationalism of the Enlightenment."

964 Fogle, Richard Harter. "The Passions of Ambrosio." THE CLASSIC BRITISH NOVEL. Ed. Howard M. Harper, Jr. and Charles Edge. Athens: University of Georgia Press, 1972.

Unusual in that Fogle attempts to judge THE MONK as a novel within a context larger than that of Gothic fiction alone; the plotting receives special attention.

965 Guthke, Karl S. ENGLISCHE VORROMANTIK UND DEUTSCHER STURM UND DRANG. Göttingen: Vandenhoeck und Ruprecht, 1958.

An important consideration of Lewis' German sources and of his impact on German literature.

966 Kiely, Robert. THE ROMANTIC NOVEL IN ENGLAND. Cambridge, Mass.: Harvard University Press, 1972.

THE MONK is among the late eighteenth-century works treated in this excellent study of the themes, conventions, and innovations of a number of disparate "romantic" novels.

967 Parreaux, André. THE PUBLICATION OF THE MONK: A LITERARY EVENT 1796-1798. Paris: Didier, 1960.

A valuable study of the stormy reception of Lewis' novel. The controversy leads Parreaux into some interesting discussions of social issues and of the changing moral and religious standards of the day. The annotated bibliography of secondary sources is helpful.

968 Peck, Louis F. "THE MONK and LE DIABLE AMOUREUX." MLN, 68 (1953), 406-8.

A brief defense of Lewis' claim that he was indebted to the French story.

969 Railo, Eino. THE HAUNTED CASTLE. London: Routledge, 1927.

See chapters II and IV for some very balanced critical judgments on Lewis' uses of Gothic themes and conventions.

970 Summers, Montague. THE GOTHIC QUEST: A HISTORY OF THE GOTHIC NOVEL. London: Fortune Press, 1938.

Ample discussion of Lewis; Summers' extravagant praise for THE MONK is curious, however, and his assumptions about Lewis' life are often unreliable.

971 Varma, Devendra P. THE GOTHIC FLAME: BEING A HISTORY OF THE GOTHIC NOVEL IN ENGLAND. London: Arthur Barker, 1957.

Includes a long discussion of THE MONK that is mostly summary and plot analysis, with glances at Lewis' sources and his use of Gothic conventions.

HENRY MACKENZIE (1745-1831)

In its time, Henry Mackenzie's THE MAN OF FEELING (1771) was the most celebrated of the "novels of sensibility," and Mackenzie himself was by some ranked alongside Richardson and Fielding as a novelist whose greatness was assured and whose fame would doubtless endure. Taste and fashion passed Mackenzie by, however, and he spent the last five decades of his long life in Edinburgh practicing law and serving the government, cultivating the friendship of literary figures, and publishing miscellaneous periodical essays and poetical dramas.

PRINCIPAL WORKS

THE MAN OF FEELING, 1771 (Novel)
THE PURSUITS OF HAPPINESS, 1771 (Poem)
THE MAN OF THE WORLD, 1773 (Novel)
JULIA DE ROUBIGNE, 1777 (Novel)
THE MIRROR, 1779-80 (Periodical)
THE LOUNGER, 1785-87 (Periodical)
ANECDOTES AND EGOTISMS, 1824-31 (Personal reminiscences)

EDITIONS

A. Collected Works

972 THE WORKS OF HENRY MACKENZIE, ESQ. 8 vols. Edinburgh, 1808.

> Still the most widely available edition, and the only one approaching completeness.

B. Individual Works

THE MAN OF FEELING

973 THE MAN OF FEELING. Ed. Hamish Miles. London: Scholartis Press, 1927.

974 THE MAN OF FEELING. Ed. Brian Vickers. Oxford English Novels. London: Oxford University Press, 1967.

> A reliable text; also includes a brief but solid critical introduction, a selective bibliography of secondary sources, and a chronology of Mackenzie's life and career.

975 THE MAN OF FEELING. FIN.

> A photofacsimile reprint of the first edition, 1771.

THE MAN OF THE WORLD

976 THE MAN OF THE WORLD. FIN.

> A photofacsimile reprint of the first edition, 1773.

LETTERS

977 HENRY MACKENZIE: LETTERS TO ELIZABETH ROSE OF KILRAVOCK, ON LITERATURE, EVENTS AND PEOPLE 1768-1815. Ed. Horst W. Drescher. Edinburgh: Oliver and Boyd, 1967.

BIBLIOGRAPHY

978 See. Nos. 979 and 981.

BIOGRAPHY

979 Barker, Gerard A. HENRY MACKENZIE. New York: Twayne, 1975.

> A readable critical biography; includes a bibliography.

980 Mackenzie, Henry. THE ANECDOTES AND EGOTISMS OF HENRY MACKENZIE. Ed. Harold William Thompson. London: Oxford University Press, 1928.

> The first complete edition of these personal reminiscences, which were composed between 1824 and 1831 and are a chief source of information about Mackenzie's life.

981 Thompson, Harold William. A SCOTTISH MAN OF FEELING. London: Oxford University Press, 1931.

> A thorough study; the best and fullest treatment of Mackenzie's life and work. Includes an extensive bibliography of works by and about Mackenzie.

CRITICAL STUDIES AND COMMENTARIES

982   Crane, Ronald S. "Suggestions toward a Genealogy of the 'Man of Feeling.'" THE IDEA OF THE HUMANITIES, I. Ed. Wayne C. Booth. Chicago: University of Chicago Press, 1967.

    The best discussion of its kind; as such, it is basic to the study of Mackenzie.

983   Foster, James R. HISTORY OF THE PRE-ROMANTIC NOVEL IN ENGLAND. New York: Modern Language Association, 1949.

    A brief but perceptive discussion of Mackenzie's novels as signs of "the rising tide of sentiment" in the 1770's.

984   Frye, Northrop. "Towards Defining an Age of Sensibility." ELH, 23 (1956), 144-52.

    An essential discussion that greatly illuminates the popular novels of sensibility published in the latter half of the eighteenth century.

985   Jenkins, Ralph E. "The Art of the Theorist: Rhetorical Structure in THE MAN OF FEELING." STUDIES IN SCOTTISH LITERATURE, 9 (1971), 3-15.

    The structural principle of the novel borrows from the sermon, and the episodes are deliberately arranged for didactic effect.

986   Kramer, Dale. "The Structural Unity of THE MAN OF FEELING." SSF, 1 (1964), 191-99.

    What unity the novel has does not derive "merely from a picaresque leading character who is associated with all of the events," but from Mackenzie's interest in and dramatization of "the theories of education of the eighteenth-century sentimental tradition."

987   Mayo, Robert D. THE ENGLISH NOVEL IN THE MAGAZINES, 1740-1815. WITH A CATALOGUE OF 1375 MAGAZINE NOVELS AND NOVELISTS. Evanston, Ill.: Northwestern University Press, 1962.

    Includes excellent treatment of Mackenzie's periodicals, THE MIRROR and THE LOUNGER.

988   Spencer, David G. "Henry Mackenzie, a Practical Sentimentalist." PLL, 3 (1967), 314-26.

    Unlike most critics, who have discovered a significant distance between Mackenzie and his novels, Spencer argues that "the philosophy of Mackenzie and the philosophy expressed in his first two books" are "identical"; the philosophy itself is that of "the golden mean--sentiment tempered with reason."

989 Tompkins, J.M.S. THE POPULAR NOVEL IN ENGLAND 1770-1800. London: Constable, 1932.

Touches upon all of Mackenzie's fiction but gives greatest attention to THE MAN OF FEELING, the work that, after Sterne, is "the most perfect and most conscious expression" of the cult of sensibility.

990 Vickers, Brian. "Introduction" to THE MAN OF FEELING. Oxford English Novels. London: Oxford University Press, 1967.

(See No. 974.) An especially able discussion of the novel and its composition.

991 Wright, Walter Francis. SENSIBILITY IN ENGLISH PROSE FICTION, 1760-1814: A REINTERPRETATION. Urbana: University of Illinois Press, 1937.

Essential to the study of Mackenzie.

MARY DELARIVIÈRE MANLEY (1672-1724)

Mary Manley--adventuress, playwright, journalist, novelist, Tory defender--
was a notorious woman who closed her life as the mistress of John Barber, a
London alderman. Swift knew and liked her, perhaps because she was a Tory
partisan; she enjoyed considerable fame as the author of the salacious QUEEN
ZARAH (1705) and NEW ATALANTIS (1709-10), both of which were thinly
disguised attacks on the Whigs and their leaders--QUEEN ZARAH was, in fact,
a scandalous assault on Sarah Churchill, Duchess of Marlborough. Manley had
an impact on the early history of the English novel, for she focused with a
vengeance on contemporary life and helped to make it the chief subject of the
novel in her day.

PRINCIPAL WORKS

LETTERS WRITTEN BY MRS. MANLEY, 1696; reissued as A STAGE COACH
        JOURNEY TO EXETER, 1725 (Fictionalized epistolary sketches)
THE SECRET HISTORY OF QUEEN ZARAH, AND THE ZARAZIANS, 1705
        (Novel/scandal chronicle)
SECRET MEMOIRS AND MANNERS OF SEVERAL PERSONS OF QUALITY . . .
        FROM THE NEW ATALANTIS, 1709 (Novel/scandal chronicle)
MEMOIRS OF EUROPE TOWARDS THE CLOSE OF THE EIGHTH CENTURY,
        1710 (Sequel to THE NEW ATALANTIS)
THE ADVENTURES OF RIVELLA, 1714 (Autobiographical novel)
LUCIUS, THE FIRST CHRISTIAN KING OF BRITAIN, 1717 (Tragedy)
THE POWER OF LOVE. IN SEVEN NOVELS, 1720 (Adaptations from Painter's
        PALACE OF PLEASURE, 1566)

EDITIONS

A. Collected Works

992 THE NOVELS OF MARY DELARIVIÈRE MANLEY. Ed. Patricia Köster.
     2 vols. Gainesville, Fla.: Scholars' Facsimiles and Reprints, 1971.

Facsimile reproductions, with a useful biographical and critical introduction and an extremely helpful index; includes all of the fiction except THE POWER OF LOVE.

B. Individual Works

QUEEN ZARAH

993 THE SECRET HISTORY OF QUEEN ZARAH, AND THE ZARAZIANS. FoN.

A photofacsimile reprint of the first edition, 1705.

NEW ATALANTIS

994 SECRET MEMOIRS AND MANNERS OF SEVERAL PERSONS OF QUALITY, OF BOTH SEXES FROM THE NEW ATALANTIS. FoN.

A photofacsimile reprint of the first edition, 1709.

ADVENTURES OF RIVELLA

995 THE ADVENTURES OF RIVELLA. FoN.

A photofacsimile reprint of the first edition, 1714.

BIOGRAPHY

996 Anderson, Paul B. "Mistress Delarivière Manley's Biography." MP, 33 (1936), 261–62.

A brief sorting of some facts from the fictions of THE ADVEN-TURES OF RIVELLA.

997 Manley, Mary Delarivière. THE ADVENTURES OF RIVELLA. London, 1714.

(See No. 995.) This fictionalized autobiography is a chief source of information about Manley's life.

998 Needham, Gwendolyn B. "Mrs. Manley: An Eighteenth-Century Wife of Bath." HLQ, 14 (1951), 259–84.

On Manley's raffish life and reputation.

CRITICAL STUDIES AND COMMENTARIES

999 Anderson, Paul B. "Delarivière Manley's Prose Fiction." PQ, 13 (1934), 168-88.

A critical survey of Manley's work, with an account of its reception.

1000 Horner, Joyce M. THE ENGLISH WOMEN NOVELISTS AND THEIR CONNECTION WITH THE FEMINIST MOVEMENT (1688-1797). Smith College Studies in Modern Languages, vol. 11, no. 1-3 (1929-30). Northampton, Mass.: 1930.

A lengthy discussion of Manley's fiction that includes a substantial account of contemporary responses to THE NEW ATALANTIS.

1001 MacCarthy, Bridget G. WOMEN WRITERS: THEIR CONTRIBUTION TO THE ENGLISH NOVEL 1621-1744. Cork, Engl.: Cork University Press, 1944.

Takes a negative view of Manley's contribution and reviles THE NEW ATALANTIS for its "endless conversations between vague individuals" and its "execrable" structure.

1002 Needham, Gwendolyn B. "Mary de la Rivière Manley, Tory Defender." HLQ, 12 (1949), 253-88.

On Manley's crucial role as a Tory satirist; THE NEW ATALANTIS cannot be overestimated for its help "in undermining public confidence in the Whigs."

1003 Richetti, John J. POPULAR FICTION BEFORE RICHARDSON: NARRATIVE PATTERNS 1700-1739. Oxford: Clarendon Press, 1969.

Chapter IV of this study offers the fullest and most detailed of all discussion of Manley--her work, its themes and conventions, and her importance as popular novelist and political satirist.

ANN RADCLIFFE (1764-1823)

Ann Radcliffe, the stay-at-home wife of a journalist, was the most popular novelist of the last decade of the eighteenth century. Her several Gothic romances captured the imagination of her audience and prompted numerous imitations. THE ROMANCE OF THE FOREST (1791) and THE MYSTERIES OF UDOLPHO (1794), her best and most successful works, combined Richardsonian themes and plotting with the effects of terror, exposing the nightmares of the unconscious for her readers' delectation. Alert to the contemporary distrust of the supernatural, Radcliffe always provided rational explanations of the strange events of her fictions.

PRINCIPAL WORKS

THE CASTLES OF ATHLIN AND DUNBAYNE, 1789 (Novel)
A SICILIAN ROMANCE, 1790 (Novel)
THE ROMANCE OF THE FOREST, 1791 (Novel)
THE MYSTERIES OF UDOLPHO, 1794 (Novel)
A JOURNEY MADE IN THE SUMMER OF 1794 THROUGH HOLLAND AND
       THE WESTERN FRONTIERS OF GERMANY, 1795
THE ITALIAN, 1797 (Novel)
POEMS, 1815
GASTON DE BLONDEVILLE, 1826 (Novel)
ST. ALBAN'S ABBEY, 1826 (Verse romance)

EDITIONS

A. Collected Works

1004 THE NOVELS OF MRS. ANN RADCLIFFE. Vol. 10. Ballantyne's Novelist's Library. London, 1821.

> This edition omits GASTON DE BLONDEVILLE and ST. ALBAN'S ABBEY; it is prefaced by Sir Walter Scott's Memoir of Radcliffe.

B. Individual Works

THE CASTLES OF ATHLIN AND DUNBAYNE

1005 THE CASTLES OF ATHLIN AND DUNBAYNE: A HIGHLAND STORY.
London: Johnson Reprint Corp., 1970.

> A reprint, in photofacsimile, of the 1796 Philadelphia edition.

1006 THE CASTLES OF ATHLIN AND DUNBAYNE: A HIGHLAND STORY.
Foreword by Frederick Shroyer. Arno Gothic Novels. New York: Arno
Press, 1972.

> A reprint of the 1821 London edition of this rare first novel.

A SICILIAN ROMANCE

1007 A SICILIAN ROMANCE. 2 vols. London: Johnson Reprint Corp., 1971.

> A reprint, in photofacsimile, of the first London edition, 1790.

1008 A SICILIAN ROMANCE. Foreword by Howard Mumford Jones; intro.
Devendra P. Varma. Arno Gothic Novels. New York: Arno Press,
1972.

> A reprint of the 1821 London edition.

ROMANCE OF THE FOREST

1009 THE ROMANCE OF THE FOREST: INTERSPERSED WITH SOME PIECES
OF POETRY. Foreword by Frederick Garber; intro. Devendra P. Varma.
Arno Gothic Novels. New York: Arno Press, 1974.

> A reprint of the 1827 London edition.

MYSTERIES OF UDOLPHO

1010 THE MYSTERIES OF UDOLPHO. Everyman's Library. 2 vols. London:
J.M. Dent, 1931.

1011 THE MYSTERIES OF UDOLPHO. A ROMANCE, INTERSPERSED WITH
SOME PIECES OF POETRY. Ed. Bonamy Dobrée. Oxford English Novels.
London: Oxford University Press, 1966.

> Includes a reliable text and an excellent critical introduction,
> together with a brief bibliographical note and a chronology of
> Radcliffe's life and career.

THE ITALIAN

1012 THE CONFESSIONAL OF THE BLACK PENITENTS. London: Folio Society, 1956.

1013 THE ITALIAN, OR THE CONFESSIONAL OF THE BLACK PENITENTS. A ROMANCE. Ed. Frederick Garber. Oxford English Novels. London: Oxford University Press, 1968.

Includes apparatus similar to that found in No. 1011.

GASTON DE BLONDEVILLE

1014 GASTON DE BLONDEVILLE: OR, THE COURT OF HENRY III. KEEPING FESTIVAL IN ARDENNE, A ROMANCE. Intro. Devendra P. Varma. Arno Gothic Novels. 2 vols. New York: Arno Press, 1972.

A reprint of the first edition, 1826.

BIBLIOGRAPHY

1015 McNutt, Dan J. THE EIGHTEENTH-CENTURY GOTHIC NOVEL: AN ANNOTATED BIBLIOGRAPHY OF CRITICISM AND SELECTED TEXTS. New York: Garland, 1975.

Includes a bibliography of Radcliffe.

1016 See No. 1018.

BIOGRAPHY

1017 Grant, Aline. ANN RADCLIFFE. Denver, Colo.: Alan Swallow, 1951.

A biography; the novels receive only superficial attention.

1018 Murray, E.B. ANN RADCLIFFE. New York: Twayne, 1972.

A critical biography; includes a bibliography.

1019 Scott, Sir Walter. Memoir of Radcliffe. THE NOVELS OF MRS. ANN RADCLIFFE. Vol. 10. Ballantyne's Novelist's Library. London, 1821.

(See No. 1004.) Scott called Radcliffe the "first poetess of romantic fiction."

1020 See No. 1026.

CRITICAL STUDIES AND COMMENTARIES

1021 Epstein, Lynne. "Mrs. Radcliffe's Landscapes: The Influence of Three Landscape Painters on Her Nature Descriptions." HARTFORD STUDIES IN LITERATURE, 1 (1969), 107-20.

> The three painters are Claude Lorrain, Salvator Rosa, and Nicolas Poussin.

1022 Foster, James R. HISTORY OF THE PRE-ROMANTIC NOVEL IN EN-GLAND. New York: Modern Language Association, 1949.

> Includes a brief but insightful overview of Radcliffe's fiction.

1023 Havens, Raymond D. "Ann Radcliffe's Nature Descriptions." MLN, 66 (1951), 251-55.

> Radcliffe's "mistaken conception" of literary art kept her from expressing in her novels what she certainly possessed, a genuine sensitivity to nature.

1024 Horner, Joyce M. THE ENGLISH WOMEN NOVELISTS AND THEIR CONNECTION WITH THE FEMINIST MOVEMENT (1688-1797). Smith College Studies in Modern Languages, vol. 11, no. 1-3 (1929-30). Northampton, Mass.: 1930.

> Provides an excellent overview of Radcliffe's works.

1025 Kiely, Robert. THE ROMANTIC NOVEL IN ENGLAND. Cambridge, Mass.: Harvard University Press, 1972.

> THE MYSTERIES OF UDOLPHO is among the late eighteenth-century works treated in this excellent study of the themes, conventions, and innovations of a number of disparate "romantic" novels.

1026 McIntyre, Clara F. ANN RADCLIFFE IN RELATION TO HER TIME. New Haven, Conn.: Yale University Press, 1920.

> Partly biographical, but mainly a study of how Radcliffe's novels navigated contemporary social, moral, and philosophical currents (without becoming propagandistic) and of how they appealed to and reinforced the taste for the emotional and the macabre in fiction.

1027 Manwaring, Elizabeth. ITALIAN LANDSCAPE IN EIGHTEENTH CENTURY ENGLAND: A STUDY CHIEFLY OF THE INFLUENCE OF CLAUDE LOR-RAIN AND SALVATOR ROSA ON ENGLISH TASTE 1700-1800. London: Frank Cass, 1925.

Radcliffe is never quite the focus, but this study is essential
to the understanding of the vogue for landscape art that prompted
and influenced her descriptions of natural scenery.

1028 Ruff, William. "Ann Radcliffe, or, The Hand of Taste." THE AGE
OF JOHNSON: ESSAYS PRESENTED TO CHAUNCEY BREWSTER TINKER.
Ed. Frederick W. Hilles. New Haven, Conn.: Yale University Press,
1949.

Radcliffe's novels can only be read today as the "embodiment
of good taste" in her own time, and indeed the moralistic
"novel of taste" is her "contribution to English literature."

1029 Summers, Montague. THE GOTHIC QUEST: A HISTORY OF THE GOTHIC
NOVEL. London: Fortune Press, 1938.

Includes ample, enthusiastic general discussion of Radcliffe's
fiction.

1030 Sypher, Wylie. "Social Ambiguity in a Gothic Novel." PARTISAN RE-
VIEW, 12 (1945), 50-60.

On THE MYSTERIES OF UDOLPHO.

1031 Tompkins, J.M.S. THE POPULAR NOVEL IN ENGLAND 1770-1800.
London: Constable, 1932.

Tompkins is more enthusiastic about Radcliffe than most who
have studied her, but she is nevertheless astute, especially
when treating the strengths of this "first poetess of romantic
fiction," who "liberated fancy and quickened colour."

1032 Ware, Malcolm. "Mrs. Radcliffe's 'Picturesque Embellishment.'" TEN-
NESSEE STUDIES IN ENGLISH, 5 (1960), 67-71.

On Radcliffe's often extravagant way with natural scenery.

1033 _____. SUBLIMITY IN THE NOVELS OF ANN RADCLIFFE: A STUDY
OF THE INFLUENCE UPON HER CRAFT OF EDMUND BURKE'S ENQUIRY.
Copenhagen: Munksgaard, 1963.

A tired subject (Radcliffe and the sublime), but freshly treated
in this small monograph; the focus on Burke as virtually the
only influence is too limiting, however.

1034 Wieten, A.A.S. MRS. RADCLIFFE--HER RELATION TOWARDS ROMAN-
TICISM. Amsterdam: H.J. Paris, 1926.

Radcliffe brought into focus the romantic tendencies of her
time, even anticipated quite directly the literary developments

(in poetry and fiction) of the early nineteenth century; thus her great popularity and the respect she earned from the likes of Scott and Coleridge. This study gives considerable attention to Radcliffe's poetry.

CLARA REEVE (1729-1807)

Clara Reeve is best remembered not for her fiction but for THE PROGRESS OF ROMANCE (1785), the first attempt to write a sustained history of prose fiction as practiced by those modern novelists whose works "sprung up" out of the "ruins" of romance. Reeve's own first novel, THE CHAMPION OF VIRTUE: A GOTHIC STORY (1777; reissued, 1778, as THE OLD ENGLISH BARON), was among the earliest narratives to anticipate directly the later development of the historical novel, and it was the first English work to take up the Gothic strain introduced in Walpole's CASTLE OF OTRANTO (1764). THE OLD ENGLISH BARON was a very popular and influential work in its day, and it is the only one of Clara Reeve's novels to be reprinted in modern times.

PRINCIPAL WORKS

ORIGINAL POEMS ON SEVERAL OCCASIONS, 1769
THE PHOENIX: OR THE HISTORY OF POLYARCHUS AND ARGENIS, by
      Barclay, 1772 (Translation)
THE CHAMPION OF VIRTUE: A GOTHIC STORY, 1777; reissued as THE OLD
      ENGLISH BARON, 1778 (Novel)
THE TWO MENTORS, 1783 (Novel)
THE PROGRESS OF ROMANCE, 1785 (Conversational history of fiction)
THE EXILES, OR MEMOIRS OF THE COUNT DE CRONSTADT, 1788 (Novel)
THE SCHOOL FOR WIDOWS, 1791 (Novel)
PLANS OF EDUCATION, 1792 (Treatise)
MEMOIRS OF SIR ROGER DE CLARENDON, 1793 (Novel)
DESTINATION: OR, MEMOIRS OF A PRIVATE FAMILY, 1799 (Novel)

EDITIONS

THE OLD ENGLISH BARON

1035 THE OLD ENGLISH BARON. Ed. James Trainer. Oxford English Novels.
    London: Oxford University Press, 1967.

Includes a brief critical introduction, a chronological record of the author's life and career, and a select bibliography; reliable text, modestly annotated.

THE PROGRESS OF ROMANCE

1036 THE PROGRESS OF ROMANCE THROUGH TIMES, COUNTRIES, AND MANNERS. New York: Garland, 1970.

A photofacsimile reprint of the first edition, 1785.

BIBLIOGRAPHY

1037 McNutt, Dan J. THE EIGHTEENTH-CENTURY GOTHIC NOVEL: AN ANNOTATED BIBLIOGRAPHY OF CRITICISM AND SELECTED TEXTS. New York: Garland, 1975.

Includes a bibliography of Reeve.

CRITICAL STUDIES AND COMMENTARIES

Reeve has attracted little attention from critics, and commentaries on her work are scarce. The standard histories of the novel should be consulted along with the few items entered here.

1038 Foster, James R. HISTORY OF THE PRE-ROMANTIC NOVEL IN ENGLAND. New York: Modern Language Association, 1949.

Includes brief but astute comments on the importance and the quality of Reeve's novels.

1039 MacCarthy, Bridget G. THE LATER WOMEN NOVELISTS, 1744–1818. New York: William Salloch, 1948.

Includes brief but perceptive discussion of Reeve's novels.

1040 Summers, Montague. THE GOTHIC QUEST: A HISTORY OF THE GOTHIC NOVEL. London: Fortune Press, 1938.

Comments helpfully on the importance of the first novelist to follow the lead of Walpole's CASTLE OF OTRANTO.

1041 Tompkins, J.M.S. THE POPULAR NOVEL IN ENGLAND 1770–1800. London: Constable, 1932.

Scattered, brief, but insightful comments on Reeve's work as novelist and literary historian.

1042 Trainer, James. "Introduction" to THE OLD ENGLISH BARON. Oxford English Novels. London: Oxford University Press, 1967.

See No. 1035.

SAMUEL RICHARDSON (1689-1761)

PRINCIPAL WORKS

THE APPRENTICE'S VADE MECUM, 1733 (Conduct book)
TOUR THRO' THE WHOLE ISLAND OF GREAT BRITAIN, by Defoe, 1738
    (Edition)
AESOP'S FABLES, translated by L'Estrange, 1740 (Revision)
THE NEGOTIATIONS OF SIR THOMAS ROE, 1740 (Edition)
PAMELA, OR VIRTUE REWARDED, Part I, 1740 (Novel)
PAMELA, Part II, 1741
LETTERS WRITTEN TO AND FOR PARTICULAR FRIENDS [FAMILIAR LETTERS],
    1741 (Manual for letter writers)
CLARISSA, OR, THE HISTORY OF A YOUNG LADY, 1747-48 (Novel)
THE HISTORY OF SIR CHARLES GRANDISON, 1753-54 (Novel)
A COLLECTION OF THE MORAL AND INSTRUCTIVE SENTIMENTS . . .
       CONTAINED IN THE HISTORIES OF PAMELA, CLARISSA, AND
       SIR CHARLES GRANDISON, 1755

EDITIONS

A. Collected Works

1043 THE WORKS OF SAMUEL RICHARDSON. Ed. Leslie Stephen. 12 vols.
London, 1883-84.

> Unlike most collected editions of Richardson's works, this one
> includes items besides the novels. The prefatory essay is often
> critically perceptive.

1044 THE NOVELS OF SAMUEL RICHARDSON. Ed. William Lyon Phelps.
19 vols. London, 1902; rpt. New York: AMS Press, 1971.

1045 THE NOVELS OF SAMUEL RICHARDSON. Ed. William King and Adrian
Bott. Shakespeare Head Edition. 18 vols. Oxford: Basil Blackwell,
1929-31.

The best of the collected editions of the novels; generally reliable texts, with all of the various prefaces and end materials published by Richardson with his novels.

B. Individual Works

PAMELA

1046 PAMELA: OR, VIRTUE REWARDED. Ed. William M. Sale, Jr. New
York: W.W. Norton, 1958.

> Part I only. Sale's introduction is an excellent critical dis-
> cussion; the text is not altogether reliable.

1047 PAMELA. Ed. Mark Kinhead-Weekes. 4 vols. Everyman's Library.
London: J.M. Dent, 1965.

> Includes part II of the novel.

1048 PAMELA: OR, VIRTUE REWARDED. Ed. T.C. Duncan Eaves and Ben D.
Kimpel. Boston: Houghton Mifflin, 1971.

> Includes the text of the first edition of part I, with the pref-
> atory matter to the first and second editions; includes also a
> fine critical introduction and a useful "Chronological Table
> of PAMELA and the PAMELA Vogue in England." This is the
> best edition presently available.

1049 PAMELA; OR, VIRTUE REWARDED. 4 vols. FIN.

> A reprint, in photofacsimile, of the rare 1801 edition, the
> last revised by Richardson; includes part I and part II of the
> novel.

FAMILIAR LETTERS

1050 FAMILIAR LETTERS ON IMPORTANT OCCASIONS. Ed. Brian W. Downs.
London: Routledge, 1928.

CLARISSA

1051 CLARISSA: OR, THE HISTORY OF A YOUNG LADY. Ed. John Butt.
4 vols. Everyman's Library. London: J.M. Dent, 1962.

> An unabridged edition.

1052 CLARISSA: OR THE HISTORY OF A YOUNG LADY. Abridged. Ed.
George Sherburn. Boston: Houghton Mifflin, 1962.

An intelligent abridgement, with a good critical introduction.

1053 CLARISSA; OR, THE HISTORY OF A YOUNG LADY. Abridged. Ed.
Philip Stevick. San Francisco: Rinehart Press, 1971.

1054 CLARISSA: PREFACE, HINTS OF PREFACES, AND POSTSCRIPT. Ed.
R.F. Brissenden. Augustan Reprint Society Publications, No. 103. Los
Angeles: William Andrews Clark Memorial Library, 1964.

A convenient gathering of materials often only partially represented in (or even entirely omitted from) editions of the novel.

SIR CHARLES GRANDISON

1055 THE HISTORY OF SIR CHARLES GRANDISON. Ed. Jocelyn Harris. 3 vols.
Oxford English Novels. London: Oxford University Press, 1972.

Includes a reliable text, together with a substantial critical
introduction, a select bibliography, and a chronology of Richardson's life and career.

LETTERS

1056 THE CORRESPONDENCE OF SAMUEL RICHARDSON. Ed. Anna L. Barbauld. 6 vols. London, 1804; rpt. New York: AMS Press, 1968.

Still the most complete collection, although there are many
omissions; the editing does not meet the standards of modern
scholarship.

1057 THE LETTERS OF DOCTOR GEORGE CHEYNE TO SAMUEL RICHARDSON.
Ed. Charles F. Mullett. Columbia: University of Missouri Press, 1943.

These letters reveal much about Richardson's health and business life; Richardson was Cheyne's patient and the publisher of
his books on medicine and natural philosophy.

1058 SELECTED LETTERS OF SAMUEL RICHARDSON. Ed. John Carroll. Oxford: Clarendon Press, 1964.

Includes 128 letters and passages from letters; the selection is
limited to "those letters or passages from the letters that bear
on the themes and characters of Richardson's novels, on his
craftsmanship and literary judgment, and on his own personality."

1059 THE RICHARDSON-STINSTRA CORRESPONDENCE AND STINSTRA'S PREF-
ACES TO CLARISSA. Ed. William C. Slattery. Carbondale: Southern
Illinois University Press, 1969.

Richardson's letters to Stinstra are an important source of information about his life; Stinstra's prefaces to his Dutch edition of CLARISSA contain important early critical commentary on the novel.

1060 See Nos. 1068 and 1142.

BIBLIOGRAPHY

1061 Carroll, John. "Richardson." THE ENGLISH NOVEL: SELECT BIBLIOGRAPHICAL GUIDES. Ed. A.E. Dyson. London: Oxford University Press, 1974.

A very selective bibliographical essay covering primary and secondary materials.

1062 Cordasco, Francesco. SAMUEL RICHARDSON: A LIST OF CRITICAL STUDIES PUBLISHED FROM 1896 TO 1946. Brooklyn, N.Y.: Long Island University Press, 1948.

An annotated list; outdated and, because of its many inaccuracies, unreliable.

1063 Sale, William M., Jr. SAMUEL RICHARDSON: A BIBLIOGRAPHICAL RECORD OF HIS LITERARY CAREER. New Haven, Conn.: Yale University Press, 1936.

Lists and descriptions of all of those works written, edited, or revised wholly or in part by Richardson; also listed and described are those works called into being by the publication of Richardson's novels. This bibliography is an invaluable resource.

1064 See Nos. 1069 and 1070.

BIOGRAPHY

1065 Brissenden, R.F. SAMUEL RICHARDSON. Writers and Their Work, No. 101. London: Longmans, Green, 1958.

A brief, useful "biocritical" introduction to Richardson.

1066 Dobson, Austin. SAMUEL RICHARDSON. London: Macmillan, 1902.

For more than thirty years after its publication, regarded as the best biography of Richardson; the criticism of the novels, especially PAMELA and GRANDISON, is extremely opinionated.

1067 Downs, Brian W. RICHARDSON. London: Routledge, 1928.

A compact critical biography.

1068 Eaves, T.C. Duncan, and Ben D. Kimpel. SAMUEL RICHARDSON: A
BIOGRAPHY. Oxford: Clarendon Press, 1971.

The standard biography. An appendix lists and locates all
letters known to have been written to or by Richardson.

1069 McKillop, Alan Dugald. SAMUEL RICHARDSON: PRINTER AND NOVEL-
IST. Chapel Hill: University of North Carolina Press, 1936.

An essential study that emphasizes Richardson's literary career;
includes a bibliography of secondary materials.

1070 Sale, William M., Jr. SAMUEL RICHARDSON, MASTER PRINTER.
Ithaca, N.Y.: Cornell University Press, 1950.

A systematic, thorough study of an important part of Richardson's life. One chapter is devoted to a list of books printed
by Richardson.

1071 Thomson, Clara L. SAMUEL RICHARDSON: A BIOGRAPHICAL AND
CRITICAL STUDY. London: Horace Marshall, 1900.

The first full-length biography of Richardson.

CRITICAL STUDIES AND COMMENTARIES

1072 Ball, Donald L. SAMUEL RICHARDSON'S THEORY OF FICTION. The
Hague: Mouton, 1971.

A dissertation, unrevised (it appears), but useful because it is
the only full-length commentary on its subject. Ball attempts
to "formulate a theory of fiction for Richardson by correlating
his statements concerning fiction, by examining carefully his
practice of fiction, and by determining from the relationship
of his statements to his practice just what he thought fiction
was and what it should do."

1073 Beasley, Jerry C. "English Fiction in the 1740's: Some Glances at the
Major and Minor Novels." SNNTS, 5 (1973), 155-75.

An attempt to show that, despite their differences, Richardson,
Fielding, and Smollett all exploited contemporary themes,
methods, and types of fiction.

1074 _____. "Romance and the 'New' Novels of Richardson, Fielding, and

Smollett." SEL, 16 (1976), 437-50.

The three major novelists of the 1740's all borrowed to some extent from the themes and conventions of romance. (See also No. 1088.)

1075 Bell, Michael Davitt. "Pamela's Wedding and the Marriage of the Lamb." PQ, 49 (1970), 100-112.

An attempt to account for the origins of Richardson's heroine, the stereotype "of romantic love," and to link the language and structure of the novel to the religious literature of the time.

1076 Black, Frank Gees. THE EPISTOLARY NOVEL IN THE LATE EIGHTEENTH CENTURY: A DESCRIPTIVE AND BIBLIOGRAPHICAL STUDY. Eugene: University of Oregon Press, 1940.

This survey quite naturally gives considerable attention to Richardson's epistolary methods and his influence.

1077 Blanchard, Frederic T. FIELDING THE NOVELIST: A STUDY IN HISTORICAL CRITICISM. New Haven, Conn.: Yale University Press, 1926.

This study of the reception and influence of Fielding's novels, from the eighteenth century through the early years of the twentieth, is also valuable to the Richardson scholar, for Richardson's reputation (as it relates to Fielding's) receives considerable attention. The bibliography of sources is extremely valuable.

1078 Brophy, Elizabeth Bergen. SAMUEL RICHARDSON: THE TRIUMPH OF CRAFT. Knoxville: University of Tennessee Press, 1974.

A full-length study of Richardson as artist; interesting, useful, and refreshing in its approach to Richardson as a writer always conscious of his art.

1079 Bullen, John S. TIME AND SPACE IN THE NOVELS OF SAMUEL RICHARDSON. Logan: Utah State University Press, 1965.

An analytical treatment of the ways in which Richardson makes artistic use of the structural and developmental devices of time and space in creating the worlds of his novels.

1080 Carroll, John. "Lovelace as Tragic Hero." UTQ, 42 (1972), 14-25.

A fine, illuminating discussion of Lovelace's development from a libertine misogynist into a tragic Tristan.

1081 _____. "Richardson at Work: Revisions, Allusions, and Quotations in

CLARISSA." STUDIES IN THE EIGHTEENTH CENTURY, II. Ed. R.F. Brissenden. Toronto: University of Toronto Press, 1973.

> An illuminating discussion of Richardson's "meticulous care" in the composition and revision of his second novel. (See also Nos. 1095, 1108, and 1135.)

1082 _____, ed. SAMUEL RICHARDSON: A COLLECTION OF CRITICAL ESSAYS. Twentieth Century Views. Englewood Cliffs, N.J.: Prentice-Hall, 1969.

> Reprinted essays by various Richardson scholars.

1083 Copeland, Edward W. "Allegory and Analogy in CLARISSA: the 'Plan' and the 'No-Plan.'" ELH, 39 (1972), 254-65.

> Allegory, a rhetorical tool, and analogy, a logical tool, work in Richardson's novel to unify it and give it power.

1084 _____. "Clarissa and Fanny Hill: Sisters in Distress." SNNTS, 4 (1972), 343-52.

> According to Copeland, Cleland's novel repeats, in parody, the themes and conventions of the early volumes of CLARISSA, although in many respects it more closely parallels the story of PAMELA. The comparison illuminates the "sexual energy that animates the rhetorical fantasies" of Richardson's characters.

1085 _____. "Samuel Richardson and Naive Allegory: Some Beauties of the Mixed Metaphor." NOVEL, 4 (1971), 231-39.

> A discussion of some of the problems Richardson made for himself in CLARISSA and (especially) PAMELA "by his failure to recognize the divergent claims of his mimetic and didactic concerns"; hence the "naive allegory" mentioned in Copeland's title.

1086 Cowler, Rosemary, ed. TWENTIETH CENTURY INTERPRETATIONS OF PAMELA. Englewood Cliffs, N.J.: Prentice-Hall, 1969.

> A collection of reprinted essays by Richardson scholars.

1087 Daiches, David. LITERARY ESSAYS. Edinburgh: Oliver and Boyd, 1956.

> The essay on Richardson is a persuasive discussion of the relationships between his first two novels and religious literature--medieval saints' lives and, to a lesser extent, Milton's epics of PARADISE LOST and PARADISE REGAINED. The novels dramatize the real world's threats to sainthood and Christian heroism.

1088 Dalziel, Margaret. "Richardson and Romance." AUMLA, 33 (1970), 5-24.

> An important discussion of Richardson's use of the conventions of prose romance. (See also No. 1074.)

1089 Day, Robert Adams. TOLD IN LETTERS: EPISTOLARY FICTION BEFORE RICHARDSON. Ann Arbor: University of Michigan Press, 1966.

> This study of more than 200 pre-Richardsonian letter fictions provides important background for the student of Richardson.

1090 Donovan, Robert Alan. THE SHAPING VISION: IMAGINATION IN THE ENGLISH NOVEL FROM DEFOE TO DICKENS. Ithaca, N.Y.: Cornell University Press, 1966.

> Includes a valuable chapter on PAMELA that deliberately skirts the usual moralistic approach and concentrates instead on "the purely social dilemma" confronting Richardson's heroine. "It is this social dilemma," states Donovan, "and Pamela's response to it, which I believe gives integrity to the novel as an artistic structure."

1091 Doody, Margaret Anne. A NATURAL PASSION: A STUDY OF THE NOVELS OF SAMUEL RICHARDSON. Oxford: Clarendon Press, 1974.

> A discussion of all of Richardson's novels, with emphasis on CLARISSA and SIR CHARLES GRANDISON. Doody explores the literary backgrounds and is especially interesting on Richardson's use of images. Love in its several kinds--eros, philia, agape--is the "natural passion" referred to in the title of this study, and Doody sees love as a central issue in the novels.

1092 Dussinger, John A. "Conscience and the Pattern of Christian Perfection in CLARISSA." PMLA, 81 (1966), 236-45.

> Emphasizes Richardson's attempt to show, through Clarissa Harlowe, how the condition of salvation proceeds from the ultimate refinement of sensibility.

1093 _____. "Richardson's 'Christian Vocation.'" PLL, 3 (1967), 3-19.

> Richardson, as a printer of numerous religious books, was keenly aware of the religious currents of his day, and these were an important influence on the meaning and the form of his novels.

1094 _____. "What Pamela Knew: An Interpretation." JEGP, 69 (1970), 377-93.

> An interesting argument suggesting that, as Richardson's novel progresses, Pamela grows in self-knowledge and hence in character.

1095 Eaves, T.C. Duncan, and Ben D. Kimpel. "The Composition of CLARISSA and Its Revisions before Publication." PMLA, 83 (1968), 416-28.

 See also Nos. 1081, 1108, and 1135.

1096 ______. "Richardson's Revisions of PAMELA." SB, 20 (1967), 61-88.

1097 Farrell, William J. "The Style and the Action in CLARISSA." SEL, 3 (1963), 365-75.

 A refreshing discussion of Richardson's stylistic versatility, especially as reflected in the "voices" of CLARISSA's many letter-writing characters.

1098 Fiedler, Leslie. LOVE AND DEATH IN THE AMERICAN NOVEL. Rev. ed. New York: Dell, 1966.

 Includes a Freudian reading of CLARISSA as a celebration of Puritan neuroses, inhibitions, and sexual fears.

1099 Golden, Morris. RICHARDSON'S CHARACTERS. Ann Arbor: University of Michigan Press, 1963.

 A psychological interpretation of the novels. Golden sees Richardson's characters as powered by a "dominance urge," a desire to rule those about them, whether for good or evil.

1100 ______. "Richardson's Repetitions." PMLA, 82 (1967), 64-67.

 "Richardson tended to use similar character types and involve them in similar situations, and this even more pervasively and significantly than has so far been noted."

1101 Hill, Christopher. "Clarissa Harlowe and Her Times." ESSAYS IN CRITICISM, 5 (1955), 315-40.

 A valuable essay on the social contexts for CLARISSA, whose theme, Hill argues, centers around contemporary commitment to the arranged marriage.

1102 Hilles, Frederick W. "The Plan of CLARISSA." PQ, 45 (1966), 236-48.

 CLARISSA is a carefully planned novel, in which Richardson echoes images, balances characters, and changes emphases to create a harmonious whole.

1103 Hornbeak, Katherine. RICHARDSON'S FAMILIAR LETTERS AND THE DOMESTIC CONDUCT BOOKS. Smith College Studies in Modern Languages, vol. 19, no. 2 (1938). Northampton, Mass.: 1937.

Still the best discussion of the relationships between Richardson's letter-writer and the popular conduct books.

1104 Hughes, Leo. "Theatrical Convention in Richardson: Some Observations on a Novelist's Technique." RESTORATION AND EIGHTEENTH-CENTURY LITERATURE: ESSAYS IN HONOR OF ALAN DUGALD McKILLOP. Ed. Carroll Camden. Chicago: University of Chicago Press, 1963.

A very balanced, judicious analysis of Richardson's borrowings from the stage. (See also Nos. 1109, 1110, and 1131.)

1105 Kearney, A.M. "CLARISSA and the Epistolary Form." ESSAYS IN CRITICISM, 16 (1966), 44-56.

Richardson's second novel makes more sophisticated use of the epistolary mode than does his first.

1106 _____. "Richardson's PAMELA: The Aesthetic Case." REL, 7 (1966), 78-90.

A balanced defense of PAMELA as the work of a careful craftsman, and hence "a much more interesting achievement" than has usually been thought.

1107 Kermode, Frank. "Richardson and Fielding." CAMBRIDGE JOURNAL, 4 (1950), 106-14.

A stimulating but prejudicial argument stressing the differences between Richardson and Fielding and exalting Richardson's searching introspection and authorial distance at the expense of Fielding's comic vision and methods. For different views of, and approaches to, the relationships between the two novelists, see Nos. 1073, 1074, 1121, and 1122.

1108 Kinhead-Weekes, Mark. "CLARISSA Restored?" RES, NS 10 (1959), 156-71.

On the question of Richardson's addition, or "restoration," of new (or previously omitted) passages to the second and subsequent editions of the novel. (See also Nos. 1081, 1095, and 1135.)

1109 _____. SAMUEL RICHARDSON: DRAMATIC NOVELIST. London: Methuen, 1973.

A comprehensive study of Richardson's fiction, with emphasis on his "dramatic" methods. Kinhead-Weekes is concerned with Richardson's vision and technique, especially as they served his moral and religious purposes, and not merely with his indebtedness to the contemporary stage. (See also Nos. 1104, 1110, and 1131.)

1110 Konigsberg, Ira. SAMUEL RICHARDSON AND THE DRAMATIC NOVEL. Lexington: University of Kentucky Press, 1968.

A study of Richardson's indebtedness to the conventions of the stage that claims too much but is nonetheless useful. (See also Nos. 1104, 1109, and 1131.)

1111 Kreissman, Bernard. PAMELA-SHAMELA: A STUDY OF THE CRITICISMS, BURLESQUES, PARODIES, AND ADAPTATIONS OF RICHARDSON'S PAMELA. Lincoln: University of Nebraska Press, 1960.

An indispensable scholarly survey.

1112 McKillop, Alan Dugald. THE EARLY MASTERS OF ENGLISH FICTION. Lawrence: University of Kansas Press, 1956.

Includes a long essay on Richardson that remains one of the very best general assessments of his work.

1113 _____. "Epistolary Technique in Richardson's Novels." RICE INSTITUTE PAMPHLETS, 38 (1951), 36-54.

The best brief discussion of this important subject. (See also Nos. 1128, 1132, and 1142.)

1114 _____. "The Personal Relations between Fielding and Richardson." MP, 28 (1931), 423-33.

The best brief discussion of this subject.

1115 _____. "Wedding Bells for PAMELA." PQ, 28 (1949), 323-25.

An account of the public reaction to Pamela's marriage.

1116 _____, ed. CRITICAL REMARKS ON SIR CHARLES GRANDISON, CLARISSA AND PAMELA. Augustan Reprint Society Publications, No. 21. Los Angeles: William Andrews Clark Memorial Library, 1950.

This 1754 pamphlet, probably by Alexander Campbell, is among the first serious critical commentaries on Richardson's novels, and it is generally hostile.

1117 Moore, Robert Etheridge. "Dr. Johnson on Fielding and Richardson." PMLA, 66 (1951), 162-81.

Moore takes the view that, despite Dr. Johnson's public comments on the two writers, Fielding's novels are much closer to

Johnson's most "deeply-felt" literary principles than are Richardson's.

1118 Morton, Donald E. "Themes and Structure in PAMELA." SNNTS, 3 (1971), 242-57.

PAMELA as "Christian art," drawing upon the Puritan tradition to supply its "sense of order."

1119 Needham, Gwendolyn B. "Richardson's Characterization of Mr. B. and Double Purpose in PAMELA." ECS, 3 (1970), 433-74.

One of the more important articles on Richardson's novel in recent years, in that it thoroughly examines the characterization of Mr. B. in his relationships with Pamela and with Richardson's moral and literary purpose.

1120 Palmer, William J. "Two Dramatists: Lovelace and Richardson in CLARISSA." SNNTS, 5 (1973), 7-21.

An interesting but debatable argument claiming that Lovelace is the "objective correlative" for Richardson's subconscious mind, and as such he, not his author, is the "playwright" in control of Richardson's "dramatic novel."

1121 Park, William. "Fielding and Richardson." PMLA, 81 (1966), 381-88.

A convincing argument that the novelists of the mid-eighteenth century shared a common body of assumptions and conventions. For a very different view of the relationships between Richardson and Fielding, see No. 1107; for views similar to those expressed in this article, see Nos. 1073, 1074, and 1122.

1122 _____. "What Was New About the 'New Species of Writing'?" SNNTS, 2 (1970), 112-30.

An attempt to justify the claims of artistic "newness" made by Richardson and Fielding, who were in many respects not so different as has sometimes been thought. (See also No. 1121.)

1123 Pierson, R.C. "The Revisions of Richardson's SIR CHARLES GRANDISON." SB, 21 (1968), 163-89.

1124 Preston, John. THE CREATED SELF: THE READER'S ROLE IN EIGHTEENTH-CENTURY FICTION. New York: Barnes and Noble, 1970.

Two chapters treating CLARISSA; excellent on the special relationships between epistolary fiction and its reader.

1125 Rabkin, Norman. "CLARISSA: A Study in the Nature of Convention." ELH, 23 (1956), 204-17.

On the tensions created by the conflict between the inner urges of the characters and the demands of propriety. Clarissa herself emerges from this discussion as less angelic than she has sometimes seemed.

1126 RICHARDSONIANA. 25 vols. SBrW.

A collection of reprints, in photofacsimile, of various works written in response to Richardson's novels, along with some minor titles by Richardson himself.

1127 Richetti, John J. POPULAR FICTION BEFORE RICHARDSON: NARRATIVE PATTERNS 1700-1739. Oxford: Clarendon Press, 1969.

A serious analysis of the characteristic plots, stereotypes, and moral concerns exhibited in early eighteenth-century fiction; important background for the study of Richardson.

1128 Roussel, Roy. "Reflections on the Letter: The Reconciliation of Distance and Presence in PAMELA." ELH, 41 (1974), 375-99.

A detailed, helpful discussion of Richardson's use of the epistolary technique, with emphasis on the problem of authorial distance and immediacy of presentation. See also Nos. 1113, 1132, and 1142.

1129 Sale, William M., Jr. "From PAMELA to CLARISSA." THE AGE OF JOHNSON: ESSAYS PRESENTED TO CHAUNCEY BREWSTER TINKER. Ed. Frederick W. Hilles. New Haven, Conn.: Yale University Press, 1949.

An extremely important essay on Richardson's increasingly sophisticated awareness of complex class issues, an awareness dramatized in CLARISSA.

1130 Sharrock, Roger. "Richardson's PAMELA: The Gospel and the Novel." DURHAM UNIVERSITY JOURNAL, 58 (1966), 67-74.

On the relations between the structure and meaning of Richardson's novel and the form and meaning of the Gospels. Sharrock stresses the essential Christianity of PAMELA.

1131 Sherburn, George. "Samuel Richardson's Novels and the Theatre: A Theory Sketched." PQ, 41 (1962), 325-29.

Suggestions concerning Richardson's novelistic use of dramatic conventions. (See also Nos. 1104, 1109, and 1110.)

1132 _____. "Writing to the Moment: One Aspect." RESTORATION AND EIGHTEENTH-CENTURY LITERATURE: ESSAYS IN HONOR OF

ALAN DUGALD McKILLOP. Ed. Carroll Camden. Chicago: University of Chicago Press, 1963.

> On Richardson's means of achieving immediacy. (See also Nos. 1113, 1128, and 1142.)

1133 Utter, Robert P., and Gwendolyn B. Needham. PAMELA'S DAUGHTERS. New York: Macmillan, 1937.

> Pamela Andrews as the ancestress of English fictional heroines; a lively and helpful study.

1134 Van Ghent, Dorothy. "On CLARISSA HARLOWE." THE ENGLISH NOVEL: FORM AND FUNCTION. New York: Rinehart, 1953.

> A provocative, but somewhat eccentric, essay on CLARISSA as "myth."

1135 Van Marter, Shirley. "Richardson's Revisions of CLARISSA in the Second Edition." SB, 26 (1973), 107-32.

> An important essay arguing that Richardson's changes for the second edition were made not merely to satisfy his readers but to accentuate the social issues dramatized by the Harlowe family. (See also Nos. 10E1, 1095, and 1108.)

1136 Watt, Ian P. "The Naming of Characters in Defoe, Richardson, and Fielding." RES, 25 (1949), 322-38.

> A discussion of the significance of names.

1137 _____. THE RISE OF THE NOVEL: STUDIES IN DEFOE, RICHARDSON AND FIELDING. London: Chatto and Windus, 1957.

> Includes important chapters on Richardson that treat his novels as products of and responses to the conflict between the individual and contemporary social values.

1138 Wendt, Allan. "Clarissa's Coffin." PQ, 39 (1960), 481-95.

> An analysis of a famous scene in CLARISSA, together with its moral and religious implications.

1139 Wilson, Stuart. "Richardson's PAMELA: An Interpretation." PMLA, 88 (1973), 79-91.

> PAMELA as a novel that can and should be taken seriously, both morally and artistically; it is a "carefully designed and formally proportioned work."

1140 Winner, Anthony. "Richardson's Lovelace: Character and Prediction." TSLL, 14 (1972), 53-75.

An interesting discussion of Lovelace as the demonic character who understands the "fallen world" of CLARISSA better than any of the other characters, including the heroine herself.

1141 Wolff, Cynthia G. SAMUEL RICHARDSON AND THE EIGHTEENTH-CENTURY PURITAN CHARACTER. Hamden, Conn.: Archon Books, 1972.

A systematic study of the sources in Puritan literature from which Richardson drew some of his methods and conceptions of character.

1142 Zirker, Malvin R. "Richardson's Correspondence: The Personal Letter as Private Experience." THE FAMILIAR LETTER IN THE EIGHTEENTH CEN-TURY. Ed. Howard Anderson et al. Lawrence: University of Kansas Press, 1966.

In an interesting way this essay, though it focuses on Richardson's private correspondence, sheds light on the epistolary method of his novels and on the personal and artistic significance of that method. See also Nos. 1113, 1128, and 1132.

CHARLOTTE SMITH (1749-1806)

Charlotte Smith, a poet and then a prolific novelist, began her career in fiction-writing as an imitator of Richardson and Burney; she later turned from sentimental themes to try her hand at Gothic romance (in THE OLD MANOR HOUSE, 1793) and political philosophy (notably in DESMOND, 1792, MARCHMONT, 1796, and THE YOUNG PHILOSOPHER, 1798). She was among the most accomplished of a large number of late-eighteenth-century women novelists.

PRINCIPAL WORKS

ELEGIAC SONNETS, AND OTHER ESSAYS, 1784
EMMELINE, THE ORPHAN OF THE CASTLE, 1788 (Novel)
ETHELINDA, OR THE RECLUSE OF THE LAKE, 1789 (Novel)
CELESTINA. A NOVEL, 1791
DESMOND. A NOVEL, 1792
THE EMIGRANTS, A POEM, 1793
THE OLD MANOR HOUSE, 1793 (Novel)
THE BANISHED MAN. A NOVEL, 1794
MONTALBERT, A NOVEL, 1795
RURAL WALKS: IN DIALOGUES, 1795-96
MARCHMONT: A NOVEL, 1796
ELEGIAC SONNETS, AND OTHER ESSAYS, Part Two, 1797
THE YOUNG PHILOSOPHER: A NOVEL, 1798
CONVERSATIONS INTRODUCING POETRY, 1804
BEACHY HEAD: WITH OTHER POEMS, 1807

EDITIONS

EMMELINE

1143 EMMELINE: THE ORPHAN OF THE CASTLE. Ed. Anne Henry Ehrenpreis. Oxford English Novels. London: Oxford University Press, 1971.

Includes an excellent critical introduction, a chronological record of Smith's life and career, and a select bibliography. The text is reliable and the notes are helpful.

DESMOND

1144 DESMOND. A NOVEL. 3 vols. FCE.

A photofacsimile reprint of the first edition, 1792.

THE OLD MANOR HOUSE

1145 THE OLD MANOR HOUSE. Ed. Anne Henry Ehrenpreis. Oxford English Novels. London: Oxford University Press, 1969.

Includes apparatus similar to that found in No. 1143. The introduction is especially fine.

1146 THE OLD MANOR HOUSE. A NOVEL. 4 vols. FCE.

A photofacsimile reprint of the first edition, 1793.

THE YOUNG PHILOSOPHER

1147 THE YOUNG PHILOSOPHER: A NOVEL. 4 vols. FCE.

A photofacsimile reprint of the first edition, 1798.

LETTERS

1148 McKillop, Alan Dugald. "Charlotte Smith's Letters." HLQ, 15 (1952), 237-55.

Smith's letters are uncollected; this essay discusses the nearly four dozen found in the Huntington Library.

1149 See No. 1155.

BIBLIOGRAPHY

1150 McNutt, Dan J. THE EIGHTEENTH-CENTURY GOTHIC NOVEL: AN ANNOTATED BIBLIOGRAPHY OF CRITICISM AND SELECTED TEXTS. New York: Garland, 1975.

Includes a bibliography of Charlotte Smith.

1151 See No. 1152.

BIOGRAPHY

1152 Hilbish, Florence M.A. CHARLOTTE SMITH, POET AND NOVELIST. Philadelphia: University of Pennsylvania Press, 1941.

A fine critical biography; includes a bibliography.

1153 Kavanagh, Julia. ENGLISH WOMEN OF LETTERS. London, 1863.

Includes a valuable biographical study of Charlotte Smith; the essay is doubly interesting because Julia Kavanagh was a friend of Charlotte Brontë.

1154 Scott, Sir Walter. "Charlotte Smith." BIOGRAPHICAL MEMOIRS OF EMINENT NOVELISTS. Edinburgh, 1834.

1155 Turner, Rufus Paul. "Charlotte Smith (1749-1806): New Light on Her Life and Literary Career." Ph.D. dissertation, University of Southern California, 1966.

A good study that, in some respects, supersedes Hilbish (No. 1152); it includes new biographical information gleaned from letters in the Yale and Huntington libraries.

CRITICAL STUDIES AND COMMENTARIES

Charlotte Smith was an important minor writer in her day, and she deserves more attention than she has received at the hands of critics. The recent publication of EMMELINE and THE OLD MANOR HOUSE in the Oxford English Novels series has made excellently edited texts available, and perhaps scholarly interest will now follow. At present, criticism of Smith's work is found primarily in the standard histories of the English novel, and these should be consulted in addition to the studies listed below.

1156 Ehrenpreis, Anne Henry. "Introduction" to EMMELINE: THE ORPHAN OF THE CASTLE. Oxford English Novels. London: Oxford University Press, 1971.

See No. 1143.

1157 _____. "Introduction" to THE OLD MANOR HOUSE. Oxford English Novels. London: Oxford University Press, 1969.

See No. 1145.

1158 Foster, James R. "Charlotte Smith, Pre-Romantic Novelist." PMLA, 43 (1928), 463-75.

An early, more ample version of the discussion of Charlotte

Smith in Foster's HISTORY OF THE PRE-ROMANTIC NOVEL
(see No. 1159).

1159 _____. HISTORY OF THE PRE-ROMANTIC NOVEL IN ENGLAND.
New York: Modern Language Association, 1949.

Brief but excellent discussion of Charlotte Smith as she figured
in the development of the "pre-romantic" novel.

1160 Fry, Carroll Lee. "Charlotte Smith, Popular Novelist." Ph.D. dissertation, University of Nebraska, 1970.

A general study of Smith's fiction, with some astute observations on her appeal to the contemporary audience.

1161 MacCarthy, Bridget G. THE LATER WOMEN NOVELISTS, 1744-1818.
New York: William Salloch, 1948.

Includes a brief but useful discussion of Charlotte Smith as she
relates to other late-eighteenth-century women novelists.

1162 Tompkins, J.M.S. THE POPULAR NOVEL IN ENGLAND 1770-1800.
London: Constable, 1932.

Brief, scattered, but sensible comments on Charlotte Smith's
many novels.

TOBIAS SMOLLETT (1721-71)

PRINCIPAL WORKS

ADVICE, 1746 (Juvenalian verse satire)
THE TEARS OF SCOTLAND, 1746 (Poem)
REPROOF, 1747 (Juvenalian verse satire)
THE ADVENTURES OF RODERICK RANDOM, 1748 (Novel)
GIL BLAS, by LeSage, 1749 (Translation)
THE REGICIDE, 1749 (Tragedy)
THE ADVENTURES OF PEREGRINE PICKLE, 1751 (Novel)
THE ADVENTURES OF FERDINAND COUNT FATHOM, 1753 (Novel)
DON QUIXOTE, by Cervantes, 1755 (Translation)
A COMPENDIUM OF AUTHENTIC AND ENTERTAINING VOYAGES, 1756
      (Edition)
THE CRITICAL REVIEW, 1756-63 (Periodical)
THE COMPLETE HISTORY OF ENGLAND, 1757-58
THE REPRISAL, 1757 (Farce)
THE ADVENTURES OF SIR LAUNCELOT GREAVES, 1760-61 (Novel)
THE BRITISH MAGAZINE, 1760-67 (Periodical)
CONTINUATION OF THE COMPLETE HISTORY OF ENGLAND, 1760-65
THE WORKS OF VOLTAIRE, 1761-65 (Edition)
THE BRITON, 1762 (Periodical)
TRAVELS THROUGH FRANCE AND ITALY, 1766
THE PRESENT STATE OF ALL NATIONS, 1768 (History)
THE HISTORY AND ADVENTURES OF AN ATOM, 1769 (Prose satire; probably
      by Smollett)
THE EXPEDITION OF HUMPHRY CLINKER, 1771 (Novel)
ODE TO INDEPENDENCE, 1773
THE ADVENTURES OF TELEMACHUS, by Fénelon, 1776 (Translation)

EDITIONS

A. Collected Works

1163 THE MISCELLANEOUS WORKS OF TOBIAS SMOLLETT, M.D., WITH

MEMOIRS OF HIS LIFE AND WRITINGS. Ed. Robert Anderson. 6 vols. Edinburgh, 1796.

The first of some seven "standard" editions of Smollett prepared by Anderson from 1796 to 1820.

1164 THE WORKS OF TOBIAS SMOLLETT, M.D., WITH MEMOIRS OF HIS LIFE. Ed. John Moore. 8 vols. London, 1797.

A rare edition that remains important because Moore was Smollett's friend.

1165 THE MISCELLANEOUS WORKS OF TOBIAS SMOLLETT. 5 vols. Edinburgh, 1809.

A rare edition, woefully incomplete, but important because it features illustrations by Thomas Rowlandson.

1166 THE WORKS OF TOBIAS SMOLLETT. Ed. Thomas Roscoe. London, 1841.

The most popular nineteenth-century edition; incomplete (in one large volume).

1167 THE WORKS OF TOBIAS SMOLLETT. Ed. George Saintsbury. 12 vols. Edinburgh, 1895.

The novels only; modernized texts.

1168 THE WORKS OF TOBIAS SMOLLETT. Ed. W.E. Henley and Thomas Seccombe. 12 vols. London, 1899-1901.

The most comprehensive edition presently available, though it is incomplete; the texts are modernized and somewhat corrupt.

1169 THE NOVELS OF TOBIAS SMOLLETT. Shakespeare Head Edition. 11 vols. Oxford: Basil Blackwell, 1925-26.

Presently, still the best and most reliable edition of the novels; will be superseded by No. 1170.

1170 THE WORKS OF TOBIAS SMOLLETT. Ed. O.M. Brack, Jr. et al. 9 vols. projected. Newark: University of Delaware Press, 1978-- .

The first scholarly edition, now in progress. Not the complete works; included will be definitive texts of the novels, as well as volumes containing the TRAVELS, the HISTORY AND ADVENTURES OF AN ATOM, and POEMS, PLAYS, AND THE BRITON.

B. Individual Works

RODERICK RANDOM

1171 RODERICK RANDOM. Ed. H.W. Hodges. Everyman's Library. London: J.M. Dent, 1927.

1172 THE ADVENTURES OF RODERICK RANDOM. London: Oxford University Press, 1930.

1173 THE ADVENTURES OF RODERICK RANDOM. Afterword by John Barth. New York: New American Library, 1964.

> Not a scholarly edition, but Barth's afterword is among the most interesting and sensible of commentaries on Smollett and his novel.

PEREGRINE PICKLE

Most editions of this work have been based on the "expurgated" second edition, 1758, in which Smollett tightened the structure of the novel and softened his satire and his attacks on some of his contemporaries.

1174 THE ADVENTURES OF PEREGRINE PICKLE. Ed. G.K. Chesterton. 2 vols. Oxford: Limited Editions Club, 1936.

> The text is that of the first edition, 1751; no scholarly apparatus.

1175 PEREGRINE PICKLE. Ed. Walter Allen. 2 vols. Everyman's Library. London: J.M. Dent, 1956.

> The text is that of the second (revised) edition, 1758; Allen's astute critical introduction is both readable and helpful.

1176 THE ADVENTURES OF PEREGRINE PICKLE, IN WHICH ARE INCLUDED MEMOIRS OF A LADY OF QUALITY. Ed. James L. Clifford. Oxford English Novels. London: Oxford University Press, 1964.

> At present, the best edition available; based on the first edition, 1751. Includes, besides Clifford's valuable critical introduction, a select bibliography, a chronological record of Smollett's life and career, and excellent explanatory notes.

FERDINAND COUNT FATHOM

1177 THE ADVENTURES OF FERDINAND COUNT FATHOM. Ed. Damian Grant.

Oxford English Novels. London: Oxford University Press, 1971.

Includes apparatus similar to that found in No. 1176; the critical introduction is very helpful.

SIR LAUNCELOT GREAVES

1178 THE LIFE AND ADVENTURES OF SIR LAUNCELOT GREAVES. Ed. David Evans. Oxford English Novels. London: Oxford University Press, 1973.

Includes apparatus similar to that found in No. 1176; the critical introduction is valuable.

TRAVELS THROUGH FRANCE AND ITALY

1179 TRAVELS THROUGH FRANCE AND ITALY. Ed. Thomas Seccombe. London: Oxford University Press, 1919.

1180 TRAVELS THROUGH FRANCE AND ITALY. Ed. James Morris. Fontwell, Sussex, Engl.: Centaur Press, 1969.

Actually a reprint from volume 11 of the Henley edition of Smollett's WORKS (No. 1168), although this borrowing is not acknowledged.

HUMPHRY CLINKER

1181 THE EXPEDITION OF HUMPHRY CLINKER. Ed. Howard Mumford Jones and Charles Lee. Everyman's Library. London: J.M. Dent, 1943.

Includes a very worthwhile, brief, critical introduction by Jones.

1182 THE EXPEDITION OF HUMPHRY CLINKER. Ed. Lewis M. Knapp. Oxford English Novels. London: Oxford University Press, 1966.

Includes a good critical introduction, and other apparatus similar to that found in No. 1176.

1183 THE EXPEDITION OF HUMPHRY CLINKER. Ed. Angus Ross. Harmondsworth, Engl.: Penguin Books, 1967.

Includes a brief but helpful critical introduction.

1184 THE EXPEDITION OF HUMPHRY CLINKER. Ed. André Parreaux. Boston: Houghton Mifflin, 1968.

Includes a good introduction.

LETTERS

1185 THE LETTERS OF TOBIAS SMOLLETT, M.D. Ed. Edward S. Noyes. Cambridge, Mass.: Harvard University Press, 1926.

> A scholarly edition; includes sixty-eight letters complete, together with fragments of several others.

1186 LETTERS OF TOBIAS GEORGE SMOLLETT: A SUPPLEMENT TO THE NOYES COLLECTION. Ed. Francesco Cordasco. Madrid: Avelino Ortega Cuesta de Sancti-Spiritus, 1950.

> Adds thirty-one letters to the Noyes collection (No. 1185); five of these (Letters 19, 26, 29, 30, and 31) are forgeries. This volume also contains a bibliography of collected editions of Smollett's works; the listing is helpful but not complete.

1187 THE LETTERS OF TOBIAS SMOLLETT. Ed. Lewis M. Knapp. Oxford: Clarendon Press, 1970.

> The standard edition.

1188 See Nos. 1198 and 1200.

BIBLIOGRAPHY

1189 Cordasco, Francesco. SMOLLETT CRITICISM, 1770-1924: A BIBLIOGRAPHY ENUMERATIVE AND ANNOTATIVE. Brooklyn, N.Y.: Long Island University Press, 1948.

> A checklist that, together with its continuation (No. 1190), provides a useful record, despite Cordasco's occasional inaccuracies. For supplementary information see Paul-Gabriel Boucé, "Smollett Criticism, 1770-1924; Corrections and Additions." N&Q, 212 (1967), 184-87. See also Korte's listing (No. 1192) for the years 1946-68.

1190 _____. SMOLLETT CRITICISM, 1925-1945: A COMPILATION. Brooklyn, N.Y.: Long Island University Press, 1947.

> A continuation of No. 1189. (See also No. 1192.)

1191 Knapp, Lewis M. "Smollett." THE ENGLISH NOVEL: SELECT BIBLIOGRAPHICAL GUIDES. Ed. A.E. Dyson. London: Oxford University Press, 1974.

> An excellent bibliographical essay covering primary and secondary materials; provides a succinct account of Smollett's reputation over the past 200 years and of trends in Smollett biography and criticism.

1192 Korte, Donald M. AN ANNOTATED BIBLIOGRAPHY OF SMOLLETT SCHOLARSHIP 1946-68. Toronto: University of Toronto Press, 1969.

> A continuation of the listings by Cordasco (Nos. 1189 and 1190).

1193 Newman, Franklin B. "A Consideration of the Bibliographical Problems Connected with the First Edition of HUMPHRY CLINKER." PBSA, 44 (1950), 340-71.

> On the complicated relationships between what appear to have been two "first" editions of Smollett's novel, with some attention to the third and fourth editions, 1771 and 1772.

1194 Norwood, L.F. "A Descriptive Bibliography of the Creative Works of Tobias Smollett." Ph.D. dissertation, Yale University, 1931.

1195 See Nos. 1186, 1197, 1208, 1209, 1224, and 1225.

BIOGRAPHY

1196 Brander, Lawrence. SMOLLETT. Writers and Their Work, No. 11. London: Longmans, Green, 1951.

> A brief, helpful "biocritical" introduction to Smollett's life and works.

1197 Hannay, David. LIFE OF TOBIAS GEORGE SMOLLETT. London, 1887.

> Still a useful account, though later biographers have found and corrected mistakes made by Hannay; includes a valuable bibliography of Smollett by John P. Anderson of the British Museum.

1198 Irving, Joseph. SOME ACCOUNT OF THE FAMILY OF SMOLLETT OF BONHILL. Dumbarton, 1860.

> Valuable for the genealogy of the Smollett family and for data from the manuscript collection at Cameron House; includes some letters.

1199 Knapp, Lewis M. TOBIAS SMOLLETT: DOCTOR OF MEN AND MANNERS. Princeton, N.J.: Princeton University Press, 1949.

> The standard biography.

1200 Melville, Lewis [L.S. Benjamin]. THE LIFE AND LETTERS OF TOBIAS SMOLLETT. London: Faber and Gwyer, 1926.

An unscholarly, unreliable study; includes a number of letters, but without annotations.

1201 Moore, John. "Memoirs." THE WORKS OF TOBIAS SMOLLETT, M.D., WITH MEMOIRS OF HIS LIFE. 8 vols. London, 1797.

(See No. 1164.) A biographical essay that is often vague, but nonetheless valuable because Moore was Smollett's friend.

1202 Spector, Robert Donald. TOBIAS GEORGE SMOLLETT. New York: Twayne, 1968.

A good critical biography, written primarily for the nonspecialist.

1203 See Nos. 1212, 1224, 1226, and 1253.

CRITICAL STUDIES AND COMMENTARIES

1204 Alter, Robert. "The Picaroon as Fortune's Plaything." ROGUE'S PROGRESS: STUDIES IN THE PICARESQUE NOVEL. Cambridge, Mass.: Harvard University Press, 1964.

Smollett's fictional view that "life is at best a paltry province" is at odds with the picaresque world view; yet of the "prominent eighteenth-century novelists in England, it was Tobias Smollett who most intentionally and explicitly sought to place his narratives in the continental tradition of the picaresque novel." This study emphasizes RODERICK RANDOM.

1205 Baker, Sheridan. "HUMPHRY CLINKER as Comic Romance." PAPERS OF THE MICHIGAN ACADEMY OF SCIENCE, ARTS AND LETTERS, 46 (1961), 645-54.

Baker borrows the term "comic romance" from Fielding and attempts to show that (like JOSEPH ANDREWS) HUMPHRY CLINKER spoofs romance, meanwhile satirizing the facades that man erects to cover his nature, which Smollett symbolizes in the bodily functions. An important article, published in an inaccessible place, but luckily reprinted in ESSAYS ON THE EIGHTEENTH-CENTURY NOVEL, ed. Robert Donald Spector (Bloomington: Indiana University Press, 1965).

1206 Beasley, Jerry C. "English Fiction in the 1740's: Some Glances at the Major and Minor Novels." SNNTS, 5 (1973), 155-75.

An attempt to show that, despite their differences, Smollett, Fielding, and Richardson all exploited contemporary themes, methods, and types of fiction.

1207 _____. "Romance and the 'New' Novels of Richardson, Fielding, and Smollett." SEL, 16 (1976), 437-50.

The three major novelists of the 1740's all borrowed to some extent from the themes and conventions of romance.

1208 Boege, Fred W. SMOLLETT'S REPUTATION AS A NOVELIST. Princeton, N.J.: Princeton University Press, 1947.

An analysis of critical attitudes toward Smollett, from the eighteenth century on; includes a bibliography.

1209 Boucé, Paul-Gabriel. THE NOVELS OF TOBIAS SMOLLETT. London: Longmans, Green, 1976.

The best full-length critical study of Smollett's fiction; contains an extensive "Select Bibliography" of Smollett studies. Translated by Boucé and Antonia White from LES ROMANS DE SMOLLETT: ÉTUDE CRITIQUE (Paris: Didier, 1971).

1210 Brack, O.M., Jr., and James B. Davis. "Smollett's Revisions of RODERICK RANDOM." PBSA, 64 (1970), 295-311.

A presentation of textual evidence to demonstrate the substantive changes made by Smollett through the first four editions of the novel.

1211 Bruce, Donald. RADICAL DOCTOR SMOLLETT. London: Gollancz, 1964.

An unscholarly, sometimes inaccurate, but often provocative work that urges a view of Smollett as a radical in reaction to contemporary scientific, medical, and intellectual currents.

1212 Buck, Howard Swazey. A STUDY IN SMOLLETT, CHIEFLY PEREGRINE PICKLE, WITH A COMPLETE COLLATION OF THE FIRST AND SECOND EDITIONS. New Haven, Conn.: Yale University Press, 1925.

A fine book, long regarded as the beginning of modern Smollett scholarship. Buck uses PEREGRINE PICKLE to correct Smollett biography and to demonstrate methods of composition; the analysis of the revision of PEREGRINE PICKLE illustrates the personal and artistic significance of the changes.

1213 Copeland, Edward [W.]. "HUMPHRY CLINKER: A Pastoral Poem in Prose." TSLL, 16 (1974), 493-501.

The benign tone of Smollett's last novel differs sharply from the caustic satire of the early works and may be accounted for in part by his interest in pastoral. HUMPHRY CLINKER may actually be described as a "comic pastoral poem in prose."

1214 Donovan, Robert Alan. THE SHAPING VISION: IMAGINATION IN THE ENGLISH NOVEL FROM DEFOE TO DICKENS. Ithaca, N.Y.: Cornell University Press, 1966.

> Includes a chapter on HUMPHRY CLINKER that argues for a thematic approach, but with emphasis on "the way the raw materials of observation are transformed by the idiosyncracies of the various observers into feelings, beliefs, and valuations which are of interest because of the special relation in which they stand to the persons who hold them."

1215 Evans, David L. "HUMPHRY CLINKER: Smollett's Tempered Augustanism." CRITICISM, 9 (1967), 257–74.

> An interesting discussion of how Smollett's last novel both exploits and transcends Augustan literary values.

1216 _____. "Peregrine Pickle: The Complete Satirist." SNNTS, 3 (1971), 258–74.

> Satiric techniques and the human implications of a satiric world view are both subject matter and theme in Smollett's second novel, and Peregrine himself is both hero and satirist.

1217 Foster, James R. "Smollett and the ATOM." PMLA, 68 (1953), 1032–46.

> An attempt to establish that Smollett was indeed the author of THE HISTORY AND ADVENTURES OF AN ATOM; the evidence is circumstantial and presumptive, but the argument is persuasive.

1218 Gassman, Byron. "The BRITON and HUMPHRY CLINKER." SEL, 3 (1963), 397–414.

> A discussion of the political background of the novel, as reflected in the BRITON.

1219 _____. "HUMPHRY CLINKER and the Two Kingdoms of George III." CRITICISM, 16 (1974), 95–108.

> In Smollett's view, the reign of George III signified England's last opportunity to realize the Augustan vision of the ideal kingdom ruled by a patriot king. HUMPHRY CLINKER dramatizes this opportunity and reveals the consequences in vulgarity and continued moral decay should the nation fail to seize it.

1220 Giddings, Robert. THE TRADITION OF SMOLLETT. London: Methuen, 1967.

> An assessment of Smollett's indebtedness to various traditions

of fiction; especially good on the picaresque.

1221 Goldberg, M.A. SMOLLETT AND THE SCOTTISH SCHOOL: STUDIES IN EIGHTEENTH-CENTURY THOUGHT. Albuquerque: University of New Mexico Press, 1959.

An approach to Smollett through the history of ideas, attempting to link his work to the Scottish Common-Sense School of empiricist philosophy.

1222 Helmick, E.T. "Voltaire and HUMPHRY CLINKER." STUDIES IN VOLTAIRE AND THE EIGHTEENTH CENTURY, 67 (1969), 59-64.

CANDIDE greatly influenced Smollett, and this accounts for some of the differences between HUMPHRY CLINKER and his earlier fiction.

1223 Iser, Wolfgang. "The Generic Control of the Aesthetic Response: An Examination of Smollett's HUMPHRY CLINKER." SOUTHERN HUMANITIES REVIEW, 3 (1969), 243-57.

An interesting discussion of Smollett's sense of genre and its impact on artistic performance and aesthetic responses.

1224 Joliat, Eugène. SMOLLETT ET LA FRANCE. Paris: Champion, 1935.

Partly biographical, but more important for its treatment of Smollett's views of, experiences in, and portrayals of France and things French in his novels and other works. Includes a useful bibliography.

1225 Jones, Claude E. SMOLLETT STUDIES. Berkeley and Los Angeles: University of California Press, 1942.

Contains two essays: "Smollett and the Navy" and "Smollett and the CRITICAL REVIEW." Both essays are useful on their subjects, but the first is superficial on the relationships between Smollett's nautical experiences and his fiction. Includes bibliographies.

1226 Kahrl, George M. TOBIAS SMOLLETT: TRAVELER-NOVELIST. Chicago: University of Chicago Press, 1945.

Kahrl's premise is that "a study of Smollett's prose fiction in terms of his varied travel interests and experiences would result in a more discriminating and just appraisal of his novels as literature." He proves the justice of his premise, especially in his treatment of Smollett's style as it was influenced by the literature and actual experience of travel and in his assessment of the uses to which Smollett put his experience in RODERICK RANDOM, PEREGRINE PICKLE, and HUMPHRY CLINKER.

1227 Knapp, Lewis M. "The Naval Scenes in RODERICK RANDOM." PMLA, 49 (1934), 593-98.

A brief discussion of the origins and the significance of the scenes relating to the novel's version of the naval expedition to Carthagena and Roderick's part in it.

1228 _____. "Smollett's Self-Portrait in THE EXPEDITION OF HUMPHRY CLINKER." THE AGE OF JOHNSON: ESSAYS PRESENTED TO CHAUNCEY BREWSTER TINKER. Ed. Frederick W. Hilles. New Haven, Conn.: Yale University Press, 1949.

An excellent essay on Smollett and Matt Bramble.

1229 Knapp, Lewis M., and Lillian de la Torre. "Smollett, MacKercher, and the Annesley Claimant." ELN, 1 (1963), 28-33.

An account of some of the facts connected with the celebrated Annesley case introduced by Smollett into PEREGRINE PICKLE.

1230 Linsalata, Carmine R. SMOLLETT'S HOAX: DON QUIXOTE IN EN-GLISH. Stanford, Calif.: Stanford University Press, 1956.

On the question of just how much of Smollett's translation is his own.

1231 McKillop, Alan Dugald. THE EARLY MASTERS OF ENGLISH FICTION. Lawrence: University of Kansas Press, 1956.

Includes a chapter on Smollett that is the best brief critical introduction to his fiction.

1232 Martz, Louis L. THE LATER CAREER OF TOBIAS SMOLLETT. New Haven, Conn.: Yale University Press, 1942.

An exhaustive critical study of the drudgery of the later years --the histories, the journalism, the editing tasks; especially valuable for the assessment of the impact of these labors on HUMPHRY CLINKER.

1233 _____. "Smollett and the Expedition to Carthagena." PMLA, 56 (1941), 428-46.

An essay that, though partly biographical, sheds light on the naval episodes in RODERICK RANDOM.

1234 Orowitz, Milton. "Smollett and the Art of Caricature." SPECTRUM, 2 (1958), 155-67.

A fine discussion of an important aspect of Smollett's methods of characterization.

1235 Paulson, Ronald. "Satire in the Early Novels of Smollett." JEGP, 59 (1960), 381-402.

> An attempt to show that RODERICK RANDOM and PEREGRINE PICKLE are Juvenalian satires in an adapted form, with the heroes as _personae_ observing vices and scourging the wicked. An altered and expanded version of this article appears in Paulson's book, SATIRE AND THE NOVEL IN EIGHTEENTH-CENTURY ENGLAND (New Haven, Conn.: Yale University Press, 1967). The book also includes a comparative discussion of Smollett and Sterne as novelistic satirists.

1236 Piper, William B. "The Large Diffused Picture of Life in Smollett's Early Novels." SP, 60 (1963), 45-56.

> On Smollett's panoramic sweep and his extraordinary range of character types and scenery.

1237 Preston, Thomas R. "Disenchanting the Man of Feeling: Smollett's FERDINAND COUNT FATHOM." QUICK SPRINGS OF SENSE: STUDIES IN THE EIGHTEENTH CENTURY. Ed. Larry S. Champion. Athens: University of Georgia Press, 1974.

> Fathom is deliberately projected as an object lesson to the "man of feeling," as an example of what most threatens goodness and benevolence. Thus Smollett "totally inverts the sentimental exemplary formula by appealing not to the alluring powers of virtue to deter vice, but to fear."

1238 _____. "Smollett and the Benevolent Misanthrope Type." PMLA, 79 (1964), 51-57.

> Especially interesting on Commodore Trunnion and Matt Bramble as type characters.

1239 _____. "The 'Stage Passions' and Smollett's Characterization." SP, 71 (1974), 105-25.

> Smollett adapts the stage device of rendering emotional states through external behavior, thus creating universal types whose emotional life is most meaningful when seen in a context of causes, effects, moral relevancy, and social implications. An interesting and helpful essay.

1240 Pritchett, V.S. THE LIVING NOVEL. New York: Reynal and Hitchcock, 1947.

> Includes a critical discussion of Smollett that is an excellent general assessment, especially interesting for its observations on links between Smollett's novels and twentieth-century fiction.

1241 Putney, Rufus. "The Plan of PEREGRINE PICKLE." PMLA, 60 (1945), 1051-65.

> An essential discussion of Smollett's second novel, which, Putney demonstrates, has a clear plan that had escaped previous commentators on the work.

1242 _____. "Smollett and Lady Vane's Memoirs." PQ, 25 (1946), 120-26.

> On the role of the "Memoirs of a Lady of Quality" in PEREGRINE PICKLE, and the question of their authorship.

1243 Read, Herbert. REASON AND ROMANTICISM: ESSAYS IN LITERARY CRITICISM. London: Faber and Gwyer, 1926.

> Includes a landmark essay that helped to establish new attitudes toward Smollett and in particular to dash complaints about his obscenity.

1244 Rothstein, Eric. SYSTEMS OF ORDER AND INQUIRY IN LATER EIGHTEENTH-CENTURY FICTION. Berkeley and Los Angeles: University of California Press, 1975.

> The circular structure, the pairing of characters, the epistolary convention, and other devices impose order upon HUMPHRY CLINKER and provide a system for the novel's inquiry into values, human feelings, and motives. A strained argument but sometimes very insightful.

1245 Rousseau, G[eorge] S., and Paul-Gabriel Boucé, eds. TOBIAS SMOLLETT: BICENTENNIAL ESSAYS PRESENTED TO LEWIS M. KNAPP. New York: Oxford University Press, 1971.

> An important collection of ten essays by Smollett scholars.

1246 Siebert, Donald T. "The Role of the Senses in HUMPHRY CLINKER." SNNTS, 6 (1974), 17-26.

> A discussion of Smollett's sense imagery as the basis of the novel's thematic commentary; the proper context for the understanding of the imagery is Lockean.

1247 Stevick, Philip. "Stylistic Energy in Early Smollett." SP, 64 (1967), 712-19.

> On the exuberance and often violent style of the early novels. "Whatever the artifice of that violent, hyperbolic style of his novels, it is in measure a spontaneous extension of a hyperbolic private style, passionate in the extreme because that is what life invites, defensive in the extreme because the writer is demonstrably menaced."

1248 Strauss, Albrecht B. "On Smollett's Language: A Paragraph in FERDI-
NAND COUNT FATHOM." STYLE IN PROSE FICTION: ENGLISH
INSTITUTE ESSAYS, 1958. New York: Columbia University Press, 1959.

An extremely valuable, precise study of Smollett's style.

1249 Thackeray, William Makepeace. THE ENGLISH HUMOURISTS OF THE
EIGHTEENTH CENTURY. Everyman's Library. London: J.M. Dent,
1929.

Lecture V (1853) includes a discussion of Smollett, in which
he is scolded for his coarseness, compared unfavorably with
Fielding, and yet praised for the amusement afforded by HUM-
PHRY CLINKER. Thackeray's views were extremely influential
in the nineteenth century.

1250 Warner, John M. "The Interpolated Narratives in the Fiction of Fielding
and Smollett: An Epistemological View." SNNTS, 5 (1973), 271-83.

Fielding's digressions, Warner believes, provide for a dialectical relationship with the main narrative, successfully supporting structures based on a principle of "epistemological uncertainty"; Smollett attempts the same, and fails in all but his
last novel (HUMPHRY CLINKER), where he finally achieves
the kind of balance Fielding had reached in JOSEPH AN-
DREWS and TOM JONES.

1251 _____. "Smollett's Development as a Novelist." NOVEL, 5 (1972),
148-61.

On Smollett's artistic growth from RODERICK RANDOM to
HUMPHRY CLINKER, with particular attention to the epistemological interests that, according to Warner, put him ahead
of his time and made him a "Pre-Romantic."

1252 West, William. "Matt Bramble's Journey to Health." TSLL, 11 (1969),
1197-1208.

Matt Bramble has grown into physical health by the end of his
journey (in HUMPHRY CLINKER) because he has learned the
value of "activity, temperance, and peace of mind."

1253 Whitridge, Arnold. TOBIAS SMOLLETT: A STUDY OF HIS MISCELLA-
NEOUS WORKS. New York: Printed for the Author, 1925.

A fairly useful general introduction for the nonspecialist; partly
biographical, with little emphasis on the novels.

LAURENCE STERNE (1713-68)

PRINCIPAL WORKS

THE LIFE AND OPINIONS OF TRISTRAM SHANDY, 1759-67 (Novel)
A POLITICAL ROMANCE [THE HISTORY OF A GOOD WARM WATCHCOAT],
    1759 (Ecclesiastical satire)
SERMONS OF MR. YORICK, 1760-69
A SENTIMENTAL JOURNEY THROUGH FRANCE AND ITALY, 1768 (Novel)
LETTERS FROM YORICK TO ELIZA [THE JOURNAL TO ELIZA], 1773 (Diary
    kept for Mrs. Elizabeth Draper)

EDITIONS

A. Collected Works

1254 THE WORKS AND LIFE OF LAURENCE STERNE. Ed. Wilbur L. Cross.
12 vols. New York: J.F. Taylor, 1904.

> This and the Shakespeare Head Edition (No. 1255) are the
> standard collections; both will be superseded by No. 1256.

1255 THE SHAKESPEARE HEAD EDITION OF THE WRITINGS OF LAURENCE
STERNE. 7 vols. Oxford: Basil Blackwell, 1926-27.

1256 A new edition of the collected works of Laurence Sterne. Ed. Melvyn
New et al. 7 vols. projected. Gainesville: University of Florida Press,
forthcoming.

> To be the definitive edition; the first volumes are expected in
> the fall of 1977.

B. Selections

1257 STERNE: MEMOIRS OF MR. LAURENCE STERNE; THE LIFE AND OPIN-

237

IONS OF TRISTRAM SHANDY; A SENTIMENTAL JOURNEY; SELECTED
SERMONS AND LETTERS. Ed. Douglas Grant. London: Reynard Library, 1950.

1258 A SENTIMENTAL JOURNEY THROUGH FRANCE AND ITALY; THE JOUR-
NAL TO ELIZA; A POLITICAL ROMANCE. Ed. Ian Jack. Oxford English Novels. London: Oxford University Press, 1968.

> A fine scholarly edition, with an excellent critical introduc-
> tion, a select bibliography, and a chronology of Sterne's life
> and career.

C. Individual Works

TRISTRAM SHANDY

1259 THE LIFE AND OPINIONS OF TRISTRAM SHANDY, GENTLEMAN. Ed.
James Aiken Work. New York: Odyssey Press, 1940.

> Still the best scholarly edition of the novel.

1260 THE LIFE AND OPINIONS OF TRISTRAM SHANDY, GENTLEMAN. Ed.
Ian [P.] Watt. Boston: Houghton Mifflin, 1965.

> A good scholarly edition, with an especially helpful critical
> introduction.

1261 THE LIFE AND OPINIONS OF TRISTRAM SHANDY, GENTLEMAN. Ed.
Graham Petrie. Harmondsworth, Engl.: Penguin Books, 1967.

> Includes an excellent critical introduction.

1262 See No. 1257.

A POLITICAL ROMANCE

1263 See No. 1258.

SENTIMENTAL JOURNEY

1264 A SENTIMENTAL JOURNEY THROUGH FRANCE AND ITALY. Ed.
Graham Petrie. Intro. A. Alvarez. Harmondsworth, Engl.: Penguin
Books, 1967.

> Includes a very helpful introduction by Alvarez; Petrie's notes
> are excellent.

1265 A SENTIMENTAL JOURNEY THROUGH FRANCE AND ITALY BY MR. YORICK. Ed. Gardner D. Stout, Jr. Berkeley and Los Angeles: University of California Press, 1967.

> The definitive edition. The introduction includes an important critical discussion of Sterne's work.

1266 A SHORT CONCORDANCE TO LAURENCE STERNE'S A SENTIMENTAL JOURNEY THROUGH FRANCE AND ITALY BY MR. YORICK. Ed. Betty B. Pasta et al. 2 vols. Princeton, N.J., and Washington, D.C.: Princeton University and the National Science Foundation, 1974.

> A computer-assisted concordance covering some 26,188 words of the original 40,635 word text. The copy-text is that of the standard edition, edited by Gardner D. Stout, Jr. (No. 1265).

1267 See Nos. 1257 and 1258.

LETTERS

1268 LETTERS BY LAURENCE STERNE. Ed. Lewis Perry Curtis. London: Oxford University Press, 1935.

> The standard edition; includes the first complete and authoritative text of THE JOURNAL TO ELIZA (see also No. 1269).

1269 THE JOURNAL TO ELIZA. Ed. Ian Jack. Oxford English Novels. London: Oxford University Press, 1968

> (See No. 1258.) This important journal, kept for Elizabeth Draper, was composed in 1767, simultaneously with a SENTIMENTAL JOURNEY. (See also No. 1268.)

1270 See No. 1257.

BIBLIOGRAPHY

1271 Cordasco, Francesco. LAURENCE STERNE: A LIST OF CRITICAL STUDIES FROM 1896 TO 1946. Brooklyn, N.Y.: Long Island University Press, 1948.

> A lengthy list, with many errors and curious omissions.

1272 Hartley, Lodwick. LAURENCE STERNE IN THE TWENTIETH CENTURY: AN ESSAY AND A BIBLIOGRAPHY OF STERNEAN STUDIES 1900-1968. Rev. ed. Chapel Hill: University of North Carolina Press, 1968.

> An indispensable work of scholarship. The "essay" is an exten-

sive discussion of trends in modern Sterne studies; the bibliography is nearly exhaustive, and it provides full and helpful annotations.

1273 Isles, Duncan. "Sterne." THE ENGLISH NOVEL: SELECT BIBLIO-GRAPHICAL GUIDES. Ed. A.E. Dyson. London: Oxford University Press, 1974.

A very helpful bibliographical essay, with unusually detailed descriptions of major works of scholarship.

1274 Yoklavich, John M. "Notes on the Early Editions of TRISTRAM SHANDY." PMLA, 63 (1948), 508-19.

The record provided by Yoklavich is especially useful for those interested in the reception of Sterne's novel.

1275 See No. 1296.

BIOGRAPHY

1276 Cash, Arthur H. LAURENCE STERNE: THE EARLY AND MIDDLE YEARS. London: Methuen, 1975.

The first installment of what will be the definitive biography when it is completed.

1277 Cross, Wilbur L. THE LIFE AND TIMES OF LAURENCE STERNE. 3rd ed., rev. New Haven, Conn.: Yale University Press, 1929.

Not a critical biography, but still an excellent account of Sterne's life.

1278 Fluchère, Henri. LAURENCE STERNE, DE L'HOMME À L'OEUVRE: BIOGRAPHIE CRITIQUE ET ESSAI D'INTERPRETATION DE TRISTRAM SHANDY. Paris: Gallimard, 1961.

The first part of this study is an excellent but brief critical biography; the second part, a close critical analysis of TRISTRAM SHANDY, has been translated by Barbara Bray as LAURENCE STERNE: FROM TRISTRAM TO YORICK. AN INTERPRETATION OF TRISTRAM SHANDY (London: Oxford University Press, 1965).

1279 Hartley, Lodwick. LAURENCE STERNE: A BIOGRAPHICAL ESSAY. Chapel Hill: University of North Carolina Press, 1968.

An introduction to Sterne biography, written for the nonspecialist.

1280 James, Overton Philip. THE RELATION OF TRISTRAM SHANDY TO THE LIFE OF STERNE. The Hague: Mouton, 1966.

> An attempt to untangle the complicated and often misunderstood relationships between Sterne's novel (especially its narrator) and his life. The emphasis is primarily biographical.

1281 Jefferson, D.W. STERNE. Writers and Their Work, No. 52. London: Longmans, Green, 1954.

> An excellent, brief "biocritical" introduction to Sterne's life and works.

1282 Piper, William B. LAURENCE STERNE. New York: Twayne, 1965.

> A good "biocritical" introduction to Sterne's life and works; useful for the specialist and the nonspecialist alike.

1283 Shaw, Margaret R.B. LAURENCE STERNE: THE MAKING OF A HUMORIST, 1713-1762. London: Richards Press, 1957.

> A "biocritical" study leading up to the early volumes of TRISTRAM SHANDY.

1284 Thomson, David. WILD EXCURSIONS: THE LIFE AND FICTION OF LAURENCE STERNE. London: Weidenfeld and Nicolson, 1972.

> A good critical biography, particularly for the nonspecialist.

CRITICAL STUDIES AND COMMENTARIES

1285 Alter, Robert. "TRISTRAM SHANDY and the Game of Love." AMERICAN SCHOLAR, 37 (1968), 316-23.

> An important discussion of Sterne's technique of witty sexual innuendo as an artistic device designed to amuse and to further the novel's philosophical statement.

1286 Anderson, Howard. "Answers to the Author of CLARISSA: Theme and Narrative Technique in TOM JONES and TRISTRAM SHANDY." PQ, 51 (1972), 859-73.

> The masterpieces of Fielding and Sterne are seen as deliberate responses, or alternatives in substance and form, to Richardson's masterpiece.

1287 _____. "Associationism and Wit in TRISTRAM SHANDY." PQ, 48 (1969), 27-41.

> A study of the complexities of the influence of Montaigne and

Locke and their importance to Sterne's novel as an expression of his wit. For Montaigne, associationism led to, and was an expression of, true wit; for Locke, associationism was a real but aberrant form of intellectual behavior.

1288 _____. "Sterne's Letters: Consciousness and Sympathy." THE FA-MILIAR LETTER IN THE EIGHTEENTH CENTURY. Ed. Howard Anderson et al. Lawrence: University of Kansas Press, 1966.

An important study of Sterne's letters as artistic creations.

1289 _____. "TRISTRAM SHANDY and the Reader's Imagination." PMLA, 86 (1971), 966-73.

Sterne implicates us, his readers, and makes us confront our-selves. His principal methods lead us to lay bare our own prejudices and our follies: we are tempted foolishly to judge situations under analysis by the characters; we are made to trip over the multiple meanings of words and to stumble into false expectations of narrative form.

1290 Baird, Theodore. "The Time-Scheme of TRISTRAM SHANDY and a Source." PMLA, 51 (1936), 803-20.

An early, systematic "straightening-out" of the chronology of Tristram's narrative.

1291 Booth, Wayne C. THE RHETORIC OF FICTION. Chicago: University of Chicago Press, 1961.

Includes a discussion of narrative technique in TRISTRAM SHANDY that is invaluable. It identifies the narrative tradi-tions in the background of Sterne's novel, analyzes in detail the function of Tristram as comic narrator, and persuasively defines the novel as a deliberately unfinished but unified and complete work of art.

1292 Cash, Arthur H. "The Birth of Tristram Shandy: Sterne and Dr. Burton." STUDIES IN THE EIGHTEENTH CENTURY. Ed. R.F. Brissenden. Can-berra: Australian National University Press, 1968.

Dr. John Burton, his obstetrical practice and his instruments, provided background for the details of Tristram's birth. A fascinating essay, and a valuable one, despite its technical content.

1293 _____. "The Lockean Psychology of TRISTRAM SHANDY." ELH, 22 (1955), 125-35.

A penetrating study, with detailed analyses of crucial passages and the issues they raise.

1294 _____. "The Sermon in TRISTRAM SHANDY." ELH, 31 (1964), 395–417.

A discussion of the appropriateness of Sterne's decision to include, verbatim, one of his own sermons in TRISTRAM SHANDY (vol. II, chap. 17). The sermon itself receives close analysis, and the effect of Cash's discussion is to comment usefully on Sterne's eccentric methods of composition.

1295 _____. STERNE'S COMEDY OF MORAL SENTIMENTS: THE ETHICAL DIMENSION OF THE JOURNEY. Pittsburgh: Duquesne University Press, 1966.

The most comprehensive study of A SENTIMENTAL JOURNEY; emphasizes Sterne's ethics as reflected in the novel, with attention to the relationship between the JOURNEY and Sterne's sermons.

1296 Cash, Arthur H., and John M. Stedmond, eds. THE WINGED SKULL: PAPERS FROM THE LAURENCE STERNE BICENTENARY CONFERENCE. Kent, Ohio: Kent State University Press, 1971.

An extremely important collection of essays by the leading modern Sterne scholars. Included are: critical discussions of the novels and their composition, considerations of Sterne's reputation in numerous foreign countries, studies of Sterne and contemporary philosophy, essays on Sterne and modern literature, and various checklists and bibliographies.

1297 Crane, Ronald S. "Suggestions toward a Genealogy of the 'Man of Feeling.'" THE IDEA OF THE HUMANITIES, I. Ed. Wayne C. Booth. Chicago: University of Chicago Press, 1967.

The very best discussion of how social, philosophical, and literary currents converged in the eighteenth century to produce the sentimental hero; essential to students of Sterne.

1298 DePorte, Michael V. NIGHTMARES AND HOBBYHORSES: SWIFT, STERNE, AND AUGUSTAN IDEAS OF MADNESS. San Marino, Calif.: Huntington Library, 1974.

An illuminating discussion of the ways in which A TALE OF A TUB and TRISTRAM SHANDY relate to eighteenth-century notions of insanity.

1299 Dilworth, Ernest N. THE UNSENTIMENTAL JOURNEY OF LAURENCE STERNE. New York: King's Crown Press, 1948.

A clever, provocative, somewhat irreverent study of Sterne (and especially A SENTIMENTAL JOURNEY) that single-mindedly pursues the argument that Sterne was mocking the sentimental tradition.

1300 Donovan, Robert Alan. THE SHAPING VISION: IMAGINATION IN THE ENGLISH NOVEL FROM DEFOE TO DICKENS. Ithaca, N.Y.: Cornell University Press, 1966.

> TRISTRAM SHANDY resists conventional critical distinctions such as "the categories of plot and character, diction and thought," but nevertheless has "an identifiable substance and form." Donovan finds Sterne's language--its ironies, its ambiguities, its richness in the rendering of consciousnesses--to be the force that gives shape and meaning to the novel.

1301 Dyson, A.E. "Sterne: The Novelist as Jester." CRITICAL QUARTERLY, 4 (1962), 309-20.

> On one aspect of Sterne's theoretical conception of the role and function of the novelist.

1302 Farrell, William J. "Nature versus Art as a Comic Pattern in TRISTRAM SHANDY." ELH, 30 (1963), 16-36.

> A thorough study of Sterne's version of a conventional theme of eighteenth-century comic literature.

1303 Fluchère, Henri. LAURENCE STERNE: FROM TRISTRAM TO YORICK. AN INTERPRETATION OF TRISTRAM SHANDY. Trans. Barbara Bray. London: Oxford University Press, 1965.

> See No. 1278.

1304 Fredman, Alice Green. DIDEROT AND STERNE. New York: Columbia University Press, 1955.

> A thorough study of the relationships between the two writers.

1305 Frye, Northrop. "Towards Defining an Age of Sensibility." ELH, 23 (1956), 144-52.

> An essential discussion; of great interest to students of Sterne, the foremost novelist of sensibility.

1306 Hall, Joan J. "The Hobbyhorsical World of TRISTRAM SHANDY." MLQ, 24 (1963), 131-43.

> A useful discussion of how the "hobbyhorse" metaphor helps to define the entire world of Sterne's novel.

1307 Hammond, Lansing van der H. LAURENCE STERNE'S SERMONS OF MR. YORICK. New Haven, Conn.: Yale University Press, 1948.

> A detailed study of the sermons, with emphasis on their literary qualities.

1308 Holtz, William V. IMAGE AND IMMORTALITY: A STUDY OF TRIS-
TRAM SHANDY. Providence, R.I.: Brown University Press, 1970.

A "sister arts" approach to TRISTRAM SHANDY: Sterne joined
the techniques of the pictorial artist (especially Hogarth) with
those of the novelist.

1309 Howes, Alan B. YORICK AND THE CRITICS: STERNE'S REPUTATION
IN ENGLAND, 1760-1868. New Haven, Conn.: Yale University Press,
1958.

An excellent study of trends in early Sterne criticism.

1310 _____, ed. STERNE: THE CRITICAL HERITAGE. London: Routledge
and Kegan Paul, 1974.

A collection of extracts from early Sterne criticism.

1311 Hunt, J.H. Leigh. ESSAY ON WIT AND HUMOUR. London, 1846.

Includes a sympathetic discussion of Sterne as a masterful comic
writer whose Uncle Toby is among the finest of all humorous
characters. For a contrary Victorian attitude toward Sterne,
see No. 1342.

1312 Hunter, J. Paul. "Response as Reformation: TRISTRAM SHANDY and
the Art of Interruption." NOVEL, 4 (1971), 132-46.

Sterne, like Fielding, uses interruption as an artful didactic
device; the technique is an alternative to straightforward moral
discourse, and its effectiveness develops from the tactic of
showing how the characters react to the interpolations.

1313 Jefferson, D.W. "TRISTRAM SHANDY and the Tradition of Learned Wit."
ESSAYS IN CRITICISM, 1 (1951), 225-48.

The tradition of "learned wit," as exemplified in such earlier
writers as Rabelais and Swift, provided the form that gives
coherence to Sterne's seemingly chaotic novel.

1314 Koppel, Gene. "Fulfillment through Frustration: Some Aspects of Sterne's
Art of the Incomplete in A SENTIMENTAL JOURNEY." SNNTS, 2
(1970), 168-72.

In A SENTIMENTAL JOURNEY sexual frustrations, like life's
other frustrations, become sources of energy, leading to an
almost spiritual kind of fulfillment.

1315 Landa, Louis A. "The Shandean Homunculus: The Background of Sterne's
'Little Gentleman.'" RESTORATION AND EIGHTEENTH-CENTURY

LITERATURE: ESSAYS IN HONOR OF ALAN DUGALD McKILLOP. Ed. Carroll Camden. Chicago: University of Chicago Press, 1963.

An excellent discussion of eighteenth-century scientific theories as they relate to TRISTRAM SHANDY.

1316 Lanham, Richard A. TRISTRAM SHANDY: THE GAMES OF PLEASURE. Berkeley and Los Angeles: University of California Press, 1973.

A fresh and important reevaluation of Sterne's novel that uses modern game theories as one means to argue that Sterne is not really "serious," not interested in profundity but in pleasure--and in this is profoundly right about man's most basic need. The concern with pleasure supports the novel's comedy and is at the heart of its major theme: "Tristram teaches us . . . that when we feel for others, we do so largely for the pleasure of the feeling. . . . We will feel for others only when we have felt enough for ourselves."

1317 Lehman, B.H. "Of Time, Personality, and the Author: A Study of TRISTRAM SHANDY: Comedy." STUDIES IN THE COMIC. Berkeley and Los Angeles: University of California Press, 1941.

An important discussion of Sterne's conception of time as it affects personality and as its manipulation makes for comic effects.

1318 McKillop, Alan Dugald. THE EARLY MASTERS OF ENGLISH FICTION. Lawrence: University of Kansas Press, 1956.

Includes a chapter on Sterne that is the best general critical introduction to his work.

1319 _____. "The Reinterpretation of Laurence Sterne." ÉTUDES ANGLAISES, 7 (1954), 36-47.

Together with astute commentary on recent (pre-1954) trends in Sterne studies, McKillop combines a host of fresh insights on Sterne's work, his ambiguity and resistance to precise interpretation, and his relations with some of his contemporaries.

1320 MacLean, Kenneth. JOHN LOCKE AND ENGLISH LITERATURE OF THE EIGHTEENTH CENTURY. New Haven, Conn.: Yale University Press, 1936.

Includes a discussion of Sterne that is one of the earliest systematic treatments of Locke's influence on TRISTRAM SHANDY, and it is still one of the best.

1321 McMaster, Juliet. "Experience to Expression: Thematic Character Contrasts in TRISTRAM SHANDY." MLQ, 32 (1971), 42-57.

Sterne's contrastive treatment of paired characters supports almost an "allegory" of the relations between the physical and the conceptual worlds.

1322 Mendilow, Adam Abraham. TIME AND THE NOVEL. London: P. Nevill, 1952.

Includes a discussion of Sterne that is still among the best treatments of the manipulations of chronological sequence in TRISTRAM SHANDY.

1323 Moglen, Helene. THE PHILOSOPHICAL IRONY OF LAURENCE STERNE. Gainesville: University of Florida Press, 1975.

A most valuable study, especially for its astute assessment of Sterne's ironic fictions in their relationships to eighteenth-century philosophy and in their anticipations of twentieth-century thought.

1324 New, Melvyn. LAURENCE STERNE AS SATIRIST: A READING OF TRISTRAM SHANDY. Gainesville: University of Florida Press, 1969.

New reads TRISTRAM SHANDY as a formal, ferocious, almost Swiftian satire that "finds its coherence not in human consciousness, but in satiric target and satiric attack." An important study, and a controversial one.

1325 Oates, J.C.T. SHANDYISM AND SENTIMENT, 1760-1800. Cambridge, Engl.: Cambridge Bibliographical Society, 1968.

A study of Sterne's influence, with emphasis on imitations of his work.

1326 Park, William. "TRISTRAM SHANDY and the New Novel of Sensibility." SNNTS, 6 (1974), 268-79.

TRISTRAM SHANDY is the most important of a group of novels in which the conventions established by Richardson, Fielding, and Smollett were changed to create the new novel of sensibility, which Park regards as a distinctive broad type within the general history of English fiction.

1327 Paulson, Ronald. SATIRE AND THE NOVEL IN EIGHTEENTH-CENTURY ENGLAND. New Haven, Conn.: Yale University Press, 1967.

Includes a discussion of Sterne that offers a useful view of TRISTRAM SHANDY as formal satire transformed; the comparisons with A TALE OF A TUB and THE MEMOIRS OF MARTINUS SCRIBLERUS are especially helpful.

1328 Petrie, Graham. "Rhetoric as Fictional Technique in TRISTRAM SHANDY." PQ, 48 (1969), 479-94.

> A helpful discussion of Sterne's novelistic uses of contemporary theories of rhetoric.

1329 Piper, William B. "Tristram Shandy's Digressive Artistry." SEL, 1 (1961), 65-76.

> A valuable study of an important aspect of Sterne's technique; the assessment of the purpose, strategy, and value of Tristram's habits of digression and interpolation is extremely helpful.

1330 Preston, John. THE CREATED SELF: THE READER'S ROLE IN EIGHTEENTH-CENTURY FICTION. New York: Barnes and Noble, 1970.

> Two chapters on TRISTRAM SHANDY provide detailed analyses of the complex narrative techniques by which Sterne manipulates his readers and of the intricate relationships among author, narrator, and reader.

1331 Price, Martin. TO THE PALACE OF WISDOM: STUDIES IN ORDER AND ENERGY FROM DRYDEN TO BLAKE. New York: Doubleday, 1964.

> By relating TRISTRAM SHANDY to RASSELAS and CANDIDE, Price attempts to show that Sterne's novel was part of a temporary movement in prose fiction toward stories incapable of resolution and therefore defiant of rational systems of thought.

1332 Putney, Rufus. "The Evolution of A SENTIMENTAL JOURNEY." PQ, 19 (1940), 349-69.

> On Sterne's composition of the work, his artistic uses of the conventions of the popular travel narrative, and (most importantly) his mockery of the sentimental tradition.

1333 _____. "Laurence Sterne: Apostle of Laughter." THE AGE OF JOHNSON: ESSAYS PRESENTED TO CHAUNCEY BREWSTER TINKER. Ed. Frederick W. Hilles. New Haven, Conn.: Yale University Press, 1949.

> A corrective to the view that Sterne was a mere sentimentalist; instead, he was a writer with a distinctively comic vision: "if the comedy of life ends in pathos, Sterne's delineation of it is comic," and therefore to "call Sterne a sentimentalist is to ignore the hard core of comic irony that made him critical of the emotional vagaries of his own life and of his imagined characters."

1334 Rothstein, Eric. SYSTEMS OF ORDER AND INQUIRY IN LATER EIGHTEENTH-

CENTURY FICTION. Berkeley and Los Angeles: University of California Press, 1975.

> Includes a chapter on TRISTRAM SHANDY arguing that the novel is unified by a set of "structural" analogies involving resemblances among family members and organically systematic relationships among episodes and volumes.

1335 Russell, H.K. "TRISTRAM SHANDY and the Technique of the Novel." SP, 42 (1945), 581-93.

> A general discussion of Sterne's work with respect to a variety of novelistic conventions.

1336 Stedmond, John M. THE COMIC ART OF LAURENCE STERNE: CONVENTION AND INNOVATION IN TRISTRAM SHANDY AND A SENTIMENTAL JOURNEY. Toronto: University of Toronto Press, 1967.

> Probably the most thoroughgoing analysis of Sterne's work: its backgrounds and sources, its styles and techniques, its comic vision and methods.

1337 STERNEIANA. 22 vols. SBrW.

> Photofacsimile reprints of a variety of eighteenth-century imitations and criticisms of Sterne's works.

1338 Stout, Gardner D., Jr. "Introduction" to A SENTIMENTAL JOURNEY THROUGH FRANCE AND ITALY BY MR. YORICK. Berkeley and Los Angeles: University of California Press, 1967.

> See No. 1265.

1339 _____. "Some Borrowings in Sterne from Rabelais and Cervantes." ELN, 3 (1965-66), 111-18.

> Emphasizes previously undiscovered indebtedness, with attention to parallel phrasing and incident.

1340 _____. "Yorick's Sentimental Journey: A Comic PILGRIM'S PROGRESS for the Man of Feeling." ELH, 30 (1963), 395-412.

> Bunyan's work provides an analogue to Sterne's, which also dramatizes a pilgrimage and is in its comic way concerned with redemption.

1341 Tave, Stuart M. THE AMIABLE HUMORIST: A STUDY IN THE COMIC THEORY AND CRITICISM OF THE EIGHTEENTH AND EARLY NINETEENTH CENTURIES. Chicago: University of Chicago Press, 1960.

> Includes a discussion of Sterne that is an impressive argument for seeing the chief figures of TRISTRAM SHANDY as part of

a tradition of comic characters who combine the heroic and the ridiculous in a mixture that makes them at once laughable and sympathetic.

1342 Thackeray, William Makepeace. THE ENGLISH HUMOURISTS OF THE EIGHTEENTH CENTURY. Everyman's Library. London: J.M. Dent, 1929.

The lecture on "Sterne and Goldsmith" includes an unflattering discussion of the author of TRISTRAM SHANDY as a vile and indecent writer. Thackeray's view was representative of a large body of Victorian critical opinion, and his lecture was very influential. For a different nineteenth-century attitude toward Sterne, see No. 1311.

1343 Traugott, John L. TRISTRAM SHANDY'S WORLD: STERNE'S PHILO-SOPHICAL RHETORIC. Berkeley and Los Angeles: University of California Press, 1954.

An influential study of Sterne's rhetorical brilliance, especially as it is informed by Lockean ideas.

1344 _____, ed. LAURENCE STERNE: A COLLECTION OF CRITICAL ESSAYS. Twentieth Century Views. Englewood Cliffs, N.J.: Prentice-Hall, 1968.

Reprinted essays by Sterne scholars.

1345 Tuveson, Ernest. "Locke and Sterne." REASON AND THE IMAGINATION: STUDIES IN THE HISTORY OF IDEAS, 1600-1800. Ed. J.A. Mazzeo. New York: Columbia University Press, 1962.

An important discussion of the relationships between Sterne and Locke, both of whom, Tuveson argues, were hostile to traditional notions of human psychology and behavior.

1346 Van Ghent, Dorothy. "On TRISTRAM SHANDY." THE ENGLISH NOVEL: FORM AND FUNCTION. New York: Rinehart, 1953.

A stimulating discussion of Sterne's method. TRISTRAM SHANDY is a "structure modeled on the operative character of consciousness," and although Sterne's interest was "not that of a theoretical psychologist," his concern was to "create a world" that has "the form of a mind."

1347 Wagoner, Mary. "Satire of the Reader in TRISTRAM SHANDY." TSLL, 7 (1966), 337-44.

An analysis of relevant passages demonstrating that throughout TRISTRAM SHANDY the reader, especially the gullible one, is among Sterne's more important targets.

1348 Watkins, Walter B.C. PERILOUS BALANCE: THE TRAGIC GENIUS OF SWIFT, JOHNSON, AND STERNE. Princeton, N.J.: Princeton University Press, 1939.

> More recent criticism has concentrated on Sterne's comic vision, but Watkins' discussion, with its emphasis on the crucial role of Yorick in TRISTRAM SHANDY, should not be overlooked.

1349 Wright, Andrew. "The Artifice of Failure in TRISTRAM SHANDY." NOVEL, 2 (1969), 212-20.

> At the end of Sterne's novel "the ordinary mendacities by which men live have been discredited, and the magnitude of life's difficulties has been exposed to view. The testing of all hypotheses has ended in failure, but in the endeavor the circle has been drawn: the effort itself has led to the making of a work of art."

JONATHAN SWIFT (1667-1745)

PRINCIPAL WORKS

THE BATTLE OF THE BOOKS, 1704 (Narrative satire)
A TALE OF A TUB, 1704 (Narrative satire)
ARGUMENT TO PROVE THAT THE ABOLISHING OF CHRISTIANITY IN EN-
        GLAND, MAY . . . BE ATTENDED WITH SOME INCONVENIENCES,
        1711 (Satirical pamphlet)
A PROPOSAL FOR CORRECTING, IMPROVING AND ASCERTAINING THE
        ENGLISH TONGUE, 1712 (Treatise)
JOURNAL TO STELLA, 1766-68 (Letters to Esther Johnson)
DRAPIER'S LETTERS, 1724 (Political pamphlets)
TRAVELS INTO SEVERAL REMOTE NATIONS OF THE WORLD [GULLIVER'S
        TRAVELS], 1726 (Novel/imaginary voyage)
A MODEST PROPOSAL, 1729 (Satirical pamphlet)

EDITIONS

A. Collected Works

1350 THE PROSE WORKS OF JONATHAN SWIFT. Ed. Herbert J. Davis.
     Shakespeare Head Edition. 14 vols. Oxford: Basil Blackwell, 1939-68.

       The standard edition; the final volume includes an index by
       William J. Kunz, Steven Hollander, and Susan Staves, as
       well as "Addenda, Errata, Corrigenda," jointly edited by Her-
       bert Davis and Irvin Ehrenpreis.

1351 THE POEMS OF JONATHAN SWIFT. Ed. Harold Williams. 2nd ed.
     3 vols. Oxford: Clarendon Press, 1958.

       The standard edition; first edition published in 1937.

1352 SWIFT: POETICAL WORKS. Ed. Herbert J. Davis. London: Oxford
     University Press, 1967.

B. Selections and Specialized Collections

1353 GULLIVER'S TRAVELS, A TALE OF A TUB, THE BATTLE OF THE BOOKS.
Ed. William A. Eddy. London: Oxford University Press, 1956.

1354 A TALE OF A TUB AND THE BATTLE OF THE BOOKS. Ed. A.C. Guthkelch and D. Nichol Smith. 2nd ed. Oxford: Clarendon Press, 1958.

> The standard edition, first published in 1920; includes an ex-
> cellent introduction and explanatory notes.

1355 GULLIVER'S TRAVELS AND OTHER WRITINGS. Ed. Louis A. Landa.
Boston: Houghton Mifflin, 1960.

> Contains a fine critical introduction and excellent notes.

1356 JONATHAN SWIFT. Ed. Kathleen Williams. London: Routledge and
Kegan Paul, 1968.

> Selections, most of them extracts, with analysis and explana-
> tory notes.

1357 THE WRITINGS OF JONATHAN SWIFT. Ed. Robert A. Greenberg and
William Piper. Norton Critical Edition. New York: W.W. Norton,
1973.

> Reliable texts of the major prose and poetry, together with
> some minor pieces; also, a gathering of background materials
> and a sampling of critical commentaries from the eighteenth
> century through the twentieth.

C. Individual Works

THE BATTLE OF THE BOOKS

1358 See Nos. 1353 and 1354.

A TALE OF A TUB

1359 A TALE OF A TUB. FoN.

> A photofacsimile reprint of the first edition, 1704.

1360 See Nos. 1353 and 1354.

GULLIVER'S TRAVELS

There is as yet no definitive edition of this work.

1361 GULLIVER'S TRAVELS: THE TEXT OF THE FIRST EDITION, WITH AN INTRODUCTION, BIBLIOGRAPHY AND NOTES. Ed. Harold Williams. London: First Editions Club, 1926.

1362 GULLIVER'S TRAVELS. Ed. Arthur E. Case. New York: Nelson, 1938.

> A good scholarly edition, very helpfully annotated.

1363 JONATHAN SWIFT: GULLIVER'S TRAVELS. Ed. Robert A. Greenberg. Norton Critical Edition. New York: W.W. Norton, 1961; rev. ed., 1970.

> Includes a reliable text, together with a selection of back-ground readings and of criticism from the eighteenth century through the twentieth.

1364 GULLIVER'S TRAVELS. Ed. Paul Turner. London: Oxford University Press, 1971.

> Includes a good critical introduction and helpful notes.

1365 See Nos. 1353 and 1355.

LETTERS AND JOURNALS

1366 THE CORRESPONDENCE OF JONATHAN SWIFT, D.D. Ed. F. Elrington Ball. 6 vols. London: G. Bell, 1910-14.

1367 JONATHAN SWIFT: JOURNAL TO STELLA. Ed. Harold Williams. 2 vols. Oxford: Clarendon Press, 1948.

> The charming and fascinating letters to Esther Johnson, composed in 1710-13; essential to Swift studies.

1368 THE CORRESPONDENCE OF JONATHAN SWIFT. Ed. Harold Williams. 5 vols. Oxford: Clarendon Press, 1963-65.

> Fine annotations and commentaries; this edition incorporates that of Ball (No. 1366), which it supersedes.

BIBLIOGRAPHY

1369 Clubb, Merrel D. "The Criticism of Gulliver's 'Voyage to the Houyhnhnms,' 1726-1914." STANFORD STUDIES IN LANGUAGE AND LITERATURE, 1941. Stanford, Calif.: Stanford University Press, 1941.

A brief bibliographical essay surveying trends and themes in this body of unusually varied criticism.

1370 Lamont, Claire. "A Checklist of Critical and Biographical Writings on Jonathan Swift, 1945-1965." FAIR LIBERTY WAS ALL HIS CRY: A TERCENTENARY TRIBUTE TO JONATHAN SWIFT, 1667-1745. Ed. A. Norman Jeffares. London: Macmillan, 1967.

Should be used along with Ricardo Quintana's accompanying bibliographical essay (see No. 1374).

1371 Landa, Louis A. "Swift." THE ENGLISH NOVEL: SELECT BIBLIO-GRAPHICAL GUIDES. Ed. A.E. Dyson. London: Oxford University Press, 1974.

An excellent bibliographical essay covering both primary and secondary sources.

1372 Landa, Louis A., and James E. Tobin. JONATHAN SWIFT: A LIST OF CRITICAL STUDIES PUBLISHED FROM 1895 TO 1945. New York: Cosmopolitan Science and Art, 1945.

A checklist, without annotations.

1373 Mayhew, George. "Recent Swift Scholarship." JONATHAN SWIFT, 1667-1967: A DUBLIN TERCENTENARY TRIBUTE. Ed. Roger McHugh and Philip Edwards. Dublin: Dolmen Press, 1967.

May be usefully read along with Quintana's appraisal of Swift studies, 1945-65 (see No. 1374).

1374 Quintana, Ricardo. "A Modest Appraisal: Swift Scholarship and Criticism, 1945-65." FAIR LIBERTY WAS ALL HIS CRY: A TERCENTE-NARY TRIBUTE TO JONATHAN SWIFT, 1667-1745. Ed. A Norman Jeffares. London: Macmillan, 1967.

(See No. 1370.) An evaluative bibliographical essay that accompanies the checklist prepared by Claire Lamont.

1375 Stathis, James J. A BIBLIOGRAPHY OF SWIFT STUDIES, 1945-1965. Nashville, Tenn.: Vanderbilt University Press, 1967.

Brief, descriptive annotations of all items listed.

1376 Teerink, Herman. A BIBLIOGRAPHY OF THE WRITINGS OF JONATHAN SWIFT. 2nd ed., rev. by A.H. Scouten. Philadelphia: University of Pennsylvania Press, 1963.

> First published in 1937; lists Swift's works, and criticism through 1895.

1377 See Nos. 1387 and 1445.

BIOGRAPHY

1378 Brain, Sir Walter Russell. "The Illness of Dean Swift." IRISH JOURNAL OF MEDICAL SCIENCE, Aug.-Sept. 1952, pp. 337-46.

> An authoritative essay that has done much to shatter old notions that Swift was insane during his last years.

1379 Davis, Herbert J. STELLA: A GENTLEWOMAN OF THE EIGHTEENTH CENTURY. New York: Macmillan, 1942.

> Brief account of Esther Johnson; indirectly sheds light on Swift as well.

1380 Ehrenpreis, Irvin. THE PERSONALITY OF JONATHAN SWIFT. London: Methuen, 1958.

> A critical biography emphasizing the ways in which the works mirror the man; a difficult and risky undertaking, very responsibly handled.

1381 _____. SWIFT: THE MAN, HIS WORKS, AND THE AGE. 3 vols. projected. Cambridge, Mass.: Harvard University Press, 1962-- .

> The standard biography, now in progress.

1382 Ferguson, Oliver W. JONATHAN SWIFT AND IRELAND. Urbana: University of Illinois Press, 1962.

> A detailed account of Swift's political and literary efforts on behalf of the Irish.

1383 Goldgar, Bertrand. THE CURSE OF PARTY: SWIFT'S RELATIONS WITH ADDISON AND STEELE. Lincoln: University of Nebraska Press, 1961.

1384 Landa, Louis A. SWIFT AND THE CHURCH OF IRELAND. Oxford: Clarendon Press, 1954.

1385 Murry, J. Middleton. SWIFT. Writers and Their Work, No. 61. Rev.

ed. London: Longmans, Green, 1966.

An excellent, brief "biocritical" introduction for the nonspecialist.

1386 Quintana, Ricardo. SWIFT: AN INTRODUCTION. London: Oxford University Press, 1955.

A brief, very readable, authoritative critical biography. (See also No. 1430.)

CRITICAL STUDIES AND COMMENTARIES

1387 Berwick, Donald M. THE REPUTATION OF JONATHAN SWIFT, 1781-1882. Philadelphia: n.p., 1941.

This Princeton University dissertation provides a detailed survey and analysis of Swift studies during the years covered, when Swift was generally regarded as low and vulgar, though brilliant; includes a valuable bibliography.

1388 Brady, Frank, ed. TWENTIETH CENTURY INTERPRETATIONS OF GULLIVER'S TRAVELS. Englewood Cliffs, N.J.: Prentice-Hall, 1968.

A selection of reprinted essays by various scholars.

1389 Bullitt, John M. JONATHAN SWIFT AND THE ANATOMY OF SATIRE: A STUDY OF SATIRIC TECHNIQUE. Cambridge, Mass.: Harvard University Press, 1953.

A fine analysis that concentrates on Swift's achievement in form instead of merely the biographical or historical circumstances motivating his satire.

1390 Carnochan, W.B. "The Complexity of Swift: Gulliver's Fourth Voyage." SP, 60 (1963), 23-44.

The Houyhnhnms represent an ideal, unattainable and perhaps undesirable in some degree, since man inevitably becomes (like Gulliver and even Swift himself) frustrated and cynical when questing after the unreachable. The Fourth Voyage is a self-portrayal of a frustrated idealist who is in part the object of the satire.

1391 _____. LEMUEL GULLIVER'S MIRROR FOR MAN. Berkeley and Los Angeles: University of California Press, 1968.

Essentially a study of Swift's satire; emphasizes the "mirror" logic created by the work's ambivalence, its "strain and counterstrain," which make Gulliver see himself (occasionally with

horror) as an object of derision. An epilogue draws comparisons with similar techniques in Joyce, Nabokov, and other
modern writers.

1392 _____. "Swift's TALE: On Satire, Negation, and the Uses of Irony."
ECS, 5 (1971), 122-44.

Irony is the "indirection that converts criticism to satire."

1393 Case, Arthur E. FOUR ESSAYS ON GULLIVER'S TRAVELS. Princeton,
N.J.: Princeton University Press, 1945.

Studies textual and critical; an important book.

1394 Clark, John R. FORM AND FRENZY IN SWIFT'S TALE OF A TUB.
Ithaca, N.Y.: Cornell University Press, 1970.

Clark sees the TALE as an exercise in mimetic art; the "regular
advancement" of its plot "raises the action to a climax and
creates a totality by that action's movement from beginning to
middle to end."

1395 Clifford, James L. "Gulliver's Fourth Voyage: 'Hard' and 'Soft' Schools
of Interpretation." QUICK SPRINGS OF SENSE: STUDIES IN THE
EIGHTEENTH CENTURY. Ed. Larry S. Champion. Athens: University
of Georgia Press, 1974.

A discussion of the scholarly debate over the interpretation of
the fourth book of GULLIVER'S TRAVELS. Clifford describes
the issues clearly and helpfully, and his argument for a legiti-
mate multiplicity of interpretations is both sensible and refreshing. (See also Nos. 1390, 1397, 1403, 1411, 1422, 1436,
1438, and 1448.)

1396 Cohan, Steven M. "Gulliver's Fiction." SNNTS, 6 (1974), 7-16.

GULLIVER'S TRAVELS no longer appeals principally as a satire,
Cohan argues, but rather as a fiction whose "psychological
structure" gives it "relevance and ties to our own world, which
are the imaginative chords it pulls upon."

1397 Crane, Ronald S. "The Houyhnhnms, the Yahoos, and the History of
Ideas." REASON AND THE IMAGINATION: STUDIES IN THE HIS-
TORY OF IDEAS, 1600-1800. Ed. J.A. Mazzeo. New York: Colum-
bia University Press, 1962.

In this and in the next article listed, Crane challenges such
arguments as those advanced by Monk (No. 1422) and Ross
(No. 1436), who approach GULLIVER'S TRAVELS as a comic
work. (See also Nos. 1395, 1403, 1438, and 1448.)

1398 _____ . "The Rationale of the Fourth Voyage." JONATHAN SWIFT: GULLIVER'S TRAVELS. Ed. Robert A. Greenberg. Norton Critical Edition. New York: W.W. Norton, 1961; rev. ed., 1970.

See also No. 1397.

1399 Darnall, F.M. "Swift's Religion." JEGP, 30 (1931), 379-82.

A brief but useful inquiry into Swift's religious views and their reflection in his major works, especially GULLIVER'S TRAVELS.

1400 DePorte, Michael V. NIGHTMARES AND HOBBYHORSES: SWIFT, STERNE, AND AUGUSTAN IDEAS OF MADNESS. San Marino, Calif.: Huntington Library, 1974.

An illuminating discussion of the ways in which A TALE OF A TUB and TRISTRAM SHANDY relate to eighteenth-century notions of insanity.

1401 Donoghue, Denis, ed. JONATHAN SWIFT: A CRITICAL ANTHOLOGY. Harmondsworth, Engl.: Penguin Books, 1971.

More than one hundred brief extracts from critical commentaries, with the coverage extending from Swift's own time through the 1960's.

1402 Ehrenpreis, Irvin. LITERARY MEANING AND AUGUSTAN VALUES. Charlottesville: University Press of Virginia, 1974.

Includes an essay on the "styles" of GULLIVER'S TRAVELS that is a valuable discussion of Swift's rhetoric and language.

1403 _____ . "The Meaning of Gulliver's Last Voyage." REL, 3 (1962), 18-38.

Brilliant reconciliation of the two prevailing views of part IV, one seeing the fourth voyage as Swift's angry outburst at human nature (as judged against the ideal of the Houyhnhnms), the other interpreting the Houyhnhnms themselves as unacceptable and Gulliver as a fool. (See also Nos. 1395, 1397, 1422, 1436, 1438, and 1448.)

1404 _____ . "The Origins of GULLIVER'S TRAVELS." PMLA, 72 (1957), 880-99.

The origins must be sought in the people Swift knew; the typical approach, "with an emphasis on manipulation of ideas, or else in terms of the techniques of fiction, usually misleads one."

1405 Elliott, Robert C. "Gulliver as Literary Artist." ELH, 19 (1952), 49-63.

On Gulliver's sometimes ambiguous function as the narrator of his own voyages; emphasizes his role as a persona. (See also No. 1406.)

1406 _____. THE POWER OF SATIRE: MAGIC, RITUAL, ART. Princeton, N.J.: Princeton University Press, 1960.

Includes a discussion of Swift that perceptively analyzes Gulliver as a persona, a deliberately "unrounded" character with little inner life, designed for specific satiric purposes.

1407 _____. "Swift's Satire: Rules of the Game." ELH, 41 (1974), 413-28.

On Swift's precision in the use of satiric techniques and his control of his devices.

1408 _____. "Swift's TALE OF A TUB: An Essay in Problems of Structure." PMLA, 66 (1951), 441-55.

An intelligent critical analysis of the strengths, ingenuities, and weaknesses of the book's problematical structure.

1409 Ewald, William B. THE MASKS OF JONATHAN SWIFT. Cambridge, Mass.: Harvard University Press, 1954.

On Swift as satirist and creator of personae; emphasizes the form of the creations, not the personality of their author.

1410 Fink, Zera S. "Political Theory in GULLIVER'S TRAVELS." ELH, 14 (1947), 151-61.

An important essay; especially helpful for the study of parts I and II of Swift's book.

1411 Foster, Milton P. A CASEBOOK ON GULLIVER AMONG THE HOUYHN-HNMS. New York: Crowell, 1961.

A useful collection of key articles in the debate over the meaning of part IV of GULLIVER'S TRAVELS.

1412 Frye, Roland M. "Swift's Yahoo and the Christian Symbols for Sin." JHI, 15 (1954), 201-17.

GULLIVER'S TRAVELS promotes a secular Christian orthodoxy.

1413 Harth, Philip. SWIFT AND ANGLICAN RATIONALISM: THE RELIGIOUS BACKGROUND OF A TALE OF A TUB. Chicago: University of Chicago Press, 1961.

A brilliant discussion demonstrating that, contrary to what was once generally assumed, the Swift of A TALE is an orthodox Anglican.

1414 Jeffares, A. Norman, ed. FAIR LIBERTY WAS ALL HIS CRY: A TER-
CENTENARY TRIBUTE TO JONATHAN SWIFT, 1667-1745. London:
Macmillan, 1967.

> Essays by various modern Swift scholars.

1415 Jones, Richard F. ANCIENTS AND MODERNS: A STUDY OF THE
BACKGROUND OF THE BATTLE OF THE BOOKS. St. Louis, Mo.:
Washington University Press, 1936; 2nd ed., 1961.

> The one indispensable work for the student of THE BATTLE OF
> THE BOOKS and A TALE OF A TUB.

1416 Kallich, Martin. THE OTHER END OF THE EGG: RELIGIOUS SATIRE
IN GULLIVER'S TRAVELS. New York: New York University Press, 1970.

> An analysis of the religious allusions in GULLIVER'S TRAVELS
> and of their function as satirical devices; the argument that in
> part IV Swift carries on a struggle against the deist heresy,
> "through the symbolic Houyhnhnms," is a matter for debate.

1417 Kliger, Samuel. "The Unity of GULLIVER'S TRAVELS." MLQ, 6 (1945),
401-15.

> An interesting and fairly influential discussion of how, despite
> the book's episodic structure, it is unified by its tone and pur-
> pose and by the presence of its central character.

1418 Landa, Louis A. "Jonathan Swift: The Critical Significance of Biographical Evidence." ENGLISH INSTITUTE ESSAYS, 1946. New York:
Columbia University Press, 1947.

> Evidence from Swift's life and career as a clergyman supports
> the view that part IV of GULLIVER'S TRAVELS is, in part,
> secular Christian apologetics--a "defence of the doctrine of
> redemption and man's need for grace."

1419 _____. "Swift, the Mysteries, and Deism." STUDIES IN ENGLISH,
UNIVERSITY OF TEXAS. Austin, 1945.

> On Swift's Christianity, and his views of deism and stoicism
> as heresies.

1420 Lee, Jae Num. SWIFT AND SCATOLOGICAL SATIRE. Albuquerque:
University of New Mexico Press, 1971.

> The only full-length study of Swift's bawdiness, his use of "sca-
> tology as an effective literary device." The discussions range
> widely, but are somewhat superficial.

1421 McHugh, Roger, and Philip Edwards, eds. JONATHAN SWIFT, 1667-1967:

A DUBLIN TERCENTENARY TRIBUTE. Dublin: Dolmen Press, 1967.

Essays (nearly a dozen of them new) by various Swift scholars.

1422 Monk, Samuel Holt. "The Pride of Lemuel Gulliver." SEWANEE RE-VIEW, 63 (1955), 48-71.

GULLIVER'S TRAVELS expresses anger, but not despair, and it is not nihilistic; rather, it is a comic work whose narrator is a ridiculous figure used by Swift as a device to "promote self-knowledge in the faith that self-knowledge will lead to right action." (See also Nos. 1395, 1397, 1403, 1436, 1438, and 1448.)

1423 Nicolson, Marjorie, and Nora M. Mohler. "The Scientific Background of Swift's 'Voyage to Laputa.'" ANNALS OF SCIENCE, 2 (1937), 299-334.

This article and No. 1424 are important studies of the follies, abuses, and pretensions of contemporary scientists; they provide important background information for the student of part III of GULLIVER'S TRAVELS.

1424 Nicolson, Marjorie, and Nora M. Mohler. "Swift's Flying Island in the 'Voyage to Laputa.'" ANNALS OF SCIENCE, 2 (1937), 405-30.

See also No. 1423.

1425 Paulson, Ronald. THE FICTIONS OF SATIRE. Baltimore: Johns Hopkins University Press, 1967.

Swift, despite the fantastic qualities of much of his satiric writing, is part of the mimetic drift of Augustan satire "away from formal satires" toward a "specifically fictional construct."

1426 _____. SATIRE AND THE NOVEL IN EIGHTEENTH-CENTURY ENGLAND. New Haven, Conn.: Yale University Press, 1967.

Paulson gives major attention to other fiction writers besides Swift, but he draws useful and intelligent distinctions between Swift's satiric fictions and those of Fielding and Smollett.

1427 _____. THEME AND STRUCTURE IN SWIFT'S TALE OF A TUB. New Haven, Conn.: Yale University Press, 1960.

A helpful, detailed discussion of the relationship between the meaning of the TALE and its intricate formal design.

1428 Pinkus, Philip. SWIFT'S VISION OF EVIL: A COMPARATIVE STUDY OF A TALE OF A TUB AND GULLIVER'S TRAVELS. Victoria, B.C.: University of Victoria Press, 1975.

A learned and persuasive study, of major importance to those interested in Swift's religion and morality.

1429 Price, Martin. SWIFT'S RHETORICAL ART: A STUDY IN STRUCTURE AND MEANING. New Haven, Conn.: Yale University Press, 1953.

A formalist approach to Swift's work, emphasizing the three great prose satires.

1430 Quintana, Ricardo. THE MIND AND ART OF JONATHAN SWIFT. London: Oxford University Press, 1936.

Widely ranging critical study of Swift and his works; mingles biography with extremely astute criticism (the latter is the main emphasis). Quintana started new trends in Swift criticism with this book, which is among the most important of all modern studies of the Dean.

1431 _____. "Situational Satire: A Commentary on the Method of Swift." UTQ, 17 (1948), 130-36.

A trend-setting article that argues for Gulliver as a persona, a character created as a part of Swift's dramatic method, and entirely separate from his author.

1432 Rawson, Claude J. "Gulliver and the Gentle Reader." IMAGINED WORLDS: ESSAYS ON SOME ENGLISH NOVELS AND NOVELISTS IN HONOUR OF JOHN BUTT. Ed. Maynard Mack and Ian Gregor. London: Methuen, 1968.

An essential essay on Swift's manipulations of his audience; the essay has subsequently appeared again in Rawson's GULLIVER AND THE GENTLE READER: STUDIES IN SWIFT AND OUR TIME (London: Routledge and Kegan Paul, 1973).

1433 _____, ed. FOCUS: SWIFT. London: Sphere Books, 1971.

Includes important essays on Swift by Rawson, John Traugott, Charles Peake, Irvin Ehrenpreis, and Ian [P.] Watt.

1434 Rogers, Pat. "Form in A TALE OF A TUB." ESSAYS IN CRITICISM, 22 (1972), 142-60.

Unlike many other modern commentators on the TALE, Rogers sees the work as deliberately dramatizing (and satirizing) "excess of form." The structure is one of "inorganic, over-developed, useless form."

1435 Rosenheim, Edward W. SWIFT AND THE SATIRIST'S ART. Chicago: University of Chicago Press, 1963.

A sophisticated, intelligent study of Swift's uses of the devices of satire; good discussion of contemporary circumstances and the ways in which they became the transformed stuff of Swift's satire, as well as its object.

1436 Ross, John R. "The Final Comedy of Lemuel Gulliver." STUDIES IN THE COMIC. Berkeley and Los Angeles: University of California Press, 1941.

At the conclusion of his TRAVELS, Gulliver becomes a ridiculous figure, the butt of satire and thus not the voice of Swift himself. (See also Nos. 1395, 1397, 1403, 1422, 1438, and 1448.)

1437 Sacks, Sheldon. FICTION AND THE SHAPE OF BELIEF: A STUDY OF HENRY FIELDING WITH GLANCES AT SWIFT, JOHNSON, AND RICHARDSON. Berkeley and Los Angeles: University of California Press, 1964.

Especially interesting on the subject of GULLIVER'S TRAVELS as an example of the "demands of satire"--the requirement that the persona of an extended satire, to be morally and satirically effective, must be a complex figure.

1438 Sherburn, George. "Errors Concerning the Houyhnhnms." MP, 56 (1958), 92-97.

An impressive refutation of the argument that part IV is essentially comic. (See also Nos. 1395, 1397, 1403, 1422, 1436, and 1448).

1439 Starkman, Miriam Kosh. SWIFT'S SATIRE ON LEARNING IN A TALE OF A TUB. Princeton, N.J.: Princeton University Press, 1950.

A detailed analysis of Swift's conservative reactions to, and satiric attacks on, a variety of things "modern"; the attack itself becomes Swift's major ordering principle in a seemingly chaotic work.

1440 Swaim, Kathleen M. A READING OF GULLIVER'S TRAVELS. The Hague: Mouton, 1972.

A discussion of the imagery in the work, with emphasis on the structural achievement. Each Voyage is studied as a discrete exploration, partly through image patterns, of an aspect of human nature--the physical, the emotional, the intellectual, the moral; the four Voyages are made to coalesce by a "framework strategy."

1441 SWIFTIANA. 19 vols. SBrW.

Photofacsimile reprints of a variety of early criticisms, commentaries, and biographies of Swift; many of these were first published during Swift's lifetime.

1442 Tuveson, Ernest. "Swift: The Dean as Satirist." UTQ, 22 (1953), 368-75.

Swift as Christian satirist, especially in GULLIVER'S TRAVELS.

1443 _____, ed. SWIFT: A COLLECTION OF CRITICAL ESSAYS. Twentieth Century Views. Englewood Cliffs, N.J.: Prentice-Hall, 1964.

Essays by various modern Swift scholars.

1444 Uphaus, Robert W. "GULLIVER'S TRAVELS, A MODEST PROPOSAL, and the Problematical Nature of Meaning." PLL, 10 (1974), 268-78.

The central subject of both works is the problematical nature of meaning, and Swift's deliberate habit of raising and then shattering reader expectations only emphasizes the difficulty of the problem.

1445 Voight, Milton. SWIFT AND THE TWENTIETH CENTURY. Detroit: Wayne State University Press, 1964.

An invaluable analytical survey of trends in Swift studies during this century; dozens of books and articles receive individual attention.

1446 Wedel, T.O. "On the Philosophical Background of GULLIVER'S TRAVELS." SP, 23 (1926), 434-50.

GULLIVER'S TRAVELS, especially part IV, is deeply rooted in orthodox Christian theology.

1447 Wilding, Michael. "The Politics of GULLIVER'S TRAVELS." STUDIES IN THE EIGHTEENTH CENTURY, II. Ed. R.F. Brissenden. Toronto: University of Toronto Press, 1973.

An attempt to place GULLIVER'S TRAVELS in a tradition of the political novel that includes "the fable and the non-naturalistic utopian narrative."

1448 Williams, Kathleen. JONATHAN SWIFT AND THE AGE OF COMPROMISE. Lawrence: University of Kansas Press, 1958.

A study of the three great prose satires; emphasizes "the writings themselves" (not the biography) and their "relation to ideas, attitudes, and literary methods" current in Swift's own day. The reading of GULLIVER'S TRAVELS is close to the interpretations of Monk (No. 1422) and Ross (No. 1436). (See also Nos. 1395, 1397, 1403, and 1438.)

1449 _____, ed. SWIFT: THE CRITICAL HERITAGE. London: Routledge and Kegan Paul, 1970.

A selection of early critical commentaries on Swift.

1450 Zimmerman, Everett. "Gulliver the Preacher." PMLA, 89 (1974), 1024-32.

Swift allows Gulliver to define a view of evil that accords with Christian tradition, but simultaneously shows us Gulliver's immoral intentions; his "preaching" is thus a pretense to disguise his own evil. An illuminating discussion.

HORACE WALPOLE (1717-97)

As the wealthy son of the great prime minister, Walpole enjoyed the advantages of leisure and famous friends. He was an inveterate letter-writer, and his COR-RESPONDENCE is among the most valuable of all sources of information about his period's leading figures in politics, society, and the arts. Walpole dabbled in painting, architecture (he rebuilt his Twickenham country house, Strawberry Hill, as a Gothic castle), historical research, publishing, and literature. THE CASTLE OF OTRANTO (1764), his only work of fiction, laid the groundwork for the later development of the Gothic novel in England.

PRINCIPAL WORKS

CATALOGUE OF THE ROYAL AND NOBLE AUTHORS OF ENGLAND, 1758
    (Literary history)
FUGITIVE PIECES IN PROSE AND VERSE, 1758 (Occasional writings)
ANECDOTES OF PAINTING IN ENGLAND, 1762-71 (Art history)
THE CASTLE OF OTRANTO, 1764 (Novel)
HISTORIC DOUBTS ON RICHARD III, 1768 (History)
THE MYSTERIOUS MOTHER, 1768 (Tragedy)
MEMOIRS, 1822-45 (Political history)

EDITIONS

A. Collected Works

1451 THE WORKS OF HORATIO WALPOLE. Ed. Mary Berry et al. 9 vols. London, 1798-1825.

B. Individual Works

THE CASTLE OF OTRANTO

1452 THE CASTLE OF OTRANTO. Ed. Oswald Doughty. London: Scholartis Press, 1929.

Includes a fine introductory essay.

1453 THE CASTLE OF OTRANTO. Ed. W.S. Lewis. Oxford English Novels. London: Oxford University Press, 1964.

Includes a fine critical introduction by the scholar who has devoted much of his career to editing Walpole's CORRESPON-DENCE (see No. 1456).

LETTERS

1454 THE LETTERS OF HORACE WALPOLE. Ed. Peter Cunningham. 9 vols. London, 1857-59.

Not the earliest collection of Walpole's letters, but the first substantial one.

1455 THE LETTERS OF HORACE WALPOLE. Ed. Mrs. Paget Toynbee. 16 vols. Oxford: Oxford University Press, 1903-5. Supplements: 3 vols., 1915-25.

For a time, this was the most scholarly and most nearly complete collection.

1456 HORACE WALPOLE'S CORRESPONDENCE. Ed. W.S. Lewis et al. New Haven, Conn.: Yale University Press, 1937-- .

This, the Yale Edition, is to be definitive; still in progress, it is likely to include some fifty volumes when completed.

1457 SELECTED LETTERS OF HORACE WALPOLE. Ed. W.S. Lewis. New Haven, Conn.: Yale University Press, 1973.

Includes 112 of the most important letters, 1736-97.

BIBLIOGRAPHY

1458 Hazen, Allen T. A BIBLIOGRAPHY OF HORACE WALPOLE. New Haven, Conn.: Yale University Press, 1948.

The standard bibliography.

1459 _____. A CATALOGUE OF HORACE WALPOLE'S LIBRARY. 3 vols. New Haven, Conn.: Yale University Press, 1969.

Includes a reprint of W.S. Lewis, HORACE WALPOLE'S LI-BRARY (Cambridge: At the University Press, 1958).

1460 McNutt, Dan J. THE EIGHTEENTH-CENTURY GOTHIC NOVEL: AN ANNOTATED BIBLIOGRAPHY OF CRITICISM AND SELECTED TEXTS. New York: Garland, 1975.

Includes a bibliography of Walpole.

BIOGRAPHY

1461 Dobson, Austin. HORACE WALPOLE: A MEMOIR. Rev. ed. London: Harper, 1910.

A readable biography, more appreciative than critical.

1462 Honour, Hugh. HORACE WALPOLE. Writers and Their Work, No. 92. London: Longmans, Green, 1958.

A brief "biocritical" study; excellent as an introduction for the nonspecialist.

1463 Kallich, Martin. HORACE WALPOLE. New York: Twayne, 1971.

Not a critical biography, but an introduction to Walpole's life, with special attention to his activities as politician and connoisseur.

1464 Ketton-Cremer, R.W. HORACE WALPOLE: A BIOGRAPHY. Rev. ed. London: Faber and Faber, 1946.

A revised edition that improves upon the original edition (1940), adds new facts, and remains a very thorough, readable critical biography.

1465 Whibley, Leonard. "The Foreign Tour of Gray and Walpole." BLACKWOOD'S MAGAZINE, 228 (1930), 813-27.

An intriguing, detailed account of the Grand Tour taken by these two friends in their youth (1739) and of its troubled conclusion in a quarrel.

CRITICAL STUDIES AND COMMENTARIES

Walpole's lone work of fiction has attracted its measure of attention from historians of the novel and (less often) from critics interested in its language and structure or its influence. OTRANTO figures importantly in the critical biographies of Walpole; these, as well as the standard histories of the novel, should be consulted in addition to the critical studies enumerated here.

1466 Dobrée, Bonamy. "Horace Walpole." RESTORATION AND EIGHTEENTH-CENTURY LITERATURE: ESSAYS IN HONOR OF ALAN DUGALD McKILLOP. Ed. Carroll Camden. Chicago: University of Chicago Press, 1963.

A very judicious critical assessment of Walpole's career and of his importance to eighteenth-century studies.

1467 Doughty, Oswald. "Introduction" to THE CASTLE OF OTRANTO. London: Scholartis Press, 1929.

See No. 1452.

1468 Ker, W.P. "Horace Walpole." COLLECTED ESSAYS, I. London: Macmillan, 1925.

A general critical discussion of Walpole's work and its importance; some attention to biography.

1469 Kiely, Robert. THE ROMANTIC NOVEL IN ENGLAND. Cambridge, Mass.: Harvard University Press, 1972.

THE CASTLE OF OTRANTO is among the eighteenth-century novels discussed. This is an excellent study, perhaps the best of its kind, that emphasizes the shared conventions, themes, and innovations of a number of disparate "romantic" novels.

1470 Lewis, W.S. "Introduction" to THE CASTLE OF OTRANTO. Oxford English Novels. London: Oxford University Press, 1964.

See No. 1453.

1471 Mehrotra, Kewal Krishna. HORACE WALPOLE AND THE ENGLISH NOVEL: A STUDY OF THE INFLUENCE OF THE CASTLE OF OTRANTO. Oxford: Basil Blackwell, 1934.

Mehrotra may occasionally claim too much in his assessment of OTRANTO's influence, but his study nonetheless succeeds in showing the very considerable historical importance of Walpole's novel.

1472 Smith, Warren H., ed. HORACE WALPOLE: WRITER, POLITICIAN, AND CONNOISSEUR: ESSAYS ON THE 250TH ANNIVERSARY OF HORACE WALPOLE'S BIRTH. New Haven, Conn.: Yale University Press, 1967.

Essays by various hands.

1473 Solomon, Stanley J. "Subverting Propriety as a Pattern of Irony in Three Eighteenth-Century Novels: THE CASTLE OF OTRANTO, VATHEK, and FANNY HILL." ERASMUS REVIEW, 1 (1971), 107-16.

An interesting and generally sound treatment of one method of irony in the three novels. Solomon perhaps assumes too much about the intentions of Walpole and Cleland.

1474 Summers, Montague. THE GOTHIC QUEST: A HISTORY OF THE GOTHIC NOVEL. London: Fortune Press, 1938.

> Gives Walpole his due as the first Gothic novelist; the assessment of OTRANTO's importance is just, and the novel is interestingly seen in terms of the history of Gothic fiction in England.

1475 Varma, Devendra P. THE GOTHIC FLAME: BEING A HISTORY OF THE GOTHIC NOVEL IN ENGLAND. London: Arthur Barker, 1957.

> Includes sections on Walpole and OTRANTO that offer a general assessment of the novel and its importance to the Gothic tradition in English fiction.

INDEX

INDEX

This index is alphabetized letter by letter.. Numbers refer to entry numbers, except that page numbers are given (in parentheses) to indicate where a title or author has been mentioned in some part of the text other than a numbered entry. The index includes all authors, editors, and translators whose names or works are mentioned in the text, as well as short titles of all books, articles, and other published works. In the case of individual authors, underlined numbers refer to main entries. For the user's convenience, a list of principal works precedes the numbered entries for each novelist included in part II of this book; items in these lists are not indexed.

A

"Abbé Prévost and the English Novel, The" 97

Abernethy, Peter L. 154

ABSTRACTS OF ENGLISH STUDIES 1, 151

ACCOMPLISHED RAKE, THE 212

ACCOUNT OF THE LIFE AND WRITINGS OF THOMAS DAY, ESQ., AN 448

ACHIEVEMENT OF SAMUEL JOHNSON, THE 887

Adams, Percy G. 81

Addison, Joseph 1383

Adelstein, Michael E. 403, 789

ADVENTURES OF CALEB WILLIAMS, THE. See CALEB WILLIAMS

ADVENTURES OF DAVID SIMPLE, THE. See DAVID SIMPLE

ADVENTURES OF EOVAII 821

ADVENTURES OF FERDINAND, COUNT FATHOM. See FERDINAND COUNT FATHOM

ADVENTURES OF HUGH TREVOR, THE 836, 848

ADVENTURES OF PEREGRINE PICKLE, THE. See PEREGRINE PICKLE

ADVENTURES OF RIVELLA, THE 995-97

ADVENTURES OF RODERICK RANDOM, THE. See RODERICK RANDOM

ADVENTURES OF SIR LAUNCELOT GREAVES, THE. See SIR LAUNCELOT GREAVES

AENEID 662, 675

AGE OF EXUBERANCE, THE 230

AGE OF JOHNSON: ESSAYS PRESENTED TO CHAUNCEY BREWSTER TINKER, THE 30, 418, 698, 800, 886, 1028, 1228, 1333

Aitken, George A. 453-55

Alden, John 482

Alexander, Boyd 282, 284, 287, 291, 294

"Allegory and Analogy in CLARISSA" 1083

Index

Allen, B. Sprague 740-41
Allen, Walter 44, 55, 724, 1175
Allott, Miriam 56
"Allusion and Analogy in the Romance of CALEB WILLIAMS" 760
Alter, Robert 45, 57, 82, 496, 594-95, 1204, 1285
Altick, Richard D. 2, 152, 217
Alvarez, A. 1264
ALWYN 848
AMELIA 130, 577, 609, 616, 624, 631, 635, 641, 656, 662, 669, 675, 685, 693
"AMELIA and Booth's Doctrine of the Passions" 609
"AMELIA and the State of Matrimony" 685
"AMELIA--The Decline of Fielding's Art" 656
AMERICAN LIBRARY RESOURCES: A BIBLIOGRAPHICAL GUIDE 6, 168
AMIABLE HUMORIST, THE 39, 681, 1341
ANATOMY OF CRITICISM 61
ANCIENTS AND MODERNS 1415
Anderson, Howard 13, 218, 596, 919, 950, 961-62, 1142, 1286-89
Anderson, John P. 1197
Anderson, Paul B. 996, 999
Anderson, Robert 1163
ANECDOTES AND EGOTISMS OF HENRY MACKENZIE, THE 980
ANNA KARENINA AND OTHER ESSAYS 380
ANNA ST. IVES (p. 161), 835, 846, 848
ANNIVERSARY PAPERS BY COLLEAGUES AND PUPILS OF GEORGE LYMAN KITTREDGE 325
ANNOTATED BIBLIOGRAPHY OF SMOLLETT SCHOLARSHIP 1946-68, AN 1192
"Annotated Checklist of the Works of William Beckford, An" 290
ANN RADCLIFFE (Grant) 1017
ANN RADCLIFFE (Murray) 1018
ANN RADCLIFFE IN RELATION TO HER TIME 1026
"Ann Radcliffe, or, The Hand of Taste" 1028

"Ann Radcliffe's Nature Descriptions" 1023
"Answers to the Author of CLARISSA" 596, 1286
ANTI-PAMELA 822
APHRA BEHN 329
"Aphra Behn's Use of Setting" 334
APOLOGY FOR THE LIFE OF MRS. SHAMELA ANDREWS, AN. See SHAMELA
"Appeal to Honor and Justice, An" 487
Appendix to THE FEMALE QUIXOTE 929, 934, 944
"Applause for Dodsley's CLEONE" 807
APPROPRIATE FORM, THE 65
Argens, Jean B. de B., marquis d' 89
"Art and Artifice in TOM JONES" 633
ART AND ILLUSION 638
"Artifice of Failure in TRISTRAM SHANDY, The" 1349
"Artistic Form of RASSELAS, The" 900
ART OF BIOGRAPHY IN EIGHTEENTH CENTURY ENGLAND, THE 190, 246
ART OF JOSEPH ANDREWS, THE 626
ART OF THE NOVEL, THE 67
"Art of the Theorist: Rhetorical Structure in THE MAN OF FEELING, The" 985
ASPECTS OF THE NOVEL 60, 507
"Associationism and Wit in TRISTRAM SHANDY" 1287
"Astrea and Celadon: An Untouched Portrait of Aphra Behn" 330
Auerbach, Erich 219
AUGUSTAN AGE, THE 17
AUGUSTAN AGE: APPROACHES TO ITS LITERATURE, LIFE, AND THOUGHT, THE 40
AUGUSTAN MILIEU: ESSAYS PRESENTED TO LOUIS A. LANDA, THE 33, 602, 654
AUGUSTAN STUDIES 920, 922
AUGUSTAN VISION, THE 36
"Au pied de la lettre: Stylistic Uncertainty in VATHEK" 309

Austen, Jane 48, 158, (p. 81),
409-10, 637, (p. 177), 940, 945
AUTHOR OF SANDFORD AND MER-
TON, THE 447
AUTHORSHIP IN THE DAYS OF
JOHNSON 224
Auty, Susan G. 83
Ayers, Robert W. 497
AZEMIA 276, 278-79

B

"Background of Fielding's Laughter,
The" 614
Backman, Sven 790
Bage, Robert (p. 53), 258-68, 753
Baine, Rodney M. 498, 842-43
Baird, Donald 154
Baird, Theodore 1290
Baker, Ernest A. 46, 315, 342, 700,
722, 948
Baker, Sheridan 84, 576, 597, 885,
1205
Balderston, Katherine C. 777, 886
Ball, Donald L. 1072
Ball, F. Elrington 1366, 1368
Banerji, H.K. 585
Barbauld, Anna L. 709, 711, 1056
Barber, John (p. 189)
BARHAM DOWNS 258
Barker, Gerard A. 742, 979
Barnett, George 85
Baron-Wilson, Margaret 952
Barrett, Charlotte 398
Barrow, Isaac 600
Barth, John 76, 1173
Bastian, Frank 499
Bate, Walter Jackson 220, 852, 887
Bateson, F.W. 162
Battestin, Martin C. 14, 558, 568,
581, 586, 598-603
BATTLE OF THE BOOKS, THE 1353-
54, 1358, 1415
Baugh, Albert C. 37
Beasley, Jerry C. 86, 153, 210,
409, 604-5, 1073-74, 1206-7
BEAUTIFUL, THE SUBLIME, AND THE
PICTURESQUE, THE 231, 241
Beckett, Juliet 726
BECKFORD 296

Beckford, William 50, 180, 209,
(p. 57), 269-312
BECKFORD AND BECKFORDISM 301
"Beckford, Byron, and Henley" 302
"Beckford's VATHEK: A Study in
Ironic Dissonance" 305
"Beckford's VATHEK and the Tradition
of Oriental Satire" 304
Behn, Aphra 107, 114, 216, (p. 63),
313-40
Bell, Howard J., Jr. 791
Bell, Inglis F. 154
Bell, Michael 606
Bell, Michael Davitt 1075
BE LOVED NO MORE 408
Benjamin, Edwin B. 500
Benjamin, L.S. See Melville, Lewis
[pseud.]
Bernbaum, Ernest 324-25
Berry, Mary 1451
Berryman, John 949
Berwick, Donald M. 1387
"Biblical Context of Johnson's RASSE-
LAS, The" 913
BIBLIOGRAPHY OF HORACE WAL-
POLE, A 1458
"Bibliography of Johnsonian Studies,
1950-1960, A" 870
BIBLIOGRAPHY OF SAMUEL JOHN-
SON, A 872
BIBLIOGRAPHY OF SWIFT STUDIES,
1945-1965, A 1375
BIBLIOGRAPHY OF THE WORKS OF
JOHN BUNYAN, A 362
BIBLIOGRAPHY OF THE WRITINGS
OF JONATHAN SWIFT, A 1376
BIBLIOGRAPHY OF THOMAS HOL-
CROFT, A 838
BIBLIOGRAPHY OF WILLIAM BECK-
FORD OF FONTHILL, A 289
BICENTENARY ESSAYS ON RASSE-
LAS 924
BIOGRAPHICAL MEMOIRS OF EMI-
NENT NOVELISTS 1154
"Birth of Tristram Shandy, The" 1292
Bissell, Frederick Olds 607
Black, Frank Gees 87, 135, 155,
1076
Black, Sidney J. 88
Blackamore, Arthur 212

Index

Blackmur, R.P. 67
Blake, William 34
Blakey, Dorothy 156, 221
Blanchard, Frederic T. 608, 1077
Bloch, Tuvia 609
Block, Andrew 157
Bloom, Edward A. 394, 397
Bloom, Lillian D. 397
Boege, Fred W. 1208
Bond, Donald F. 37, 158, 178, 189
Bonheim, Helmut W. 159
Booth, Wayne C. 21, 58, 158, 160,
   610, 982, 1291, 1297
Bosse, Malcolm J. 210, 211
Boswell, James (p. 87), 874, 879,
   913
Bott, Adrian 1045
Boucé, Paul-Gabriel 1189, 1209,
   1245
Boulton, James T. 458, 467, 743,
   888
"Bourgeois Picaroon, A" 496
Boyce, Benjamin 89, 501
Brack, O.M., Jr. 875-76, 1170,
   1210
Bradbrook, Frank W. 410, 940
Bradbury, Malcolm 430
Brady, Frank 1388
Brailsford, H.N. 733
Brain, Sir Walter Russell 1378
Brander, Lawrence 1196
Braudy, Leo 90-91, 431, 611
BRAVO OF VENICE, THE 951
Bray, Barbara 1278
Brissenden, R.F. 15-16, 47, 1054,
   1065, 1081, 1292, 1447
Bristow, Christopher 474
BRITISH AUTHORS BEFORE 1800: A
   BIOGRAPHICAL DICTIONARY 10
BRITISH LIBRARY RESOURCES: A
   BIBLIOGRAPHICAL GUIDE 7, 169
BRITISH MUSEUM GENERAL CATA-
   LOGUE OF PRINTED BOOKS 3,
   161
BRITISH NOVEL THROUGH JANE
   AUSTEN, THE 158
BRITON, THE 1170, 1218
"BRITON and HUMPHRY CLINKER,
   The" 1218
Brockman, Harold A.N. 295

Bronson, Bertrand H. 854
Brontë, Charlotte 1153
Brooke, Henry (p. 69), 341-49
Brooks, Douglas 92, 569, 571, 612
Brooks, Peter 963
Brophy, Elizabeth Bergen 1078
Brown, Ford K. 734
Brown, Homer O. 502
Brown, John 358, 364
Browning, D.C. 477
Bruce, Donald 1211
Buck, Howard Swazey 1212
Bullen, John S. 1079
Bullitt, John M. 1389
"Bunyan" (Sharrock) 363
BUNYAN (Talon) 367
Bunyan, John 41, 54, 170, 350-90,
   1340
"Bunyan and Spenser" 373
"Bunyan and the Autobiographer's Ar-
   tistic Purpose" 381
"Bunyan and the English Emblem Writ-
   ers" 383
BUNYAN CHARACTERS 390
"Bunyan, Mr. Ignorance, and the
   Quakers" 376
"Bunyan's Giant Despair" 374
"Bunyan's HOLY WAR: A Study in
   Christian Experience" 379
Burgess, Anthony 474
Burke, Edmund 27, 205, (p. 81),
   752, 754, 1033
BURKE NEWSLETTER 205
Burney, Charles (p. 81)
Burney, Fanny 30, 107, 218 (p. 81),
   391-421, 829, (p. 219)
Burns, Robert 32
Burton, Dr. John 1292
Butt, John 17, 587, 1051. See also
   IMAGINED WORLDS
Byrd, Max 18, 222, 503
Byron, George Gordon, Lord 302,
   (p. 181)

C

CALEB WILLIAMS 50, 130, (p. 139),
   722-25, 743, 745-46, 749-52,
   755-57, 760, 762
"CALEB WILLIAMS: The Bondage of
   Truth" 762

CALIPH OF FONTHILL, THE 295
CAMBRIDGE BIBLIOGRAPHY OF EN-
GLISH LITERATURE, THE 162,
187
Camden, Carroll 1104, 1132, 1315,
1466
Cameron, William J. 326
CAMILLA (p. 81), 397
Campbell, Alexander 1116
CANDIDE 863, 1222, 1331
"Canon and Chronology of William
Godwin's Early Works, The" 730
CAPTAIN SINGLETON 464-66, 537
Carnochan, W.B. 1390-92
Carroll, John 1058, 1061, 1080-82
Carter, K. Odell 717
Case, Arthur E. 1362, 1393
CASEBOOK ON GULLIVER AMONG
THE HOUYHNHNMS, A 1411
Cash, Arthur H. 1276, 1292-96
CASTLE OF OTRANTO, THE 50,
(p. 199), 1040, (p. 269), 1452-
53, (p. 271), 1467, 1469-71,
1473-75
CASTLES OF ATHLIN AND DUN-
BAYNE, THE 1005-6
CATALOG OF THE DEFOE COLLEC-
TION IN THE BOSTON PUBLIC
LIBRARY, A 482
"Catalogue of English Prose Fiction,
1470-1832" 176
CATALOGUE OF HORACE WAL-
POLE'S LIBRARY, A 1459
CATALOGUE OF THE BURNEY FAM-
ILY CORRESPONDENCE, A 401
Cauthen, I.B., Jr. 613
CAVALCADE OF THE ENGLISH
NOVEL 55, 195
CBEL. See CAMBRIDGE BIBLIOGRA-
PHY OF ENGLISH LITERATURE,
THE
Cecil, David 411
CECILIA (p. 81), 395-96, 409, 420
Cervantes, Miguel de 54, 63, 122,
138, 626, 628, (p. 153), 942,
1230, 1339
CHAMPION, THE 560, 698
Champion, Larry S. 19, 635, 644,
1237, 1395
CHAMPION OF VIRTUE, THE. See
OLD ENGLISH BARON, THE

Chandler, Frank Wadleigh 59
"Change in the Criticism of the Novel
after 1760" 123
Chapin, Chester F. 889
Chapman, Guy 270, 281, 283, 289,
296
Chapman, R.W. 853, 859, 865, 868
CHAPTER IN FICTION, THE 76
CHARACTER AND THE NOVEL 66
Charlotte, Queen (p. 81)
CHARLOTTE RAMSAY LENNOX 939,
947
"Charlotte Smith" 1154
CHARLOTTE SMITH, POET AND
NOVELIST 1152
"Charlotte Smith, Popular Novelist"
1160
"Charlotte Smith, Pre-Romantic Nov-
elist" 1158
"Charlotte Smith (1749-1806)" 1155
"Charlotte Smith's Letters" 1148
Chaucer, Geoffrey 63
"Checklist of Critical and Biographi-
cal Writings on Jonathan Swift,
1945-1965, A" 1370
CHECK LIST OF ENGLISH PROSE
FICTION, 1700-1739, A 178
CHECK LIST OF PROSE FICTION
PUBLISHED IN ENGLAND, 1740-
1749, A 153
CHECKLIST OF THE WRITINGS OF
DANIEL DEFOE, A 484
Chesterton, G.K. 1174
Cheyne, George 1057
CHOICE OF LIFE, THE 908
Churchill, Sarah, Duchess of Marl-
borough (p. 189)
CITIZEN OF THE WORLD, THE 769-
71
CLARISSA 54, 128, (p. 87), 432,
580, 596, (p. 135), 1051-54, 1059,
1080-81, 1083-85, 1087, 1091-92,
1095, 1097-98, 1101-2, 1105,
1108, 1116, 1120, 1124-25, 1129,
1134-35, 1138, 1140, 1286
"CLARISSA: A Study in the Nature
of Convention" 1125
CLARISSA: PREFACE, HINTS OF
PREFACES, AND POSTSCRIPT 1054
"Clarissa and Fanny Hill" 432, 1084

Index

"CLARISSA and the Epistolary Form" 1105

"Clarissa Harlowe and Her Times" 1101

"CLARISSA Restored?" 1108

"Clarissa's Coffin" 1138

Clark, John R. 1394

Clarke, Samuel 600, 671

CLASSIC BRITISH NOVEL, THE 964

Cleland, John 25, (p. 87), 422-41, 1084

CLEONE 807

Clifford, James L. 20, 223, 869-71, 877, 1176, 1395

Clubb, Merrel D. 1369

Cobb, Joann P. 744

Cohan, Steven M. 1396

Colby, Elbridge 838-40

Cole, G.D.H. 477

Coleridge, Samuel Taylor (p. 139), 1034

Coley, William B. 558, 614

COLLECTED ESSAYS, I (Ker) 1468

COLLECTED LETTERS OF OLIVER GOLDSMITH, THE 777

COLLECTED WORKS OF OLIVER GOLDSMITH 767

Collins, Arthur S. 224

COLONEL JACK 455, 473, 515

"Colonel Jacque: Defoe's Definition of the Complete Gentleman" 515

COLUMELLA (p. 153), 811

COMEDY AND SOCIETY FROM CONGREVE TO FIELDING 31, 648

"Comedy of RASSELAS, The" 926

COMIC ART OF LAURENCE STERNE, THE 1336

"Comic Celebrant of Life in TOM JONES, The" 630

"Comic Prose Epic or Comic Romance" 627

"Comic Resolution in Fielding's JOSEPH ANDREWS" 679

COMIC SPIRIT OF EIGHTEENTH-CENTURY NOVELS, THE 83

COMPLETE WORKS OF HENRY FIELDING, ESQ., THE (Henley) 557

COMPLETE WORKS OF JOHN BUNYAN, THE (Offor) 350

COMPLETE WORKS OF JOHN BUNYAN, THE (Stebbing) 351

"Complexity of Swift, The" 1390

"Composition of CLARISSA and Its Revisions before Publication, The" 1095

Conant, Martha Pike 93, 163, 303, 890

"Concept of Plot and the Plot of TOM JONES, The" 617

"Conclusion of Defoe's ROXANA, The" 509

CONFESSIONAL OF THE BLACK PENITENTS, THE. See ITALIAN, THE

Congreve, William 31

"Conscience and the Pattern of Christian Perfection in CLARISSA" 1092

"Conscious Irony in MOLL FLANDERS" 520

"Consideration of the Bibliographical Problems Connected with the First Edition of HUMPHRY CLINKER, A" 1193

CONSOLIDATOR, THE 460

Cooke, Arthur L. 615

Coolidge, John S. 616

Copeland, Edward W. 432, 1083-85, 1213

Cordasco, Francesco 164, 582, 1062, 1186, 1189-90, 1192, 1271

CORRESPONDENCE OF JONATHAN SWIFT, THE (Ball) 1366, 1368

CORRESPONDENCE OF JONATHAN SWIFT, THE (Williams) 1368

CORRESPONDENCE OF SAMUEL RICHARDSON, THE 709, 1056

COUNTRY AND THE CITY, THE 43

Courtney, W.P. 868, 872

COVENT-GARDEN JOURNAL, THE 559, 942

Coventry, Francis (p. ix), 652

Cowler, Rosemary 1086

Cox, Edward Godfrey 165

CRAFT OF FICTION, THE 70

Crane, Ronald S. 21, 150, 225, 617, 778, 982, 1297, 1397-98

CREATED SELF, THE 128, 530, 663, 1124, 1330

"Crime and Punishment in Defoe's ROXANA" 521

CRITICAL REMARKS ON SIR CHARLES
GRANDISON, CLARISSA AND
PAMELA 1116
CRITICAL REVIEW, THE 1225
"Criticism of Gulliver's 'Voyage to
the Houyhnhnms,' 1726-1914, The"
1369
CRITICS AND CRITICISM: ANCIENT
AND MODERN 617
Croix, Pétis de la. See de la Croix,
Pétis
Cross, Wilbur L. (p. 115), 588,
590, 670, 710-11, 1254, 1277
Crouch, William G. 262
Crowley, J. Donald 462
Cruttwell, Patrick 745
Cunningham, Peter 1454
CURSE OF PARTY, THE 1383
Curtis, Lewis Perry 1268

D

Dahl, Curtis 792
Daiches, David 1087
Dalziel, Margaret 929, 941, 1088
DANIEL DEFOE (Boulton) 458
"Daniel Defoe" (Novak) 484
DANIEL DEFOE: A COLLECTION
OF CRITICAL ESSAYS 503
DANIEL DEFOE: A CRITICAL STUDY
544
DANIEL DEFOE: A STUDY IN
CONFLICT 489
DANIEL DEFOE: CITIZEN OF THE
MODERN WORLD 491
DANIEL DEFOE: HIS LIFE AND RE-
CENTLY DISCOVERED WRITINGS
1716-1729 490
DANIEL DEFOE: HIS MIND AND
HIS ART 540
DANIEL DEFOE AND MIDDLE-CLASS
GENTILITY 493
DANIEL DEFOE AND THE SUPERNA-
TURAL 498
DANIEL DEFOE ET SES ROMANS
488
DANIEL DEFOE'S MANY VOICES
511
Darbee, Richard H. 347
D'Arblay, General Alexandre (p. 81)

D'Arblay, Mme. See Burney, Fanny
D'Argens, Marquis. See Argens,
Jean B. de B., marquis d'
Darnall, F.M. 1399
DAVID SIMPLE (p. 135), 700-702,
713-14
Davis, Herbert J. 1350, 1352, 1379
Davis, James B. 1210
Davys, Mary 212
Day, Robert Adams 94, 135, 166,
1089
Day, Thomas (p. 91), 442-52
DEAN AND THE ANARCHIST, THE
759
Deane, Seamus 836
"Deathless Lady" 441
"Defoe" (Novak) 485
DEFOE (Sutherland) 494
DEFOE (Sutherland, Writers and Their
Work) 495
Defoe, Daniel 19-20, 34, 43, 48-49,
52, 54, 57, 63, 65, 71, 76, 92,
115, 128, 134, 137, 142, 148,
170, 337, 440, (p. 95), 453-553,
644, 690, 1136
DEFOE: THE CRITICAL HERITAGE
536
DEFOE AND CASUISTRY 541
DEFOE AND SPIRITUAL AUTOBIOG-
RAPHY 542
DEFOE AND THE NATURE OF MAN
522
DEFOE AND THE NOVEL 552
DEFOE IN THE PILLORY AND OTHER
STUDIES 518
"Defoe's CAPTAIN SINGLETON: A
Reassessment with Observations"
537
"Defoe's 'Indifferent Monitor': The
Complexity of MOLL FLANDERS"
523
"Defoe's JOURNAL OF THE PLAGUE
YEAR Reconsidered" 499
DEFOE'S NARRATIVES 533
"Defoe's Prose Style" 543
"Defoe's Reaction to Enlightened Secu-
larism: A JOURNAL OF THE
PLAGUE YEAR" 513
"Defoe's Theory of Fiction" 524
"Defoe's Use of Irony" 525

Index

"Defoe, Swift, and Fielding: Notes on the Retirement Theme" 644

DEGREE OF PRUDERY: A BIOGRAPHY OF FANNY BURNEY, A 406

de la Croix, Pétis 921

"Delarivière Manley's Prose Fiction" 999

de la Torre, Lillian 1229

DePorte, Michael V. 18, 22, 226, 1298, 1400

Derrick, Samuel 89

"Descriptive Bibliography of the Creative Works of Tobias Smollett, A" 1194

DESERTED VILLAGE, THE 791

"DESERTED VILLAGE and Goldsmith's Social Doctrines, THE" 791

DESMOND (p. 219), 1144

"Development of Techniques in Fielding's Comedies" 625

DIABLE AMOUREUX, LE 968

DIARIES, PRAYERS, AND ANNALS 866

DIARY AND LETTERS OF MADAME D'ARBLAY, THE 398

Dickens, Charles 48, 637, 748

DICTIONARY OF NATIONAL BIOGRAPHY 4

Diderot, Denis 1304

DIDEROT AND STERNE 1304

Digeon, Aurélien 618

Dilworth, Ernest N. 1299

DISCOURSE OF THE MIND IN EIGHTEENTH-CENTURY FICTION, THE 96

"Disenchanting the Man of Feeling" 1237

"Displaced Self in the Novels of Daniel Defoe, The" 502

DISSERTATION ABSTRACTS INTERNATIONAL 5, 167

Dobrée, Bonamy 23, 359, 1011, 1466

Dobson, Austin 391, 398, 404, 589, 770, 772, 781, 1066, 1461

DR. JOHNSON: HIS LIFE IN LETTERS 867

DR. JOHNSON AND FANNY BURNEY 419

"Dr. Johnson as Equivocator" 911

"Dr. Johnson on Fielding and Richardson" 655, 910, 1117

"Dr. Johnson on Prose Fiction" 909

Dodsley, Robert 807

Donoghue, Denis 1401

Donovan, Robert Alan 48, 504, 619, 1090, 1214, 1300

DON QUIXOTE 54, 122, 628, 942, 1230

Doody, Margaret Anne 1091

Dostoyevsky, Fyodor 748

Dottin, Paul 488

Doughty, Oswald 773, 1452, 1467

Downs, Brian W. 1050, 1067

Downs, Robert B. 6-7, 168-69

Draper, Mrs. Elizabeth 1269

DREAMS, WAKING THOUGHTS AND INCIDENTS 286

Drescher, Horst W. 977

Dryden, John 32, 34, 214

"Duality of Theme in THE VICAR OF WAKEFIELD" 789

Dudden, F. Homes 590

Dumas, D. Gilbert 746

Duncan, Jeffrey L. 95

DUNCIAD, THE (p. 157)

Dussinger, John A. 96, 1092-94

Dyson, A.E. 170, 363, 485, 581, 620, 1061, 1191, 1273, 1301, 1371

Dyson, Anne Jane 154

E

Eagle, Dorothy 8

EARLY BIOGRAPHIES OF SAMUEL JOHNSON, THE 875

EARLY DIARY OF FRANCES BURNEY, THE 399

"Early Editions and Issues of THE MONK, The" 957

EARLY MASTERS OF ENGLISH FICTION, THE 115, 516, 649, 1112, 1231, 1318

EARLY OPPOSITION TO THE ENGLISH NOVEL 143

Eaves, T.C. Duncan 1048, 1068, 1095-96

ECONOMICS AND THE FICTION OF DANIEL DEFOE 526

Eddy, William A. 1353
Edge, Charles 964
"Educational Theory and Human Nature in Fielding's Works" 646
EDUCATION AND ENLIGHTENMENT IN THE WORKS OF WILLIAM GODWIN 758
Edwards, Philip 1373, 1421
Ehrenpreis, Anne Henry 1143, 1145, 1156-57
Ehrenpreis, Irvin 24, 621, 1350, 1380-81, 1402-4, 1433
EIGHTEENTH CENTURY, THE 158
EIGHTEENTH CENTURY: A CURRENT BIBLIOGRAPHY, THE 171
EIGHTEENTH CENTURY BACKGROUND, THE 255
EIGHTEENTH CENTURY BIBLIOGRAPHIES 164
EIGHTEENTH-CENTURY BRITISH NOVELISTS ON THE NOVEL 85
EIGHTEENTH-CENTURY ENGLISH LITERATURE: MODERN ESSAYS IN CRITICISM 20
EIGHTEENTH CENTURY ENGLISH NOVEL IN FRENCH TRANSLATION: A BIBLIOGRAPHICAL STUDY, THE 193
EIGHTEENTH-CENTURY GOTHIC NOVEL: AN ANNOTATED BIBLIOGRAPHY OF CRITICISM AND SELECTED TEXTS, THE 180, 292, 956, 1015, 1037, 1150, 1460
"Eighteenth-Century 'Histories' as a Fictional Mode" 88
EIGHTEENTH-CENTURY STUDIES 198
Elliott, Robert C. 505, 1405-8
Ellis, Annie Raine 395, 399
Ellis, Frank 506
Ellis, Havelock 810
ELOQUENT "I," THE 41, 388
Emerson, O.F. 858
EMILE (p. 69), (p. 91), 452
EMMA (p. 81), 945
EMMELINE 1143, (p. 221), 1156
Empson, William 622
Emslie, Macdonald 793
END OF OBSCENITY, THE 437
England, Martha Winburn 718
ENGLAND IN THE REIGN OF CHARLES II 242

ENGLAND IN TRANSITION 228
ENGLAND'S WEALTHIEST SON 294
ENGLISCHE VORROMANTIK UND DEUTSCHER STURM UND DRANG 965
ENGLISH BIOGRAPHY BEFORE 1700 247
ENGLISH BOOK TRADE, THE 243
"English Circulating Libraries, 1725-1750" 116
ENGLISH COMMON READER, THE 217
ENGLISH COUNTRY SQUIRE, THE 136
"English Fiction in the 1740's" 86, 604, 1073, 1206
ENGLISH FICTION TO 1820 IN THE UNIVERSITY OF PENNSYLVANIA LIBRARY 173
ENGLISH HUMOURISTS OF THE EIGHTEENTH CENTURY, THE 683, 1249, 1342
ENGLISH LANDED SOCIETY IN THE EIGHTEENTH CENTURY 240
ENGLISH LITERATURE FROM DRYDEN TO BURNS 32
ENGLISH LITERATURE IN THE EARLY EIGHTEENTH CENTURY, 1700-1740 23
ENGLISH LITERATURE OF THE LATE SEVENTEENTH CENTURY 38
ENGLISH LITERATURE, 1789-1815 35
ENGLISH LITERATURE, 1660-1800: A BIBLIOGRAPHY OF MODERN STUDIES 171
ENGLISH NOVEL: A PANORAMA, THE 53, 55, 191
ENGLISH NOVEL: A SHORT CRITICAL HISTORY, THE 44, 55
ENGLISH NOVEL: FORM AND FUNCTION, THE 54, 387, 547, 686, 1134, 1346
ENGLISH NOVEL: SELECT BIBLIOGRAPHICAL GUIDES, THE 170, 363, 485, 581, 1061, 1191, 1273, 1371
ENGLISH NOVEL BEFORE RICHARDSON: A CHECKLIST OF TEXTS AND CRITICISMS TO 1970, THE 159

ENGLISH NOVEL EXPLICATION:
CRITICISMS TO 1972 154
ENGLISH NOVEL EXPLICATION:
SUPPLEMENT I 154
ENGLISH NOVEL 1578-1956: A
CHECKLIST OF TWENTIETH-
CENTURY CRITICISMS, THE 154
"English Novel from 1731 to 1740,
The" 103
ENGLISH NOVEL IN THE MAGA-
ZINES, 1740-1815, THE 119,
181, 987
ENGLISH NOVEL, 1740-1850: A
CATALOGUE, THE 157
ENGLISH PROSE FICTION, 1700-
1800, IN THE UNIVERSITY OF
ILLINOIS LIBRARY 179
ENGLISH PROSE FICTION, 1600-
1700: A CHRONOLOGICAL
CHECKLIST 183
"English Short Fiction in the Seven-
teenth Century" 120
ENGLISH THEORIES OF THE NOVEL
101
ENGLISH TRAVELLER AND THE
MOVEMENT OF IDEAS, 1660-
1732, THE 227
ENGLISH WOMEN NOVELISTS, THE
107, 335, 415, 712, 831, 943,
1000, 1024
ENGLISH WOMEN OF LETTERS 1153
ENGLISH WRITERS OF THE EIGH-
TEENTH CENTURY 912
ENLIGHTENMENT ESSAYS 199
ENQUIRY CONCERNING THE PRIN-
CIPLES OF POLITICAL JUSTICE.
See POLITICAL JUSTICE
EPIC STRAIN IN THE ENGLISH
NOVEL, THE 78
EPIC TO NOVEL 118
EPISODES OF VATHEK, THE 270,
274-75
EPISTOLARY NOVEL: ITS ORIGIN,
DEVELOPMENT, DECLINE, AND
RESIDUARY INFLUENCE, THE 135
EPISTOLARY NOVEL IN THE LATE
EIGHTEENTH CENTURY, THE 87,
135, 155, 1076
"Epistolary Technique in Richardson's
Novels" 1113

Epstein, Lynne 1021
Epstein, William 429
"Equation of Love and Money in
MOLL FLANDERS, The" 517
Erickson, James P. 412, 829-30
"Errors Concerning the Houyhnhnms"
1438
Esdaile, Arundell 172
ESSAY ON THE HISTORY AND RE-
ALITY OF APPARITIONS, AN 498
"Essay on the Life and Genius of
Henry Fielding, Esq." 554
ESSAY ON THE NEW SPECIES OF
WRITING FOUNDED BY MR.
FIELDING, AN 652
ESSAY ON WIT AND HUMOUR 1311
ESSAYS IN CRITICISM AND RE-
SEARCH 921
ESSAYS ON THE EIGHTEENTH-
CENTURY NOVEL 137, 1205
Evans, David L. 1178, 1215-16
Evans, Frank B. III 747
EVELINA (p. 81), 391-94, 409,
412, 417-18, 420-21, 829
"EVELINA and BETSY THOUGHTLESS"
412, 829
"EVELINA Revisited" 417
EVERGREEN TREE OF DIABOLICAL
KNOWLEDGE, THE 254
"Evolution of A SENTIMENTAL JOUR-
NEY, The" 1332
Ewald, William B. 1409
EXCURSION A ALCOBACA ET BA-
TALHA 283
EXEMPLARY MR. DAY, THE 449
EXPEDITION OF HUMPHRY CLINKER,
THE. See HUMPHRY CLINKER
EXPERIENCE IN THE NOVEL 104
"Experience of Character in the En-
glish Gothic Novel, The" 104
"Experience to Expression: Thematic
Character Contrasts in TRISTRAM
SHANDY" 1321

F

FABLE'S END 73
FAIR JILT, THE 318
FAIR LIBERTY WAS ALL HIS CRY
1370, 1374, 1414

FAMILIAR LETTER IN THE EIGH-
TEENTH CENTURY, THE 218,
1142, 1288
FAMILIAR LETTERS 1050, 1103
FANNY BURNEY (Adelstein) 403
FANNY BURNEY (Dobson) 404
"Fanny Burney and Jane Austen's
PRIDE AND PREJUDICE" 409
"Fanny Burney and the Courtesy
Books" 414
FANNY BURNEY, NOVELIST 421
"Fanny Burney's EVELINA" 418
FANNY HILL 25, (p. 87), 422-23,
(p. 88), 430-41, 546, 1084
"FANNY HILL and Materialism" 431
"FANNY HILL and the Comic Novel"
430
Farrell, William J. 623, 1097, 1302
FARTHER ADVENTURES OF ROBIN-
SON CRUSOE, THE (p. 97)
Faulkner, Peter 835
FEMALE HUSBAND AND OTHER
WRITINGS, THE 561
FEMALE QUIXOTE, THE (p. 177),
929-30, 934, 941-46
FEMALE SPECTATOR, THE 823
FEMINIST CONTROVERSY IN EN-
GLAND 1788-1810, THE 209
FERDINAND COUNT FATHOM 1177,
1237, 1248
Ferguson, Oliver W. 1382
FICTION AND THE READING PUB-
LIC 235
FICTION AND THE SHAPE OF BE-
LIEF 131, 672, 916, 1437
FICTIONS OF SATIRE, THE 126,
1425
Fiedler, Leslie 1098
"Fielding" (Battestin) 581
FIELDING (Butt) 587
Fielding, Henry 14, 16, 19-20, 30-
31, 39, 43, 48-49, 52, 54, 57-
58, 75, 78, 83-84, 86, 91-92,
95, 109, 115, 124-28, 130-32,
134, 137, 141, 148, 170, 212,
548, (p. 111), 554-699, (p. 135),
700-702, (p. 157), (p. 160), 910,
(p. 177), 942, (p. 185), 1073-74,
1107, 1111, 1114, 1117, 1121-22,
1136, 1205-7, 1249-50, 1286,
1312, 1326, 1426

Fielding, Sarah 107, 114, (p. 135),
700-716
FIELDING: A COLLECTION OF
CRITICAL ESSAYS 660
FIELDING: THE CRITICAL HERITAGE
661
FIELDING: TOM JONES 621
"Fielding and 'Conservation of Char-
acter'" 616
"Fielding and Richardson" 124, 657,
1121
"Fielding and the Authorship of
SHAMELA" 697
"Fielding and the Meaning of History"
680
FIELDING AND THE NATURE OF
THE NOVEL 594
"Fielding, Square, and the Fitness of
Things" 671
"Fielding's AMELIA: An Interpreta-
tion" 675
"Fielding's AMELIA: Dramatic and
Authorial Narration" 631
FIELDING'S ART OF FICTION 641
"Fielding's Changing Politics and JO-
SEPH ANDREWS" 586
"Fielding's Definition of Wisdom"
598
"Fielding's Digressions in JOSEPH
ANDREWS" 613
"Fielding's Early Aesthetic and Tech-
nique" 667
"Fielding's Irony: Its Method and Ef-
fects" 634
"Fielding's Knowledge of History and
Biography" 688
FIELDING'S MORAL PSYCHOLOGY
629
"Fielding's Novel About Novels" 642
"Fielding's Novels: Selected Criti-
cism (1940-1969)" 583
"Fielding's Revisions of JOSEPH AN-
DREWS" 599
"Fielding's Social Outlook" 676
FIELDING'S THEORY OF THE NOVEL
607
FIELDING THE NOVELIST 608, 1077
"Final Comedy of Lemuel Gulliver,
The" 1436
Fink, Zera S. 1410

FIRST AMERICAN NOVELIST?, THE 938

Fish, Stanley E. 370

Fitzgerald, Brian 489

FLEETWOOD 728

Fleisher, David 735

Fletcher, Theodore T. 263

FLOWERING OF THE NOVEL, THE 210

Fluchère, Henri 1278, 1303

FOCUS: SWIFT 1433

Fogle, Richard Harter 964

Folkenflik, Robert 624

Folsom, James K. 304

FOOL OF QUALITY, THE (p. 69), 341-42, 348

"Foreign Tour of Gray and Walpole, The" 1465

FORM AND FRENZY IN SWIFT'S TALE OF A TUB 1394

"Form in A TALE OF A TUB" 1434

"Form of the Sentimental Novel, The" 90

Forrest, James F. 361

Forster, E.M. 60, 507

Forster, John 782

FORTUNATE FOUNDLINGS, THE 824

FORTUNES AND MISFORTUNES OF THE FAMOUS MOLL FLANDERS, THE. See MOLL FLANDERS

Foster, James R. 97-98, 264, 348, 450, 794, 983, 1022, 1038, 1158-59, 1217

Foster, Milton P. 1411

FOUNDATIONS OF THE NOVEL 211

FOUR BEFORE RICHARDSON 212, 819

FOUR ESSAYS ON GULLIVER'S TRAVELS 1393

"'Fourth Son of the Mighty Emperor, The'" 907

FOUR YEARS VOYAGES OF CAPTAIN GEORGE ROBERTS, THE 479

Foxon, David 25, 433-34

"Framework of SHAMELA, The" 668

Frantz, R.W. 227

Fredman, Alice Green 1304

FRENCH REVOLUTION AND THE EN-GLISH NOVEL, THE 100, 749, 844

Friedman, Arthur 767, 775, 778

FROM CLASSIC TO ROMANTIC 220

"From PAMELA to CLARISSA" 1129

Fry, Carroll Lee 1160

Frye, Northrop 26, 61, 150, 984, 1305

Frye, Roland M. 371, 1412

"Fulfillment through Frustration" 1314

Furbank, P.N. 748

Fussell, Paul 27, 891

G

Gallaway, W.F. 795

Garber, Frederick 1009, 1013

Garnett, Richard 269, 768

Garrick, David (p. 87)

Gassman, Byron 1218-19

GASTON DE BLONDEVILLE 1004, 1014

Gay, John 14

Gecker, Sidney 173

Gemmett, Robert J. 275, 286, 290

GENERAL HISTORY OF THE PYRATES, A 480

"Generality and Particularity in Johnson's Thought" 915

"Generic Control of the Aesthetic Response, The" 1223

GENRE 200

GENTLEMAN'S MAGAZINE, 1731-51: THE LISTS OF BOOKS, COLLECTED WITH ANNUAL INDEXES AND THE INDEX TO THE FIRST TWENTY YEARS COMPILED BY EDWARD KIMBER (1752), THE 174

George, M. Dorothy 228-29

George II (p. 69), 1219

Gerin, Winifred 405

Gibbon, Edward 91, 214

Gibbs, J.M.W. 766

Gibson, Daniel, Jr. 372

Giddings, Robert 1220

Gignilliat, George Warren 447

Gildon, Charles 313

GOD, MAN AND SATAN 371

Godwin, William 50, 100, 130, 209, (p. 53), 266, (p. 139), 717-63, (p. 161), 841, 844-46

Godber, Joyce 365
GODWIN AND MARY 729
GODWIN CRITICISM: A SYNOPTIC
    BIBLIOGRAPHY 731
"Godwin's CALEB WILLIAMS" 752
"Godwin's Changing Conception of
    CALEB WILLIAMS" 756
"Godwin's Later Novels" 761
"Godwin's Literary Theory" 266, 753,
    845
GODWIN'S MORAL PHILOSOPHY
    755
"Godwin's Novels" 748
"Godwin's Novels and POLITICAL
    JUSTICE" 744
"Godwin's Reading in Burke" 754
Goggin, L.P. 625
Goldberg, Homer 626-28
Goldberg, M.A. 1221
Golden, Morris 629, 1099-1100
Golder, Harold 373-74
Goldgar, Bertrand 1383
GOLDSMITH 784
Goldsmith, Oliver 14, 95-96, 764-
    803
GOLDSMITH: SELECTED WORKS
    768
GOLDSMITH: THE CRITICAL HERI-
    TAGE 802
"Goldsmith, the Good-Natured Man"
    800
GOLDSMITH: THE VICAR OF WAKE-
    FIELD 793
Gombrich, E.H. 638
GOTHIC BIBLIOGRAPHY, A 194
GOTHIC FLAME, THE 147, 312,
    971, 1475
GOTHIC NOVELS 213
GOTHIC QUEST, THE 140, 970,
    1029, 1040, 1474
"Gothic Versus Romantic: A Revalua-
    tion of the Gothic Novel" 110
Gotlieb, Howard B. 291
Gove, Philip Babcock 62, 99, 175
GOVERNESS, THE 703
Grabo, C.H. 265
GRACE ABOUNDING TO THE CHIEF
    OF SINNERS 353, 356, 381,
    388

Graham, Kenneth W. 305
Grant, Aline 1017
Grant, Damian 1177
Grant, Douglas 1257
Graves, Richard (p. 153), 804-15
Graves, William 211
Gray, Thomas 1465
GREAT CHAIN OF BEING, THE 236
GREAT TRADITION, THE 51
Greaves, Richard L. 375
Green, F.C. 28
Greenberg, Robert A. 1357, 1363,
    1398
Greene, Donald J. 230, 870-71,
    878, 892-93
Greenough, C.N. 176
Gregor, Ian 52, 545, 633, 927,
    1432
Gregory, Allene 100, 749, 844
Greiner, Walter F. 101
Grey, Jill E. 703
Grieder, Josephine 102, 211
Grimsditch, Herbert 271
Gross, Harvey 750
Grossvogel, David I. 63
Grundy, Isobel 591
Grylls, Rosalie Glynn 736
Guffey, George Robert 332
"Gulliver and the Gentle Reader"
    1432
GULLIVER AND THE GENTLE READER:
    STUDIES IN SWIFT AND OUR
    TIME 1432
"Gulliver as Literary Artist" 1405
"Gulliver's Fiction" 1396
"Gulliver's Fourth Voyage: 'Hard'
    and 'Soft' Schools of Interpretation"
    1395
GULLIVER'S TRAVELS 24, 1353,
    1355, 1361-65, 1388, 1390-91,
    1393, 1395-99, 1402-6, 1410-12,
    1416-18, 1422-24, 1428, 1431-32,
    1436-38, 1440, 1442, 1444, 1446-
    48, 1450
"GULLIVER'S TRAVELS, A MODEST
    PROPOSAL, and the Problematical
    Nature of Meaning" 1444
GULLIVER'S TRAVELS AND OTHER
    WRITINGS 1355

GULLIVER'S TRAVELS, A TALE OF A TUB, THE BATTLE OF THE BOOKS 1353

"Gulliver the Preacher" 1450

GUSTAVUS VASA (p. 69)

Guthke, Karl S. 954, 965

Guthkelch, A.C. 1354

Guthrie, William B. 630

H

Haas, Gaylord R. 103

Hagstrum, Jean H. 894

Hahn, Emily 406

Hale, Will T. 413

Halewood, William 508

Hall, Joan J. 1306

Halperin, John 64

Hammond, Lansing van der H. 1307

HANDBOOK TO LITERATURE, A 9

Hannay, David 1197

Hardin, Richard F. 376

Hardy, Barbara 65

Hardy, John P. 861

Hargreaves, Henry A. 327, 333

Harper, Howard M., Jr. 964

Harris, Jocelyn 1055

Harrison, Frank M. 362, 364

Harrison, G.B. 359, 366

Hart, Francis R. 104

Harth, Philip 29, 1413

Hartley, Cecil 442

Hartley, Lodwick 1272, 1279

Harvey, Paul 8

Harvey, W.J. 66

Hassall, Anthony 624, 631

Hatfield, Glenn W. 632

HAUNTED CASTLE, THE 969

Havens, Raymond D. 1023

Haviland, Thomas Philip 105

Hawkins, Sir John 879

Haycraft, Howard 10

Haywood, Eliza 114, 129, 212, 412, (p. 157), 816-34

Hazen, Allen T. 868, 1458-59

Hazlitt, William (p. 139), 737, 840

Healey, George Harris 481

Heidler, Joseph Bunn 106

Helmick, E.T. 1222

Hemlow, Joyce 400-401, 407, 414

Henley, Samuel 269, 272-73, 302, 311

Henley, William E. 557, 1168, 1180

"Henley's Share in Beckford's VATHEK" 311

HENRIETTA 931

HENRY BROOKE 345

"Henry Brooke: A Study of His Ideas and of His Position in the Pre-Romantic Movement" 347

HENRY FIELDING (Dobson) 589

HENRY FIELDING (Rawson) 664

HENRY FIELDING: A CRITICAL ANTHOLOGY 666

HENRY FIELDING: A LIST OF CRITICAL STUDIES PUBLISHED FROM 1895 TO 1946 582

HENRY FIELDING AND THE AUGUSTAN IDEAL UNDER STRESS 665

HENRY FIELDING AND THE DRY MOCK 647

HENRY FIELDING AND THE LANGUAGE OF IRONY 632

"Henry Fielding and the Writers of Romance" 615

"Henry Fielding: Christian Censor" 698

HENRY FIELDING: HIS LIFE, WORKS, AND TIMES 590

HENRY FIELDING: MASK AND FEAST 699

HENRY FIELDING: NOVELIST AND MAGISTRATE 592

HENRY FIELDING: PLAYWRIGHT, JOURNALIST, AND MASTER OF THE ART OF FICTION 585

HENRY FIELDING: THE TENTATIVE REALIST 638

"Henry Fielding's Comic Romances" 597

HENRY FIELDING'S THEORY OF THE COMIC PROSE EPIC 684

HENRY MACKENZIE 979

"Henry Mackenzie, a Practical Sentimentalist" 988

HENRY MACKENZIE: LETTERS TO ELIZABETH ROSE 977

HERMSPRONG (p. 53), 259-60

"Heroic Allusion in TOM JONES" 673

"H.F.'s Meditations: A JOURNAL OF THE PLAGUE YEAR" 553

Hilbish, Florence M.A. 1152, 1155

Hill, Charles Jarvis 807, 809, 811

Hill, Christopher 1101

Hill, G.B. 874

Hill, Rowland M. 334

Hilles, Frederick W. 30, 418, 633, 698, 769, 774, 796, 800, 886, 895-96, 1028, 1102, 1228, 1333

Hipple, Walter J. 231, 241

HISTORICAL SOURCES OF DEFOE'S JOURNAL OF THE PLAGUE YEAR, THE 519

HISTORIES AND NOVELS OF THE LATE INGENIOUS MRS. BEHN, THE 313, 324, 328

HISTORY AND ADVENTURES OF AN ATOM, THE 1170, 1217

HISTORY AND REMARKABLE LIFE OF . . . COLONEL JACQUE. See COLONEL JACK

HISTORY, FROM 1700 TO 1800, OF ENGLISH CRITICISM OF PROSE FICTION, THE 106

HISTORY OF A GOOD WARM WATCHCOAT, THE. See POLITICAL ROMANCE, A

HISTORY OF ENGLAND 252

HISTORY OF ENGLISH THOUGHT IN THE EIGHTEENTH CENTURY 248

HISTORY OF FANNY BURNEY, THE 407

HISTORY OF HENRY FIELDING, THE (p. 115), 588, 590, 670, 710

HISTORY OF JEMMY AND JENNY JESSAMY, THE 826

HISTORY OF LITTLE JACK, THE 444

HISTORY OF MISS BETSY THOUGHTLESS, THE 412, 829

HISTORY OF MODERN CRITICISM, 1750-1950, A 252

HISTORY OF OPHELIA, THE 707

HISTORY OF POMPEY THE LITTLE 652

HISTORY OF RASSELAS, PRINCE OF ABYSSINIA, THE. See RASSELAS

HISTORY OF SANDFORD AND MER-

TON, THE (p. 91), 442-43, 447, 450-52

HISTORY OF SIR CHARLES GRANDISON, THE 1055, 1066, 1091, 1116, 1123

HISTORY OF THE ADVENTURES OF JOSEPH ANDREWS, THE. See JOSEPH ANDREWS

HISTORY OF THE COUNTESS OF DELLWYN, THE 706

HISTORY OF THE ENGLISH NOVEL, THE 46

"History of the Life and Memoirs of Mrs. Behn, The" 313, 324, 328

HISTORY OF THE NUN, THE 216, 322

HISTORY OF THE PRE-ROMANTIC NOVEL IN ENGLAND 98, 264, 348, 450, 794, 983, 1022, 1038, 1158-59

HISTORY OF TOM JONES, THE. See TOM JONES

Hoadly, Benjamin 600

Hobbes, Thomas 629

"Hobbyhorsical World of TRISTRAM SHANDY, The" 1306

Hodges, H.W. 1171

Hodgkin, John 289

Hogarth, William 1308

Holcroft, Thomas 100, (p. 139), 749, 753, (p. 161), 835-50

"Holcroft's Influence on POLITICAL JUSTICE" 846

Hollander, John 435

Hollander, Steven 1350

Holman, C. Hugh 9

Holtz, William V. 1308

HOLY WAR, THE (p. 74), 360-61, 379

Honour, Hugh 1462

Hopkins, Robert H. 797

"Horace Walpole" (Dobrée) 1466

HORACE WALPOLE (Honour) 1462

HORACE WALPOLE (Kallich) 1463

"Horace Walpole" (Ker) 1468

HORACE WALPOLE: A BIOGRAPHY 1464

HORACE WALPOLE: A MEMOIR 1461

Index

HORACE WALPOLE: WRITER, POLITICIAN, AND CONNOISSEUR 1472

HORACE WALPOLE AND THE ENGLISH NOVEL 1471

HORACE WALPOLE'S CORRESPONDENCE (p. 269), 1453, 1456

HORACE WALPOLE'S LIBRARY 1459

Hornbeak, Katherine 1103

Horner, Joyce M. 107, 335, 415, 712, 831, 943, 1000, 1024

"Houyhnhnms, the Yahoos, and the History of Ideas, The" 1397

Howes, Alan B. 1309-10

Hughes, Helen Sard 108-9

Hughes, Leo 1104

Hughes, Peter 232

Hume, David 91, 747, 755

Hume, Robert D. 110, 509

Humphreys, A.R. 571, 574, 577, 634

HUMPHRY CLINKER 130, 689, 1181-84, 1193, 1205, 1213-15, 1218-19, 1222-23, 1226, 1228, 1232, 1244, 1246, 1249-52

"HUMPHRY CLINKER: A Pastoral Poem in Prose" 1213

"HUMPHRY CLINKER: Smollett's Tempered Augustanism" 1215

"HUMPHRY CLINKER and the Two Kingdoms of George II" 1219

"HUMPHRY CLINKER as Comic Romance" 1205

Hunt, J.H. Leigh 1311

Hunter, J. Paul 470, 508, 510, 635-36, 1312

Hunting, Robert 798

Hutchens, Eleanor Newman 637

Hutcheson, Francis 755

Hutchins, Henry C. 483

I

IDEA OF THE HUMANITIES, THE 21, 982, 1297

"Ideas of Romance in Eighteenth-Century Fiction" 84

"Illness of Dean Swift, The" 1378

ILLUSTRATED ENGLISH SOCIAL HISTORY 253

IMAGE AND IMMORTALITY 1308

"Imaginary Islands and Real Beasts: The Imaginative Genesis of ROBINSON CRUSOE" 527

IMAGINARY VOYAGE IN PROSE FICTION, THE 62, 99, 175

IMAGINED WORLDS: ESSAYS ON SOME ENGLISH NOVELS AND NOVELISTS IN HONOUR OF JOHN BUTT 52, 545, 633, 927, 1432

"Imlac and the Business of a Poet" 919

IMOGEN 718

"Imprisonments of John Bunyan, The" 365

Inchbald, Elizabeth (p. ix)

INCOMPARABLE APHRA, THE 331

INDEX TO DEFOE'S REVIEW 457

"Influence of the AENEID on Fielding's AMELIA, The" 662

"In Praise of RASSELAS" 927

"Interpolated Narratives in the Fiction of Fielding and Smollett, The" 689, 1250

"Interpolated Stories in JOSEPH ANDREWS, The" 628

"Interpolated Tales in JOSEPH ANDREWS Again, The" 612

"Interpositions of Providence and the Design of Fielding's Novels" 695

"Introduction" to A SENTIMENTAL JOURNEY 1338

"Introduction" to DAVID SIMPLE 713

"Introduction" to EMMELINE 1156

"Introduction" to THE CASTLE OF OTRANTO (Doughty) 1467

"Introduction" to THE CASTLE OF OTRANTO (Lewis) 1470

INTRODUCTION TO THE ENGLISH NOVEL, AN 49

"Introduction" to THE FEMALE QUIXOTE 941

"Introduction" to THE MAN OF FEELING 990

"Introduction" to THE MONK 961

"Introduction" to THE OLD ENGLISH BARON 1042

"Introduction" to THE OLD MANOR HOUSE 1157

"Introduction" to THE SPIRITUAL QUIXOTE 815
"Introduction" to THE VICAR OF WAKEFIELD 796
IRONY IN TOM JONES 637
Irving, Joseph 1198
Irving, Washington 783
Irwin, George 880
Irwin, Michael 638
Irwin, William R. 639-40
Iser, Wolfgang 1223
Isles, Duncan E. 929, 933-35, 937, 944, 1273
ITALIAN, THE 1012-13
ITALIAN LANDSCAPE IN EIGHTEENTH CENTURY ENGLAND 238, 1027
ITALIAN LETTERS 719
ITALY, WITH SKETCHES OF SPAIN AND PORTUGAL 280

J

Jack, Ian 1258, 1269
Jack, Jane 476
JAMAICA LADY, THE 212
James, E. Anthony 511
James, Henry 67, 70
James, Overton Philip 1280
JAMES WALLACE 258
JANE AUSTEN AND HER PREDECESSORS 410, 940
"Jane Austen and THE FEMALE QUIXOTE" 945
Jeffares, A. Norman 784, 1370, 1414
Jefferson, D.W. 799, 1281, 1313
Jenkins, Brian 862
Jenkins, H.D. 897
Jenkins, Ralph E. 512, 985
Jensen, Gerard E. 559, 942
Jobe, Alice 583
JOHN BUNYAN (Greaves) 375
JOHN BUNYAN (Sharrock) 384
JOHN BUNYAN (Winslow) 369
JOHN BUNYAN: A STUDY IN PERSONALITY 366
JOHN BUNYAN: HIS LIFE, TIMES, AND WORK 364
JOHN BUNYAN, MECHANICK PREACHER 386

JOHN BUNYAN: THE MAN AND HIS WORKS 368
JOHN CLELAND: IMAGES OF A LIFE 429
"John Cleland and The Publication of MEMOIRS OF A WOMAN OF PLEASURE" 433
JOHN LOCKE AND ENGLISH LITERATURE OF THE EIGHTEENTH CENTURY 237, 1320
Johnson, Clifford 513
Johnson, Esther 1367, 1379
Johnson, Maurice 641
Johnson, R. Brimley 396, 704
Johnson, Samuel 20, 42, 52, 96, 130-31, 201, 214, 224, (p. 81), 419, 655, (p. 165), 851-928, (p. 177), 929, 934, 937, 1117, 1331
JOHNSON: THE CRITICAL HERITAGE 888
"Johnson and Charlotte Lennox" 937
JOHNSON AS CRITIC 857
JOHNSON, BOSWELL AND THEIR CIRCLE: ESSAYS PRESENTED TO LAWRENCE FITZROY POWELL IN HONOUR OF HIS EIGHTY-FOURTH BIRTHDAY 895, 905
JOHNSONIANA 898
"Johnsonian Bibliography" 868
JOHNSONIAN GLEANINGS 882
JOHNSONIAN NEWS LETTER 201, 899
JOHNSONIAN STUDIES 870
JOHNSONIAN STUDIES, 1887-1950 869
JOHNSON READER, A 855
"Johnson's Vile Melancholy" 886
Joliat, Eugène 1224
JONATHAN SWIFT 1356
JONATHAN SWIFT: A CRITICAL ANTHOLOGY 1401
JONATHAN SWIFT: A LIST OF CRITICAL STUDIES PUBLISHED FROM 1895 TO 1945 1372
JONATHAN SWIFT: GULLIVER'S TRAVELS 1363, 1398
JONATHAN SWIFT: JOURNAL TO STELLA 1367
"Jonathan Swift: The Critical Significance of Biographical Evidence" 1418

JONATHAN SWIFT AND IRELAND
1382
JONATHAN SWIFT AND THE AGE
OF COMPROMISE 1448
JONATHAN SWIFT AND THE
ANATOMY OF SATIRE 1389
JONATHAN SWIFT, 1667-1967: A
DUBLIN TERCENTENARY TRIBUTE
1373, 1421
JONATHAN WILD (p. 114), 570-
72, 623, 634, 639, 647, 665,
692
Jones, B. Maelor 592
Jones, Claude E. 561, 1225
Jones, Emrys 900
Jones, Howard Mumford 1008, 1181
Jones, Richard F. 1415
Jones, S. Paul 177
JOSEPH ANDREWS 558, 567-69,
586-87, 594, 599-600, 607, 612-
13, 619, 626-28, 641, 647, 679,
682, 684, 689, 691, (p. 135),
1205, 1250
"Joseph as Hero in JOSEPH AN-
DREWS" 682
JOURNAL (Beckford) 291
JOURNAL OF A VOYAGE TO LIS-
BON 557, 571, 578
JOURNAL OF A WEST-INDIA PRO-
PRIETOR 953
JOURNAL OF NARRATIVE TECH-
NIQUE 202
JOURNAL OF THE PLAGUE YEAR,
A 474-75, 499, 513, 519, 553
JOURNAL OF WILLIAM BECKFORD
IN PORTUGAL AND SPAIN,
1787-1788, THE 282
JOURNALS AND LETTERS OF FANNY
BURNEY, THE 400
JOURNAL TO ELIZA, THE 1258,
1268-69
Joyce, James 1391
JULIET GRENVILLE (p. 69), 343
"Justice to CALEB WILLIAMS" 742

K

Kahrl, George M. 1226
Kallich, Martin 1416, 1463
Kaplan, Fred 642

Karl, Frederick R. 111
Kaufmann, U. Milo 377
Kauvar, Elaine M. 945
Kavanagh, Julia 1153
Kay, Donald 112
Kearney, A.M. 1105-6
Keeling, Cecil 260
Keir, James 448
Kelley, Robert E. 875-76
Kellogg, Robert 74
Kelly, Edward 472
Kelman, John 378
Kelsall, Malcolm 701, 713
Kenney, William 901
Ker, W.P. 1468
Kermode, Frank 68, 643, 1107
Kettle, Arnold 49
Ketton-Cremer, R.W. 1464
Kiely, Robert 50, 306, 751, 966,
1025, 1469
Kimber, Edward 174
Kimpel, Ben D. 1048, 1068, 1095-96
King, William 1045
Kingsley, Charles 341-42
Kinhead-Weekes, Mark 1047, 1108-9
Kirk, Clara M. 785
Kittredge, George Lyman. See AN-
NIVERSARY PAPERS BY COL-
LEAGUES AND PUPILS OF
GEORGE LYMAN KITTREDGE
Kliger, Samuel 233, 1417
Knapp, Lewis M. 1182, 1187, 1191,
1199, 1227-29. See also TOBIAS
SMOLLETT: BICENTENNIAL ESSAYS
Knowles, A.S., Jr. 644
Kolb, Gwin J. 158, 860, 902-4
Konigsberg, Ira 1110
Koonce, Howard L. 514
Koppel, Gene 1314
Korshin, Paul J. 234, 438
Korte, Donald M. 1189, 1192
Köster, Patricia 992
Kramer, Dale 986
Kreissman, Bernard 645, 1111
Kropf, C.R. 646
Krutch, Joseph Wood 881
Kumar, Shiv K. 465
Kunitz, Stanley J. 10
Kunz, William J. 1350

L

LADY CHATTERLEY'S LOVER 437

Lafayette, Comtesse de 63

Lamont, Claire 1370, 1374

Lamont, Daniel 379

Landa, Louis A. 171, 475, 1315, 1355, 1371-72, 1384, 1418-19. See also AUGUSTAN MILIEU

Landsdown, Charlotte 285

LANGUAGE OF FICTION 69

LANGUAGE OF POLITICS, THE 743

Lanham, Richard A. 1316

"Large Diffused Picture of Life in Smollett's Early Novels, The" 1236

Lascelles, Mary 873, 905

LATER CAREER OF TOBIAS SMOLLETT, THE 1232

LATER EIGHTEENTH CENTURY, THE 42

LATER WOMEN NOVELISTS, 1744-1818, THE 113, 416, 946, 1039, 1161

LAURENCE STERNE 1282

LAURENCE STERNE: A BIOGRAPHICAL ESSAY 1279

LAURENCE STERNE: A COLLECTION OF CRITICAL ESSAYS 1344

LAURENCE STERNE: A LIST OF CRITICAL STUDIES FROM 1896 TO 1946 1271

"Laurence Sterne: Apostle of Laughter" 1333

LAURENCE STERNE AS SATIRIST 1324

LAURENCE STERNE: DE L'HOMME A L'OEUVRE 1278

LAURENCE STERNE: FROM TRISTRAM TO YORICK 1278, 1303

LAURENCE STERNE IN THE TWENTIETH CENTURY 1272

LAURENCE STERNE'S SERMONS OF MR. YORICK 1307

LAURENCE STERNE: THE EARLY AND MIDDLE YEARS 1276

LAURENCE STERNE: THE MAKING OF A HUMORIST 1283

Lawrence, D.H. 437

Leavis, F.R. 51, 380

Leavis, Q.D. 235

Lee, Charles 1181

Lee, Jae Num 1420

Lee, Sophia (p. ix)

Lee, William 490

Lehman, B.H. 1317

LEMUEL GULLIVER'S MIRROR FOR MAN 1391

Lennox, Charlotte Ramsay 107, (p. 177), 929-47

"Lennox Collection, The" 933

"Lesson of AMELIA, The" 635

LETTERS OF DANIEL DEFOE, THE 481

LETTERS OF DOCTOR GEORGE CHEYNE TO SAMUEL RICHARDSON, THE 1057

LETTERS OF HORACE WALPOLE, THE (Cunningham) 1454

LETTERS OF HORACE WALPOLE, THE (Toynbee) 1455

LETTERS OF LAURENCE STERNE 1268

LETTERS OF SAMUEL JOHNSON, THE 865

LETTERS OF TOBIAS GEORGE SMOLLETT: A SUPPLEMENT TO THE NOYES COLLECTION 1186

LETTERS OF TOBIAS SMOLLETT, THE (Knapp) 1187

LETTERS OF TOBIAS SMOLLETT, M.D., THE (Noyes) 1185-86

Levine, George R. 647

Levy, Herman Mittle, Jr. 276

Lewis, Matthew Gregory 50, 180, (p. 181), 948-71

Lewis, W.S. 1453, 1456-57, 1459, 1470

Leyburn, Ellen Douglas 906

LIBERAL IMAGINATION, THE 79

LIBERTINE LITERATURE IN ENGLAND, 1660-1745 25, 434

LIFE, ADVENTURES, AND PYRACIES OF THE FAMOUS CAPTAIN SINGLETON, THE. See CAPTAIN SINGLETON

LIFE AND CORRESPONDENCE OF M.G. LEWIS, THE 952

LIFE AND DEATH OF MR. BADMAN, THE (p. 74), 358-59

LIFE AND LETTERS OF BECKFORD 297

LIFE AND LETTERS OF TOBIAS SMOLLETT, THE 1200
LIFE AND OPINIONS OF TRISTRAM SHANDY, THE. See TRISTRAM SHANDY
"Life and Plays of Mrs. Behn, The" 327
LIFE AND ROMANCES OF MRS. ELIZA HAYWOOD, THE 828
LIFE AND STRANGE SURPRIZING ADVENTURES OF ROBINSON CRUSOE, THE. See ROBINSON CRUSOE
LIFE AND TIMES OF LAURENCE STERNE, THE 1277
LIFE AND TIMES OF OLIVER GOLDSMITH, THE 782
LIFE AND TIMES OF SEVEN MAJOR BRITISH WRITERS, THE 214
"Life and Works of Sarah Fielding, The" 711
LIFE AT FONTHILL, 1807-1822 284
LIFE OF BECKFORD 298
"Life of Dr. Oliver Goldsmith, The" (Percy) 786
LIFE OF HARRIOT STUART, THE (p. 177)
LIFE OF MATTHEW GREGORY LEWIS, A 959
LIFE OF MR. JONATHAN WILD THE GREAT, THE. See JONATHAN WILD
LIFE OF OLIVER GOLDSMITH, THE (Dobson) 781
LIFE OF OLIVER GOLDSMITH, THE (Irving) 783
LIFE OF OLIVER GOLDSMITH, THE (Prior) 787
LIFE OF SAMUEL JOHNSON, L.L.D., THE (Boswell) 874, 913
LIFE OF SAMUEL JOHNSON, LLD., THE (Hawkins) 879
LIFE OF THOMAS HOLCROFT, THE 840
LIFE OF TOBIAS GEORGE SMOLLETT 1197
LIFE OF WILLIAM GODWIN, THE 734
LIFE'S PROGRESS THROUGH THE PASSIONS 825

LIMITS OF THE NOVEL 63
Lingham, P.R.A. 425
Link, Frederick M. 329
Linsalata, Carmine R. 1230
LIST OF ENGLISH TALES AND PROSE ROMANCES PRINTED BEFORE 1740, A 172
LIST OF FRENCH PROSE FICTION FROM 1700 TO 1750, A 177
LITERARY AND SOCIAL CRITICISM OF HENRY FIELDING 563
LITERARY CAREER OF RICHARD GRAVES, THE 809
LITERARY ESSAYS 1087
LITERARY HISTORY OF ENGLAND, A 37
LITERARY MEANING AND AUGUSTAN VALUES 24, 1402
LITERARY PORTRAITS IN THE NOVELS OF HENRY FIELDING 677
"Literary Reputation of Aphra Behn, The" 339
LITERATURE OF ROGUERY, THE 59
Littlejohn, David 867
LIVES OF CLEOPATRA AND OCTAVIA, THE 704-5
LIVES OF THE POETS, THE 857
LIVING NOVEL, THE 451, 1240
Lobo, Father Jerome 906
Locke, John 237, 629, 1246, 1287, 1293, 1320, 1343, 1345
Locke, Miriam A. 562
"Locke and Sterne" 1345
"Lockean Psychology of TRISTRAM SHANDY, The" 1293
Lockhart, Donald M. 907
Lockwood, Thomas 661
Lodge, David 69
Loftis, John 31, 648
LONDON LIFE IN THE EIGHTEENTH CENTURY 229
Londsdale, Roger 272
Lorrain, Claude 238, 1021, 1027
LOUNGER, THE 987
LOVE AND DEATH IN THE AMERICAN NOVEL 1098
LOVE IN EXCESS (p. 157)
Lovejoy, Arthur O. 236
"Lovelace as Tragic Hero" 1080
Lowth, William 913

Lubbock, Percy 70
LUCK AT LAST 212
Luria, Gina 209
Lyons, N.J. 812
Lyttelton, George, Lord (p. 69)

M

McAdam, Edward L., Jr. 580, 800, 855, 866
McBurney, William Harlin 178-79, 212, 515, 819
MacCarthy, Bridget G. 113-14, 336, 416, 714, 832, 946, 1001, 1039, 1161
McCracken, David 266, 725, 752-54, 845
McHugh, Roger 1373, 1421
McIntosh, Carey 908
McIntyre, Clara F. 1026
Mack, Maynard 52, 545, 567, 633, 927, 1432
Mackenzie, Henry (p. 185), 972-91
McKillop, Alan Dugald 32, 115-16, 516, 649-52, 1069, 1112-16, 1148, 1231, 1318. See also RESTORATION AND EIGHTEENTH-CENTURY LITERATURE
Mackinnon, Sir Frank D. 392
MacLean, Kenneth 237, 1320
McMaster, Juliet 517, 1321
McNutt, Dan J. 180, 292, 956, 1015, 1037, 1150, 1460
MADAME D'ARBLAY'S PLACE IN THE DEVELOPMENT OF THE ENGLISH NOVEL 413
Mahmoud, Fatma Moussa 307
Major, John Campbell 117
MAKING OF JONATHAN WILD, THE 639
Mallarmé, Stephen 308
Malone, Kemp 417
Mandel, Barrett S. 381
Mandeville, Bernard 629
Manley, Mary Delariviere 89, 107, 114, 129, (p. 189), 992-1003
"Manners, Morals, and The Novel" 79
MAN OF FEELING, THE (p. 185), 973-75, 985-86, 989-90

MAN OF THE WORLD, THE 976
"Manuscript of M.G. Lewis's THE MONK, The" 962
MAN VERSUS SOCIETY IN EIGHTEENTH-CENTURY BRITAIN 223
Manwaring, Elizabeth 238, 1027
MARCHMONT (p. 219)
Maresca, Thomas E. 118
MARIANNE 109
Marivaux, Pierre de 109, 626
Marken, Jack W. 718, 730
Marlborough, Sarah Churchill, Duchess of. See Churchill, Sarah
MARRIAGE: FIELDING'S MIRROR OF MORALITY 696
Martz, Louis L. 418, 1232-33
"Mary de la Rivière Manley, Tory Defender" 1002
Marzials, Sir Frank T. 274
MASKS OF JONATHAN SWIFT, THE 1409
"Matrimonial Theme of Defoe's ROXANA, The" 528
"Matt Bramble's Journey to Health" 1252
Mayhew, George 1373
Maynadier, Gustavus H. 454, 938
Mayo, Robert D. 119, 181, 987
Mazzeo, J.A. 239, 1345, 1397
"Meaning of Gulliver's Last Voyage, The" 1403
Mehrotra, Kewal Krishna 1471
Melville, Lewis [pseud.] 274, 297, 1200
"Memoir" of Mrs. Radcliffe 1004, 1019
MEMOIR of Robert Bage 258
"Memoir" of Tobias Smollett 1201
MEMOIRS OF A CAVALIER 467-68, 538
MEMOIRS OF A CERTAIN ISLAND ADJACENT TO THE KINGDOM OF UTOPIA 817
MEMOIRS OF A COXCOMB 424-26
MEMOIRS OF A WOMAN OF PLEASURE. See FANNY HILL
"MEMOIRS OF A WOMAN OF PLEASURE: Pornography and the Mid-Eighteenth-Century English Novel" 438

MEMOIRS OF EUROPE. See NEW ATALANTIS, THE

MEMOIRS OF MARTINUS SCRIBLERUS, THE 1327

MEMOIRS OF MR. LAURENCE STERNE 1257

MEMOIRS OF THE LATE THOMAS HOLCROFT 840

MEMOIRS OF WILLIAM BECKFORD OF FONTHILL 300

Mendilow, Adam Abraham 1322

MERCENARY LOVER, THE 818

Metzger, Lore 320

MHRA ANNUAL BIBLIOGRAPHY OF ENGLISH LANGUAGE AND LITERATURE 182

Middendorf, John H. 912

"Middle-Class Reader and the English Novel, The" 108

"Miguel de Cervantes and the English Novel" 138

Miles, Hamish 973

Miller, Henry 437

Miller, Henry Knight 33, 602, 653-54

Miller, Stuart 71

Milne, George 855

Milton, John 371, 1087

MIMESIS: THE REPRESENTATION OF REALITY IN WESTERN LITERATURE 219

MIND AND ART OF JONATHAN SWIFT, THE 1430

MINERVA PRESS, 1790-1820, THE 156, 221

Mingay, G.E. 240

MINUET 28

MIRROR, THE 987

MISCELLANEOUS WORKS OF JOHN BUNYAN, THE 352, (p. 74)

MISCELLANEOUS WORKS OF OLIVER GOLDSMITH, THE 764, 786

MISCELLANEOUS WORKS OF OLIVER GOLDSMITH, THE (Prior) 765

MISCELLANEOUS WORKS OF TOBIAS SMOLLETT, THE 1165

MISCELLANEOUS WORKS OF TOBIAS SMOLLETT, M.D., THE (Anderson) 1163

MISCELLANIES (Fielding) (p. 114), 692

Misenheimer, James B., Jr. 909

Mish, Charles C. 120, 183, 216, 322

MR. REVIEW: DANIEL DEFOE AS AUTHOR OF THE REVIEW 492

"Mrs. Behn's Biography a Fiction" 324

"Mrs. Behn's OROONOKO" 325

"Mistress Delarivière Manley's Biography" 996

"Mrs. Manley: An Eighteenth-Century Wife of Bath" 998

MRS. RADCLIFFE--HER RELATION TOWARDS ROMANTICISM 1034

"Mrs. Radcliffe's Landscapes" 1021

"Mrs. Radcliffe's 'Picturesque Embellishment'" 1032

MLA ABSTRACTS OF ARTICLES IN SCHOLARLY JOURNALS 11, 184

MLA INTERNATIONAL BIBLIOGRAPHY OF BOOKS AND ARTICLES 11, 184

"Mock-Heroic Form of JONATHAN WILD, The" 623

MODERN NOVEL WRITING 276-77

"Modest Appraisal: Swift Scholarship and Criticism, 1945-65, A" 1374

MODEST PROPOSAL, A 1444

Moglen, Helene 1323

Mohler, Nora M. 1423-24

MOLL FLANDERS 54, 71, 128, 440, 469-72, 493, 496, 501, 504-5, 507, 514, 517, 520, 523, 528-31, 535, 542, 546-47, 549-50

"MOLL FLANDERS and FANNY HILL: A Comparison" 440, 546

"MOLL FLANDERS as a Structure of Topics" 529

"Moll's Muddle: Defoe's Use of Irony in MOLL FLANDERS" 514

MONK, THE 50, (p. 181), 948-50, 957, 961-64, 966-68, 970-71

Monk, Samuel Holt 231, 241, 473, 1397, 1422, 1448. See also STUDIES IN CRITICISM AND AESTHETICS, 1660-1800

"MONK and LE DIABLE AMOUREUX, THE" 968

Monro, D.H. 755
Montague, Edwine 418
Montaigne, Michel 1287
Moore, John 1164, 1201
Moore, John Robert 484, 491, 518
Moore, Robert Etheridge 655, 910, 1117
"Moral Allegory of JONATHAN WILD, The" 692
MORAL BASIS OF FIELDING'S ART, THE 600
"Moral Function of Thwackum, Square, and Allworthy, The" 678
Morgan, Charlotte E. 121, 185
Morris, James 1180
Morrissey, L.J. 436
Morton, Donald E. 1118
MOUNT HENNETH 258
Mozart, Wolfgang Amadeus (p. 57)
Muir, Edwin 72
Mullett, Charles F. 1057
Murphy, Arthur 554-56
Murray, E.B. 1018
Murry, J. Middleton 1385
Mutter, R.P.C. 575
Myers, Mitzi 756
"My Servant Caleb" 757
MYSTERIES OF UDOLPHO, THE 50, (p. 181), (p. 193), 1010-11, 1025, 1030

N

Nabokov, Vladimir 1391
"Naked Virtue of Amelia, The" 693
"Naming of Characters in Defoe, Richardson, and Fielding, The" 548, 690, 1136
NARRATIVE FORM IN HISTORY AND FICTION 91, 611
"Narrative Technique in TOM JONES" 687
NATIONAL UNION CATALOGUE, THE 12, 186
NATURAL PASSION, A 1091
"Nature and Development of the Quixote Figure in the Eighteenth-Century English Novel, The" 122
"Nature and Modes of Narrative Fiction, The" 80

NATURE OF NARRATIVE, THE 74
"Nature versus Art as a Comic Pattern in TRISTRAM SHANDY" 1302
"Naval Scenes in RODERICK RANDOM, The" 1227
NCBEL. See NEW CAMBRIDGE BIBLIOGRAPHY OF ENGLISH LITERATURE, THE
Needham, Gwendolyn B. 146, 998, 1002, 1119, 1133
NEW APPROACHES TO EIGHTEENTH-CENTURY LITERATURE 29
NEW ATALANTIS, THE (p. 189), 994, 1000-1002
NEW CAMBRIDGE BIBLIOGRAPHY OF ENGLISH LITERATURE, THE 162, 187
New edition of the collected works of Daniel Defoe, projected, A 456
New edition of the collected works of Laurence Sterne, A 1256
"New Evidence of the Realism of Mrs. Behn's OROONOKO" 333
"New Letter from Fielding, A" 580
NEW LIGHT ON APHRA BEHN 326
NEW LIGHT ON DR. JOHNSON 896
New, Melvyn 1256, 1324
Newman, Franklin B. 1193
"New Verse by Henry Fielding" 591
Nicholson, Watson 519
Nicolson, Marjorie 1423-24
Niehus, Edward L. 122
NIGHTMARES AND HOBBYHORSES 22, 226, 1298, 1400
"No Romantick Absurdities or Incredible Fictions" 906
NORTHANGER ABBEY 945
Norwood, L.F. 1194
"Note on the Drama and the Novel: Fielding's Contribution, A" 606
"Note on the Realism of Mrs. Behn's OROONOKO, A" 340
"Notes on the Early Editions of TRISTRAM SHANDY" 1274
Novak, Maximillian E. 456, 484-85, 520-27
NOVEL: A FORUM ON FICTION 203

NOVEL AND ROMANCE, 1700–1800 149, 196

NOVEL IN ENGLAND 1700-1775, THE 210, 211

NOVEL IN LETTERS, THE 215

NOVEL IN MOTLEY, THE 75, 133, 674

NOVELISTS ON THE NOVEL 56

"'Novel,' 'Romance,' and Popular Fiction in the First Half of the Eighteenth Century" 132

"Novels of Eliza Haywood, The" 830

NOVELS OF FIELDING, THE 618

NOVELS OF MARY DELARIVIERE MANLEY, THE 992

NOVELS OF MRS. ANN RADCLIFFE, THE 1004

NOVELS OF MRS. APHRA BEHN, THE 315

"Novels of Robert Bage, The" 262

NOVELS OF SAMUEL RICHARDSON, THE (Phelps) 1044

NOVELS OF SAMUEL RICHARDSON, THE (Shakespeare Head Edition) 1045

NOVELS OF SMOLLETT, THE 1209

"Novels of Thomas Holcroft, The" 842

NOVELS OF TOBIAS SMOLLETT, THE 1169

Noyes, Edward S. 1185-86

NUMBER AND PATTERN IN THE EIGHTEENTH-CENTURY NOVEL 92

O

Oates, J.C.T. 1325

"Observations on THE VICAR OF WAKEFIELD" 799

OCCASIONAL FORM 636

Offor, George 350

O'Flaherty, Patrick 911

"Of Time, Personality, and the Author" 1317

Ogg, David 242

OLD ENGLISH BARON, THE (p. 199), 1035, 1042

"Old Last Act: Some Observations on FANNY HILL, The" 435

OLD MANOR HOUSE, THE (p. 219), 1145-46, (p. 221), 1157

O'Leary, Ralph Dorman. See STUDIES IN ENGLISH IN HONOR OF . . .

Oliver, John W. 298

"Oliver Goldsmith" (Friedman) 778

OLIVER GOLDSMITH (Kirk) 785

OLIVER GOLDSMITH (Wardle) 788

"Oliver Goldsmith" (Williams) 780

OLIVER GOLDSMITH: A GEORGIAN STUDY 801

OLIVER GOLDSMITH: HIS LIFE AND WORKS 803

OLIVER GOLDSMITH BIBLIOGRAPHICALLY AND BIOGRAPHICALLY CONSIDERED 779

"On CALEB WILLIAMS" 745

"On CLARISSA HARLOWE" 1134

"On MOLL FLANDERS" 547

"On Smollett's Language" 1248

"On the Genesis of PILGRIM'S PROGRESS" 372

"On the Philosophical Background of GULLIVER'S TRAVELS" 1446

"On THE PILGRIM'S PROGRESS" 387

"On TOM JONES" 686

"On TRISTRAM SHANDY" 1346

ORIENTAL TALE IN ENGLAND IN THE EIGHTEENTH CENTURY, THE 93, 163, 303, 890

"Origins of GULLIVER'S TRAVELS, The" 1404

OROONOKO (p. 63), 316, 318-20, 325, 330, (p. 66), 333, 337-38, 340

"Oroonoko and Crusoe's Man Friday" 337

OROONOKO AND OTHER PROSE NARRATIVES 316

"OROONOKO in France in the XVIIIth Century" 338

Orowitz, Milton 1234

OTHER END OF THE EGG, THE 1416

"Other Letters in the Lennox Collection" 934

Ousby, Ian 757

OXFORD COMPANION TO ENGLISH LITERATURE, THE 8

OXFORD HISTORY OF ENGLISH
    LITERATURE, THE   23, 35, 38

P

Pagliaro, Harold   578, 912
Palmer, Eustace   656
Palmer, Helen H.   154
Palmer, William J.   1120
PAMELA   146, (p. 87), 432, 619,
    645, (p. 135), 822, 1046-49,
    1066, 1075, 1084-87, 1090,
    1094, 1096, 1106, 1111, 1115-
    16, 1118-19, 1128-30, 1133,
    1139
PAMELA'S DAUGHTERS   146, 1133
PAMELA-SHAMELA   645, 1111
"Pamela's Wedding and the Marriage
    of the Lamb"   1075
"'Paradise' in Abyssinia and the
    'Happy Valley' in RASSELAS, The"
    902
PARADISE LOST   371, 1087
PARADISE REGAINED   1087
Park, William   123-25, 657-58,
    1121-22, 1326
Parreaux, André   283, 299, 967,
    1184
PARTIAL MAGIC   45
Pascal, Roy   382
"Passions of Ambrosio, The"   964
Pasta, Betty B.   1266
Patrick, Simon   913
"Patterns of Disguise in THE VICAR
    OF WAKEFIELD"   792
Paul, C. Kegan   738, 841
Paulson, Ronald   126-27, 659-61,
    1235, 1327, 1425-27
Payne, William L.   457, 492
Peacock, Mabel   360
Peake, Charles   856, 1433
Pearce, Roy Harvey   104
Peck, Louis F.   949, 959, 968
"Peculiar Phase of the Theory of Re-
    alism in Pre-Richardsonian Fiction,
    A"   144
Percy, Thomas   764, 786
PEREGRINE PICKLE   1174-76, 1212,
    1216, 1226, 1229, 1235, 1241-42
"Peregrine Pickle: The Complete Sat-

irist"   1216
PERILOUS BALANCE   1348
PERSIAN TALES   921
PERSONALITY OF JONATHAN
    SWIFT, THE   1380
"Personal Relations between Fielding
    and Richardson, The"   650, 1114
Peterson, Spiro   528
Petrie, Graham   1261, 1264, 1328
Phelps, Robert   317
Phelps, William Lyon   1044
PHILIDORE AND PLACENTIA   212,
    819
PHILOSOPHICAL ENQUIRY INTO
    THE ORIGIN OF OUR IDEAS OF
    THE SUBLIME AND BEAUTIFUL,
    A   1033
PHILOSOPHICAL IRONY OF LAU-
    RENCE STERNE, THE   1323
PICARESQUE NOVEL, THE   71
"Picaroon as Fortune's Plaything, The"
    1204
"Picaroon Domesticated, The"   595
Pierson, R.C.   1123
PILGRIM'S PROGRESS, THE (Bunyan)
    54, (p. 74), 353, 355-58, 365,
    370-72, 377-78, 380, 382-85,
    387-89, 1340
"Pilgrim's Progress, The" (Leavis)
    380
PILGRIM'S PROGRESS AND TRADI-
    TIONS IN PURITAN MEDITATION,
    THE   377
Pinkus, Philip   1428
Piper, William B.   529, 1236, 1282,
    1329, 1357
Pitcher, Edward W.   119
"Plan of CLARISSA, The"   1102
"Plan of PEREGRINE PICKLE, The"
    1241
Plant, Marjorie   243
Platt, Harrison Gray, Jr.   330
PLAYS, HISTORIES, AND NOVELS
    OF THE INGENIOUS MRS. APHRA
    BEHN, THE   314
"Plot of TOM JONES, The"   617
Plumb, J.H.   244, 570
"Poems in THE VICAR OF WAKE-
    FIELD, The"   798
POEMS OF JONATHAN SWIFT, THE
    1351

POETS AND STORY-TELLERS 411
POLITICAL JUSTICE (p. 139), 717, 720-21, 735, 744, 747, 846
POLITICAL ROMANCE, A 1258, 1263
"Political Theory in GULLIVER'S TRAVELS" 1410
POLITICS IN LITERATURE IN THE NINETEENTH CENTURY 849
"Politics of GULLIVER'S TRAVELS, The" 1447
POLITICS OF SAMUEL JOHNSON, THE 892
Pollin, Burton R. 718-19, 731, 758
Pope, Alexander 14, 204, 214, (p. 69), (p. 157)
POPULAR FICTION BEFORE RICH-ARDSON 129, 534, 833, 1003, 1127
POPULAR NOVEL IN ENGLAND 1770-1800, THE 145, 268, 349, 420, 814, 850, 989, 1031, 1041, 1162
Poussin, Nicolas 1021
Powell, Lawrence Fitzroy 874. See also JOHNSON, BOSWELL AND THEIR CIRCLE
POWER OF LOVE, THE 992
POWER OF SATIRE, THE 1406
Powers, Lyall H. 662
PREFACES TO FICTION 89
"Preface" to VATHEK 308
"Present Tense in THE PILGRIM'S PROGRESS, The" 382
Preston, John 128, 530, 663, 1124, 1330
Preston, Thomas R. 913, 1237-39
Preu, James A. 759
Prévost d'Exiles, Antoine F., Abbé 97
Price, Martin 34, 531, 1331, 1429
PRIDE AND PREJUDICE (p. 81), 409, 945
"Pride of Lemuel Gulliver, The" 1422
Priestley, Mary 823
Priestly, F.E.L. 720
Primer, Irwin 718
Prior, Sir James 765, 787
Pritchett, V.S. 451, 1240

"Probable and the Marvelous in TOM JONES, The" 694
"Profit and Loss of Moll Flanders, The" 535
"Progress in THE PILGRIM'S PROGRESS" 370
PROGRESS OF ROMANCE, THE (p. 199), 1036
PROSE STYLE OF SAMUEL JOHNSON, THE 928
PROSE WORKS OF JONATHAN SWIFT, THE 1350
PROVIDENCE OF WIT, THE 14
PUBLICATION OF THE MONK, THE 967
"Purpose and Narration in Fielding's AMELIA" 624
"Pursuer and the Pursued, The" 750
Putney, Rufus 1241-42, 1332-33

Q

Quennell, Peter 422
"Question of Emotion in Defoe, The" 501
QUICK SPRINGS OF SENSE 19, 635, 644, 1237, 1395
Quintana, Ricardo 801, 1370, 1373-74, 1386, 1430-31

R

Rabelais, François 1313, 1339
Rabkin, Norman 1125
Radcliffe, Ann 30, 50, 180 (p. 181), (p. 193), 1004-34
RADICAL DOCTOR SMOLLETT 1211
Railo, Eino 969
Raleigh, John Henry 532
RAMBLER NO. 4 (p. 165)
RASH RESOLVE, THE 816
RASSELAS (Johnson) 130, (p. 165), 854, 856, 858-64, 873, 885-86, 889-91, 894-95, 897, 900-904, 906-8, 911-22, 924-27, 1331
"RASSELAS" (Tillotson) 920
"RASSELAS, an 'Uninstructive Tale'" 895
"RASSELAS: A Rejoinder" 873
"RASSELAS: Psychological Irony and Romance" 885

"RASSELAS: Purchase Price, Proprietors, and Printings" 903

RASSELAS AND ESSAYS 856

"RASSELAS and the Persian Tales" 921

"RASSELAS and the Theme of Diversification" 901

RASSELAS, POEMS, AND SELECTED PROSE 854

"Rasselas Returns--to What?" 918

"Rationale of the Fourth Voyage, The" 1398

Rawson, Claude J. 664-66, 1432-33

Raynal, Margaret Isabel 715

Read, Herbert 1243

Reade, Aleyn Lyell 882

"Reader, the General, and the Particular: Johnson and Imlac in Chapter Ten of RASSELAS, The" 925

READER'S GUIDE TO THE EIGHTEENTH-CENTURY ENGLISH NOVEL, A 111

READING OF GULLIVER'S TRAVELS, A 1440

REASON AND ROMANTICISM 1243

REASON AND THE IMAGINATION 239, 1345, 1397

"Recent Critical Fortunes of MOLL FLANDERS, The" 549

"Recent Studies in the Restoration and Eighteenth Century" 188

"Recent Swift Scholarship" 1373

RECOLLECTIONS OF AN EXCURSION TO THE MONASTERIES OF ALCOBACA AND BATALHA 287

RECOLLECTIONS OF THE LATE WILLIAM BECKFORD 285

Redding, Cyrus 300

Reeve, Clara 180, (p. 199), 1035-42

REFERENCE GUIDE TO THE LITERATURE OF TRAVEL, A 165

"Reflections on the Letter" 1128

REFLECTIONS ON THE REVOLUTION IN FRANCE 752

"Reinterpretation of Laurence Sterne, The" 1319

"Relation of Defoe's Fiction to His Non-Fictional Writings, The" 545

RELATION OF TRISTRAM SHANDY TO THE LIFE OF STERNE, THE 1280

"Religion and Invention in ROBINSON CRUSOE" 508

RELIGIOUS LIBERALISM IN EIGHTEENTH-CENTURY ENGLAND 249

RELIGIOUS THOUGHT OF SAMUEL JOHNSON, THE 889

RELUCTANT PILGRIM, THE 510

Rembar, Charles 437

Renwick, W.L. 35

REPUTATION OF JONATHAN SWIFT, 1781-1882, THE 1387

"Response as Reformation: TRISTRAM SHANDY and the Art of Interruption" 1312

RESTORATION AND EIGHTEENTH-CENTURY LITERATURE: ESSAYS IN HONOR OF ALAN DUGALD MCKILLOP 1104, 1132, 1315, 1466

RESTORATION AND EIGHTEENTH CENTURY (1660-1789), THE 37, 189

RESTORATION PROSE FICTION, 1666-1700: AN ANTHOLOGY OF REPRESENTATIVE PIECES 216, 322

REVIEW OF THE AFFAIRS OF FRANCE, A 457, 492

Review of THE FEMALE QUIXOTE 942

"Revisions of Richardson's SIR CHARLES GRANDISON, The" 1123

Reynolds, Joshua (p. 81)

RHETORICAL WORLD OF AUGUSTAN HUMANISM, THE 27

"Rhetoric as Fictional Technique in TRISTRAM SHANDY" 1328

RHETORIC OF FICTION, THE 58, 160, 610, 1291

Rhys, Ernest 393

"Richard Graves and THE SPIRITUAL QUIXOTE" 810

"Richardson" (Carroll) 1061

RICHARDSON (Downs) 1067

Richardson, Samuel 16, 29, 30, 43, 47-49, 54, 84, 86, 94, 96, 109,

115, 124-25, 128-29, 131-32,
137, 144, 146, 148, 159, 166,
170, 212, 214, 218, (p. 81),
421, (p. 87), 432, 548, 580,
596, 604-5, 608, 619, 643, 645,
650, 655, 657-58, 690-91,
(p. 135), 709, (p. 157), 822,
(p. 160), 910, (p. 177), 929,
934, (p. 185), (p. 193), 1043-
1142, (p. 219), 1206-7, 1286,
1326

"Richardson and Fielding" 643, 1107
"Richardson and Romance" 1088
"Richardson at Work: Revisions, Allusions, and Quotations in CLARISSA" 1081
RICHARDSONIANA 1126
"Richardson's Characterization of Mr. B. and Double Purpose in PAMELA" 1119
RICHARDSON'S CHARACTERS 1099
"Richardson's 'Christian Vocation'" 1093
"Richardson's Correspondence" 1142
RICHARDSON'S FAMILIAR LETTERS AND THE DOMESTIC CONDUCT BOOKS 1103
"Richardson's Lovelace: Character and Prediction" 1140
"Richardson's PAMELA: An Interpretation" 1139
"Richardson's PAMELA: The Aesthetic Case" 1106
"Richardson's PAMELA: The Gospel and the Novel" 1130
"Richardson's Repetitions" 1100
"Richardson's Revisions of CLARISSA in the Second Edition" 1135
"Richardson's Revisions of PAMELA" 1096
RICHARDSON-STINSTRA CORRESPONDENCE AND STINSTRA'S PREFACES TO CLARISSA, THE 1059
Richetti, John J. 129, 533-34, 833, 1003, 1127
Richter, David H. 73
Rieger, James Henry 309
RISE OF THE NOVEL, THE 148, 550, 627, 691, 1137

RISE OF THE NOVEL OF MANNERS, THE 121, 185
ROAD: A STUDY OF JOHN BUNYAN'S PILGRIM'S PROGRESS, THE 378
Robbe-Grillet, Alain 63
"Robert Bage, a Forgotten Novelist" 265
"Robert Bage: A Representative Revolutionary Novelist" 263
"Robert Bage, Novelist of Ideas" 267
ROBERT DRURY'S JOURNAL AND OTHER STUDIES 538
"Robert Mayo's THE ENGLISH NOVEL IN THE MAGAZINES, 1740-1815: New Facts" 119
Roberts, Sydney Castle 883
ROBINSON CRUSOE 337, 461-63, 483, 497, 500-501, 506, 508, 510, 527, 534, 542, 550-51
"ROBINSON CRUSOE: 'Allusive Allegorick History'" 497
ROBINSON CRUSOE AND ITS PRINTING, 1719-1731 483
"ROBINSON CRUSOE as a Myth" 551
RODERICK RANDOM 71, 1171-73, 1204, 1210, 1226-27, 1233, 1235, 1251
Rogal, Samuel J. 535
Rogers, Pat 36, 478, 536, 1434
Rogers, Winfield H. 667
ROGUE'S PROGRESS 57, 82, 496, 595, 1204
ROLE OF PERSONAL MEMOIRS IN ENGLISH BIOGRAPHY AND NOVEL, THE 117
"Role of the Senses in HUMPHRY CLINKER, The" 1246
"Romance and the 'New' Novels of Richardson, Fielding, and Smollett" 605, 1074, 1207
ROMANCE OF THE FOREST, THE (p. 193), 1009
ROMANCES AND NARRATIVES BY DANIEL DEFOE 453-55
"'Roman de Longue Haleine' on English Soil, The" 105
LES ROMANS DE FIELDING 618
LES ROMANS DE SMOLLETT 1209

ROMANTIC NOVEL IN ENGLAND, THE 50, 306, 751, 966, 1025, 1469
Rosa, Salvator 238, 1021, 1027
Roscoe, Thomas 555, 1166
Rose, Elizabeth 977
Rosenheim, Edward W. 1435
Ross, Angus 461, 1183
Ross, John R. 1397, 1436, 1448
Rothstein, Eric 33, 130, 668-69, 760, 914, 1244, 1334
Rousseau, George S. 33, 802, 1245
Rousseau, Jean Jacques (p. 69), (p. 91), 452, 750
Roussel, Roy 1128
Rowlandson, Thomas 1165
ROXANA 476, 501, 509, 512, 521, 528, 532
ROYAL SLAVE, THE. See OROONOKO
Ruff, William 1028
Rundus, Raymond J. 670
"Rural Ideal in Eighteenth-Century Fiction, The" 95
Russell, H.K. 1335
Ruthven, K.K. 671
Rymer, Michael 813

S

Sachs, Arieh 915
Sackett, S.J. 560
Sacks, Sheldon 131, 672, 916, 1437
Sade, Marquis de 47
Sadler, Michael 452
ST. ALBAN'S ABBEY 1004
ST. LEON 726-27, 755
Saintsbury, George 577, 1167
Sale, William M., Jr. 1046, 1063, 1070, 1129
SAMUEL JOHNSON (Greene) 878
SAMUEL JOHNSON (Krutch) 881
SAMUEL JOHNSON (Roberts) 883
SAMUEL JOHNSON (Wain) 884
SAMUEL JOHNSON: A COLLECTION OF CRITICAL ESSAYS 893
SAMUEL JOHNSON: A PERSONALITY IN CONFLICT 880
SAMUEL JOHNSON: A SURVEY AND BIBLIOGRAPHY OF CRITICAL STUDIES 871

SAMUEL JOHNSON AND THE LIFE OF WRITING 891
SAMUEL JOHNSON AND THE PROBLEM OF EVIL 917
SAMUEL JOHNSON'S EARLY BIOGRAPHIES 876
SAMUEL JOHNSON'S LITERARY CRITICISM 894
SAMUEL JOHNSON THE MORALIST 923
SAMUEL RICHARDSON (Brissenden) 1065
SAMUEL RICHARDSON (Dobson) 1066
SAMUEL RICHARDSON: A BIBLIOGRAPHICAL RECORD OF HIS LITERARY CAREER 1063
SAMUEL RICHARDSON: A BIOGRAPHICAL AND CRITICAL STUDY 1071
SAMUEL RICHARDSON: A BIOGRAPHY 1068
SAMUEL RICHARDSON: A COLLECTION OF CRITICAL ESSAYS 1082
SAMUEL RICHARDSON: A LIST OF CRITICAL STUDIES PUBLISHED FROM 1896 TO 1946 1062
SAMUEL RICHARDSON: DRAMATIC NOVELIST 1109
SAMUEL RICHARDSON: PRINTER AND NOVELIST 1069
SAMUEL RICHARDSON: THE TRIUMPH OF CRAFT 1078
"Samuel Richardson and Naive Allegory" 1085
SAMUEL RICHARDSON AND THE DRAMATIC NOVEL 1110
SAMUEL RICHARDSON AND THE EIGHTEENTH-CENTURY PURITAN CHARACTER 1141
SAMUEL RICHARDSON, MASTER PRINTER 1070
"Samuel Richardson's Novels and the Theatre" 1131
SAMUEL RICHARDSON'S THEORY OF FICTION 1072
"Satire and Comedy in the Works of Henry Fielding" 640
SATIRE AND THE NOVEL IN EIGHTEENTH-CENTURY ENGLAND 127, 659, 1235, 1327, 1426

Index

"Satire in the Early Novels of Smol-
lett" 1235
"Satire of the Reader in TRISTRAM
SHANDY" 1347
"Satiric and Comic Theory in Relation
to Fielding" 620
"Satiric Technique in THE SPIRITUAL
QUIXOTE" 813
Scarron, Paul 626
Schiller, Friedrich (p. 181)
Schlatter, Richard B. 245
Scholes, Robert 74
Schonhorn, Manuel 456, 480, 537,
673
Schroyer, Frederick 1006
Schulz, Dieter 132
Schwartz, Richard B. 917
"Scientific Background of Swift's
'Voyage to Laputa,' The" 1423
Scott, Sir H.W. 449
Scott, Sarah (p. ix)
Scott, Temple 779
Scott, Sir Walter 48, 258 (p. 181),
(p. 185), 1004, 1019, 1034, 1154
SCOTTISH MAN OF FEELING, A
981
Scouten, A.H. 1376
SCRIBLERIAN, THE 204
Scudéry, Georges de 89
Scurr, Helen Margaret 345
Seccombe, Thomas 1168, 1179
Secord, Arthur W. 457, 538-39
SECRET HISTORY OF QUEEN ZARAH,
THE (p. 189), 993
SECRET HISTORY OF THE PRESENT
INTRIGUES OF THE COURT OF
CARAMANIA, THE 820
SECRET MEMOIRS AND MANNERS
OF SEVERAL PERSONS OF QUAL-
ITY, OF BOTH SEXES FROM THE
NEW ATALANTIS. See NEW
ATALANTIS, THE
Seeber, Edward D. 337-38
SELECTED LETTERS OF HORACE
WALPOLE 1457
SELECTED LETTERS OF SAMUEL
RICHARDSON 1058
SELECTED POETRY AND PROSE OF
DANIEL DEFOE 459
SELECTED WRITINGS OF THE IN-

GENIOUS MRS. APHRA BEHN
317
SELECTIONS FROM SAMUEL JOHN-
SON 853
SELECTIVE BIBLIOGRAPHY FOR THE
STUDY OF ENGLISH AND AMERI-
CAN LITERATURE 2, 152
SELF-CONSUMING ARTIFACTS 370
Selkirk, Alexander 461
Sells, Arthur Lytton 803
Sen, Sri C. 540
SENSE OF AN ENDING, THE 68
SENSIBILITY IN ENGLISH PROSE
FICTION, 1760-1814 150, 991
"Sentimentalism of Goldsmith, The"
795
SENTIMENTAL JOURNEY, A 1257-
58, 1264-67, 1269, 1295, 1299,
1314, 1332, 1336, 1340
SERIOUS REFLECTIONS OF ROBIN-
SON CRUSOE (p. 97)
"Sermon in TRISTRAM SHANDY, The"
1294
SERMONS OF MR. YORICK 1307
SEVEN XVIIITH CENTURY BIBLIOG-
RAPHIES 780
SEVENTEENTH CENTURY BACK-
GROUND, THE 256
Shaftesbury, Anthony Ashley Cooper,
Earl of 614, 629
SHAKESPEARE HEAD EDITION OF
THE NOVELS AND SELECTED
WRITINGS OF DANIEL DEFOE,
THE 455
SHAKESPEARE HEAD EDITION OF
THE WRITINGS OF LAURENCE
STERNE, THE 1254-55
SHAMELA (p. 111), 564-66, 568-69,
641, 645, 668, 674, 697
"Shandean Homunculus, The" 1315
SHANDYISM AND SENTIMENT,
1760-1800 1325
SHAPING VISION, THE 48, 504,
619, 1090, 1214, 1300
Sharrock, Roger 352-53, 355, 363,
383-85, 1130
Shaw, Margaret R.B. 1283
Shea, John S. 13, 919
Shebbeare, John (p. ix)
Sheffey, Ruthe T. 339

Shelley, Percy Bysshe (p. 139), 733, 747, (p. 181)
SHELLEY, GODWIN, AND THEIR CIRCLE 733
"Shelley, Godwin, Hume, and the Doctrine of Necessity" 747
Shenstone, William (p. 153), 811
"Shenstone and Richard Graves's COLUMELLA" 811
Shepperson, Archibald Bolling 75, 133, 674
Sherbo, Arthur 134
Sherburn, George 37, 189, 573, 675-76, 723, 761, 918, 1052, 1131-32, 1438
Sheridan, Frances (p. ix)
Shesgreen, Sean 677-78
SHE STOOPS TO CONQUER 769
Shinagel, Michael 438, 463, 493
SHORT CONCORDANCE TO LAURENCE STERNE'S A SENTIMENTAL JOURNEY, A 1266
SHORTER NOVELS 319
SHORTEST WAY WITH THE DISSENTERS, THE 454
SHORT FICTION IN THE SPECTATOR 112
Shugrue, Michael F. 210, 211, 459
SICILIAN ROMANCE, A 1007-8
Siebert, Donald T. 1246
Singer, Godfrey Frank 135
SIR LAUNCELOT GREAVES 1178
SIR ROBERT WALPOLE 244
"Situational Satire: A Commentary on the Method of Swift" 1431
Sitwell, Sacheverell 301
Slagle, Kenneth Chester 136
Slattery, William C. 1059
Slepian, B. 436
Small, Miriam R. 939, 947
Smith, Charlotte 180, 209, (p. 219), 1143-62
Smith, David Nichol 872, 1354. See also STUDIES IN THE EIGHTEENTH CENTURY and STUDIES IN THE EIGHTEENTH CENTURY II
Smith, Warren H. 1472
SMOLLETT (Brander) 1196
"Smollett" (Knapp) 1191
Smollett, Tobias 19, 30, 48, 57,

71, 83-84, 86, 92, 95, 115, 126-27, 130, 137, 170, 212, (p. 81), 421, 604-5, 689, 1073-74, 1163-1253, 1326, 1426
"Smollett and Lady Vane's Memoirs" 1242
"Smollett and the Art of Caricature" 1234
"Smollett and the ATOM" 1217
"Smollett and the Benevolent Misanthrope Type" 1238
"Smollett and the CRITICAL REVIEW" 1225
"Smollett and the Expedition to Carthagena" 1233
"Smollett and the Navy" 1225
SMOLLETT AND THE SCOTTISH SCHOOL 1221
SMOLLETT CRITICISM, 1925-1945 1190
SMOLLETT CRITICISM, 1770-1924 1189
"Smollett Criticism, 1770-1924: Corrections and Additions" 1189
SMOLLETT ET LA FRANCE 1224
"Smollett, MacKercher, and the Annesley Claimant" 1229
"Smollett's Development as a Novelist" 1251
SMOLLETT'S HOAX: DON QUIXOTE IN ENGLISH 1230
SMOLLETT'S REPUTATION AS A NOVELIST 1208
"Smollett's Revisions of RODERICK RANDOM" 1210
"Smollett's Self-Portrait in THE EXPEDITION OF HUMPHRY CLINKER" 1228
SMOLLETT STUDIES 1225
"Social Ambiguity in a Gothic Novel" 1030
SOCIAL IDEAS OF RELIGIOUS LEADERS, 1660-1688, THE 245
Solomon, Stanley J. 310, 439, 1473
SOME ACCOUNT OF THE FAMILY OF SMOLLETT OF BONHILL 1198
"Some Aspects of the Background of RASSELAS" 897
"Some Borrowings in Sterne from Rabelais and Cervantes" 1339

Index

"Some Functions of Rhetoric in TOM JONES" 653

"Some Recent Views of TOM JONES" 651

"Some Unpublished Letters of M.G. Lewis" 954

SOPHIA 932

Southey, Robert (p. 181)

SPECTATOR, THE 112

Spector, Robert Donald 137, 1202, 1205

Spencer, David G. 988

Spenser, Edmund 373

Spilka, Mark 679

SPIRIT OF THE AGE, THE 737

"Spiritual Autobiography in THE PIL-GRIM'S PROGRESS" 385

SPIRITUAL QUIXOTE, THE (p. 153), 804-6, 810, 812-13, 815

"SPIRITUAL QUIXOTE: A New Key to the Characters in Graves's Novel, The" 812

"'Stage Passions' and Smollett's Characterization, The" 1239

Stallbaumer, Virgil R. 846-48

Stamper, Rexford 762

Starkie, Walter F. 138

Starkman, Miriam Kosh 1439

Starr, George A. 471, 508, 541-43

Stathis, James J. 1375

Stauffer, Donald A. 190, 246-47

Staves, Susan 1350

Stebbing, Henry 351

Stedmond, John M. 1296, 1336

Steele, Sir Richard 1383

STELLA: A GENTLEWOMAN OF THE EIGHTEENTH CENTURY 1379

Stephen, Leslie 248, 556-57, 763, 1043

"Sterne" (Isles) 1273

STERNE (Jefferson) 1281

Sterne, Laurence 15-16, 19-20, 22, 30, 34, 39, 45, 48-49, 54, 58, 63, 83, 92, 95-96, 115, 126-28, 130, 137, 170, 214, 237, 239, (p. 69), 596, 900, 989, 1235, 1254-1349

STERNE: MEMOIRS OF MR. LAURENCE STERNE; THE LIFE AND OPINIONS OF TRISTRAM SHANDY; A SENTIMENTAL JOURNEY; SELECTED SERMONS AND LETTERS 1257

STERNE: THE CRITICAL HERITAGE 1310

"Sterne: The Novelist as Jester" 1301

STERNEIANA 1337

STERNE'S COMEDY OF MORAL SENTIMENTS 1295

"Sterne's Letters: Consciousness and Sympathy" 1288

Stevenson, Lionel 46, 53, 55, 191

Stevick, Philip 76-77, 192, 680, 1053, 1247

Stinstra, Johannes 1059

Stout, Gardner D., Jr. 1265-66, 1338-40

Strauss, Albrecht B. 1248

Streeter, Harold Wade 193

Stromberg, Roland N. 249

"Structural Patterns of Control in RASSELAS" 912

"Structural Unity of THE MAN OF FEELING, The" 986

"Structure of RASSELAS, The" 904

"Structure of ROXANA, The" 512

STRUCTURE OF THE NOVEL, THE 72

STUDIES IN BURKE AND HIS TIME 205, 250

STUDIES IN CHANGE AND REVOLUTION 234, 438

STUDIES IN CRITICISM AND AESTHETICS, 1660-1800: ESSAYS IN HONOR OF SAMUEL HOLT MONK 13, 919

STUDIES IN EIGHTEENTH-CENTURY CULTURE 206, 251

STUDIES IN ENGLISH IN HONOR OF RALPH DORMAN O'LEARY AND SELDEN LINCOLN WHITCOMB 897

STUDIES IN ENGLISH LITERATURE, 1500-1900 207

STUDIES IN THE COMIC 1317, 1436

STUDIES IN THE EIGHTEENTH CENTURY 15, 1292

STUDIES IN THE EIGHTEENTH CENTURY NOVEL 134

STUDIES IN THE EIGHTEENTH CEN-
TURY II 16, 1081, 1447
STUDIES IN THE NARRATIVE METHOD
OF DEFOE 539
STUDIES IN THE NOVEL 139, 208
STUDIES OF A BIOGRAPHER 763
STUDY IN SMOLLETT, CHIEFLY PER-
EGRINE PICKLE, A 1212
"Study of Sarah Fielding's Novels, A"
715
STUDY OF THE SOURCES OF BUN-
YAN'S ALLEGORIES, A 389
"Style and Structure and Their Import
in Defoe's ROXANA" 532
"Style and the Action in CLARISSA,
The" 1097
STYLE IN PROSE FICTION 1248
"Stylistic Energy in Early Smollett"
1247
SUBLIME: A STUDY OF CRITICAL
THEORIES IN XVIII-CENTURY
ENGLAND, THE 231, 241
SUBLIMITY IN THE NOVELS OF
ANN RADCLIFFE 1033
"Subverting Propriety as a Pattern of
Irony in Three Eighteenth-Century
Novels" 310, 439, 1473
"Suggestions toward a Genealogy of
the 'Man of Feeling'" 21, 225,
982, 1297
Summers, Montague 140, 194, 316,
970, 1029, 1040, 1474
Sutherland, James R. 38, 464, 469,
494-95, 544-45
Sutherland, John H. 267
Swaim, Kathleen M. 1440
Swedenberg, Hugh T. 141-42, 525
"Swift" (Landa) 1371
SWIFT (Murry) 1385
Swift, Jonathan 16, 19, 20, 22,
24, 27, 52, 127, 131, 142, 170,
204, 214, 239, 614, 644, 759,
(p. 189), 1313, 1327, 1350-1450
SWIFT: A COLLECTION OF CRITI-
CAL ESSAYS 1443
SWIFT: AN INTRODUCTION 1386
SWIFT: POETICAL WORKS 1352
SWIFT: THE CRITICAL HERITAGE
1449
"Swift: The Dean as Satirist" 1442

SWIFT: THE MAN, HIS WORKS,
AND THE AGE 1381
"Swift, the Mysteries, and Deism"
1419
SWIFT AND ANGLICAN RATIONAL-
ISM 1413
SWIFT AND SCATOLOGICAL SATIRE
1420
SWIFT AND THE CHURCH OF IRE-
LAND 1384
SWIFT AND THE SATIRIST'S ART
1435
SWIFT AND THE TWENTIETH CEN-
TURY 1445
SWIFTIANA 1441
"Swift's Flying Island in the 'Voyage
to Laputa'" 1424
"Swift's Religion" 1399
SWIFT'S RHETORICAL ART 1429
"Swift's Satire: Rules of the Game"
1407
SWIFT'S SATIRE ON LEARNING IN
A TALE OF A TUB 1439
"Swift's TALE: On Satire, Negation,
and the Uses of Irony" 1392
"Swift's TALE OF A TUB: An Essay
in Problems of Structure" 1408
SWIFT'S VISION OF EVIL 1428
"Swift's Yahoo and the Christian Sym-
bols for Sin" 1412
"Symbolic Elements in ROBINSON
CRUSOE" 500
Sypher, Wylie 340, 1030
SYSTEMS OF ORDER AND INQUIRY
130, 669, 760, 914, 1244, 1334

T

TALE OF A TUB, A 22, 1327, 1353-
54, 1359-60, 1392, 1394, 1400,
1408, 1413, 1415, 1427-28, 1434,
1439
TALE OF A TUB AND THE BATTLE
OF THE BOOKS, A 1354
TALES OF WONDER (p. 181)
Talon, Henri A. 367-68
Taube, Myron 440, 546
Tave, Stuart M. 39, 681, 1341
Taylor, Dick, Jr. 682
Taylor, John Tinnon 143

Index

Teerink, Herman 1376
Teissedou, Janie 849
Thackeray, William Makepeace 48, 637, 683, 1249, 1342
"Theatrical Convention in Richardson" 1104
THEME AND STRUCTURE IN SWIFT'S TALE OF A TUB 1427
"Themes and Structure in PAMELA" 1118
THEORY OF LITERATURE 80
THEORY OF THE EPIC IN ENGLAND 1650-1800, THE 141
THEORY OF THE NOVEL, THE 77, 192
THEORY OF THE NOVEL: NEW ESSAYS, THE 64
THINGS AS THEY ARE. See CALEB WILLIAMS
"Things As They Were" 746
THIS SINGULAR TALE 790
THOMAS DAY: AN ENGLISH DISCIPLE OF ROUSSEAU 452
THOMAS HOLCROFT AND THE REVOLUTIONARY NOVEL 843
"Thomas Holcroft: A Radical Novelist" 849
"Thomas Holcroft as a Novelist" 848
"Thomas Holcroft: A Satirist in the Stream of Sentimentalism" 847
"Thomas Holcroft, Man of Letters" 839
Thompson, Harold William 980-81
Thompson, Karl F. 302, 311
Thompson, Ralph 441
Thomson, Clara L. 1071
Thomson, David 1284
Thomson, Hugh 391
Thornbury, Ethel M. 684
Thorpe, James 356
Thrale, Mrs. Hester Lynch (p. 81)
Tieck, Ludwig (p. 181)
Tieje, Arthur Jerrold 144
Tillotson, Geoffrey 862, 919-22
Tillotson, John 600
Tillyard, E.M.W. 78
TIME AND SPACE IN THE NOVELS OF SAMUEL RICHARDSON 1079
TIME AND THE NOVEL 1322
"Time in RASSELAS" 922

"Time-Scheme of TRISTRAM SHANDY and a Source, The" 1290
Tindall, William York 386
Tinker, Chauncey Brewster 419. See also AGE OF JOHNSON
TOBIAS GEORGE SMOLLETT 1202
TOBIAS SMOLLETT: A STUDY OF HIS MISCELLANEOUS WORKS 1253
TOBIAS SMOLLETT: BICENTENNIAL ESSAYS PRESENTED TO LEWIS M. KNAPP 1245
TOBIAS SMOLLETT: DOCTOR OF MEN AND MANNERS 1199
TOBIAS SMOLLETT: TRAVELER-NOVELIST 1226
Tobin, James E. 1372
Todd, William B. 957
TOLD IN LETTERS 94, 135, 166, 1089
"TOM JONES" (Empson) 622
TOM JONES (Fielding) 54, 128, 558, 573-76, 594-96, 598, 601-3, 610, 617, 621-22, 630, 633, 637, 641-42, 651, 653-54, 659, 663, 670, 673, 678, 683-84, 686-87, 689, 694, (p. 135), 1250, 1286
"TOM JONES: The Argument of Design" 602
"Tom Jones and 'His Egyptian Majesty'" 601
"TOM JONES in Adaptation" 670
Tompkins, J.M.S. 145, 268, 349, 420, 814, 850, 989, 1031, 1041, 1162
Torre, Lillian de la. See de la Torre, Lillian
TO THE PALACE OF WISDOM 34, 531, 1331
Tourtellot, A.B. 408
TOUR THRO' THE WHOLE ISLAND OF GREAT BRITAIN, A 477-78
"Towards Defining an Age of Sensibility" 26, 984, 1305
Towers, A.R. 685
Toynbee, Mrs. Paget 1455
Tracy, Clarence 805, 815
TRADITION OF SMOLLETT, THE 1220
Trainer, James 1035, 1042

TRANSLATIONS OF FRENCH SENTI-
MENTAL PROSE FICTION IN LATE
EIGHTEENTH-CENTURY ENGLAND
102
"Translations of the Vie de Marianne
and their Relation to Contemporary
English Fiction" 109
Trask, Willard R. 219
Traugott, John L. 1343-44, 1433
TRAVEL-DIARIES OF WILLIAM BECK-
FORD, THE 281
TRAVELERS AND TRAVEL-LIARS,
1660-1800 81
TRAVELS INTO SEVERAL REMOTE
NATIONS OF THE WORLD. See
GULLIVER'S TRAVELS
TRAVELS THROUGH FRANCE AND
ITALY (Smollett) 1170, 1179-80
Trevelyan, George Macaulay 252-53
Trilling, Lionel 79
TRISTRAM SHANDY 22, 45, 54,
128, 130, (p. 69), 596, 900,
1257, 1259-62, 1274, 1278,
1280, 1283, 1285-87, 1289-94,
1298, 1300, 1302-3, 1306, 1308,
1312-13, 1315-17, 1320-22, 1324-
31, 1334-36, 1341-43, 1346-49
TRISTRAM SHANDY: THE GAMES
OF PLEASURE 1316
"TRISTRAM SHANDY and the Game
of Love" 1285
"TRISTRAM SHANDY and the New
Novel of Sensibility" 1326
"TRISTRAM SHANDY and the Reader's
Imagination" 1289
"TRISTRAM SHANDY and the Tech-
nique of the Novel" 1335
"TRISTRAM SHANDY and the Tradi-
tion of Learned Wit" 1313
"Tristram Shandy's Digressive Artistry"
1329
TRISTRAM SHANDY'S WORLD 1343
Trollope, Anthony 332
TROPIC OF CANCER 437
TRUE-BORN ENGLISHMAN, THE
454
TRUE GENIUS OF OLIVER GOLD-
SMITH, THE 797
TRUE PATRIOT, THE 562
Turner, Paul 1364

Turner, Rufus Paul 1155
Tuveson, Ernest 1345, 1442-43
TWENTIETH CENTURY INTERPRETA-
TIONS OF GULLIVER'S TRAVELS
1388
TWENTIETH CENTURY INTERPRETA-
TIONS OF MOLL FLANDERS 505
TWENTIETH CENTURY INTERPRETA-
TIONS OF PAMELA 1086
TWENTIETH CENTURY INTERPRETA-
TIONS OF ROBINSON CRUSOE
506
TWENTIETH CENTURY INTERPRETA-
TIONS OF TOM JONES 603
"Two Dramatists: Lovelace and Rich-
ardson in CLARISSA" 1120
TWO ENGLISH NOVELISTS: APHRA
BEHN AND ANTHONY TROLLOPE
332

U

"Unity of GULLIVER'S TRAVELS, The"
1417
"Unpublished Johnson Letters" 935
UNSENTIMENTAL JOURNEY OF
LAURENCE STERNE, THE 1299
Uphaus, Robert W. 1444
USES OF IRONY, THE 142, 525
Utter, Robert P. 146, 1133

V

Van Ghent, Dorothy 54, 387, 547,
686, 1134, 1346
Van Marter, Shirley 1135
Van Thal, Herbert 724
VARIED PATTERN, THE 232
Varma, Devendra P. 147, 213, 254,
312, 726, 951, 971, 1008-9,
1014, 1475
VATHEK 50, (p. 57), 269-75, 299,
(p. 61), 303-6, 308-12
VICAR OF WAKEFIELD, THE 769,
772-76, 789-99, 801
VICAR OF WAKEFIELD AND OTHER
WRITINGS, THE 769
Vickers, Brian 974, 990
VIE DE MARIANNE. See MARIANNE
Virgil 662, 675

Index

"Virtue and Terror: THE MONK"
963
VIRTUE IN DISTRESS 47
VISITS TO BEDLAM 18, 222
"Voices of Henry Fielding: Style in
TOM JONES, The" 654
Voight, Milton 1445
Voitle, Robert 923
Voltaire 863, 1222, 1331
"Voltaire and HUMPHRY CLINKER"
1222
Vopat, James B. 687
VOYAGES OF MR. JOB VINEGAR,
THE 560
VOYAGE TO ABYSSINIA 906

W

Wagenknecht, Edward 55, 195
Wagoner, Mary 1347
Wahba, Magdi 870, 924
Wain, John 857, 884
Wall, Barbara 368
Wallace, Robert M. 688
Walpole, Horace 50, 180, (p. 199),
1040, (p. 269), 1451-75
Walpole, Sir Robert 244, (p. 69),
586, 591, (p. 269)
WANDERER, THE (p. 81)
Warburton, William 89
Wardle, Ralph M. 729, 788
Ware, Malcolm 1032-33
Warner, John M. 689, 1250-51
Warren, Austin 80
Watkins, Walter B.C. 1348
Watson, George 187
Watt, Ian P. 40, 148, 548-51, 564,
627, 690-91, 1136-37, 1260, 1433
Webber, Joan 41, 388
"Wedding Bells for PAMELA" 1115
Wedel, T.O. 1446
Weinbrot, Howard D. 925
Wellek, René 42, 80
Wendt, Allan 692-93, 1138
Werner, Herman Oscar, Jr. 711
Wesley, John (p. 69)
WESLEYAN EDITION OF THE WORKS
OF HENRY FIELDING, THE
(p. 111), 558-59
Wess, Robert V. 694

West, William 1252
Wharey, J.B. 355, 389
"What Is FANNY HILL?" 436
"What Pamela Knew: An Interpreta-
tion" 1094
"What Was New About the 'New Spe-
cies of Writing'?" 125, 658, 1122
Whibley, Charles 804
Whibley, Leonard 1465
Whicher, George Frisbie 828
"Whig Aesthetics: A Phase of
Eighteenth-Century Taste" 233
WHIG SUPREMACY: 1714-1760, THE
257
Whitcomb, Selden Lincoln. See
STUDIES IN ENGLISH IN HONOR
OF . . .
White, Eugene 421
Whitefield, George (p. 153)
Whitley, Alvin 926
Whitridge, Arnold 1253
Whyte, Alexander 390
Wieten, A.A.S. 1034
WILD EXCURSIONS 1284
Wilding, Michael 1447
Wilkins, Vaughan 259
Wilkins, W.M. 779
Willey, Basil 255-56
WILLIAM BECKFORD, AUTEUR DE
VATHEK 299
WILLIAM BECKFORD OF FONTHILL
291
WILLIAM BECKFORD OF FONTHILL:
BICENTENARY ESSAYS 307
"William Godwin" 737
WILLIAM GODWIN: A BIOGRAPHI-
CAL STUDY 739
WILLIAM GODWIN: A STUDY IN
LIBERALISM 735
WILLIAM GODWIN AND HIS WORLD
736
"William Godwin and the Stage" 740
"William Godwin as a Sentimentalist"
741
WILLIAM GODWIN, HIS FRIENDS
AND CONTEMPORARIES 738,
841
"William Godwin, Philosopher and
Novelist" 743
"William Godwin's Novels" 763

Williams, Aubrey 695
Williams, Basil 257
Williams, David 232
Williams, Harold 1351, 1361, 1367-68
Williams, Ioan 149, 196, 563
Williams, Iolo A. 780
Williams, Kathleen 1356, 1448-49
Williams, Murial Brittain 696
Williams, Raymond 43
Wilson, Mona 953
Wilson, Stuart 1139
Wimsatt, W.K. 927-28
WINGED SKULL, THE 1296
Winner, Anthony 1140
Winslow, Ola E. 369
Wolff, Cynthia G. 1141
Wollstonecraft, Mary (p. 139), 729
WOMEN WRITERS 114, 336, 714, 832, 1001
Woodcock, George 331, 739
Woods, Charles B. 697
Work, James Aiken 698, 1259
WORKS AND LIFE OF LAURENCE STERNE, THE 1254
WORKS OF APHRA BEHN, THE 316
WORKS OF DANIEL DEFOE, THE 454
WORKS OF HENRY FIELDING, ESQ., THE (Murphy) 554-55
WORKS OF HENRY FIELDING, ESQ., THE (Roscoe) 555
WORKS OF HENRY FIELDING, ESQ., THE (Stephen) 556
WORKS OF HENRY MACKENZIE, ESQ., THE 972
WORKS OF HORATIO WALPOLE, THE 1451
WORKS OF OLIVER GOLDSMITH, THE 766
WORKS OF SAMUEL JOHNSON, THE (Yale) 852, 866

WORKS OF SAMUEL JOHNSON, L.L.D., THE 851
WORKS OF SAMUEL RICHARDSON, THE 1043
WORKS OF TOBIAS SMOLLETT, THE (Brack) 1170
WORKS OF TOBIAS SMOLLETT, THE (Henley and Seccombe) 1168, 1180
WORKS OF TOBIAS SMOLLETT, THE (Roscoe) 1166
WORKS OF TOBIAS SMOLLETT, THE (Saintsbury) 1167
WORKS OF TOBIAS SMOLLETT, M.D., WITH MEMOIRS OF HIS LIFE, THE (Moore) 1164, 1201
Wright, Andrew 2, 152, 332, 699, 1349
Wright, Walter Francis 150, 991
WRITINGS OF JONATHAN SWIFT, THE 1357
"Writing to the Moment: One Aspect" 1132
Würzbach, Natascha 215

Y

YEAR'S WORK IN ENGLISH STUDIES, THE 197
Yoklavich, John M. 1274
YORICK AND THE CRITICS 1309
"Yorick's Sentimental Journey" 1340
YOUNG FANNY BURNEY, THE 405
YOUNG PHILOSOPHER, THE (p. 219), 1147
YOUNG SAM JOHNSON 877

Z

Zimmerman, Everett 552-53, 1450
Zirker, Malvin R. 1142